D1058573

SPORTING LITERATURE

SPORTING LITERATURE

An Anthology

CHOSEN BY
VERNON SCANNELL

OXFORD UNIVERSITY PRESS
1987

Oxford University Press, Walton Street, Oxford OX2 6DP
Oxford New York Toronto
Delhi Bombay Calcutta Madras Karachi
Petaling Jaya Singapore Hong Kong Tokyo
Nairobi Dar es Salaam Cape Town
Melbourne Auckland
and associated companies in
Beirut Berlin Ibadan Nicosia

Oxford is a trade mark of Oxford University Press

British Library Cataloguing in Publication Data
Sporting literature: an anthology.
1. English literature 2. Sports — Literary collections
I. Scannell, Vernon
802'.8'0355 PR1111.S/
ISBN 0–19–212250–9

Typeset by Promenade Graphics
Printed in Great Britain by
Butler & Tanner Ltd
Frome and London

CONTENTS

III · We'll to the River

IV · At the Races

V · In the Ring

VI · The Football War

VII · Bat and Pad

IX · Bowls and Tennis

X · In and On the Water

XI · We Run because We Must

XII · Men and Mountains

INTRODUCTION

SPORTING activities of one kind or another have long been a prominent feature of English social life and, indeed, accounts of competitive athletic games are to be found in the records of all the world's cultures from as far back in time as historians can with any confidence trace. The earliest references to sport in ancient Greece deal with funeral games, as for instance in Homer's description in the *Iliad*, xxiii, of the games — or *agones* — at the funeral of Patroclus, and there are few games or sports, even in the twentieth century, which in their performance do not contain some element of ritual. It is partly because of this ritualistic quality and the fact that many, if not all, sports may easily be seen to contain strong metaphorical or allegorical possibilities, and partly because sport, simply as an enjoyable pastime, is an important form of human activity, that so many authors have felt the need to write about it. Not all of these writers have composed simple and joyful celebrations of the sport they have taken for their subject. Some may seize upon a popular activity such as hunting or fishing and explore it as a metaphor which will effectively communicate concerns of a quite different kind from those usually associated with the sport. Others may attack with the barbs of satire or the cudgels of direct condemnation sports which they regard as foolish or humanly degrading and wicked practices, but whatever the author's purpose or purposes he will fail to engage his reader's interest unless his knowledge and observation of the subject is accurate and vividly communicated. But before venturing any more generalizations on the subject of literature and sport I must set out the scope and limits of this anthology.

I have taken the term 'Sport' to include all of those physical or non-sedentary activities which involve some kind of competition or the pursuit of a quarry. My definition of competition naturally includes the obvious trials of skill and fitness between opposing teams or individuals in such sports as soccer and boxing, but I also intend the word to accommodate other pastimes such as mountain-climbing, solo swimming, skating and fishing, activities where the participant is competing not against a fellow-sportsman but against a physical obstacle, the natural elements, another species, or against the adversary within himself, his fear, lack of resolution, stamina or experience. Some readers may be disappointed to find that there are no works here dealing with a sport which they enjoy, as either spectator or participant, motor-racing, for example, or skiing. This is not because I am indifferent to the attractions of the neglected sport, but simply because I have found no literature of any real merit which is suitable for anthologizing.

The temptation to use translations from the sporting literature of other languages was strong, as was the impulse to print poetry and prose by authors from the United States but, reluctantly, I decided to confine the contents of this anthology to British writers with the small exception of three brief translations, one from Latin and two from the Greek Anthology, and the splendid poem by the American, Elizabeth Bishop, 'The Fish'. There is, of course, much fine literature on sport from the pens of American writers: a selection of excellent sporting prose could be compiled from the work of Hemingway alone. But this very profusion of excellence, allied to the fact that a good deal of transatlantic sporting literature deals with games and rites unfamiliar to most British readers, resulted in my decision to concentrate on our native authors. I have divided their works into thematic groups — hunting, stalking and shooting, combat sports, ball-games, water sports, and so on — and within the sections, although the order is roughly chronological, I have sometimes broken the continuity in favour of an interesting juxtaposition of styles or treatment. The section called *An Assembly of Animals* contains work which deals with blood-sports other than that of riding to hounds (the theme of the first section), with shooting, bull-fighting, badger-baiting, hawking and so on, or writings in which the emphasis is on the animal, whether victim or predator, rather than the human activity in which it is involved. It also includes examples of sporting animals featured in fable and legend.

Sport in its various forms is not merely an agreeable, diverting and apparently indispensable feature of human life, it always possesses in some degree not only the ritualistic elements mentioned above, but a language of considerable vigour and one which lends itself naturally to the figurative. It is a commonplace to mention the sporting origin of so many of our popular vernacular metaphors: from horse-racing are derived *heavy-going*, *outsider*, *rushing one's fences*, *backing a loser*; from boxing *toeing the line* (a term from the old bare-knuckle prize-fighting rules), *up to the mark* (same source), *below the belt*, *a knock-out*, *clean contest*; from cricket *to be stumped*, *a sticky wicket*, *hit for six*, *caught out* and so on. What is perhaps less obvious is the way in which authors have turned to sports for the more complex metaphorical purposes of creating extended allegories of mankind's vital concerns with love, reflection and action, ambition, betrayal, fear and triumph, life and death. In the first section, *From a View to the Death*, the reader will find poems in which the allegorical meaning is quite plain (in John Gay's Fable, 'The Hound and the Huntsman', for instance), but even in other pieces which seem simply to describe, embody and celebrate the exhilaration of the Hunt, there are often found undertones of something less jovial and robust, something deeper and darker. We see man, the predator, and the death of his prey is not symbolic but real. And in those works where the hunt is employed as a metaphor for the pursuit of love, man may still be the predator and mortality, in however shadowy a form, is always present. Even that familiar song, 'John Peel', which I thought I remembered as quite a jolly celebration of its subject, turned out, on reacquaintance, to be something rather more ambiguous. There is a note of desperation in its jollity and death's cold and ironic chime is struck repeatedly through the verses.

While I have laid some stress on the fact that sporting literature may well carry symbolic undertones I have not included work which simply makes passing reference to a sport, perhaps in the form of an illustrative simile. It is important that the author should be primarily concerned with communicating the reality of the sporting activity he is dealing with, and that he should write about it with authority. At this point perhaps I should offer an apology or explanation for the presence in this book of a number of my own poems. I recall with premonitory trepidation a review of *A Little Treasury of Modern Poetry* compiled by an American, Oscar Williams. A compatriot, the critic and poet, Randall Jarrell, in his assessment of the book, mentioned that Oscar Williams had included nine (presumably treasurable) poems of his own as compared with five from the pen of Thomas Hardy. 'It takes a lot of courage to like your own poetry almost twice as well as Hardy's,' reflected Jarrell. Well, I do not include my poems because I like them twice as well, or even half as well, as anyone else's, but because they deal with a sport about which I know quite a lot (I am willing to take a substantial bet that I am the only published poet who has owned a professional boxer's licence from the British Boxing Board of Control), and I hope that something of this knowledge of a game, the true nature of which few people who have not practised it even begin to understand, will convey to the reader at least some sense of authenticity.

In his *Varieties of Religious Experience* William James wrote: 'One hears of the mechanical equivalent of heat. What we now need to discover in the social realm is the moral equivalent of war: something heroic that will speak to men as universally as war does, yet will be as compatible with their spiritual selves as war has proved itself to be incompatible.' I feel fairly sure that James would have rejected the notion that combative sport — rugger, soccer, wrestling, boxing — and perhaps the testing of the solitary individual on mountain-face or at sea could provide, if not a perfect moral equivalent of war, at least an approximation to one. However that may be, for very many people sport of some kind supplies a spectacle of human endeavour which thrills and inspires with a display of competitive strife, cruelty, courage, narrative and ritual as well as providing a special kind of sensuous and aesthetic satisfaction. Despite the cynical exploitation of both athlete and public which is an almost inevitable consequence of professionalism and big business, sport, like art, is practised for its own sake and the committed athlete, whether amateur or professional, personifies that complete dedication and ultimate self-abnegation that are also central to the nature of the artist, and we are exalted by his example. Not all of the contributions to this anthology are intended to exalt; some are ironic others overtly condemnatory. A few are amiably comic while others are objectively descriptive. The mix is richly varied. I hope it will provide stimulus and sustenance for most appetites.

VERNON SCANNELL

PROLOGUE

Verses on Games

(*To 'An Almanac of Twelve Sports', by W. Nicholson*, 1898)

Here is a horse to tame—
Here is a gun to handle—
God knows you can enter the game
If you'll only pay the same,
And the price of the game is a candle—
A single flickering candle!

JANUARY (*Hunting*)

Certes, it is a noble sport,
And men have quitted selle and swum for't.
But I am of the meeker sort
And I prefer Surtees in comfort.

Reach me my *Handley Cross* again,
My run, where never danger lurks, is
With Jorrocks and his deathless train—
Pigg, Binjimin, and Artaxerxes.

FEBRUARY (*Coursing*)

Most men harry the world for fun—
Each man seeks it a different way,
But 'of all the daft devils under the sun,
A greyhound's the daftest,' says Jorrocks J.

MARCH (*Racing*)

The horse is ridden—the jockey rides—
The backers back—the owners own—
But . . . there are lots of things besides,
And *I* should let this game alone.

APRIL (*Rowing*)

The Pope of Rome he could not win
From pleasant meats and pleasant sin
These who, replying not, submit
Unto the curses of the Pit
Which that stern Coach (oh, greater shame)
Flings forth by number not by name.
Can Triple Crown or Jesuit's oath
Do what one wrathful trainer doth?

MAY (*Fishing*)

Behold a parable. A fished for B
C took her bait; her heart being set on D.
Thank Heaven who cooled your blood and cramped
your wishes,
Men and not Gods torment you, little fishes!

JUNE (*Cricket*)

Thank God who made the British Isles
And taught me how to play,
I do not worship crocodiles,
Or bow the knee to clay!
Give me a willow wand and I
With hide and cork and twine
From century to century
Will gambol round my shrine!

JULY (*Archery*)

The child of the Nineties considers with laughter
The maid whom his sire in the Sixties ran after,
While careering himself in pursuit of a girl whom
The Twenties will dub a 'last-century heirloom'.

AUGUST (*Coaching*)

The Pious Horse to church may trot,
A maid may work a man's salvation. . . .
Four horses and a girl are not,
However, roads to reformation.

SEPTEMBER (*Shooting*)

'Peace upon Earth, Goodwill to men'
So greet we Christmas Day!
Oh, Christian, load your gun and then,
Oh, Christian, out and slay.

OCTOBER (*Golf*)

Why Golf is Art and Art is Golf
We have not far to seek—
So much depends upon the lie,
So much upon the cleek.

NOVEMBER (*Boxing*)

Read here the moral roundly writ
For him who into battle goes—
Each soul that, hitting hard or hit,
Endureth gross or ghostly foes.
Prince, blown by many overthrows
Half blind with shame, half choked with dirt,
Man cannot tell, but Allah knows
How much the other side was hurt!

DECEMBER
(*Skating*)

Over the ice she flies
   Perfect and poised and fair.
Stars in my true-love's eyes
   Teach me to do and dare.
Now will I fly as she flies—
   Woe for the stars that misled.
Stars I beheld in her eyes
   Now do I see in my head!

Now we must come away.
   What are you out of pocket?
'Sorry to spoil your play
But somebody says we must pay,
   And the candle's down to the socket—
      Its horrible tallowy socket.

RUDYARD KIPLING (1863–1936)

I

From a View to the Death

The Hunt Is Up

The hunt is up, the hunt is up,
  And it is well nigh day;
And Harry our King is gone hunting
  To bring his deer to bay.

The east is bright with morning light,
  And darkness it is fled;
And the merry horn wakes up the morn
  To leave his idle bed.

Behold the skies with golden dyes
  Are glowing all around;
The grass is green, and so are the treen
  All laughing at the sound.

The horses snort to be at sport,
  The dogs are running free,
The woods rejoice at the merry noise
  Of *Hey tantara tee ree!*

The sun is glad to see us clad
  All in our lusty green,
And smiles in the sky as he riseth high
  To see and to be seen.

Awake all men, I say again,
  Be merry as you may;
For Harry our King is gone hunting,
  To bring his deer to bay.

ANONYMOUS (16th century)

Rustic Song

(from *The Sun's Darling*)

Haymakers, rakers, reapers, and mowers,
  Wait on your Summer-Queen!
Dress up with musk-rose her eglantine bowers,
  Daffodils strew the green!
    Sing, dance, and play,
    'Tis holiday!
  The sun does bravely shine
  On our ears of corn.
    Rich as a pearl
    Comes every girl.
  This is mine, this is mine, this is mine.
Let us die ere away they be borne.

Bow to our Sun, to our Queen, and that fair one
  Come to behold our sports:
Each bonny lass here is counted a rare one,
  As those in princes' courts.
    These and we
    With country glee,
  Will teach the woods to resound,
  And the hills with echoes hollow.
    Skipping lambs
    Their bleating dams
  'Mongst kids shall trip it round;
For joy thus our wenches we follow.

Wind jolly huntsmen, your neat bugles shrilly,
  Hounds make a lusty cry;
Spring up, you falconers, partridges freely,
  Then let your brave hawks fly!
    Horses amain,
    Over ridge, over plain,
  The dogs have the stag in chase:
  'Tis a sport to content a king.
    So ho! ho! through the skies
    How the proud bird flies,
  And sousing, kills with a grace!
Now the deer falls; hark! how they ring.

THOMAS DEKKER (1570–1632)

From *Venus and Adonis*

'Thou hadst been gone,' quoth she, 'sweet boy, ere this,
But that thou told'st me thou wouldst hunt the boar.
O, be advised: thou know'st not what it is
With javelin's point a churlish swine to gore,
    Whose tushes never sheathed he whetteth still,
    Like to a mortal butcher, bent to kill.

'On his bow-back he hath a battle set
Of bristly pikes, that ever threat his foes;
His eyes, like glow-worms, shine when he doth fret;
His snout digs sepulchres where'er he goes;
    Being moved, he strikes whate'er is in his way,
    And whom he strikes his crooked tushes slay.

'His brawny sides, with hairy bristles armed,
Are better proof than thy spear's point can enter;
His short thick neck cannot be easily harmed;
Being ireful, on the lion he will venture:
    The thorny brambles and embracing bushes,
    As fearful of him, part; through whom he rushes

'Alas, he nought esteems that face of thine,
To which Love's eyes pay tributary gazes;
Nor thy soft hands, sweet lips and crystal eyne,
Whose full perfection all the world amazes;
    But having thee at vantage—wondrous dread!—
    Would root these beauties as he roots the mead.

'O, let him keep his loathsome cabin still;
Beauty hath nought to do with such foul fiends:
Come not within his danger by thy will;
They that thrive well take counsel of their friends.
    When thou didst name the boar, not to dissemble,
    I fear'd thy fortune, and my joints did tremble.

'Didst thou not mark my face? was it not white?
Saw'st thou not signs of fear lurk in mine eye?
Grew I not faint? and fell I not downright?
Within my bosom, whereon thou dost lie,
    My boding heart pants, beats, and takes no rest,
    But, like an earthquake, shakes thee on my breast.

'For where Love reigns, disturbing Jealousy
Doth call himself Affection's sentinel;
Gives false alarms, suggested mutiny,
And in a peaceful hour doth cry 'Kill, kill!'
    Distempering gentle Love in his desire,
    As air and water do abate the fire.

'This sour informer, this bate-breeding spy,
This canker that eats up Love's tender spring,
This carry-tale, dissentious Jealousy,
That sometime true news, sometime false doth bring,
    Knocks at my heart, and whispers in mine ear,
    That if I love thee, I thy death should fear:

'And more than so, presenteth to mine eye
The picture of an angry-chafing boar,
Under whose sharp fangs on his back doth lie
An image like thyself, all stain'd with gore;
    Whose blood upon the fresh flowers being shed
    Doth make them droop with grief and hang the head.

'What should I do, seeing thee so indeed,
That tremble at the imagination?
The thought of it doth make my faint heart bleed,
And fear doth teach it divination:
    I prophesy thy death, my living sorrow,
    If thou encounter with the boar to-morrow.

'But if thou needs wilt hunt, be ruled by me;
Uncouple at the timorous flying hare,
Or at the fox which lives by subtlety,
Or at the roe which no encounter dare:
    Pursue these fearful creatures o'er the downs,
    And on thy well-breath'd horse keep with thy hounds.

'And when thou hast on foot the purblind hare,
Mark the poor wretch, to overshoot his troubles,
How he outruns the wind, and with what care
He cranks and crosses with a thousand doubles:
    The many musits through the which he goes
    Are like a labyrinth to amaze his foes.

'Sometime he runs among a flock of sheep,
To make the cunning hounds mistake their smell,
And sometime where earth-delving conies keep,
To stop the loud pursuers in their yell;
 And sometime sorteth with a herd of deer:
 Danger deviseth shifts: wit waits on fear:

'For there his smell with others being mingled,
The hot scent-snuffing hounds are driven to doubt,
Ceasing their clamorous cry till they have singled
With much ado the cold fault cleanly out;
 Then do they spend their mouths: Echo replies,
 As if another chase were in the skies.

'By this, poor Wat, far off upon a hill,
Stands on his hinder legs with listening ear,
To hearken if his foes pursue him still;
Anon their loud alarums he doth hear;
 And now his grief may be compared well
 To one sore sick that hears the passing-bell.

'Then shalt thou see the dew-bedabbled wretch
Turn, and return, indenting with the way;
Each envious brier his weary legs doth scratch,
Each shadow makes him stop, each murmur stay:
 For misery is trodden on by many,
 And being low never relieved by any.

WILLIAM SHAKESPEARE (1564–1616)

'Hare-Hunting'

Hark! from yon covert, where those tow'ring oaks
Above the humble copse aspiring rise,
What glorious triumphs burst in ev'ry gale
Upon our ravished ears! The hunters shout,
The clanging horns swell their sweet-winding notes,
The pack wide-op'ning load the trembling air
With various melody; from tree to tree
The propagated cry redoubling bounds,
And wingèd zephyrs waft the floating joy
Through all the regions near. Afflictive birch
No more the schoolboy dreads, his prison broke,
Scamp'ring he flies, nor heeds his master's call.

The weary traveller forgets his road,
And climbs th' adjacent hill; the ploughman leaves
Th' unfinished furrow; nor his bleating flocks
Are now the shepherd's joy; men, boys and girls
Desert th' unpeopled village; and wild crowds
Spread o'er the plain, by the sweet frenzy seized.
Look, how she pants! and o'er yon op'ning glade
Slips glancing by; while at the further end
The puzzling pack unravel wile by wile
Maze within maze. The covert's utmost bound
Slyly she skirts; behind them cautious creeps,
And, in that very track so lately stained
By all the steaming crowd, seems to pursue
The foes she flies. Let cavillers deny
That brutes have reason; sure 'tis something more,
'Tis heav'n directs, and stratagems inspires
Beyond the short extent of human thought.
But hold—I see her from the covert break:
Sad on yon little eminence she sits;
Intent she listens with one ear erect,
Pond'ring, and doubtful what new course to take,
And how t' escape the fierce bloodthirsty crew,
That still urge on, and still in volleys loud
Insult her woes, and mock her sore distress.
As now in louder peals the loaded winds
Bring on the gath'ring storm, her fears prevail;
And o'er the plain, and o'er the mountain's ridge,
Away she flies; nor ships with wind and tide,
And all their canvas wings, scud half so fast.
Once more, ye jovial train, your courage try,
And each clean courser's speed. We scour along,
In pleasing hurry and confusion tossed,
Oblivion to be wished. The patient pack
Hang on the scent unwearied, up they climb,
And ardent we pursue; our lab'ring steeds
We press, we gore; till once the summit gained,
Painfully panting, there we breathe awhile;
Then like a foaming torrent, pouring down
Precipitant, we smoke along the vale.

WILLIAM SOMERVILLE (1675–1742), from *The Chase*, ii

The Hound and the Huntsman

Impertinence at first is borne
With heedless slight, or smiles of scorn;
Teased into wrath, what patience bears
The noisy fool who perseveres?
  The morning wakes, the huntsman sounds,
At once rush forth the joyful hounds.
They seek the wood with eager pace,
Through bush, through brier, explore the chase.
Now scattered wide, they try the plain,
And snuff the dewy turf in vain.
What care, what industry, what pains!
What universal silence reigns.
  Ringwood, a dog of little fame,
Young, pert, and ignorant of game,
At once displays his babbling throat;
The pack, regardless of the note,
Pursue the scent; with louder strain
He still persists to vex the train.
  The huntsman to the clamour flies;
The smacking lash he smartly plies.
His ribs all welked, with howling tone
The puppy thus expressed his moan:
  'I know the music of my tongue
Long since the pack with envy stung.
What will not spite? These bitter smarts
I owe to my superior parts.'
  'When puppies prate,' the huntsman cried,
'They show both ignorance and pride:
Fools may our scorn, not envy raise,
For envy is a kind of praise.
Had not thy forward noisy tongue
Proclaimed thee always in the wrong,
Thou might'st have mingled with the rest,
And ne'er thy foolish nose confess'd.
But fools, to talking ever prone,
Are sure to make their follies known.'

JOHN GAY (1685–1732), from *Fables*

The Three Huntsmen

There were three jovial Welshmen,
As I have heard men say,
And they would go a-hunting, boys,
Upon St David's Day.
And all the day they hunted,
But nothing could they find,
Except a ship a-sailing,
A sailing with the wind.
And a-hunting they did go.

One said it surely was a ship,
The second he said, Nay;
The third declared it was a house
With the chimney blown away.
Then all the night they hunted,
And nothing could they find,
Except the moon a-gliding,
A-gliding with the wind.
And a-hunting they did go.

One said it surely was the moon,
The second he said, Nay;
The third declared it was a cheese
The half o't cut away.
Then all next day they hunted,
And nothing could they find,
Except a hedgehog in a bush,
And that they left behind.
And a-hunting they did go.

One said it was a hedgehog,
The second he said, Nay;
The third, it was a pincushion,
The pins stuck in wrong way.
Then all next day they hunted,
And nothing could they find,
Except a hare in a turnip field,
And that they left behind.
And a-hunting they did go.

One said it surely was a hare,
  The second he said, Nay;
The third, he said it was a calf,
  And the cow had run away.
Then all next day they hunted,
  And nothing could they find,
But one owl in a holly-tree
  And that they left behind.
    And a-hunting they did go.

One said it surely was an owl,
  The second he said, Nay;
The third said 'twas an aged man
  Whose beard was growing grey.
Then all three jovial Welshmen
  Came riding home at last,
'For three days we have nothing killed,
  And never broke our fast!'
    And a-hunting they did go.

ANONYMOUS (?14th–15th century)

From *The Birth of the Squire: an Eclogue*

(*in imitation of the* Pollio *of Virgil*)

Ye sylvan Muses, loftier strains recite,
Not all in shades, and humble cotts delight.
Hark! the bells ring; along the distant grounds
The driving gales convey the swelling sounds;
Th' attentive swain, forgetful of his work,
With gaping wonder, leans upon his fork.
What sudden news alarms the waking morn?
To the glad Squire a hopeful heir is born.
Mourn, mourn, ye stags; and all ye beasts of chase,
This hour destruction brings on all your race:
See the pleas'd tenants duteous off'rings bear,
Turkeys and geese and grocer's sweetest ware;
With the new health the pond'rous tankard flows,
And old October reddens ev'ry nose.
Beagles and spaniels round his cradle stand,
Kiss his moist lip and gently lick his hand;

October] a beer or ale brewed in October

He joys to hear the shrill horn's ecchoing sounds,
And learns to lisp the names of all the hounds.
With frothy ale to make his cup o'er-flow,
Barley shall in paternal acres grow;
The bee shall sip the fragrant dew from flow'rs,
To give metheglin for his morning hours;
For him the clustring hop shall climb the poles,
And his own orchard sparkle in his bowles.
  His sire's exploits he now with wonder hears,
The monstrous tales indulge his greedy ears;
How when youth strung his nerves and warm'd his veins,
He rode the mighty Nimrod of the plains:
He leads the staring infant through the hall,
Points out the horny spoils that grace the wall;
Tells, how this stag thro' three whole Countys fled,
What rivers swam, where bay'd, and where he bled.
Now he the wonders of the fox repeats,
Describes the desp'rate chase, and all his cheats;
How in one day beneath his furious speed,
He tir'd seven coursers of the fleetest breed:
How high the pale he leapt, how wide the ditch,
When the hound tore the haunches of the witch!
These stories which descend from son to son,
The forward boy shall one day make his own.

JOHN GAY

John Peel

D'ye ken John Peel with his coat so gay?
D'ye ken John Peel at the break of the day?
D'ye ken John Peel when he's far, far away,
With his hounds and his horn in the morning?
  'Twas the sound of his horn called me from my bed,
  And the cry of his hounds has me oft-times led,
  For Peel's *View-hollo* would awaken the dead,
  Or a fox from his lair in the morning.

D'ye ken that bitch whose tongue is death?
D'ye ken her sons of peerless faith?
D'ye ken that a fox with his last breath
Cursed them all as he died in the morning?

Yes, I ken John Peel and Ruby too
Ranter and Royal and Bellman as true;
From the drag to the chase, from the chase to a view,
From a view to the death in the morning.

And I've followed John Peel both often and far
O'er the rasper-fence and the gate and the bar,
From Low Denton Holme up to Scratchmere Scar
When we vied for the brush in the morning.

Then here's to John Peel with my heart and soul,
Come fill—fill to him another strong bowl:
And we'll follow John Peel through fair and through foul,
While we're waked by his horn in the morning.
'Twas the sound of his horn called me from my bed,
And the cry of his hounds has me oft-times led,
For Peel's *View-hollo* would awaken the dead
Or a fox from his lair in the morning.

JOHN WOODCOCK GRAVES (1795–1886)

My Heart's in the Highlands

My heart's in the Highlands, my heart is not here;
My heart's in the Highlands a chasing the deer;
Chasing the wild deer, and following the roe;
My heart's in the Highlands, wherever I go.—

Farewell to the Highlands, farewell to the North;
The birth-place of valour, the country of worth:
Wherever I wander, wherever I rove,
The hills of the Highlands for ever I love.—

Farewell to the mountains high cover'd with snow;
Farewell to the Straths and green valleys below;
Farewell to the forests and wild-hanging woods;
Farewell to the torrents and loud-pouring floods.—

My heart's in the Highlands, my heart is not here,
My heart's in the Highlands a chasing the deer:
Chasing the wild deer, and following the roe;
My heart's in the Highlands, wherever I go.—

ROBERT BURNS (1759–96)

From *Autumn*

The stag, too, singled from the herd, where long
He ranged the branching monarch of the shades,
Before the tempest drives. At first, in speed
He sprightly puts his faith, and, roused by fear,
Gives all his swift aerial soul to flight.
Against the breeze he darts, that way the more
To leave the lessening murderous cry behind.
Deception short! though, fleeter than the winds
Blown o'er the keen-aired mountain by the North,
He bursts the thickets, glances through the glades,
And plunges deep into the wildest wood.
If slow, yet sure, adhesive to the track
Hot-steaming, up behind him come again
The inhuman rout, and from the shady depth
Expel him, circling through his every shift.
He sweeps the forest oft; and sobbing sees
The glades, mild opening to the golden day,
Where in kind contest with his butting friends
He wont to struggle, or his loves enjoy.
Oft in the full-descending flood he tries
To lose the scent, and lave his burning sides—
Oft seeks the herd; the watchful herd, alarmed,
With selfish care avoid a brother's woe.
What shall he do? His once so vivid nerves,
So full of buoyant spirit, now no more
Inspire the course; but fainting, breathless toil
Sick seizes on his heart: he stands at bay,
And puts his last weak refuge in despair.
The big round tears run down his dappled face;
He groans in anguish; while the growling pack,
Blood-happy, hang at his fair jutting chest,
And mark his beauteous chequered sides with gore.

JAMES THOMSON (1700–48), *The Seasons*

From *The Wild Huntsman*

The Wildgrave winds his bugle-horn,
To horse, to horse! halloo, halloo!
His fiery courser snuffs the morn,
And thronging serfs their lord pursue.

The eager pack, from couples freed,
 Dash through the bush, the brier, the brake;
While, answering hound, and horn, and steed,
 The mountain echoes startling wake.

The beams of God's own hallow'd day
 Had painted yonder spire with gold,
And, calling sinful man to pray,
 Loud, long, and deep the bell had toll'd.

But still the Wildgrave onward rides;
 Halloo, halloo! and hark again!
When, spurring from opposing sides,
 Two Stranger Horsemen join the train.

Who was each Stranger, left and right,
 Well may I guess, but dare not tell;
The right-hand steed was silver white,
 The left, the swarthy hue of hell.

The right-hand Horseman, young and fair;
 His smile was like the morn of May;
The left, from eye of tawny glare,
 Shot midnight lightning's lurid ray.

He waved his huntsman's cap on high,
 Cried, 'Welcome, welcome, noble lord!
What sport can earth, or sea, or sky,
 To match the princely chase, afford?'

'Cease thy loud bugle's clanging knell,'
 Cried the fair youth, with silver voice;
'And for devotion's choral swell,
 Exchange the rude unhallow'd noise.

'To-day, the ill-omen'd chase forbear,
 Yon bell yet summons to the fane;
To-day the Warning Spirit hear,
 To-morrow thou mayst mourn in vain.'

'Away, and sweep the glades along!'
 The Sable Hunter hoarse replies;
'To muttering monks leave matin-song,
 And bells, and books, and mysteries.'

The Wildgrave spurr'd his ardent steed,
And, launching forward with a bound,
'Who, for thy drowsy priestlike rede,
Would leave the jovial horn and hound?

'Hence, if our manly sport offend!
With pious fools go chant and pray:
Well hast thou spoke, my dark-brow'd friend:
Halloo, halloo! and hark away!'

The Wildgrave spurr'd his courser light,
O'er moss and moor, o'er holt and hill;
And on the left and on the right,
Each Stranger Horseman follow'd still.

Upsprings, from yonder tangled thorn,
A stag more white than mountain snow;
And louder rung the Wildgrave's horn,
'Hark forward, forward! holla, ho!'

A heedless wretch has cross'd the way;
He gasps the thundering hoofs below;—
But, live who can, or die who may,
Still, 'forward, forward!' on they go.

See, where yon simple fences meet,
A field with Autumn's blessings crown'd:
See, prostrate at the Wildgrave's feet,
A husbandman with toil embrown'd:

'O mercy, mercy, noble lord!
Spare the poor's pittance,' was his cry,
'Earn'd by the sweat these brows have pour'd,
In scorching hour of fierce July.'

Earnest the right-hand Stranger pleads,
The left still cheering to the prey;
The impetuous Earl no warning heeds,
But furious holds the onward way.

'Away, thou hound! so basely born,
Or dread the scourge's echoing blow!'
Then loudly rung his bugle-horn,
'Hark forward, forward! holla, ho!'

So said, so done: A single bound
  Clears the poor labourer's humble pale;
Wild follows man, and horse, and hound,
  Like dark December's stormy gale.

And man and horse, and hound and horn,
  Destructive sweep the field along;
While, joying o'er the wasted corn,
  Fell Famine marks the maddening throng.

Again uproused, the timorous prey
  Scours moss and moor, and holt and hill;
Hard run, he feels his strength decay,
  And trusts for life his simple skill.

Too dangerous solitude appear'd;
  He seeks the shelter of the crowd;
Amid the flock's domestic herd
  His harmless head he hopes to shroud.

O'er moss and moor, and holt and hill,
  His track the steady blood-hounds trace;
O'er moss and moor, unwearied still,
  The furious Earl pursues the chase.

Full lowly did the herdsman fall;
  'O spare, thou noble Baron, spare
These herds, a widow's little all;
  These flocks, an orphan's fleecy care!'

Earnest the right-hand Stranger pleads,
  The left still cheering to the prey;
The Earl nor prayer nor pity heeds,
  But furious keeps the onward way.

'Unmanner'd dog! To stop my sport
  Vain were thy cant and beggar whine,
Though human spirits, of thy sort,
  Were tenants of these carrion kine!'

Again, he winds his bugle-horn,
  'Hark forward, forward! holla, ho!'
And through the herd, in ruthless scorn,
  He cheers his furious hounds to go.

In heaps the throttled victims fall;
  Down sinks their mangled herdsman near;
The murderous cries the stag appal.
  Again he starts, new-nerved by fear.

SIR WALTER SCOTT (1771–1832)

The Fox Hunters

What Gods are these? Bright red, or white and green,
Some of them jockey-capp'd and some in hats,
The gods of vermin have their runs, like rats.
Each has six legs, four moving, pendent two,
Like bottled tails, the tilting four between.
Behold Land-Interest's compound Man-and-Horse,
Which so enchants his outraged helot-crew,
Hedge-gapping, with his horn, and view-halloo,
O'er hunter's clover—glorious broom and gorse!
The only crop his godship ever grew:
Except his crop of hate, and smouldering ire,
And cloak'd contempt, of coward insult born,
And hard-faced labour, paid with straw for corn,
And fain to reap it with a scythe of fire.

EBENEZER ELLIOT (1781–1849)

'A Foreigner Rides to Hounds'

A fox-hunt to a foreigner is strange;
  'Tis also subject to the double danger
Of tumbling first and having in exchange
  Some pleasant jesting at the awkward stranger.
But Juan had been early taught to range
  The wilds, as doth an Arab turned avenger,
So that his horse or charger, hunter, hack
Knew that he had a rider on his back.

And now in this new field, with some applause,
  He cleared hedge, ditch and double post and rail
And never craned and made but few *faux pas*
  And only fretted when the scent 'gan fail.
He broke, 'tis true, some statutes of the laws
  Of hunting, for the sagest youth is frail,
Rode o'er the hounds, it may be, now and then,
And once o'er several country gentlemen.

But on the whole to general admiration
  He acquitted both himself and horse. The squires
Marvelled at merit of another nation.
  The boors cried, 'Dang it, who'd have thought it?' Sires,
The Nestors of the sporting generation,
  Swore praises and recalled their former fires.
The huntsman's self relented to a grin
And rated him almost a whipper-in.

Such were his trophies, not of spear and shield,
  But leaps and bursts and sometimes fox's brushes.
Yet I must own—although in this I yield
  To patriot sympathy a Briton's blushes—
He thought at heart like courtly Chesterfield,
  Who after a long chase o'er hills, dales, bushes,
And what not, though he rode beyond all price,
Asked next day, 'If men ever hunted twice?'

LORD BYRON (1788–1824), *Don Juan*, canto xiv

'The Meet'

They reach the meet—a wayside public-house on a common, before which the hounds with their attendants and some fifty or sixty horsemen, many of them in scarlet, were assembled. Jorrocks was received with the greatest cordiality, amid whoops and holloas, and cries of 'now Twankay!—now Sugar!—now Figs!' Waving his hand in token of recognition, he passed on and made straight for Tom Hill, with a face full of importance, and nearly rode over a hound in his hurry. 'Now, Tom,' said he, with the greatest energy, 'do, my good fellow, strain every nerve to show sport to-day.—A gentleman has come all the way from the north-east side of the town of Boroughbridge, in the county of York, to see our excellent 'ounds, and I would fain have him galvanised.—Do show us a run, and let it end with blood, so that he may have something to tell the natives when he gets back to his own parts. That's him, see, sitting under the yew-tree, in a bottle-green coat with basket buttons, just striking a light on the pommel of his saddle to indulge in a fumigation.—Keep your eye on him all day, and if you can lead him over an awkward place, and get him a purl, so much the better.—If he'll risk his neck I'll risk my 'oss's.'

The Yorkshireman, having lighted his cigar and tightened his girths, rode leisurely among the horsemen, many of whom were in eager council, and a gentle breeze wafted divers scraps of conversation to his ear.

What is that hound got by? No. How is that horse bred? No. What sport had you on Wednesday? No. Is it a likely find to-day? No, no, no; it was not where the hounds, but what the Consols, left off at; what the four per cents, and not the four horses, were up to; what the condition of the money, not the horse, market. 'Anything doing in Danish bonds, sir?' said one. 'You must do it by lease and release, and levy a fine,' replied another. Scott *v.* Brown, crim. con. to be heard on or before Wednesday next.—Barley thirty-two to forty-two.—Fine upland meadow and rye grass hay, seventy to eighty.—The last pocket of hops I sold brought seven pounds fifteen shillings. Sussex bags six pounds ten shillings.—There were only twenty-eight and a quarter ships at market, 'and coals are coals.' 'Glad to hear it, sir, for half the last you sent me were slates.'—'Best qualities of beef four shillings and eightpence a stone—mutton three shillings and eightpence, to four shillings and sixpence.—He was exceedingly ill when I paid my last visit—I gave him nearly a stone of Epsom-salts, and bled him twice.—This horse would suit you to a T, sir, but my skip-jack is coming out on one at two o'clock that can carry a house.—See what a bosom this one's got.—Well, Gunter, old boy, have you iced your horse to-day?—Have you heard that Brown and Co. are in the *Gazette*? No, which Brown—not John Brown? No, William Brown. What, Brown of Goodman's Fields? No, Brown of —— Street—Brown*e* with an *e*; you know the man I mean.—Oh, Lord, ay, the man wot used to be called Nosey Browne.' A general move ensued, and they left 'the meet'.

'Vere be you going to turn out pray, sir, may I inquire?' said a gentleman in green to the huntsman, as he turned into a field. 'Turn out,' said he, 'why, ye don't suppose we be come calf-hunting, do ye? We throws off some two stones'-throw from here, if so be you mean what cover we are going to draw.' 'No,' said green-coat, 'I mean where do you turn out the stag?'—'D—n the stag, we know nothing about such matters,' replied the huntsman. 'Ware wheat! ware wheat! ware wheat!' was now the general cry, as a gentleman in nankeen pantaloons and Hessian boots with long brass spurs, commenced a navigation across a sprouting crop. 'Ware wheat, ware wheat!' replied he, considering it part of the ceremony of hunting, and continued his forward course. 'Come to my side,' said Mr ——, to the whipper-in, 'and meet that gentleman as he arrives at yonder gate; and keep by him while I scold you.'—'Now, sir, most particularly d—n you, for riding slap-dash over the young wheat, you most confounded insensible ignorant tinker, isn't the headland wide enough both for you and your horse, even if your spurs were as long again as they are?' Shouts of 'Yooi over, over, over hounds—try for him—yoicks— wind him! good dogs—yoicks! stir him up—have at him there!'—here interrupted the jaw-bation, and the whip rode off shaking his sides with laughter. 'Your horse has got a stone in each forefoot, and a thorn in his near hock,' observed a dentist to a wholesale haberdasher from Ludgate Hill, 'allow me to extract them for you—no pain, I assure—over before you know it.' 'Come away, hounds! come away!' was heard, and presently the huntsman, with some of the pack at his horse's heels, issued from the wood playing *Rule, Britannia!* on a key-bugle, while the cracks of heavy-thonged whips warned the stragglers and loiterers to follow. 'Music hath charms to soothe the savage beast,' observed Jorrocks, as he tucked the laps of his frock over his thighs, 'and I hope we shall find before long, else that quarter of house-lamb will be utterly ruined. Oh, dear, they are going below hill I do believe! why we shall never get home to-day, and I told Mrs Jorrocks half-past five to a minute, and I invited old Fleecy, who is a most punctual man.'

Jorrocks was right in his surmise. They arrived on the summit of a range of steep hills commanding an extensive view over the neighbouring country—almost, he said, as far as the sea-coast. The huntsman and hounds went down, but many of the field held a council of war on the top. 'Well! who's going down?' said one. 'I shall wait for the next turn,' said Jorrocks, 'for my horse does not like collar work.' 'I shall go this time,' said another 'and the rest next.' 'And so will I,' said a third, 'for mayhap there will be no second turn.' 'Ay,' added a fourth, 'and he may go the other way, and then where shall we all be?' 'Poh!' said Jorrocks, 'did you ever know a Surrey fox not take to the hills?—If he does not, I'll eat him without mint sauce,' again harping on the quarter of lamb. Facilis descensus Averni—two thirds of the field went down, leaving Jorrocks, two horse-dealers in scarlet, three chicken-butchers, half a dozen swells in leathers, a whip, and the Yorkshireman on the summit. 'Why don't you go with the hounds?' inquired the latter of the whip. 'Oh, I wait here, sir,' said he, 'to meet Tom Hills as he comes up, and to give him a fresh horse.' 'And who is Tom Hills?' inquired the Yorkshireman. 'Oh, he's our huntsman,' replied he; 'you know Tom, don't you?' 'Why, I can't say I do, exactly,' said he; 'but tell me, is he called Hills because he rides up and down these hills, or is that his real name?' 'Hought! you know as well as I do,' said he, quite indignantly, 'that Tom Hills is his name.'

The hounds, with the majority of the field, having effected the descent of the hills, were now trotting on in the valley below, sufficiently near, however, to allow our hill party full view of their proceedings. After drawing a couple of osier-beds blank, they assumed a line parallel to the hills, and moved on to a wood of about ten acres, the west end of which terminated in a natural gorse. 'They'll find there to a certainty,' said Mr Jorrocks, pulling a telescope out of his breeches' pocket, and adjusting the sight. 'Never saw it blank but once, and that was the werry day the commercial panic of twenty-five commenced.—I remember making an entry in my ledger when I got home to that effect. Humph!' continued he, looking through the glass, 'they are through the wood, though, with a challenge.—Now, my booys, push him out of the gorse! Let's see vot you're made of.—There goes the first 'ound in.— It's Galloper, I believe.—I can almost see the bag of shot round his neck.—Now they all follow.—One—two—three—four—five—all together, my beauties! Oh, vot a sight! Peckham's cap's in the air, and it's a find, by heavens!' Mr Jorrocks is right.—The southerly wind wafts up the fading notes of the 'Huntsman's Chorus' in *Der Freischutz* and confirms the fact.—Jorrocks is in ecstasies.—'Now,' said he, clawing up his breeches (for he dispenses with the article of braces when out hunting), 'that's what I calls fine. Oh, beautiful! beautiful!—Now, follow me if you please, and if yon gentleman in drab does not shoot the fox, he will be on the hills before long.' Away they scampered along the top of the ridge, with a complete view of the operations below. At length Jorrocks stopped, and pulling the telescope out, began making an observation. 'There he is, at last,' cried he, 'just crossed the corner of yon green field—now he creeps through the hedge by the fir-tree, and is in the fallow one. Yet, stay—that's no fox—it's a hare: and yet Tom Hills makes straight for the spot—and did you hear that loud tally-ho? Oh! gentlemen, gentlemen, we shall be laughed to scorn—what can they be doing—see, they take up the scent, and the whole pack have joined in chorus. Great heavens, it's no more a fox than I am!—No more brush than a badger! Oh dear! oh, dear! that I should live to see my old friends, the Surrey fox'ounds, 'unt hare, and that too in the presence of a stranger.' The animal made direct for the hills—whatever it was, the hounds were on good terms with it, and got away in good form. The sight was splendid—all the field got well off, nor between the cover and the hills was there sufficient space for tailing. A little elderly gentleman, in a pepper-and-salt coat, led the way gallantly—then came the scarlets—then the darks—and then the fustian-clad countrymen. Jorrocks was in a shocking state, and rolled along the hill-tops, almost frantic. The field reached the bottom, and the foremost commenced the steep ascent.

'Oh, Tom Hills!—Tom Hills!—"what are you at? what are you arter?" demanded Jorrocks, as he landed on the top. 'Here's a gentleman come all the way from the north-east side of the town of Boroughbridge, in the county of York, to see our excellent 'ounds, and here you are running a hare. Oh, Tom Hills! Tom Hills! ride forward, ride forward, and whip them off, ere we eternally disgrace ourselves.' 'Oh,' says Tom, laughing, 'he's a fox! but he's so tarnation frightened of our hounds, that his brush dropped off through very fear, as soon as ever he heard us go into the wood; if you go back, you'll find it somewhere, Mr Jorrocks; haw, haw, haw! No fox indeed!' said he.—'Forrard, hounds, forrard!' And away he went—caught the old whipper-in, dismounted him in a twinkling, and was on a fresh horse with his hounds in full cry. The line of flight was still along the hill-tops, and all eagerly pressed on, making a goodly rattle over the beds of flints. A check ensued. 'The guard on yonder nasty Brighton coach has frightened him with his horn,' said Tom; 'now we must make a cast up to yonder garden, and see if he's taken shelter among the geraniums in the greenhouse. As little damage as possible, gentlemen, if you please, in riding through the nursery grounds. Now, hold hard, sir—pray do—there's no occasion for you to break the kale pots; he can't be under them. Ah, yonder he goes, the tailless beggar; did you see him as he stole past the corner out of the early-cabbage bed? Now bring on the hounds, and let us press him towards London.'

'See the conquering hero comes,' sounded through the avenue of elms as Tom dashed forward with the merry, merry pack. 'I shall stay on the hills,' said one, 'and be ready for him as he comes back; I took a good deal of the shine out of my horse in coming up this time.' ' I think I will do the same,' said two or three more. 'Let's be doing,' said Jorrocks, ramming his spurs into his nag to seduce him into a gallop, who after sending his heels in the air a few times in token of his disapprobation of such treatment, at last put himself into a round-rolling sort of canter, which Jorrocks kept up by dint of spurring and dropping his great bastinaderer of a whip every now and then across his shoulders. Away they go pounding together!

The line lies over flint fallows occasionally diversified with a turnip-field or market-garden, and every now and then a 'willa' appears, from which emerge footmen in jackets, and in yellow, red and green plush breeches, with no end of admiring housemaids, governesses, and nurses with children in their arms.

R. S. Surtees (1805–64), from *The Yorkshireman and the Surrey*

The Find

Yon sound's neither sheep-bell nor bark,
They're running—they're running. Go hark!
The sport may be lost by a moment's delay;
So whip up the puppies and scurry away,
Dash down through the cover by dingle and dell,
There's gate at the bottom—I know it full well;
And they're running—they're running,
Go hark!

They're running—they're running. Go hark!
One fence and we're out of the park;
Sit down in your saddles and race at the brook,
Then smash at the bullfinch; no time for a look;
Leave cravens and skirters to dangle behind;
He's away for the moors in the teeth of the wind,
And they're running—they're running,
Go hark!

They're running—they're running. Go hark!
Let them run on and run till it's dark!
Well with them we are, and well with them we'll be,
While there's wind in our horses and daylight to see:
Then shog along homeward, chat over the fight,
And bear in our dreams the sweet music all night
Of—They're running—they're running,
Go hark!

CHARLES KINGSLEY (1819–75)

Tally-Ho!

There are soul-stirring clouds in the fiddle and flute,
When dancing begins in the hall,
And a goddess in muslin, that's likely to suit,
Is the mate of your choice for the ball;
But the player may strain every finger in vain,
And the fiddler may rosin his bow,
Nor flourish nor string such a rapture shall bring,
As the music of sweet Tally-Ho!

There's a melody, too, in the whispering trees
When day has gone down in the West,
And a lullaby soft in the sigh of the breeze
That hushes the woods to their rest;
There are madrigals fair in the voices of air,
In the stream with its ripple and flow,
But a merrier tune shall delight us at noon,
In the music of sweet Tally-Ho!

When autumn is flaunting his banner of pride
For glory that summer has fled,
Arrayed in the robes of his royalty, dyed
In tawny and orange and red;
When the oak is yet rife with the vigour of life,
Though his acorns are dropping below,
Through bramble and brake shall the echoes awake,
To the ring of a clear Tally-Ho!

'A fox, for a hundred!' they know it, the pack,
  Old Chorister always speaks true,
And the Whip from his corner is told to come back,
  And forbid to go on for a view.
Now the varmint is spied, as he crosses the ride,
  A tough old campaigner I trow—
Long, limber, and grey, see him stealing away
  —Half a minute!—and then—Tally-Ho!

Mark Fanciful standing, all eye and all ear,
  One second, ere wild for the fun,
She is lashing along with the pace of a deer,
  Her comrades to join in the run.
Your saddle you grip, gather bridle and whip,
  Give your hunter the office to go,
In his rush through the air little breath is to spare
  For the cheer of your wild Tally-Ho!

At the end of the wood the old farmer in brown,
  On the back of his good little mare,
Shows a grin of delight and a jolly bald crown,
  As he holds up his hat in the air;
Though at heart he's as keen as if youth were still green,
  Yet (a secret all sportsmen should know)
Not a word will he say till the fox is away,
  Then he gives you a real Tally-Ho!

There's a scent, you may swear, by the pace that they drive,
  You must tackle to work with a will,
For as sure as you stand in your stirrups alive,
  It's a case of a run and a kill!
So I wish you good speed, a good line, and a lead,
  With the luck of each fence where it's low,
Not the last of the troop, may you hear the Who-Whoop,
  Well pleased as you heard Tally-Ho!

G. J. WHYTE-MELVILLE (1821–78)

'A Pleasant Duty'

The time went very pleasantly. Some adventures I had;—two of which I told in the *Tales of All Countries*, under the names of *The O'Conors of Castle Conor*, and *Father Giles of Ballymoy*. I will not swear to every detail in these stories, but the main purport of each is true. I could tell many others of the same nature, were this the place for them. I found that the surveyor to whom I had been sent kept a pack of hounds, and therefore I bought a hunter. I do not think he liked it, but he could not well complain. He never rode to hounds himself, but I did; and then and thus began one of the great joys of my life. I have ever since been constant to the sport, having learned to love it with an affection which I cannot myself fathom or understand. Surely no man has laboured at it as I have done, or hunted under such drawbacks as to distances, money, and natural disadvantages. I am very heavy, very blind, have been—in reference to hunting—a poor man, and am now an old man. I have often had to travel all night outside a mail-coach, in order that I might hunt the next day. Nor have I ever been in truth a good horseman. And I have passed the greater part of my hunting life under the discipline of the Civil Service. But it has been for more than thirty years a duty to me to ride to hounds; and I have performed that duty with a persistent energy. Nothing has ever been allowed to stand in the way of hunting,—neither the writing of books, nor the work of the Post Office, nor other pleasures. As regarded the Post Office, it soon seemed to be understood that I was to hunt; and when my services were re-transferred to England, no word of difficulty ever reached me on the subject. I have written on very many subjects, and on most of them with pleasure; but on no subject with such delight as that of hunting. I have dragged it into many novels,—into too many no doubt,—but I have always felt myself deprived of a legitimate joy when the nature of the tale has not allowed me a hunting chapter. Perhaps that which gave me the greatest delight was the description of a run on a horse accidentally taken from another sportsman,—a circumstance which occurred to my dear friend Charles Buxton, who will be remembered as one of the members for Surrey.

ANTHONY TROLLOPE (1815–82), *An Autobiography*

Friday, 7 March 1873

In the afternoon I drove to Whitney Rectory in the dog-cart to dine and sleep. An April day and showers and shine with exquisitely clear views of the mountains and two beautiful rainbows. Before dinner Emily, Jane and Armine Dew walked with me up through the steep hanging wood above the railway, carpeted with primroses upbreaking through the earth. After dinner Henry Dew told us some of his old hunting reminiscences of the days when he rode with the Maesllwch fox-hounds.

Charles Lacy was out with the Radnorshire and West Herefordshire fox-hounds when they met at Cabalva last Wednesday. He gave an amusing description of the run. Old Tom Evans, the tailor, of Cwm Ithel on Clyro Hill, was once a running huntsman with the Clyro harriers, and very keen after the sport. When he heard the hunting horns along the hill on

Wednesday the old hunting instinct in him awoke like a giant refreshed. He scrambled on to his old pony and rode furiously into the middle of the pack hat in hand hooping and holloing and laying the hounds on the scent as of yore. Colonel Price the MFH was greatly enraged. 'Man! Man!' he shouted. 'Where are you going, man? Come from those hounds!' But the tailor maddened with the chase was deaf to all entreaties and commands. He careered along among and over the hounds, hooping, holloing and waving his hat till the enraged MFH charged him and knocked tailor and pony head over heels. Nothing daunted however the tailor scrambled on to his beast again and he and his pony were second in at the death, close at the heels of the MFH.

Charles Lacy said the bag fox had been kept in a dark cellar so long that he was dazed and half blind when he was turned out. After they had killed the bag fox they tried for a wild one at Dolbedwyn, where some poultry had been stolen by a fox.

FRANCIS KILVERT (1840–79), *Diary*

A Runnable Stag

When the pods went pop on the broom, green broom,
   And apples began to be golden-skinned,
We harboured a stag in the Priory coomb,
   And we feathered his trail up-wind, up-wind,
   We feathered his trail up-wind—
      A stag of warrant, a stag, a stag,
      A runnable stag, a kingly crop,
      Brow, bay and tray and three on top,
      A stag, a runnable stag.

Then the huntsman's horn rang yap, yap, yap,
   And 'Forwards' we heard the harbourer shout;
But 'twas only a brocket that broke a gap
   In the beechen underwood, driven out,
   From the underwood antlered out
      By warrant and might of the stag, the stag,
      The runnable stag, whose lordly mind
      Was bent on sleep, though beamed and tined
      He stood, a runnable stag.

So we tufted the covert till afternoon
  With Tinkerman's Pup and Bell-of-the-North;
And hunters were sulky and hounds out of tune
  Before we tufted the right stag forth,
  Before we tufted him forth,
    The stag of warrant, the wily stag,
    The runnable stag with his kingly crop,
    Brow, bay and tray and three on top,
    The royal and runnable stag.

It was Bell-of-the-North and Tinkerman's Pup
  That stuck to the scent till the copse was drawn.
'Tally ho! tally ho!' and the hunt was up,
  The tufters whipped and the pack laid on,
  The resolute pack laid on,
    And the stag of warrant away at last,
    The runnable stag, the same, the same,
    His hoofs on fire, his horns like flame,
    A stag, a runnable stag.

'Let your gelding be: if you check or chide
  He stumbles at once and you're out of the hunt;
For three hundred gentlemen, able to ride,
  On hunters accustomed to bear the brunt,
  Accustomed to bear the brunt,
    Are after the runnable stag, the stag,
    The runnable stag with his kingly crop,
    Brow, bay and tray and three on top,
    The right, the runnable stag.'

By perilous paths in coomb and dell,
  The heather, the rocks, and the river-bed,
The pace grew hot, for the scent lay well,
  And a runnable stag goes right ahead,
  The quarry went right ahead—
    Ahead, ahead, and fast and far;
    His antlered crest, his cloven hoof,
    Brow, bay and tray and three aloof,
    The stag, the runnable stag.

For a matter of twenty miles and more,
  By the densest hedge and the highest wall,
Through herds of bullocks he baffled the lore
  Of harbourer, huntsman, hounds and all,
  Of harbourer hounds and all—

The stag of warrant, the wily stag,
For twenty miles, and five and five,
He ran, and he never was caught alive,
This stag, this runnable stag.

When he turned at bay in the leafy gloom,
In the emerald gloom where the brook ran deep,
He heard in the distance the rollers boom,
And he saw in a vision of peaceful sleep,
In a wonderful vision of sleep,
A stag of warrant, a stag, a stag,
A runnable stag in a jewelled bed,
Under the sheltering ocean dead,
A stag, a runnable stag.

So a fateful hope lit up his eye,
And he opened his nostrils wide again,
And he tossed his branching antlers high
As he headed the hunt down the Charlock glen,
As he raced down the echoing glen
For five miles more, the stag, the stag,
For twenty miles, and five and five,
Not to be caught now, dead or alive,
The stag, the runnable stag.

Three hundred gentlemen, able to ride,
Three hundred horses as gallant and free,
Beheld him escape on the evening tide,
Far out till he sank in the Severn Sea,
Till he sank in the depths of the sea—
The stag, the buoyant stag, the stag
That slept at last in a jewelled bed
Under the sheltering ocean spread,
The stag, the runnable stag.

JOHN DAVIDSON (1857–1909)

From *Reynard the Fox*

Meanwhile the fox passed Nonesuch Farm,
Keeping the spinney on his right.
Hounds raced him here with all their might
Along the short firm grass, like fire.
The cowman viewed him from the byre

Lolloping on, six fields ahead,
Then hounds, still carrying such a head
It made him stare, then Rob on Pip,
Sailing the great grass like a ship,
Then grand Maroon in all his glory,
Sweeping his strides, his great chest hoary
With foam fleck and the pale hill-marl.
They strode the Leet, they flew the Snarl,
They knocked the nuts at Nonesuch Mill,
Raced up the spur of Gallows Hill
And viewed him there. The line he took
Was Tineton and the Pantry Brook,
Going like fun and hounds like mad.
Tom glanced to see what friends he had
Still within sight, before he turned
The ridge's shoulder; he discerned,
One field away, young Cothill sailing
Easily up. Pete Gurney failing.

Hugh Colway quartering on Sir Peter,
Bill waiting on the mare to beat her,
Sal Ridden skirting to the right.
A horse, with stirrups flashing bright
Over his head at every stride,
Looked like the Major's; Tom espied
Far back a scarlet speck of man
Running, and straddling as he ran.
Charles Copse was up, Nob Manor followed,
Then Bennett's big-boned black that wallowed,
Clumsy, but with the strength of ten.
Then black and brown and scarlet men,
Brown horses, white and black and grey,
Scattered a dozen fields away.
The shoulder shut the scene away.

* * * * * * *

From the Gallows Hill to the Tineton Copse
There were ten ploughed fields, like ten full-stops,
All wet red clay, where a horse's foot
Would be swathed, feet thick, like an ash-tree root.
The fox raced on, on the headlands firm,
Where his swift feet scared the coupling worm;
The rooks rose raving to curse him raw,
He snarled a sneer at their swoop and caw.

Then on, then on, down a half-ploughed field
Where a ship-like plough drove glitter-keeled,
With a bay horse near and a white horse leading,
And a man saying 'Zook', and the red earth bleeding.
He gasped as he saw the ploughman drop
The stilts and swear at the team to stop.
The ploughman ran in his red clay clogs,
Crying, 'Zick un, Towzer; zick, good dogs!'
A couple of wire-haired lurchers lean
Arose from his wallet, nosing keen;
With a rushing swoop they were on his track,
Putting chest to stubble to bite his back.
He swerved from his line with the curs at heel,
The teeth as they missed him clicked like steel.
With a worrying snarl, they quartered on him,
While the ploughman shouted, 'Zick; upon him.'

* * * * * * *

The lurcher dogs soon shot their bolt,
And the fox raced on by the Hazel Holt,
Down the dead grass tilt to the sandstone gash
Of the Pantry Brook at Tineton Ash.
The loitering water, flooded full,
Had yeast on its lip like raddled wool,
It was wrinkled over with Arab script
Of eddies that twisted up and slipped
The stepping-stones had a rush about them,
So the fox plunged in and swam without them.

* * * * * * *

He crossed to the cattle's drinking shallow,
Firmed up with rush and the roots of mallow;
He wrung his coat from his draggled bones
And romped away for the Sarsen Stones.

* * * * * * *

A sneaking glance with his ears flexed back
Made sure that his scent had failed the pack,
For the red clay, good for corn and roses,
Was cold for scent and brought hounds to noses

* * * * * * *

He slackened pace by the Tineton Tree
(A vast hollow ash-tree grown in three),
He wriggled a shake and padded slow,
Not sure if the hounds were on or no.

* * * * * * *

A horn blew faint, then he heard the sounds
Of a cantering huntsman, lifting hounds;
The ploughman had raised his hat for sign,
And the hounds were lifted and on his line.
He heard the splash in the Pantry Brook,
And a man's voice: 'Thiccy's the line he took.'
And a clear 'Yoi doit!' and a whimpering quaver,
Though the lurcher dogs had dulled the savour.

* * * * * * *

The fox went off while the hounds made halt,
And the horses breathed and the field found fault,
But the whimpering rose to a crying crash
By the hollow ruin of Tineton Ash.

Then again the kettledrum horsehooves beat,
And the green blades bent to the fox's feet,
And the cry rose keen not far behind
Of the 'Blood, blood, blood,' in the foxhounds' mind.

* * * * * * *

The fox was strong, he was full of running,
He could run for an hour and then be cunning,
But the cry behind him made him chill,
They were nearer now and they meant to kill.
They meant to run him until his blood
Clogged on his heart as his brush with mud,
Till his back bent up and his tongue hung flagging,
And his belly and brush were filthed from dragging.
Till he crouched stone-still, dead-beat and dirty,
With nothing but teeth against the thirty.
And all the way to that blinding end
He would meet with men and have none his friend:
Men to holloa and men to run him,
With stones to stagger and yells to stun him;
Men to head him, with whips to beat him,
Teeth to mangle and mouths to eat him.

And all the way, that wild high crying,
To cold his blood with the thought of dying,
The horn and the cheer, and the drum-like thunder
Of the horsehooves stamping the meadow under.
He upped his brush and went with a will
For the Sarsen Stones on Wan Dyke Hill.

JOHN MASEFIELD (1878–1967)

St Valentine's Day

Today, all day, I rode upon the down,
With hounds and horsemen, a brave company.
On this side in its glory lay the sea,
On that the Sussex weald, a sea of brown.
The wind was light, and brightly the sun shone,
And still we galloped on from gorse to gorse.
And once, when checked, a thrush sang, and my horse
Pricked his quick ears as to a sound unknown.
I knew the Spring was come. I knew it even
Better than all by this, that through my chase
In bush and stone and hills and sea and heaven
I seemed to see and follow still your face.
Your face my quarry was. For it I rode,
My horse a thing of wings, myself a god.

WILFRID SCAWEN BLUNT (1840–1922)

'The Stag at Eve'

I

The stag at eve had drunk his fill,
Where danced the moon on Monan's rill,
And deep his midnight lair had made
In lone Glenartney's hazel shade;
But, when the sun his beacon red
Had kindled on Benvoirlich's head,
The deep-mouth'd bloodhound's heavy bay
Resounded up the rocky way,
And faint, from farther distance borne,
Were heard the clanging hoof and horn.

II

As Chief, who hears his warder call,
'To arms! the foemen storm the wall,'
The antler'd monarch of the waste
Sprung from his heathery couch in haste.
But, ere his fleet career he took,
The dew-drops from his flanks he shook;
Like crested leader proud and high,
Toss'd his beam'd frontlet to the sky;
A moment gazed adown the dale,
A moment snuff'd the tainted gale
A moment listen'd to the cry,
That thicken'd as the chase drew nigh;
Then, as the headmost foes appear'd,
With one brave bound the copse he clear'd,
And, stretching forward free and far,
Sought the wild heaths of Uam-Var.

III

Yell'd on the view the opening pack;
Rock, glen, and cavern, paid them back;
To many a mingled sound at once
The awaken'd mountain gave response.
A hundred dogs bay'd deep and strong,
Clatter'd a hundred steeds along,
Their peal the merry horns rung out,
A hundred voices join'd the shout;
With hark and whoop and wild halloo,
No rest Benvoirlich's echoes knew.
Far from the tumult fled the roe,
Close in her covert cower'd the doe;
The falcon, from her cairn on high,
Cast on the rout a wondering eye,
Till far beyond her piercing ken
The hurricane had swept the glen.
Faint and more faint, its failing din
Return'd from cavern, cliff, and linn,
And silence settled, wide and still,
On the lone wood and mighty hill.

IV

Less loud the sounds of silvan war
Disturb'd the heights of Uam-Var,
And roused the cavern, where, 'tis told,
A giant made his den of old;

For ere that steep ascent was won,
High in his pathway hung the sun,
And many a gallant, stay'd perforce,
Was fain to breathe his faltering horse,
And of the trackers of the deer,
Scarce half the lessening pack was near;
So shrewdly on the mountain side
Had the bold burst their mettle tried.

V

The noble stag was pausing now
Upon the mountain's southern brow,
Where broad extended, far beneath,
The varied realms of fair Menteith.
With anxious eye he wander'd o'er
Mountain and meadow, moss and moor,
And ponder'd refuge from his toil
By far Lochard or Aberfoyle.
But nearer was the copsewood grey,
That waved and wept in Loch-Achray,
And mingled with the pine-trees blue
On the bold cliffs of Benvenue.
Fresh vigour with the hope return'd,
With flying foot the heath he spurn'd,
Held westward with unwearied race,
And left behind the panting chase.

VI

'Twere long to tell what steeds gave o'er,
As swept the hunt through Cambusmore:
What reins were tighten'd in despair,
When rose Benledi's ridge in air;
Who flagg'd upon Bochastle's heath,
Who shunn'd to stem the flooded Teith,—
For twice that day, from shore to shore,
The gallant stag swam stoutly o'er.
Few were the stragglers, following far,
That reach'd the lake of Vennachar;
And when the Brigg of Turk was won,
The headmost horseman rode alone.

VII

Alone, but with unbated zeal,
That horseman plied the scourge and steel;

For jaded now, and spent with toil,
Emboss'd with foam, and dark with soil,
While every gasp with sobs he drew,
The labouring stag strain'd full in view.
Two dogs of black Saint Hubert's breed,
Unmatch'd for courage, breath, and speed,
Fast on his flying traces came,
And all but won that desperate game;
For, scarce a spear's length from his haunch,
Vindictive toil'd the bloodhounds stanch;
Nor nearer might the dogs attain,
Nor farther might the quarry strain.
Thus up the margin of the lake,
Between the precipice and brake,
O'er stock and rock their race they take.

VIII

The Hunter mark'd that mountain high,
The lone lake's western boundary,
And deem'd the stag must turn to bay,
Where that huge rampart barr'd the way;
Already glorying in the prize,
Measured his antlers with his eyes;
For the death-wound and death-halloo,
Muster'd his breath, his whinyard drew;—
But thundering as he came prepared,
With ready arm and weapon bared,
The wily quarry shunn'd the shock,
And turn'd him from the opposing rock;
Then, dashing down a darksome glen,
Soon lost to hound and hunter's ken,
In the deep Trosachs' wildest nook
His solitary refuge took.
There, while close couch'd, the thicket shed
Cold dews and wild-flowers on his head,
He heard the baffled dogs in vain
Rave through the hollow pass amain,
Chiding the rocks that yell'd again.

IX

Close on the hounds the hunter came,
To cheer them on the vanish'd game;
But, stumbling in the rugged dell,
The gallant horse exhausted fell.

The impatient rider strove in vain
To rouse him with the spur and rein,
For the good steed, his labours o'er,
Stretch'd his stiff limbs, to rise no more;
Then, touch'd with pity and remorse,
He sorrow'd o'er the expiring horse:
'I little thought, when first thy rein
I slack'd upon the banks of Seine,
That Highland eagle e'er should feed
On thy fleet limbs, my matchless steed!
Woe worth the chase, woe worth the day,
That costs thy life, my gallant grey!'

SIR WALTER SCOTT, from *The Lady of the Lake*

The Fall of the Deer

[From an old MS.]

Now the loud Crye is up, and harke!
The barkye Trees give back the Bark;
The House Wife heares the merrie rout,
And runnes,—and lets the beere run out,
Leaving her Babes to weepe,—for why?
She likes to heare the Deer Dogges crye,
And see the wild Stag how he stretches
The naturall Buck-skin of his Breeches,
Running like one of Human kind
Dogged by fleet Bailiffes close behind—
As if he had not payde his Bill
For Ven'son, or was owing still
For his two Hornes, and soe did get
Over his Head and Ears in Debt;—
Wherefore he strives to paye his Waye
With his long Legges the while he maye:—
But he is chased, like Silver Dish,
As well as anye Hart may wish
Except that one whose Heart doth beat
So faste it hasteneth his feet;—
And runninge soe, he holdeth Death
Four Feet from him,—till his Breath
Faileth, and slacking Pace at last,
From runninge slow he standeth faste,
With hornie Bayonettes at baye,
To baying Dogges around, and they

Pushing him sore, he pusheth sore,
And goreth them that seeke his Gore,
Whatever Dogge his Horne doth rive
Is dead—as sure as he's alive!
Soe that courageous Hart doth fight
With Fate, and calleth up his might
And standeth stout that he maye fal
Bravelye, and be avenged of all,
Nor like a Craven yeeld his Breath
Under the Jawes of Dogges and Death!

THOMAS HOOD (1799–1845)

A Scene [after Hunting] at Swallowfield in Berkshire

Dr Thirlby There's pleasure, sure, in being clad in green,
Which none but huntsmen know. How did my limbs
Exult, to find themselves disrobed of black!
What is the scold of bedmakers to that
Harmonious pack! or what the solemn note
Of beadle Simpson to our huntsman shrill!
I felt unusual courage when the fox,
Wiliest of creatures, stared me in the face
(Through enterprise or fear, I cannot tell);
But sure the beast was hideous. Yet I stood
Undaunted, at the time that Whaley's self
Fled in dismay, and sought the neighbouring copse.
Had not my noblest champion, generous Dodd,
Spurred to my aid, that moment were my last.

Whaley You wrong me, Doctor, by the manes great
Of my all-trading sire: I ne'er was deemed
A coward; no, not when the gander dire,
Furious with poked-out neck and flapping wings,
Assailed me sore perplexed; but soon the gaggling
Monster a victim fell to stone or stick.
Then call it caution; for believe me, sirs,
I took the grinning monster for a wolf.

Mr Dodd gives Whaley a slap on the face, and says,

Thou art the vilest coward that e'er lived;
I saw thee as thou fled'st, and if my sense
Divined aright, methought I smelt thee too.
In vain the standing corn opposed my speed,
In vain the farmer swore; nor hedge nor oaths
Deterred me; hedge I broke, and oaths returned
With recompense, and came in need extreme

To save my friend, waging unequal war.
But thy o'er-wearied spirits ask recruit.
A cordial for the Doctor!—As for him,
I'll make example dire, and to be rued
By cowards yet unborn; that all may learn
Boldness and enterprise, and fear to fear.
Here, take him hence!

Whaley Ah me! how happy once!

Exit

Dodd O for invention to chastise the crime!
Through all my house, through kitchen, pantry, hall,
To grooms, and cook, and butler, be it known
That 'tis my pleasure Whaley fast this day;
And whoso'er clandestine shall appease
His longing maw, himself shall fast I swear.

Dr Thirlby Consider, sir, lest indignation, just
In principle, transport you to pronounce
A sentence too severe, and o'er-proportioned
To the transgression (foul, I must confess);
But must not mercy whisper to the thought
A mulct less rigid?

Dodd Doctor, this age,
This dastard and fox-fearing age, demands
Severity and rigour.
Farrel, be thou the bearer of my will!

Whaley in his apartments. To him Farrel.

Farrel Excuse me, sir, if duty bids me speak
What kindness would conceal. Thus said my master:
'Through all my house, through kitchen, pantry, hall,
To grooms, and cook, and butler, be it known
That 'tis my pleasure Whaley fast this day;
And whoso'er clandestine shall appease
His longing maw, himself shall fast I swear.'

Whaley O Mr Farrel,
Supreme of valets, gently hast thou told
Thy message, which would else in telling wound,
And in performing end me. Some few hours
Pass, and you'll see my hunger-quaking cheeks,
And my loose skin, descending and unnerved,
Apron my nether parts. But I submit,
And will prepare, if possible, to fast. *Exit Farrel.*

Whaley solus Nimrod, I hate thee, premier hunter vile,
Beast of a man! and of all other beasts,
The fox is my aversion. Brute accursed,
Lamb-eating, narrow-snouted, stinking villain!

Author of all my sorrows! but for him
I yet had flourished, unimpeached of fear.
  Yet why the fox accused? how could he help
My trembling nature's fault, not his? or how
Contrive not to be taken for a wolf?
'Tis I, I only am to blame. O cowardice!
What ills dost thou create? But chief of thee,
Of thee I most complain, O want of food!
I've often heard, indeed, of that word *fast*,
But never yet the meaning could devise.
Ah! by severe experience now I feel
To fast is to abstain from meat and drink.
Happy the meagre, cloistered man resigned!
He at set periods, by spare diet taught,
Can his commanded appetites renounce,
And pine with voluntary want. But I,
Pampered, and sleek, and jovial, ill can brook
Th' abstemious trial. Flesh and blood can't bear it.
I will not fast. How not? ah! there's the question,
While surly grooms each avenue secure.
For twice twelve livelong hours must I then rue
Hunger and thirst, and my delighted spirits,
So oft in nectar bathed, exhausted flag!
Must I then lose thee, burgundy; nor taste
Delicious morsels, carp, or hare, or quail?
Unfortunate! Ev'n now perhaps the guests
At the thronged board make merry with my woes.
One asks with sneering purport, 'Where is Whaley?'
'Dining with good Duke Humphrey,' cries another.
Pratt smiles malignantly, and Davies grins
At my undoing; nay, perchance he rhymes
(Vile bard!), and on my ruin builds his song.
  No more—I'll to the window. Beauteous scene
Of water and of hills, of lawns and trees,
What respite can ye give to lean distress?
And you, plump deer, that scud along the lawn,
Serve but to raise my venison appetite!
  Am I deceived, or through the waving boughs
An alehouse sign peeps forth?—I'm not deceived,
For through the boughs an alehouse sign peeps forth;
Would I were there!—but ah! what gulf 's between!
When will tomorrow come?——

Bell rings to dinner. Whaley faints away.

SNEYD DAVIES (1709–69)

From *Epistle To Miss Blount, on her leaving the Town, after the Coronation*

Some Squire, perhaps, you take a delight to rack;
Whose game is Whisk, whose treat a toast in sack,
Who visits with a gun, presents you birds,
Then gives a smacking buss, and cries—No words!
Or with his hound comes hollowing from the stable,
Makes love with nods, and knees beneath a table;
Whose laughs are hearty, tho' his jests are coarse,
And loves you best of all things—but his horse.

ALEXANDER POPE (1688–1744)

'Hail, Happy Britain!'

Hail, happy Britain! highly-favoured isle,
And Heaven's peculiar care! To thee 'tis given
To train the sprightly steed, more fleet than those
Begot by winds, or the celestial breed
That bore the great Pelides through the press
Of heroes armed, and broke their crowded ranks;
Which proudly neighing, with the sun begins
Cheerful his course; and ere his beams decline,
Has measured half thy surface unfatigued.
In thee alone, fair land of liberty!
Is bred the perfect hound, in scent and speed
As yet unrivalled, while in other climes
Their virtue fails, a weak degenerate race.
In vain malignant steams, and winter fogs
Load the dull air, and hover round our coasts,
The huntsman ever gay, robust, and bold,
Defies the noxious vapour, and confides
In this delightful exercise, to raise
His drooping head and cheer his heart with joy.
Ye vigorous youths, by smiling Fortune blest
With large demesnes, hereditary wealth,
Heaped copious by your wise forefathers' care,
Hear and attend! while I the means reveal
To enjoy those pleasures, for the weak too strong,
Too costly for the poor; to rein the steed
Swift-stretching o'er the plain, to cheer the pack
Opening in concerts of harmonious joy,

But breathing death. What though the gripe severe
Of brazen-fisted Time, and slow disease
Creeping through every vein, and nerve unstrung,
Afflict my shattered frame, undaunted still,
Fixed as a mountain ash, that braves the bolts
Of angry Jove; though blasted, yet unfallen;
Still can my soul in Fancy's mirror view
Deeds glorious once, recal the joyous scene
In all its splendours decked, o'er the full bowl
Recount my triumphs past, urge others on
With hand and voice, and point the winding way:
Pleased with that social sweet garrulity,
The poor disbanded veteran's sole delight.

WILLIAM SOMERVILLE, from *The Chase*

An Elegy on the Death of Dobbin, the Butterwoman's Horse

The death of faithful Dobbin I deplore;
Dame Jolt's brown horse, old Dobbin, is no more.
The cruel Fates have snapped his vital thread,
And Gammer Jolt bewails old Dobbin dead.
From stony Cudham down to watery Cray,
This honest horse brought butter every day,
Fresh butter meet to mix with nicest rolls,
And sometimes eggs, and sometimes geese and fowls;
And though this horse to stand had ne'er a leg,
He never dropped a goose, or broke an egg.
Ye maids of Cray your buttered rolls deplore,
Dame Jolt's brown horse, old Dobbin, is no more.

Oft did the squire, that keeps the great hall-house,
Invite the willing vicar to a goose;
For goose could make his kindred Muse aspire
From earth to air, from water to the fire;
But now, alas! his towering spirit's fled,
His Muse is foundered, for poor Dobbin's dead.
Last Friday was a luckless day, I wot,
For Friday last lean Dobbin went to pot;
No drinks could cherish, no prescriptions save;
In C——n's hounds he found a living grave:
Weep all, and all (except sad dogs) deplore,
Dame's Jolt's brown horse, old Dobbin, is no more.

Skulk, Reynard, skulk in the securest grounds,
Now Dobbin hunts thee in the shape of hounds.
Late sure but slow he marched as foot could fall,
Sure to march slow whene'er he marched at all;
Now fleeter than the pinions of the wind,
He leaves the huntsman and the hunt behind,
Pursues thee o'er the hills and down the steep,
Through the rough copse, wide woods and waters deep,
Along th' unbounded plain, along the lea,
But has no pullet and no goose for thee.
Ye dogs, ye foxes, howl for Dobbin dead,
Nor thou, O Muse, disdain the tear to shed;
Ye maids of Cray your buttered rolls deplore,
Dame Jolt's brown horse, old Dobbin, is no more.

FRANCIS FAWKES (1720–77)

On the Death of Echo,
A Favourite Beagle

Silent at last, beneath the silent ground,
Here Echo lives, no unsubstantial sound
Nor babbling mimic—but a Beagle fleet
With drooping ears, keen nose, and nimble feet.
In the glad Chase she raised her merry voice
And made her name-sake of the woods rejoice,
But now dumb Death has chok'd poor Echo's cry
And to no call can Echo more reply—

HARTLEY COLERIDGE (1796–1849)

Simon Lee,
The Old Huntsman

with an incident in which he was concerned.

In the sweet shire of Cardigan,
Not far from pleasant Ivor-hall,
An Old Man dwells, a little man,
'Tis said he once was tall.
Full five-and-thirty years he lived
A running Huntsman merry;
And still the centre of his cheek
Is blooming as a cherry.

No man like him the horn could sound,
And hill and valley rang with glee
When Echo bandied, round and round,
The halloo of Simon Lee.
In those proud days, he little cared
For husbandry or tillage;
To blither tasks did Simon rouse
The sleepers of the village.

He all the country could outrun,
Could leave both man and horse behind;
And often, ere the chase was done,
He reeled and was stone-blind.
And still there's something in the world
At which his heart rejoices;
For when the chiming hounds are out,
He dearly loves their voices!

But, oh the heavy change!—bereft
Of health, strength, friends, and kindred, see!
Old Simon to the world is left
In liveried poverty.
His Master's dead,—and no one now
Dwells in the Hall of Ivor;
Men, dogs, and horses, all are dead;
He is the sole survivor.

WILLIAM WORDSWORTH

The Ballad of the Foxhunter

'Lay me in a cushioned chair;
Carry me, ye four,
With cushions here and cushions there,
To see the world once more.

'To stable and to kennel go;
Bring what is there to bring;
Lead my Lollard to and fro,
Or gently in a ring.

'Put the chair upon the grass:
Bring Rody and his hounds,
That I may contented pass
From these earthly bounds.'

His eyelids droop, his head falls low,
His old eyes cloud with dreams;
The sun upon all things that grow
Falls in sleepy streams.

Brown Lollard treads upon the lawn,
And to the armchair goes,
And now the old man's dreams are gone,
He smooths the long brown nose.

And now moves many a pleasant tongue
Upon his wasted hands,
For leading aged hounds and young
The huntsman near him stands.

'Huntsman Rody, blow the horn,
Make the hills reply.'
The huntsman loosens on the morn
A gay wandering cry.

Fire is in the old man's eyes,
His fingers move and sway,
And when the wandering music dies
They hear him feebly say,

'Huntsman Rody, blow the horn,
Make the hills reply.'
'I cannot blow upon my horn,
I can but weep and sigh.'

Servants round his cushioned place
Are with new sorrow wrung;
Hounds are gazing on his face,
Aged hounds and young.

One blind hound only lies apart
On the sun-smitten grass;
He holds deep commune with his heart:
The moments pass and pass;

The blind hound with a mournful din
Lifts slow his wintry head;
The servants bear the body in;
The hounds wail for the dead.

W. B. Yeats (1865–1939)

The Stable Path

The last red rose on the arch has faded,
  The border has mourned for its last white flower;
The dahlias droop where the frost has raided,
  The grass is wet with the autumn shower;
Dull are the paths with their leaf-strewn gravel,
  Cold is the wind as it wanders by,
Still there's a path that a man can travel
  Happy at heart though the roses die.

The path to the stable!—Though summer be ended,
  Though down through the garden no bird be astir,
This path has new melodies tunefully blended—
  The flick of a whip with the clink of a spur!
So—on through the yew-trees where shadows strike chiller,
  Across the paved court-yard, at last to the stall
Where, pawing in eagerness, chained on the pillar
  Stands, champing his bit-bars, the Pearl of them All!

WILL H. OGILVIE (1869–1963)

A Single Hound

When the opal lights in the West had died
  And night was wrapping the red ferns round,
As I come home by the woodland side
  I heard the cry of a single hound.

The huntsman had gathered his pack and gone;
  The last late hoof had echoed away;
The horn was twanging a long way on
  For the only hound that was still astray.

While, heedless of all but the work in hand,
  Up through the brake where the brambles twine,
Crying his joy to a drowsy land
  Javelin drove on a burning line.

The air was sharp with a touch of frost,
  The moon came up like a wheel of gold;
The wall at the end of the woods he crossed
  And flung away on the open wold.

And long as I listened beside the stile
The larches echoed that eerie sound:
Steady and tireless, mile on mile,
The hunting cry of a single hound.

WILL H. OGILVIE

The Old Squire

I like the hunting of the hare
Better than that of the fox;
I like the joyous morning air,
And the crowing of the cocks.

I like the calm of the early fields,
The ducks asleep by the lake,
The quiet hour which Nature yields,
Before mankind is awake.

I like the pheasants and feeding things
Of the unsuspicious morn;
I like the flap of the wood-pigeon's wings
As she rises from the corn.

I like the blackbird's shriek, and his rush
From the turnips as I pass by,
And the partridge hiding her head in a bush,
For her young ones cannot fly.

I like these things, and I like to ride,
When all the world is in bed,
To the top of the hill where the sky grows wide,
And where the sun grows red.

The beagles at my horse heels trot,
In silence after me;
There's Ruby, Roger, Diamond, Dot,
Old Slut and Margery,

A score of names well-used and dear,
The names my childhood knew;
The horn, with which I rouse their cheer,
Is the horn my father blew.

I like the hunting of the hare
   Better than that of the fox;
The new world still is all less fair
   Than the old world it mocks.

I covet not a wider range
   Than these dear manors give;
I take my pleasures without change,
   And as I lived I live.

I leave my neighbours to their thought;
   My choice it is, and pride,
On my own lands to find my sport,
   In my own fields to ride.

The hare herself no better loves
   The field where she was bred,
Than I the habit of these groves,
   My own inherited.

I know my quarries every one,
   The meuse where she sits low;
The road she chose to-day was run
   A hundred years ago.

The lags, the gills, the forest ways,
   The hedgerows one and all,
These are the kingdoms of my chase,
   And bounded by my wall;

Nor has the world a better thing,
   Though one should search it round,
Than thus to live one's own sole king,
   Upon one's own sole ground.

I like the hunting of the hare;
   It brings me, day by day,
The memory of old days as fair,
   With dead men past away.

To these, as homeward still I ply
   And pass the churchyard gate,
Where all are laid as I must lie,
   I stop and raise my hat.

I like the hunting of the hare;
    New sports I hold in scorn.
I like to be as my fathers were,
    In the days ere I was born.

WILFRID SCAWEN BLUNT

II

An Assembly of Animals

The Companyes of Bestys and Foule

An Herde of swannys
An Herde of cranys
An Herde of corlewys
An Herde of wrennys
A Nye of fesauntys
A Bevy of quayles
A Sege of herons
A Sege of bytourys
A Sorde or a Sute of malards
A Mustre of pecockys
A Walke of snytes
An Exaltynge of larkys
A Cherme of golfynches
A Flyghte of dovves
An Unkyndnes of ravens
A Clayterynge of choughes
A Dyssymulacion of byrdes
A Bevy of conyes
A Cowple of spanellys
A Tryppe of haarys
A Gagle of geys
A Brode of hennys
A Badelynge of dokys
A Covy of pertryches
A Sprynge of telys
A Deseerte of lapwynges
A Falle of wodcockes
A Congregacion of plovers
A Coverte of cootes
A Duell of turtylles

telys] teals

A Tygendis of pyes
A Flyght of swalowes
A Buyldynge of rokys
A Murmuracion of stares
A Nest of rabettys.

DAME JULIANA BERNERS (1486), *The Boke of St Albans*

From *The Squyre of Low Degree*

'To-morowe ye shall on hunting fare,
And ride, my doughter, in a chare;
It shal be covered with velvet reede,
And clothes of fine golde al about your hed,
With damaske white and asure-blewe,
Wel diapred with lillies newe;
Your pomelles shal be ended with gold,
Your chaines enameled many a folde;
Your mantel of riche degree,
Purpil palle and ermine free;
Jennettes of Spaine, that been so wight,
Trapped to the ground with velvet bright.
Ye shall have harpe, sautry, and songe,
And other mirthes you amonge.
Ye shall have rumney and malmesine,
Both ypocrasse and vernage wine,
Mountrose and wine of Greke,
Both algarde and respice eke,
Antioche and bastarde,
Piment also and garnarde,
Wine of Greke and muscadell,
Both clare, piment, and rochell;
The reed your stomake to defye,
And pottes of osey set you by.
You shall have venison ybake,

stares] starlings

chare] carriage diapred] patterned pomelles] ornamental knobs degree] quality purpil palle and ermine free] rich crimson cloth and noble ermine Jennettes] light horses wight] swift trapped] decked sautry] psaltery rumney and malmesine] sweet Grecian wine and Malmsey ypocrasse and vernage] spiced wine and sweet Italian wine algarde and respice] Algarve wine and red wine Antioche and bastarde] tonic wine and sweet Spanish Piment and garnarde] spiced wine and ?Granada wine rochel] wine of La Rochelle reed your stomake to defye] red wine to aid digestion osey] Alsace

The best wilde foule that may be take;
A lese of grehound with you to strike,
And hert and hinde and other like.
Ye shal be set at such a trist
That herte and hinde shall come to your fist;
Your disease to drive you fro
To here the bugles there yblow,
With their bugles in that place,
And sevenscore raches at his rechase.
Homward thus shall ye ride,
On hauking by the rivers side,
With goshauke and with gentil fawcon,
With egle-horne and merlyon.

ANONYMOUS (14th century)

'A Wood near Athens'

Horns winded within.
Enter Theseus, Hippolyta, Egeus, and train.

The. Go, one of you, find out the forester;
For now our observation is perform'd;
And since we have the vaward of the day,
My love shall hear the music of my hounds.
Uncouple in the western valley; let them go:
Dispatch, I say, and find the forester. [*Exit an Attendant.*
We will, fair queen, up to the mountain's top,
And mark the musical confusion
Of hounds and echo in conjunction.

Hip. I was with Hercules and Cadmus once,
When in a wood of Crete they bay'd the bear
With hounds of Sparta: never did I hear
Such gallant chiding; for, besides the groves,
The skies, the fountains, every region near
Seem'd all one mutual cry: I never heard
So musical a discord, such sweet thunder.

The. My hounds are bred out of the Spartan kind,
So flew'd, so sanded; and their heads are hung
With ears that sweep away the morning dew;
Crook-knee'd, and dew-lapp'd like Thessalian bulls;

lese of greyhound with you to strike] three greyhounds to run with you trist] hunting station disease] melancholy bugles] hunting horns bugles] ?beagles raches at his rechase] hounds at his recall gentil fawcon] noble falcon egle-horne and merlyon] ?kind of hawk and merlin

Slow in pursuit, but match'd in mouth like bells,
Each under each. A cry more tuneable
Was never holla'd to, nor cheer'd with horn,
In Crete, in Sparta, nor in Thessaly:
Judge when you hear.

WILLIAM SHAKESPEARE, *A Midsummer Night's Dream*

The Care of Hounds

A good keeper of Houndes should be gratious, curteous, and gentle, loving his dogges of a naturall disposition, and he ought to be both well footed and well winded, aswell to fill his horne as his bottell: the first thing whiche he ought to do when he riseth, is to go see his Houndes, to make their lodging cleane, and to dresse them as the case shall require: after he hath so clensed them, he ought to take his horne and and sounde three or foure tymes the call, to the ende he may comforte them and call them to him: and when he shall see them all aboute hym, then shall he couple them, and in couplyng them he muste take good heede that he couple not the Dogges together, for feare least they fight one with another, and if there be any yong houndes, it shalbe good to couple them with the olde bitches, to teache them to followe: when they are all well coupled, the keeper muste fill two great bagges or pockets with small bones, and other good morsels, as fishe, or horse feete fried, fatte roste meates, and such like, then he shall breake all into small gobbets into his bagges, and hang one bagge about his owne necke, and give another unto one of his companions, that done, he must take two wispes of cleane straw and put them under his gyrdell, with a little brush or duster to rubbe and duste his houndes when they shall come into the fielde: the other Huntesmen or varlettes whiche shalbe with him ought to do asmuch. Afterwards every man shal take a fayre wande in his hande, and let one go before to call the houndes unto him, another shall come behind which shall jerke them forwardes, and if there be two others, they shall go on eche side, and so all foure togither shall go leade the houndes through the greene Corne fieldes and through the medowes, aswell to feede them, as for to teach them to knowe theyr voyce, making them to passe through the heardes of sheepe and other suche like beastes, to accustome them, and to make them to know them: and if there be any dogge that is so il taught as he would runne at a sheepe or any such tame beast, you must couple him with a ramme or a stoute Sheepe, and with your wande you muste all to pay him and beate him a good while, crying and threatening to the ende that another time he may know the rate of suche as use it.

GEORGE TURBERVILLE (1540–1610), from
The Noble Arte of Venerie or Hunting (1576)

'Before an Alehouse on a Heath'

Horns winded. Enter a Lord from hunting, with his train.

Lord. Huntsman, I charge thee, tender well my hounds:
Brach Merriman, the poor cur is emboss'd;
And couple Clowder with the deep-mouth'd brach.
Saw'st thou not, boy, how Silver made it good
At the hedge-corner, in the coldest fault?
I would not lose the dog for twenty pound.
First Hun. Why, Belman is as good as he, my lord:
He cried upon it as the merest loss,
And twice today picked out the dullest scent:
Trust me, I take him for the better dog.
Lord. Thou art a fool: if Echo were as fleet,
I would esteem him worth a dozen such.
But sup them well and look unto them all:
Tomorrow I intend to hunt again.
First Hun. I will, my lord.

WILLIAM SHAKESPEARE, *The Taming of the Shrew*

'Hawking'

When making for the brook, the Falconer doth espy
On river, plash, or mere, where store of fowl doth lie:
Whence forcéd over land, by skilful Falconers' trade:
A fair convenient flight, may easily be made.
He whistleth off his hawks, whose nimble pinions straight,
Do work themselves by turns, into a stately height:
And if that after check, the one or both do go,
Sometimes he them the lure, sometimes doth water show;
The trembling fowl that hear the jigging hawk-bells ring,
And find it is too late to trust then to their wing,
Lie flat upon the flood, whilst the high-mounted hawks,
Then being lords alone, in their etherial walks,
Aloft so bravely stir, their bells so thick that shake;
Which when the Falconer sees, that scarce one plane they make,
The gallant'st birds, saith he, that ever flew on wing,
And swears there is a flight, were worthy of a King.
Then making to the flood, to cause the fowls to rise,
The fierce and eager hawks, down thrilling from the skies,
Make sundry canceleers e'er they the fowl can reach,

plane] glide canceleers] turns on the wing

Which then to save their lives, their wings do lively stretch.
But when the whizzing bells the silent air do cleave,
And that their greatest speed, them vainly do deceive,
And the sharp cruel hawks, they at their backs do view,
Themselves for very fear they instantly ineawe.
  The hawks get up again into their former place,
And ranging here and there, in that their airy race,
Still as the fearful fowl attempt to 'scape away,
With many a stooping brave, them in again they lay.
But when the Falconers take their hawking-poles in hand,
And crossing of the brook, do put it over land,
The hawk gives it a souse, that makes it to rebound,
Well-near the height of man, sometime above the ground;
Oft takes a leg, or wing, oft takes away the head,
And oft from neck to tail, the back in two doth shred.
With many a Wo-ho-ho, and jocond lure again,
When he his quarry makes upon the grassy plain.

MICHAEL DRAYTON (1563–1631), from *Polyolbion*

The Eagle, and the Assembly of Animals

As Jupiter's all-seeing eye
Surveyed the worlds beneath the sky,
From this small speck of earth were sent,
Murmurs and sounds of discontent;
For every thing alive complained,
That he the hardest life sustained.
Jove calls his eagle. At the word
Before him stands the royal bird.
The bird, obedient, from heav'n's height,
Downward directs his rapid flight;
Then cited every living thing,
To hear the mandates of his king.
  'Ungrateful creatures, whence arise
These murmurs which offend the skies?
Why this disorder? say the cause:
For just are Jove's eternal laws.
Let each his discontent reveal;
To yon sour dog, I first appeal.'
  'Hard is my lot,' the hound replies,
'On what fleet nerves the greyhound flies,

ineawe] plunge into the water   souse] swoop

While I, with weary step and slow,
O'er plains and vales, and mountains go.
The morning sees my chase begun,
Nor ends it till the setting sun.'
'When,' says the greyhound, 'I pursue,
My game is lost, or caught in view;
Beyond my sight the prey's secure:
The hound is slow, but always sure.
And had I his sagacious scent,
Jove ne'er had heard my discontent.'
The lion craved the fox's art;
The fox, the lion's force and heart:
The cock implored the pigeon's flight,
Whose wings were rapid, strong, and light:
The pigeon strength of wing despised,
And the cock's matchless valour prized:
The fishes wished to graze the plain;
The beasts to skim beneath the main.
Thus, envious of another's state,
Each blamed the partial hand of Fate.
The bird of heaven then cried aloud,
'Jove bids disperse the murm'ring crowd;
The god rejects your idle prayers.
Would ye, rebellious mutineers,
Entirely change your name and nature,
And be the very envied creature?
What, silent all, and none consent!
Be happy then, and learn content:
Nor imitate the restless mind,
And proud ambition, of mankind.'

JOHN GAY, from *Fables*

'Otter Hunt'

One labour yet remains, celestial Maid!
Another element demands thy song.
No more o'er craggy steeps, through coverts thick
With pointed thorn, and briers intricate,
Urge on with horn and voice the painful pack:
But skim with wanton wing th' irriguous vale,
Where winding streams amid the flowery meads
Perpetual glide along; and undermine
The caverned banks, by the tenacious roots

Of hoary willows arched; gloomy retreat
Of the bright scaly kind; where they at will,
On the green wat'ry reed their pasture graze,
Suck the moist soil, or slumber at their ease,
Rocked by the restless brook, that draws aslope
Its humid train, and laves their dark abodes.
Where rages not oppression? Where, alas!
Is innocence secure? Rapine and spoil
Haunt ev'n the lowest deeps; seas have their sharks,
Rivers and ponds inclose the rav'nous pike;
He in his turn becomes a prey; on him
The amphibious otter feasts. Just is his fate
Deserved; but tyrants know no bounds; nor spears
That bristle on his back, defend the perch
From his wide greedy jaws; nor burnished mail
The yellow carp; nor all his arts can save
Th' insinuating eel, that hides his head
Beneath the slimy mud; nor yet escapes
The crimson-spotted trout, the river's pride,
And beauty of the stream. Without remorse,
This midnight pillager ranging around,
Insatiate swallows all. The owner mourns
Th' unpeopled rivulet, and gladly hears
The huntsman's early call, and sees with joy
The jovial crew, that march upon its banks
In gay parade, with bearded lances armed.
This subtle spoiler of the beaver kind,
Far off, perhaps, where ancient alders shade
The deep still pool; within some hollow trunk
Contrives his wicker couch: whence he surveys
His long purlieu, lord of the stream, and all
The finny shoals his own. But you, brave youths,
Dispute the felon's claim; try every root,
And every reedy bank; encourage all
The busy-spreading pack, that fearless plunge
Into the flood, and cross the rapid stream.
Bid rocks and caves, and each resounding shore,
Proclaim your bold defiance; loudly raise
Each cheering voice, till distant hills repeat
The triumphs of the vale. On the soft sand
See there his seal impressed! and on that bank
Behold the glitt'ring spoils, half-eaten fish,
Scales, fins, and bones, the leavings of his feast.
Ah! on that yielding sag-bed, see, once more
His seal I view. O'er yon dank rushy marsh
The sly goose-footed prowler bends his course,

And seeks the distant shallows. Huntsman, bring
Thy eager pack; and trail him to his couch.
Hark! the loud peal begins, the clam'rous joy,
The gallant chiding, loads the trembling air.
Ye Naiads fair, who o'er these floods preside,
Raise up your dripping heads above the wave,
And hear our melody. Th' harmonious notes
Float with the stream; and ev'ry winding creek
And hollow rock, that o'er the dimpling flood
Nods pendant; still improve from shore to shore
Our sweet reiterated joys. What shouts!
What clamour loud! What gay heart-cheering sounds
Urge through the breathing brass their mazy way!
Nor choirs of Tritons glad with sprightlier strains
The dancing billows, when proud Neptune rides
In triumph o'er the deep. How greedily
They snuff the fishy steam, that to each blade
Rank-scenting clings! See! how the morning dews
They sweep, that from their feet besprinkling drop
Dispersed, and leave a track oblique behind.
Now on firm land they range; then in the flood
They plunge tumultuous; or through reedy pools
Rustling they work their way: no holt escapes
Their curious search. With quick sensation now
The fuming vapour stings; flutter their hearts,
And joy redoubled bursts from every mouth
In louder symphonies. Yon hollow trunk,
That with its hoary head incurved, salutes
The passing wave, must be the tyrant's fort,
And dread abode. How these impatient climb,
While others at the root incessant bay:
They put him down. See, there he dives along!
The ascending bubbles mark his gloomy way.
Quick fix the nets, and cut off his retreat
Into the shelt'ring deeps. Ah, there he vents!
The pack lunge headlong, and protended spears
Menace destruction: while the troubled surge
Indignant foams, and all the scaly kind
Affrighted, hide their heads. Wild tumult reigns,
And loud uproar. Ah, there once more he vents!
See, that bold hound has seized him; down they sink,
Together lost: but soon shall he repent
His rash assault. See there escaped, he flies
Half-drowned, and clambers up the slipp'ry bank
With ouze and blood distained. Of all the brutes,
Whether by Nature formed, or by long use,

This artful diver best can bear the want
Of vital air. Unequal is the fight,
Beneath the whelming element. Yet there
He lives not long; but respiration needs
At proper intervals. Again he vents;
Again the crowd attack. That spear has pierced
His neck; the crimson waves confess the wound.
Fixed is the bearded lance, unwelcome guest,
Where'er he flies; with him it sinks beneath,
With him it mounts; sure guide to every foe.
Inly he groans; nor can his tender wound
Bear the cold stream. Lo! to yon sedgy bank
He creeps disconsolate; his numerous foes
Surround him, hounds and men. Pierced through and through,
On pointed spears they lift him high in air;
Wriggling he hangs, and grins, and bites in vain.
Bid the loud horns, in gaily warbling strains,
Proclaim the felon's fate; he dies, he dies.
  Rejoice, ye scaly tribes, and leaping dance
Above the wave, in sign of liberty
Restored; the cruel tyrant is no more.
Rejoice, secure and blessed; did not as yet
Remain, some of your own rapacious kind;
And man, fierce man, with all his various wiles.

WILLIAM SOMERVILLE, from *The Chase*

'The Sylvan War'

Ye vig'rous Swains! while Youth ferments your Blood,
And purer Spirits swell the sprightly Flood,
Now range the Hills, the gameful Woods beset,
Wind the shrill Horn, or spread the waving Net.
When milder Autumn Summer's Heat succeeds,
And in the new-shorn Field the Partridge feeds,
Before his Lord the ready Spaniel bounds,
Panting with Hope, he tries the furrow'd Grounds,
But when the tainted Gales the Game betray,
Couch'd close he lyes, and meditates the Prey;
Secure they trust th'unfaithful Field, beset,
Till hov'ring o'er 'em sweeps the swelling Net.
Thus (if small Things we may with great compare)
When *Albion* sends her eager Sons to War,
Some thoughtless Town, with Ease and Plenty blest,
Near, and more near, the closing lines invest;

Sudden they seize th'amaz'd, defenceless Prize,
And high in Air *Britannia*'s Standard flies.
See! from the Brake the whirring Pheasant springs,
And mounts exulting on triumphant Wings;
Short is his Joy! he feels the fiery Wound,
Flutters in Blood, and panting beats the Ground.
Ah! what avail his glossie, varying Dyes,
His Purple Crest, and Scarlet-circled Eyes,
The vivid Green his shining Plumes unfold;
His painted Wings, and Breast that flames with Gold?
Nor yet, when moist *Arcturus* clouds the Sky,
The Woods and Fields their pleasing Toils deny.
To Plains with well-breath'd Beagles we repair,
And trace the Mazes of the circling Hare.
(Beasts, urg'd by us, their Fellow Beasts pursue,
And learn of Man each other to undo.)
With slaught'ring Guns th'unweary'd Fowler roves,
When Frosts have whiten'd all the naked Groves;
Where Doves in Flocks the leafless Trees o'ershade,
And lonely Woodcocks haunt the watry Glade.
He lifts the Tube, and levels with his Eye;
Strait a short Thunder breaks the frozen Sky.
Oft, as in Airy Rings they skim the Heath,
The clam'rous Lapwings feel the Leaden Death:
Oft as the mounting Larks their Notes prepare,
They fall, and leave their little Lives in Air.
In genial Spring, beneath the quiv'ring Shade
Where cooling Vapours breathe along the Mead,
The patient Fisher takes his silent Stand
Intent, his Angle trembling in his Hand;
With Looks unmov'd, he hopes the Scaly Breed,
And eyes the dancing Cork and bending Reed.
Our plenteous Streams a various Race supply;
The bright-ey'd Perch with Fins of *Tyrian* Dye,
The silver Eel, in shining Volumes roll'd,
The yellow Carp, in Scales bedrop'd with Gold,
Swift Trouts, diversify'd with Crimson Stains,
And Pykes, the Tyrants of the watry Plains.
Now *Cancer* glows with *Phœbus'* fiery Car;
The Youth rush eager to the Sylvan War;
Swarm o'er the Lawns, the Forest Walks surround,

Volumes] coils, folds, convolutions, especially of a serpent Now *Cancer* glows] the sun (Phoebus's car) is in the constellation of the Twins (zodiacal sign of Gemini) from about 21 May to 22 June. It enters the constellation of the Crab (Cancer) at the summer solstice 22 June.

Rowze the fleet Hart, and chear the opening Hound.
Th'impatient Courser pants in ev'ry Vein,
And pawing, seems to beat the distant Plain,
Hills, Vales, and Floods appear already crost,
And ere he starts, a thousand Steps are lost.
See! the bold Youth strain up the threatning Steep,
Rush thro' the Thickets, down the Vallies sweep,
Hang o'er their Coursers Heads with eager Speed,
And Earth rolls back beneath the flying Steed.
Let old *Arcadia* boast her ample Plain,
Th' Immortal Huntress, and her Virgin Train;
Nor envy *Windsor*! since thy Shades have seen
As bright a Goddess, and as chast a Queen;
Whose Care, like hers, protects the Sylvan Reign,
The Earth's fair Light, and Empress of the Main.

ALEXANDER POPE, from *Windsor Forest*

'The Transformation of Actaeon into a Stag'

In a fair chase a shady mountain stood,
Well stored with game, and marked with trails of blood.
Here did the huntsmen till the heat of day
Pursue the stag, and load themselves with prey;
When thus Actaeon calling to the rest:
'My friends,' says he, 'our sport is at the best;
The sun is high advanced, and downward sheds
His burning beams directly on our heads;
Then, by consent, abstain from farther spoils,
Call off the dogs, and gather up the toils;
And ere tomorrow's sun begins his race,
Take the cool morning to renew the chase.'
They all consent, and in a cheerful train
The jolly huntsmen, loaden with the slain,
Return in triumph from the sultry plain.
Down in a vale with pine and cypress clad,
Refreshed with gentle winds, and brown with shade,

Rowze] technical hunting term: 'to rouse a hart, is to raise him from his harbour'. opening] giving tongue Whose Care, like hers] allusion to the interest taken by Queen Anne in hunting

The chaste Diana's private haunt, there stood
Full in the centre of the darksome wood
A spacious grotto, all around o'ergrown
With hoary moss, and arched with pumice-stone.
From out its rocky clefts the waters flow,
And trickling swell into a lake below.
Nature had everywhere so played her part,
That everywhere she seemed to vie with art.
Here the bright goddess, toiled and chafed with heat,
Was wont to bathe her in the cool retreat.
  Here did she now with all her train resort,
Panting with heat, and breathless from the sport;
Her armour-bearer laid her bow aside,
Some loosed her sandals, some her veil untied;
Each busy nymph her proper part undressed;
While Crocalé, more handy than the rest,
Gathered her flowing hair, and in a noose
Bound it together, whilst her own hung loose.
Five of the more ignoble sort by turns
Fetch up the water, and unlade their urns.
  Now all undressed the shining goddess stood,
When young Actaeon, wildered in the wood,
To the cool grot by his hard fate betrayed,
The fountains filled with naked nymphs surveyed.
The frighted virgins shrieked at the surprise,
(The forest echoed with their piercing cries,)
Then in a huddle round their goddess pressed:
She, proudly eminent above the rest,
With blushes glowed; such blushes as adorn
The ruddy welkin, or the purple morn;
And though the crowding nymphs her body hide,
Half backward shrunk, and viewed him from aside.
Surprised, at first she would have snatched her bow,
But sees the circling waters round her flow;
These in the hollow of her hand she took,
And dashed them in his face, while thus she spoke:
'Tell if thou canst the wondrous sight disclosed,
A goddess naked to thy view exposed.'
  This said, the man began to disappear
By slow degrees, and ended in a deer.
A rising horn on either brow he wears,
And stretches out his neck, and pricks his ears;
Rough is his skin, with sudden hairs o'ergrown,
His bosom pants with fears before unknown.
Transformed at length, he flies away in haste,
And wonders why he flies away so fast.

But as by chance, within a neighbouring brook,
He saw his branching horns and altered look,
Wretched Actaeon! in a doleful tone
He tries to speak, but only gave a groan;
And as he wept, within the watery glass
He saw the big round drops, with silent pace,
Run trickling down a savage hairy face.
What should he do? Or seek his old abodes,
Or herd among the deer, and skulk in woods?
Here shame dissuades him, there his fear prevails,
And each by turns his aching heart assails.
  As he thus ponders, he behind him spies
His opening hounds, and now he hears their cries:
A generous pack, or to maintain the chase,
Or snuff the vapour from the scented grass.
  He bounded off with fear, and swiftly ran
O'er craggy mountains, and the flowery plain;
Through brakes and thickets forced his way, and flew
Through many a ring, where once he did pursue.
In vain he oft endeavoured to proclaim
His new misfortune, and to tell his name;
Nor voice nor words the brutal tongue supplies;
From shouting men, and horns, and dogs he flies,
Deafened and stunned with their promiscuous cries.
When now the fleetest of the pack, that pressed
Close at his heels, and sprung before the rest,
Had fastened on him, straight another pair
Hung on his wounded haunch, and held him there,
Till all the pack came up, and every hound
Tore the sad huntsman, grovelling on the ground,
Who now appeared but one continued wound.
With dropping tears his bitter fate he moans,
And fills the mountain with his dying groans.
His servants with a piteous look he spies,
And turns about his supplicating eyes.
His servants, ignorant of what had chanced,
With eager haste and joyful shouts advanced,
And called their lord Actaeon to the game;
He shook his head in answer to the name;
He heard, but wished he had indeed been gone,
Or only to have stood a looker-on.
But, to his grief, he finds himself too near,
And feels his ravenous dogs with fury tear
Their wretched master, panting in a deer.

JOSEPH ADDISON (1672–1719)

From *Autumn*

Here the rude clamour of the sportsman's joy,
The gun fast-thundering and the winded horn,
Would tempt the Muse to sing the rural game,—
How, in his mid career, the spaniel, struck
Stiff by the tainted gale, with open nose
Outstretched and finely sensible, draws full,
Fearful, and cautious on the latent prey
As in the sun the circling covey bask
Their varied plumes, and, watchful every way,
Through the rough stubble turn the secret eye.
Caught in the meshy snare, in vain they beat
Their idle wings, entangled more and more:
Nor, on the surges of the boundless air
Though borne triumphant, are they safe; the gun,
Glanced just, and sudden, from the fowler's eye,
O'ertakes their sounding pinions, and again
Immediate brings them from the towering wing
Dead to the ground; or drives them wide-dispersed,
Wounded and wheeling various down the wind.

JAMES THOMSON, *The Seasons*

'The Vultures' View of Man'

A shepherd of Bohemia has, by long abode in the forests, enabled himself to understand the voice of birds; at least he relates with great confidence a story of which the credibility may be considered by the learned.

'As I was sitting,' said he, 'within a hollow rock, and watching my sheep that fed in the valley, I heard two vultures interchangeably crying on the summit of the cliff. Both voices were earnest and deliberate. My curiosity prevailed over my care of the flock; I climbed slowly and silently from crag to crag, concealed among the shrubs, till I found a cavity where I might sit and listen without suffering, or giving disturbance.

'I soon perceived that my labour would be well repaid; for an old vulture was sitting on a naked prominence, with her young about her, whom she was instructing in the arts of a vulture's life, and preparing, by the last lecture, for their final dismission to the mountains and the skies.

' "My children," said the old vulture, "you will the less want my instructions because you have had my practice before your eyes; you have seen me snatch from the farm the household fowl, you have seen me seize the leveret in the bush, and the kid in the pasture, you know how to fix your talons, and how to balance your flight when you are laden with your prey. But you remember the taste of more delicious food; I have often regaled you with the flesh of man."

' "Tell us," said the young vultures, "where man may be found, and how he may be known; his flesh is surely the natural food of a vulture. Why have you never brought a man in your talons to the nest?"

' "He is too bulky," said the mother; "when we find a man, we can only tear away his flesh, and leave his bones upon the ground."

' "Since man is so big," said the young ones, "how do you kill him? You are afraid of the wolf and of the bear; by what power are vultures superior to man; is man more defenceless than a sheep?"

' "We have not the strength of man," returned the mother, "and I am sometimes in doubt whether we have the subtlety; and the vultures would seldom feast upon his flesh, had not Nature, that devoted him to our uses, infused into him a strange ferocity, which I have never observed in any other being that feeds upon the earth. Two herds of men will often meet and shake his earth with noise, and fill the air with fire. When you hear noise and see fire which flashes along the ground, hasten to the place with your swiftest wing, for men are surely destroying one another; you will then find the ground smoking with blood and covered with carcasses, of which many are dismembered and mangled for the convenience of the vulture."

' "But when men have killed their prey," said the pupil, "why do they not eat it? When the wolf has killed a sheep, he suffers not the vulture to touch it till he has satisfied himself. Is not man another kind of wolf?"

' "Man," said the mother, "is the only beast who kills that which he does not devour, and this quality makes him so much a benefactor to our species."

' "If men kill our prey and lay it in our way," said the young one, "what need shall we have of labouring for ourselves?"

' "Because man will, sometimes," replied the mother, "remain for a long time quiet in his den. The old vultures will tell you when you are to watch his motions. When you see men in great numbers moving close together, like a flight of storks, you may conclude that they are hunting, and that you will soon revel in human blood."

' "But still," said the young one, "I would gladly know the reason of this mutual slaughter. I could never kill what I could not eat."

' "My child," said the mother, "this is a question which I cannot answer, though I am reckoned the most subtle bird of the mountain. When I was young I used frequently to visit the eyrie of an old vulture who dwelt upon the Carpathian rocks; he had made many observations; he knew the places that afforded prey round his habitation, as far in every direction as the strongest wing can fly between the rising and setting of the summer sun; he had fed year after year on the entrails of men. His opinion was that men had only the appearance of animal life, being really vegetables with a power of motion; and that as the boughs of an oak are dashed together by the storm, that swine may fatten upon the falling acorns, so men are by some unaccountable power driven one against another, till they lose their motion, that vultures may be fed. Others think they have observed something of contrivance and policy among these mischievous beings, and those that hover more closely round them pretend that there is, in every herd, one that gives directions to the rest, and seems to be more eminently delighted with a wide carnage. What it is that entitles him to such pre-eminence we know not; he is seldom the biggest or the swiftest, but he shows by his eagerness and diligence that he is, more than any of the others, a friend to vultures." '

SAMUEL JOHNSON (1709–84), *The Idler*, no. 22 (9 September 1750)

'Tom Caught Trespassing'

Little Jones went one day a shooting with the gamekeeper; when happening to spring a covey of partridges near the border of that manor over which Fortune, to fulfil the wise purposes of Nature, had planted one of the game consumers, the birds flew into it, and were marked (as it is called) by the two sportsmen, in some furze bushes, about two or three hundred paces beyond Mr Allworthy's dominions.

Mr Allworthy had given the fellow strict orders, on pain of forfeiting his place, never to trespass on any of his neighbours; no more on those who were less rigid in this matter than on the lord of this manor. With regard to others, indeed, these orders had not been always very scrupulously kept; but as the disposition of the gentleman with whom the partridges had taken sanctuary was well known, the gamekeeper had never yet attempted to invade his territories. Nor had he done it now, had not the younger sportsman, who was excessively eager to pursue the flying game, over-persuaded him; but Jones being very importunate, the other, who was himself keen enough after the sport, yielded to his persuasions, entered the manor, and shot one of the partridges.

The gentleman himself was at that time on horse-back, at a little distance from them; and hearing the gun go off, he immediately made towards the place, and discovered poor Tom; for the gamekeeper had leapt into the thickest part of the furze-brake, where he had happily concealed himself.

The gentleman having searched the lad, and found the partridge upon him, denounced great vengeance, swearing he would acquaint Mr Allworthy. He was as good as his word: for he rode immediately to his house, and complained of the trespass on his manor in as high terms and as bitter language as if his house had been broken open, and the most valuable furniture stole out of it. He added, that some other person was in his company, though he could not discover him; for that two guns had been discharged almost in the same instant. And, says he, 'We have found only this partridge, but the Lord knows what mischief they have done.'

At his return home, Tom was presently convened before Mr Allworthy. He owned the fact, and alledged no other excuse but what was really true, viz., that the covey was originally sprung in Mr Allworthy's own manor.

Tom was then interrogated who was with him, which Mr Allworthy declared he was resolved to know, acquainting the culprit with the circumstance of the two guns, which had been deposed by the squire and both his servants; but Tom stoutly persisted in asserting that he was alone; yet, to say the truth, he hesitated a little at first, which would have confirmed Mr Allworthy's belief, had what the squire and his servants said wanted any further confirmation.

The gamekeeper, being a suspected person, was now sent for, and the question put to him; but he, relying on the promise which Tom had made him, to take all upon himself, very resolutely denied being in company with the young gentleman, or indeed having seen him the whole afternoon.

Mr Allworthy then turned towards Tom, with more than usual anger in his countenance, and advised him to confess who was with him; repeating, that he was resolved to know. The lad, however, still maintained his resolution, and was dismissed with much wrath by Mr Allworthy, who told him he should have to the next morning to consider of it, when he should be questioned by another person, and in another manner.

Poor Jones spent a very melancholy night; and the more so as he was without his usual companion; for Master Blifil was gone abroad on a visit with his mother. Fear of the punishment he was to suffer was on this occasion his least evil; his chief anxiety being, lest his constancy should fail him, and he should be brought to betray the gamekeeper, whose ruin he knew must now be the consequence.

Nor did the gamekeeper pass his time much better. He had the same apprehensions with the youth; for whose honour he had likewise a much tenderer regard than for his skin.

In the morning, when Tom attended the reverend Mr Thwackum, the person to whom Mr Allworthy had committed the instruction of the two boys, he had the same questions put to him by that gentleman which he had been asked the evening before, to which he returned the same answers. The consequence of this was, so severe a whipping, that it possibly fell little short of the torture with which confessions are in some countries extorted from criminals.

Tom bore his punishment with great resolution; and though his master asked him, between every stroke, whether he would not confess, he was contented to be flead rather than betray his friend, or break the promise he had made.

The gamekeeper was now relieved from his anxiety, and Mr Allworthy himself began to be concerned at Tom's sufferings: for besides that Mr Thwackum, being highly enraged that he was not able to make the boy say what he himself pleased, had carried his severity much beyond the good man's intention, this latter began now to suspect that the squire had been mistaken; which his extreme eagerness and anger seemed to make probable; and as for what the servants had said in confirmation of their master's account, he laid no great stress upon that. Now, as cruelty and injustice were two ideas of which Mr Allworthy could by no means support the consciousness a single moment, he sent for Tom, and after many kind and friendly exhortations, said, 'I am convinced, my dear child, that my suspicions have wronged you; I am sorry that you have been so severely punished on this account.' And at last gave him a little horse to make him amends; again repeating his sorrow for what had past.

HENRY FIELDING (1707–54), *The History of Tom Jones*

Noon

Enough! Enough! no longer we pursue
The scattered covey in the tainted dew.
No more we charge, nor new excursions make,
Nor beat the copse, the bean-field, nor the brake.
O pleasing sport! far better prized than wealth!
Thou spring of spirits, and thou source of health,
Thou giv'st, when thus our leisure we employ,
To life the relish and the zest to joy,
O may I still on rural pleasures bent,
Rove devious in sequester'd fields of Kent;
Ease, study, exercise successive blend,
Nor want the blessing of a cheerful friend!

Forbear, my dogs! now mid-day heats prevail,
The scent grows languid in the sultry gale;
Herds seek the shades where cooling fountains well,
And sweet the music of your noon-tide bell.

FRANCIS FAWKES

'The Badger'

The badger grunting on his woodland track
With shaggy hide and sharp nose scrowed with black
Roots in the bushes and the woods and makes
A great hugh burrow in the ferns and brakes
With nose on ground he runs a awkard pace
And anything will beat him in the race
The shepherds dog will run him to his den
Followed and hooted by the dogs and men
The woodman when the hunting comes about
Go round at night to stop the foxes out

And hurrying through the bushes ferns and brakes
Nor sees the many hol[e]s the badger makes
And often through the bushes to the chin
Breaks the old holes and tumbles headlong in

When midnight comes a host of dogs and men
Go out and track the badger to his den
And put a sack within the hole and lye
Till the old grunting badger passes bye
He comes and hears they let the strongest loose
The old fox hears the noise and drops the goose
The poacher shoots and hurrys from the cry
And the old hare half wounded buzzes bye
They get a forked stick to bear him down
And clapt the dogs and bore him to the town
And bait him all the day with many dogs
And laugh and shout and fright the scampering hogs
He runs along and bites at all he meets
They shout and hollo down the noisey streets

He turns about to face the loud uproar
And drives the rebels to their very doors
The frequent stone is hurled where ere they go
When badgers fight and every ones a foe
The dogs are clapt and urged to join the fray
The badger turns and drives them all away
Though scar[c]ely half as big dimute and small
He fights with dogs for hours and beats them all
The heavy mastiff savage in the fray
Lies down and licks his feet and turns away
The bull dog knows his match and waxes cold
The badger grins and never leaves his hold
He drive[s] the crowd and follows at their heels
And bites them though the drunkard swears and reels

The frighted women takes the boys away
The blackguard laughs and hurrys on the fray
He trys to reach the woods a awkard race
But sticks and cudgels quickly stop the chace
He turns agen and drives the noisey crowd
And beats the many dogs in noises loud
He drives away and beats them every one
And then they loose them all and set them on
He falls as dead and kicked by boys and men
Then starts and grins and drives the crowd agen
Till kicked and torn and beaten out he lies
And leaves his hold and cackles groans and dies

Some keep a baited badger tame as hog
And tame him till he follows like the dog
They urge him on like dogs and show fair play
He beats and scarcely wounded goes away
Lapt up as if asleep he scorns to fly
And siezes any dog that ventures nigh
Clapt like a dog he never bites the men
But worrys dogs and hurrys to his den
They let him out and turn a barrow down
And there he fights the pack of all the town
He licks the patting hand and trys to play
And never trys to bite or run away
And runs away from noise in hollow tree[s]
Burnt by the boys to get a swarm of bees

JOHN CLARE (1792–1864)

'Bull Fight'

Hushed is the din of tongues—on gallant steeds,
With milk-white crest, gold spur, and light-poised lance,
Four cavaliers prepare for venturous deeds
And lowly-bending to the lists advance;
Rich are their scarfs, their chargers featly prance:
If in the dangerous game they shine to-day,
The crowd's loud shout and ladies' lovely glance,
Best prize of better acts! they bear away;
And all that kings or chiefs e'er gain their toils repay.

In costly sheen and gaudy cloak arrayed,
But all afoot, the light-limbed Matadore
Stands in the centre, eager to invade
The lord of lowing herds; but not before
The ground, with cautious tread, is traversed o'er,
Lest aught unseen should lurk to thwart his speed:
His arms a dart, he fights aloof, nor more
Can Man achieve without the friendly steed—
Alas! too oft condemned for him to bear and bleed.

Thrice sounds the Clarion; lo! the signal falls,
The den expands, and Expectation mute
Gapes round the silent circle's peopled walls:
Bounds with one lashing spring the mighty brute,
And, wildly staring, spurns, with sounding foot,

The sand, nor blindly rushes on his foe:
Here, there, he points his threatening front, to suit
His first attack, wide-waving to and fro
His angry tail; red rolls his eye's dilated glow.

Sudden he stops—his eye is fixed—away—
Away, thou heedless boy! prepare the spear;
Now is thy time, to perish, or display
The skill that yet may check his mad career!
With well-timed croupe the nimble coursers veer;
On foams the Bull, but not unscathed he goes;
Streams from his flank the crimson torrent clear:
He flies, he wheels, distracted with his throes;
Dart follows dart—lance, lance—loud bellowings speak his woes.

Again he comes; nor dart nor lance avail,
Nor the wild plunging of the tortured horse;
Though Man and Man's avenging arms assail,
Vain are his weapons, vainer is his force.
One gallant steed is stretched a mangled corse;
Another, hideous sight! unseamed appears,
His gory chest unveils life's panting source;
Though death-struck, still his feeble frame he rears;
Staggering, but stemming all, his Lord unharmed he bears.

Foiled, bleeding, breathless, furious to the last.
Full in the centre stands the Bull at bay,
'Mid wounds, and clinging darts, and lances brast
And foes disabled in the brutal fray:
And now the Matadores around him play,
Shake the red cloak, and poise the ready brand:
Once more through all he bursts his thundering way—
Vain rage! the mantle quits the conynge hand,
Wraps his fierce eye—'tis past—he sinks upon the sand!

Where his vast neck just mingles with the spine,
Sheathed in his form the deadly weapon lies.
He stops—he starts—disdaining to decline:
Slowly he falls, amidst triumphant cries,
Without a groan, without a struggle dies.
The decorated car appears—on high
The corse is piled—sweet sight for vulgar eyes—
Four steeds that spurn the rein, as swift as shy,
Hurl the dark bulk along, scarce seen in dashing by.

LORD BYRON, *Childe Harold's Pilgrimage*

'The Bull Apis Makes his Début in Spain'

'Villamarti's troupe stood ready for his second bull. The gates opened, and we saw Apis, beautifully balanced on his feet, peer coquettishly round the corner, as though he were at home. A picador—a mounted man with the long lance-goad—stood near the barrier on his right. He had not even troubled to turn his horse, for the capeadors—the men with the cloaks—were advancing to play Apis—to feel his psychology and intentions, according to the rules that are made for bulls who do not think. . . . I did not realize the murder before it was accomplished! The wheel, the rush, the oblique charge from behind, the fall of horse and man were simultaneous. Apis leaped the horse, with whom he had no quarrel, and alighted, all four feet together (it was enough), between the man's shoulders, changed his beautiful feet on the carcass, and was away, pretending to fall nearly on his nose. Do you follow me? In that instant, by that stumble, he produced the impression that his adorable assassination was a mere bestial blunder. Then, Monsieur, I began to comprehend that it was an artist we had to deal with. He did not stand over the body to draw the rest of the troupe. He chose to reserve that trick. He let the attendants bear out the dead, and went on to amuse himself among the capeadors. Now to Apis, trained among our children in the yards, the cloak was simply a guide to the boy behind it. He pursued, you understand, the person, not the propaganda—the proprietor, not the journal. If a third of our electors of France were as wise, my friend! . . . But it was done leisurely, with humour and a touch of truculence. He romped after one man's cloak as a clumsy dog might do, but I observed that he kept the man on his terrible left side. Christophe whispered to me: "Wait for his mother's kick. When he has made the fellow confident it will arrive." It arrived in the middle of a gambol. My God! He lashed out in the air as he frisked. The man dropped like a sack, lifted one hand a little towards his head, and—that was all. So you see, a body was again at his disposition; a second time the cloaks ran up to draw him off, but, a second time, Apis refused his grand scene. A second time he acted that his murder was accident and—he convinced his audience! It was as though he had knocked over a bridge-gate in the marshes by mistake. Unbelievable? I saw it.'

The memory sent Monsieur Voiron again to the champagne; and I accompanied him.

'But Apis was not the sole artist present. They say Villamarti comes of a family of actors. I saw him regard Apis with a new eye. He, too, began to understand. He took his cloak and moved out to play him before they should bring on another picador. He had his reputation. Perhaps Apis knew it. Perhaps Villamarti reminded him of some boy with whom he had practised at home. At any rate Apis permitted it—up to a certain point; but he did not allow Villamarti the stage. He cramped him throughout. He dived and plunged clumsily and slowly, but always with menace and always closing in. We could see that the man was conforming to the bull—not the bull to the man; for Apis was playing him towards the centre of the ring, and, in a little while—I watched his face—Villamarti knew it. But I could not fathom the creature's motive. "Wait," said old Christophe. "He wants that picador on the white horse yonder. When he reaches his proper distance he will get him. Villamarti is his cover. He used me once that way." And so it was, my friend! With the clang of one of our own Seventy-fives, Apis dismissed Villamarti with his chest—breasted him over—and had arrived at his objective near the barrier. The same oblique charge; the head carried low for the sweep of the horns; the immense sideways fall of the horse, broken-legged and half-paralysed; the senseless man on the ground, and—behold Apis between them, backed against the barrier—his right covered by the horse; his left by the body of the man at his feet. The simplicity of it! Lacking the carts and tractors of his early parade-grounds he, being a genius, had extemporized with the materials at hand, and dug himself in. The troupe closed up again, their left wing broken by the kicking horse, their right immobilized by the man's body which Apis bestrode with significance. Villamarti almost threw himself between the horns, but—it was more an appeal than an attack. Apis refused him. He held his base. A picador was sent at him—necessarily from the front, which alone was open. Apis charged—he who, till then, you realize, had not used the horn! The horse went over backwards, the man half beneath him. Apis halted, hooked him under the heart, and threw him to the barrier. We heard his head crack, but he was dead before he hit the wood. There was no demonstration from the audience. They, also, had begun to realize this Foch among bulls! The arena occupied itself again with the dead. Two of the troupe irresolutely tried to play him—God knows in what hope!—but he moved out to the centre of the ring. "Look!" said Christophe. "Now he goes to clean himself. That always frightened me." He knelt down; he began to clean his horns. The earth was hard. He worried at it in an ecstasy of absorption. As he laid his head along and rattled his ears, it was as though he were interrogating the Devils themselves upon their secrets, and always saying impatiently: "Yes, I know that—and *that*—and *that*! Tell me more—*more*!" In the silence that covered us, a woman cried: "He digs a grave! Oh, Saints, he digs a grave!" Some others echoed this—not loudly—as a wave echoes in a grotto of the sea.

'And when his horns were cleaned, he rose up and studied poor Villamarti's troupe, eyes in eyes, one by one, with the gravity of an equal in intellect and the remote and merciless resolution of a master in his art. This was more terrifying than his toilette.'

'And they—Villamarti's men?' I asked.

'Like the audience, were dominated. They had ceased to posture, or stamp, or address insults to him. They conformed to him. The two other matadores stared. Only Chisto, the oldest, broke silence with some call or other, and Apis turned his head towards him. Otherwise he was isolated, immobile—sombre—meditating on those at his mercy. Ah!

'For some reason the trumpet sounded for the *banderillas*—those gay hooked darts that are planted in the shoulders of bulls who do not think, after their neck-muscles are tired by lifting horses. When such bulls feel the pain, they check for an instant, and, in that instant, the men step gracefully aside. Villamarti's banderillero answered the trumpet mechanically—like one condemned. He stood out, poised the darts and stammered the usual patter of invitation. . . . And after? I do not assert that Apis shrugged his shoulders, but he reduced the episode to its lowest elements, as could only a bull of Gaul. With his truculence was mingled always—owing to the shortness of his tail—a certain Rabelaisian abandon, especially when viewed from the rear. Christophe had often commented upon it. Now, Apis brought that quality into play. He circulated round that boy, forcing him to break up his beautiful poses. He studied him from various angles, like an incompetent photographer. He presented to him every portion of his anatomy except his shoulders. At intervals he feigned to run in upon him. My God, he was cruel! But his motive was obvious. He was playing for a laugh from the spectators which should synchronize with the fracture of the human morale. It was achieved. The boy turned and ran towards the barrier. Apis was on him before the laugh ceased; passed him; headed him—what do I say?—herded him off to the left, his horns beside and a little in front of his chest: he did not intend him to escape into a refuge. Some of the troupe would have closed in, but Villamarti cried: "If he wants him he will take him. Stand!" They stood. Whether the boy slipped or Apis nosed him over I could not see. But he dropped, sobbing. Apis halted like a car with four brakes, struck a pose, smelt him very completely and turned away. It was dismissal more ignominious than degradation at the head of one's battalion. The representation was finished. Remained only for Apis to clear his stage of the subordinate characters.

'Ah! His gesture then! He gave a dramatic start—this Cyrano of the Camargue—as though he was aware of them for the first time. He moved. All their beautiful breeches twinkled for an instant along the top of the barrier. He held the stage alone! But Christophe and I, we trembled! For, observe, he had now involved himself in a stupendous drama of which he only could supply the third act. And, except for an audience on the razor-edge of emotion, he had exhausted his material. Molière himself—we have forgotten, my friend, to drink to the health of that great soul—might have been at a loss. And Tragedy is but a step behind Failure. We could see the four or five Civil Guards, who are sent always to keep order, fingering the breeches of their rifles. They were but waiting a word from the Mayor to fire on him, as they do sometimes at a bull who leaps the barrier among the spectators. They would, of course, have killed or wounded several people—but that would not have saved Apis.'

Monsieur Voiron drowned the thought at once, and wiped his beard.

'At that moment Fate—the Genius of France, if you will—sent to assist in the incomparable finale, none other than Chisto, the eldest, and I should have said (but never again will I judge!) the least inspired of all; mediocrity itself, but at heart—and it is the heart that conquers always, my friend—at heart an artist. He descended stiffly into the arena, alone and assured. Apis regarded him, his eyes in his eyes. The man took stance, with his cloak, and called to the bull as to an equal: "Now, Señor, we will show these honourable caballeros something together." He advanced thus against this thinker who at a plunge—a kick—a thrust—could, we all knew, have extinguished him. My dear friend, I wish I could convey to you something of the unaffected bonhomie, the humour, the delicacy, the consideration bordering on respect even, with which Apis, the supreme artist, responded to this invitation. It was the Master, wearied after a strenuous hour in the atelier, unbuttoned and at ease with some not inexpert but limited disciple. The telepathy was instantaneous between them. And for good reason! Christophe said to me: "All's well. That Chisto began among the bulls. I was sure of it when I heard him call just now. He has been a herdsman. He'll pull it off." There was a little feeling and adjustment, at first, for mutual distances and allowances.

'Oh, yes! And here occurred a gross impertinence of Villamarti. He had, after an interval, followed Chisto—to retrieve his reputation. My Faith! I can conceive the elder Dumas slamming his door on an intruder precisely as Apis did. He raced Villamarti into the nearest refuge at once. He stamped his feet outside it, and he snorted: "Go! I am engaged with an artist." Villamarti went—his reputation left behind for ever.

'Apis returned to Chisto saying: "Forgive the interruption. I am not always master of my time, but you were about to observe, my dear confrère . . .?" Then the play began. Out of compliment to Chisto, Apis chose as his objective (every bull varies in this respect) the inner edge of the cloak—that nearest to the man's body. This allows but a few millimetres clearance in charging. But Apis trusted himself as Chisto trusted him, and, this time, he conformed to the man, with inimitable judgement and temper. He allowed himself to be played into the shadow or the sun, as the delighted audience demanded. He raged enormously; he feigned defeat; he despaired in statuesque abandon, and thence flashed into fresh paroxysms of wrath—but always with the detachment of the true artist who knows he is but the vessel of an emotion whence others, not he, must drink. And never once did he forget that honest Chisto's cloak was to him the gauge by which to spare even a hair on the skin. He inspired Chisto too. My God! His youth returned to that meritorious beef-sticker—the desire, the grace, and the beauty of his early dreams. One could almost see that girl of the past for whom he was rising, rising to these present heights of skill and daring. It was his hour too—a miraculous hour of dawn returned to gild the sunset. All he knew was at Apis' disposition. Apis acknowledged it with all that he had learned at home, at Arles and in his lonely murders on our grazing-grounds. He flowed round Chisto like a river of death—round his knees, leaping at his shoulders, kicking just clear of one side or the other of his head; behind his back, hissing as he shaved by; and once or twice—inimitable!—he reared wholly up before him while Chisto slipped back from beneath the avalanche of that instructed body.

Those two, my dear friend, held five thousand people dumb with no sound but of their breathings—regular as pumps. It was unbearable. Beast and man realized together that we needed a change of note—a *détente*. They relaxed to pure buffoonery. Chisto fell back and talked to him outrageously. Apis pretended he had never heard such language. The audience howled with delight. Chisto slapped him; he took liberties with his short tail, to the end of which he clung while Apis pirouetted; he played about him in all postures; he had become the herdsman again—gross, careless, brutal, but comprehending. Yet Apis was always the more consummate clown. All that time (Christophe and I saw it) Apis drew off towards the gates of the *toril* where so many bulls enter but—have you ever heard of one that returned? *We* knew that Apis knew that as he had saved Chisto, so Chisto would save him. Life is sweet to us all; to the artist who lives many lives in one, sweetest. Chisto did not fail him. At the last, when none could laugh any longer, the man threw his cape across the bull's back, his arm round his neck. He flung up a hand at the gate, as Villamarti, young and commanding but *not* a herdsman, might have raised it, and he cried: "Gentlemen, open to me and my honourable little donkey." They opened—I have misjudged Spaniards in my time!—those gates opened to the man and the bull together, and closed behind them. And then? From the Mayor to the Guardia Civil they went mad for five minutes, till the trumpets blew and the fifth bull rushed out—an unthinking black Andalusian. I suppose some one killed him. My friend, my very dear friend, to whom I have opened my heart, I confess that I did not watch. Christophe and I, we were weeping together like children of the same Mother. Shall we drink to Her?'

RUDYARD KIPLING, from *The Bull that Thought*

From *'The Pickwick Club'*

'Hallo!' said Mr Pickwick in his turn: seeing that his companion was armed with a gun, and that another lay ready on the grass. 'What's going forward?'

'Why, your friend and I,' replied the host, 'are going out rook-shooting before breakfast. He's a very good shot, an't he?'

'I've heard him say he's a capital one,' replied Mr Pickwick; 'but I never saw him aim at anything.'

'Well,' said the host, 'I wish he'd come. Joe—Joe!'

The fat boy, who under the exciting influence of the morning did not appear to be more than three parts and a fraction asleep, emerged from the house.

'Go up, and call the gentleman, and tell him he'll find me and Mr Pickwick in the rookery. Show the gentleman the way there; d'ye hear?'

The boy departed to execute his commission; and the host, carrying both guns like a second Robinson Crusoe, led the way from the garden.

'This is the place,' said the old gentleman, pausing after a few minutes' walking, in an avenue of trees. The information was unnecessary; for the incessant cawing of the unconscious rooks sufficiently indicated their whereabout.

The old gentleman laid one gun on the ground, and loaded the other.

'Here they are,' said Mr Pickwick; and as he spoke, the forms of Mr Tupman, Mr Snodgrass, and Mr Winkle appeared in the distance. The fat boy, not being quite certain which gentleman he was directed to call, had with peculiar sagacity, and to prevent the possibility of any mistake, called them all.

'Come along,' shouted the old gentleman, addressing Mr Winkle; 'a keen hand like you ought to have been up long ago, even to such poor work as this.'

Mr Winkle responded with a forced smile, and took up the spare gun with an expression of countenance which a metaphysical rook, impressed with a foreboding of his approaching death by violence, may be supposed to assume. It might have been keenness, but it looked remarkably like misery.

The old gentleman nodded; and two ragged boys who had been marshalled to the spot under the direction of the infant Lambert, forthwith commenced climbing up two of the trees.

'What are those lads for?' inquired Mr Pickwick abruptly. He was rather alarmed; for he was not quite certain but that the distress of the agricultural interest, about which he had often heard a great deal, might have compelled the small boys attached to the soil to earn a precarious and hazardous subsistence by making marks of themselves for inexperienced sportsmen.

'Only to start the game,' replied Mr Wardle, laughing.

'To what?' inquired Mr Pickwick.

'Why, in plain English to frighten the rooks.'

'Oh! is that all?'

'You are satisfied?'

'Quite.'

'Very well. Shall I begin?'

'If you please,' said Mr Winkle, glad of any respite.

'Stand aside, then. Now for it.'

The boy shouted, and shook a branch with a nest on it. Half-a-dozen young rooks in violent conversation, flew out to ask what the matter was. The old gentleman fired by way of reply. Down fell one bird, and off flew the others.

'Take him up, Joe,' said the old gentleman.

There was a smile upon the youth's face as he advanced. Indistinct visions of rook-pie floated through his imagination. He laughed as he retired with the bird—it was a plump one.

'Now, Mr Winkle,' said the host, reloading his own gun. 'Fire away.'

Mr Winkle advanced, and levelled his gun. Mr Pickwick and his friends cowered involuntarily to escape damage from the heavy fall of rooks, which they felt quite certain would be occasioned by the devastating barrel of their friend. There was a solemn pause—a shout—a flapping of wings—a faint click.

'Hallo!' said the old gentleman.

'Won't it go?' inquired Mr Pickwick.

'Missed fire,' said Mr Winkle, who was very pale: probably from disappointment.

'Odd,' said the old gentleman, taking the gun. 'Never knew one of them miss fire before. Why, I don't see anything of the cap.'

'Bless my soul,' said Mr Winkle. 'I declare I forgot the cap!'

The slight omission was rectified. Mr Pickwick crouched again. Mr Winkle stepped forward with an air of determination and resolution; and Mr Tupman looked out from behind a tree. The boy shouted; four birds flew out. Mr Winkle fired. There was a scream as of an individual—not a rook—in corporeal anguish. Mr Tupman had saved the lives of innumerable unoffending birds by receiving a portion of the charge in his left arm.

To describe the confusion that ensued would be impossible. To tell how Mr Pickwick in the first transports of his emotion called Mr Winkle 'Wretch!' how Mr Tupman lay prostrate on the ground; and how Mr Winkle knelt horror-stricken beside him; how Mr Tupman called distractedly upon some feminine Christian name, and then opened first one eye, and then the other, and then fell back and shut them both;—all this would be as difficult to describe in detail, as it would be to depict the gradual recovering of the unfortunate individual, the binding up of his arm with pocket-handkerchiefs, and the conveying him back by slow degrees supported by the arms of his anxious friends.

CHARLES DICKENS (1812–70), *Pickwick Papers*

Nature and the Gamekeeper

The changes in the fauna of the inland counties brought about by the favour shown to certain species are very remarkable. The alterations caused by the preservation of pheasants have reached their limit. No further effects are likely to be produced, even if pheasant-preserving should be carried to a still greater extent, which itself is improbable. One creature at least, the pine-marten, has been exterminated over Southern England, and is now only to be seen—in the stuffed state—in museums. It may be roughly described as a large tree-weasel, and was shot down on account of its habit of seizing pheasants at roost. The polecat is also practically extinct, though occasional specimens are said to occur. These two animals could not be allowed to exist in any preserve. But it is in the list of birds that the change is most striking. Eagles are gone: if one is seen it is a stray from Scotland or Wales; and so are the buzzards, except from the moors. Falcons are equally rare: the little merlin comes down from the north now and then, but the peregrine falcon as a resident or regular visitor is extinct. The hen-harrier is still shot at intervals; but the large hawks have ceased out of the daily life, as it were, of woods and fields. Horned owls are becoming rare; even the barn-owl has all but disappeared from some districts, and the wood-owl is local. The raven is extinct—quite put out. The birds are said to exist near the sea-coast; but it is certain that any one may walk over inland country for years without seeing one. These, being all more or less birds of prey, could not but be excluded from pheasant-covers. All these birds, however, would probably resume their ancient habitations in the course of five-and-twenty years if permitted to do so. They exist plentifully at no great distance—judged as such strong flyers judge distance; and if they found that they were unmolested they would soon come back from the extremities of the land.

But even more remarkable than the list of birds driven away is the list of those creatures, birds and animals, which have stood their ground in spite of traps, guns, and dogs. Stoats and weasels are always shot when seen, they are frequently trapped, and in every manner hunted to the death and their litters destroyed—the last the more effectual method of extermination. But in spite of the unceasing enmity directed against them, stoat and weasel remain common. They still take their share of game, both winged and ground. Stoat and weasel will not be killed out. As they are both defenceless creatures, and not even swift of foot, being easily overtaken in the open, their persistent continuance is curious. If any reason can be assigned for it, it must be because they spend much of their time in buries, where they are comparatively safe, and because they do not confine themselves to woods, but roam cornfields and meadows. Certainly, if man has tried to exterminate any creature, he has tried his hardest to get rid of these two, and has failed. It is even questionable whether their numbers show any appreciable diminution. Kept down to the utmost in one place, they flourish in another. Kestrel and sparrowhawk form a parallel among winged creatures. These two hawks have been shot, trapped, and their eggs destroyed unsparingly: they remain numerous just the same. Neither of them choose inaccessible places for their eyries; neither of them rear large broods. The sparrowhawk makes a nest in a tree, often in firs; the kestrel lays in old rooks', crows', or magpies' nests. Both the parents are often shot on or near the nest, and the eggs broken. Sometimes the young are permitted to grow large enough to fly, and are then shot down after the manner of rook-shooting. Nevertheless kestrels are common, and sparrowhawks, if not quite so numerous, are in no degree uncommon. Perhaps the places of those killed are supplied by birds from the great woods, moors, and mountains of the north.

A third instance is the crow. Hated by all gamekeepers, and sportsmen, by farmers, and every one who has anything to do with country life, the crow survives. Cruel tyrant as he is to every creature smaller than himself, not a voice is raised in his favour. Yet crows exist in considerable numbers. Shot off in some places, they are recruited again from others where there is less game preservation. The case of the crow, however, is less striking than that of the two hawks; because the crow is a cosmopolitan bird, and if every specimen in the British Isles were destroyed today, there would be an influx from abroad in a very short time. The crow is, too, partly a sea-coast feeder, and so escapes. Still, to any one who knows how determined is the hostility to his race shown by all country people, his existence in any number must be considered remarkable. His more powerful congener the raven, as has been pointed out, is practically extinct in southern counties, and no longer attacks the shepherd's weakly lambs. Why, then, does the crow live on? Wherever a pair of ravens do exist the landowner generally preserves them now, as interesting representatives of old times. They are taken care of; people go to see them; the appearance of eggs in the nest is recorded. But the raven does not multiply. Barn-owls live on, though not in all districts. Influenced by the remonstrance of naturalists, many gentlemen have stopped the destruction of owls; but a custom once established is not easily put an end to.

Jays and magpies have also been subjected to a bitter warfare of extermination. Magpies are quite shot off some places; in others they exist sparingly; here and there they may be found in fair numbers. Occasionally their nests are preserved—indeed, the growing tendency is to spare. Still, they have been shot off rigorously, and have survived it. So have jays. In large woods—particularly where there is much fir—jays are so numerous that to destroy them seems almost impossible. Another bird that has defied the gun and trap is the green woodpecker, which used to be killed for alleged destruction of timber. Woodpeckers are not now so ceaselessly killed, though the old system of slaying them is common enough. They have defied not only gun and trap, but the cunning noose placed at the mouth of their holes.

Twenty creatures, furred and feathered, have undergone severe persecution since the extension of pheasant-covers, and of these the first nine have more or less succumbed—namely, pine-marten, polecat, eagle, buzzard, falcon, kite, horned owl, harrier, and raven. The remaining eleven have survived—namely, stoat, weasel, rat, crow, kestrel, sparrow-hawk, brown and barn owl, jay, magpie, and woodpecker. . . . One new bird has also been introduced into Scotland—in this case a re-introduction. The magnificent capercailzie is now flourishing again in the north, to the honour of those who laboured for its restoration. In these notes I have not included attempts at acclimatisation, as that of the wild turkey from North America, which has partly succeeded. Beavers, too, have been induced to resume possession of their ancient streams under careful supervision, but they are outside present consideration. While England has thus lost some species and suffered a diminution of several, other countries have been supplied from our streams and woods and hedgerows. England has sent the sparrow to the United States and Australia; also the nightingale, rabbit, salmon, trout, and sweet-briar.

It is quite open to argument that pheasant-covers have saved as well as destroyed. Wood-pigeons could scarcely exist in such numbers without the quiet of preserved woods to breed in; nor could squirrels. Nor can the rarity of such birds as the little bearded tit be charged on game. The great bustard, the crane, and bittern have been driven away by cultivation. The crane, possibly, has deserted us wilfully; since civilisation in other countries has not destroyed it. And then the fashion of making natural history collections has much extended of recent years: so much so, that many blame too ardent collectors for the increasing rarity of birds like the crossbill, waxwing, hoopoe, golden oriole, and others which seem to have once visited this country more commonly than at present.

RICHARD JEFFERIES (1848–87), *The Life of the Fields*

Inishmaan

I have come over again to Inishmaan, and this time I had fine weather for my passage. The air was full of luminous sunshine from the early morning, and it was almost a summer's day when I set sail at noon with Michael and two other men who had come over for me in a curagh.

The wind was in our favour, so the sail was put up and Michael sat in the stern to steer with an oar, while I rowed with the others.

We had had a good dinner and drink, and were wrought up by this sudden revival of summer to a dreamy voluptuous gaiety that made us shout with exultation to hear our voices passing out across the blue twinkling of the sea.

Even after the people of the south island, these men of the Inishmaan seemed to be moved by strange archaic sympathies with the world. Their mood accorded itself with wonderful fineness to the suggestions of the day, and their ancient Gaelic seemed so full of divine simplicity that I would have liked to turn the prow to the west and row with them for ever.

I told them I was going back to Paris in a few days to sell my books and my bed, and that then I was coming back to grow as strong and simple as they were among the islands of the west.

When our excitement sobered down, Michael told me that one of the priests had left his gun at our cottage and given me leave to use it till he returned to the island. There was another gun and a ferret in the house also, and he said that as soon as we got home he was going to take me out fowling on rabbits.

A little later in the day we set off, and I nearly laughed to see Michael's eagerness that I should turn out a good shot.

We put the ferret down in a crevice between two bare sheets of rock, and waited. In a few minutes we heard rushing paws underneath us, then a rabbit shot up straight into the air from the crevice at our feet and set off for a wall that was a few feet away. I threw up the gun and fired.

'Buail tu é,' screamed Michael at my elbow as he ran up the rock. I had killed it.

We shot seven or eight more in the next hour, and Michael was immensely pleased. If I had done badly I think I should have had to leave the islands. The people would have despised me. A 'duine uasal' who cannot shoot seems to these descendants of hunters a fallen type who is worse than an apostate.

J. M. SYNGE (1871–1909), from *The Aran Islands*

Partridges

Here they lie mottled to the ground unseen,
This covey linked together from the nest.
The nosing pointers put them from their rest,
The wings whirr, the guns flash and all has been.

The lucky crumple to the clod, shot clean,
The wounded drop and hurry and lie close;
The sportsmen praise the pointer and his nose,
Until he scents the hiders and is keen.

Tumbled in bag with rabbits, pigeons, hares,
The crumpled corpses have forgotten all
The covey's joys of strong or gliding flight.

But when the planet lamps the coming night,
The few survivors seek those friends of theirs;
The twilight hears and darkness hears them call.

JOHN MASEFIELD

At Hurlingham

This was dear Willy's brief dispatch,
A curt and yet a cordial summons;—
'Do come! I'm in tomorrow's match,
And see us whip the *Faithful Commons.*'
We trundled out behind the bays,
Through miles and miles of brick and garden;
Mama was dresst in mauve and maize,—
Of course I wore my *Dolly Varden*.

A charming scene, and lovely too,
The paddock's full, the band is playing
Boulotte's song in *Barbe bleu*;
And what are all these people saying?
They flirt! they bet! there's Linda Reeves
Too lovely! I'd give worlds to borrow
Her yellow rose with russet leaves!—
I'll wear a yellow rose tomorrow!

And there are May and Algy Meade;
How proud she looks on her promotion!
The ring must be amused indeed
And edified by such devotion!
I wonder if she ever guess'd!
I wonder if he'll call on Friday!
I often wonder which is best!—
I only hope my hair is tidy!

Some girls repine, and some rejoice,
And some get bored, but I'm contented
To make my destiny my choice,—
I'll never dream that I've repented.
There's something sad in *lov'd and cross'd*,
For all the fond, fond hope that rings it:
There's something sweet in 'Loved and lost'—
And Oh, how sweetly Alfred sings it.

I'll own I'm bored with *handicaps*!
Bluerocks! (they always are 'bluerock'-ing!)—
With May, a little bit, perhaps,—
And yon Faust's *teufelshund* is shocking!
Bang . . . bang . . .! That's Willy! There's his bird,
Blithely it cleaves the skies above me!
He's missed all ten! He's too absurd!—
I hope he'll always, always love me!

We've lost! To tea, then back to town;
  The crowd is laughing, eating, drinking:
The moon's eternal eyes look down,—
  Of what can yon sad moon be thinking?
Oh, but for some good fairy's wand,—
  This pigeoncide is worse than silly,
But still I'm very, very fond
  Of Hurlingham, and tea,—and Willy.

FREDERICK LOCKER-LAMPSON (1821–95)

Hunting Season

A shot: from crag to crag
  The tell-tale echoes trundle;
Some feathered he-or-she
  Is now a lifeless bundle
And, proud into a kitchen, some
Example of our tribe will come.

Down in the startled valley
  Two lovers break apart:
He hears the roaring oven
  Of a witch's heart;
Behind his murmurs of her name
She sees a marksman taking aim.

Reminded of the hour
  And that his chair is hard,
A deathless verse half done,
  One interrupted bard
Postpones his dying with a dish
Of several suffocated fish.

W. H. AUDEN (1907–73)

III

We'll to the River

'Alexandria. Cleopatra's Palace'

Enter Cleopatra, Charmian, Iras, and Alexas.

Cleo. Give me some music; music, moody food
Of us that trade in love.
All. The music, ho!
Enter Mardian the Eunuch.
Cleo. Let it alone; let's to billiards: come, Charmian.
Char. My arm is sore: best play with Mardian.
Cleo. As well a woman with an eunuch play'd
As with a woman. Come, you'll play with me, sir?
Mar. As well as I can, madam.
Cleo. And when good will is show'd, though 't come too short,
The actor may plead pardon. I'll none now:
Give me mine angle; we'll to the river: there,
My music playing far off, I will betray
Tawny-finn'd fishes; my bended hook shall pierce
Their slimy jaws, and as I draw them up,
I'll think them every one an Antony,
And say 'Ah, ha! you're caught.'
Char. 'Twas merry when
You wager'd on your angling; when your diver
Did hang a salt-fish on his hook, which he
With fervency drew up.
Cleo. That time—O times!—
I laugh'd him out of patience, and that night
I laugh'd him into patience; and next morn,
Ere the ninth hour, I drunk him to his bed;
Then put my tires and mantles on him, whilst
I wore his sword Philippan.

WILLIAM SHAKESPEARE, *Antony and Cleopatra*

The Bait

Come live with me and be my love,
And we will some new pleasures prove,
Of golden sands and crystal brooks,
With silken lines and silver hooks.

There will the river whisp'ring run,
Warm'd by the eyes more than the Sun;
And there the enamell'd fish will stay,
Begging themselves they may betray.

When thou wilt swim in that live bath,
Each fish, which ev'ry channel hath,
Most am'rously to thee will swim,
Gladder to catch thee, than thou him.

If thou, to be so seen, beest loath,
By sun or moon, thou dark'ness both,
And if mine eyes have leave to see,
I need not their light, having thee.

Let others freeze with Angling-reeds,
And cut their legs with shells and weeds;
Or treach'rously poor fish beset,
With strangling snares, or windowy net.

Let coarse bold hands, from slimy nest,
The bedded fish in banks outwrest;
Let curious traitors sleave silk flies,
To 'witch poor wand'ring fishes' eyes.

For thee, thou need'st no such deceit,
For thou thyself art thine own bait:
That fish that is not catched thereby,
Is wiser far, Alas! than I.

JOHN DONNE (1572–1631)

From *To Penshurst*

Thy copse, too, named of Gamage, thou hast there,
  That never fails to serve thee seasoned deer
When thou wouldst feast or exercise thy friends.
  The lower land, that to the river bends,

Thy sheep, thy bullocks, kine and calves do feed;
  The middle grounds thy mares and horses breed.
Each bank doth yield thee conies, and the tops,
  Fertile of wood, Ashour and Sidney's copse,
To crown thy open table, doth provide
  The purpled pheasant with the speckled side;
The painted partridge lies in every field,
  And for thy mess is willing to be killed.
And if the high-swoll'n Medway fail thy dish,
  Thou hast thy ponds that pay thee tribute fish:
Fat, aged carps, that run into thy net;
  And pikes, now weary their own kind to eat,
As loath the second draught or cast to stay,
  Officiously, at first, themselves betray;
Bright eels, that emulate them, and leap on land
  Before the fisher, or into his hand.

BEN JONSON (1572–1637)

'Hunting by Water'

Fishing is a kind of hunting by water, be it with nets, weels, baits, angling, or otherwise, and yields all out as much pleasure to some men as dogs or hawks, 'when they draw their fish upon the bank,' saith Nic. Henselius, *Silesiographiæ, cap.* 3, speaking of that extraordinary delight his countrymen took in fishing and in making of pools. James Dubravius, that Moravian, in his book *de pisc.*, telleth how, travelling by the highway side in Silesia, he found a nobleman, 'booted up to the groins,' wading himself, pulling the nets, and labouring as much as any fisherman of them all: and when some belike objected to him the baseness of his office, he excused himself, 'that if other men might hunt hares, why should not he hunt carps? Many gentlemen in like sort with us will wade up to the arm-holes upon such occasions, and voluntarily undertake that, to satisfy their pleasure, which a poor man for a good stipend would scarce be hired to undergo. Plutarch, in his book *de soler. animal.*, speaks against all fishing, 'as a filthy, base, illiberal employment, having neither wit nor perspicacity in it, nor worth the labour.' But he that shall consider the variety of baits for all seasons, and pretty devices which our anglers have invented, peculiar lines, false flies, several sleights, etc., will say that it deserves like commendation, requires as much study and perspicacity as the rest, and is to be preferred before many of them. Because hawking and hunting are very laborious, much riding, and many dangers accompany them; but this is still and quiet: and if so be the angler catch no fish, yet he hath a wholesome walk to the brookside, pleasant shade by the sweet silver streams; he hath good air, and sweet smells of fine fresh meadow flowers, he hears the melodious harmony of birds, he sees the swans, herons, ducks, water-hens, coots, etc., and many other fowl, with their brood, which he thinketh better than the noise of hounds, or blast of horns, and all the sport that they can make.

ROBERT BURTON (1577–1640), *The Anatomy of Melancholy*

The Angler's Dinner

Now as an *Angler* melancholy standing
Upon a greene bancke yeelding roome for landing,
A wrigling yealow worme thrust on his hooke,
Now in the midst he throwes, then in a nooke:
Here puls his line, there throwes it in againe,
Mendeth his Corke and Baite, but all in vaine,
He stands long viewing of the curled streame;
At last a hungry *Pike*, or well-growne *Breame*
Snatch at the worme, and hasting fast away,
He knowing it, a Fish of stubborne sway
Puls up his rod, but soft: (as having skill)
Wherewith the hooke fast holds the Fishes gill.
Then all his line he freely yeeldeth him,
Whilst furiously all up and downe doth swimme
Th'insnared Fish, here on the top doth scud,
There underneath the banckes, then in the mud;
And with his franticke fits so scares the shole,
That each one takes his *hyde*, or starting hole:
By this the *Pike* cleane wearied, underneath
A *Willow* lyes, and pants (if Fishes breath)
Wherewith the *Angler* gently puls him to him,
And Least his hast might happen to undoe him,
Layes downe his rod, then takes his line in hand,
And by degrees getting the Fish to land,
Walkes to another Poole; at length is winner
Of such a dish as served him for his dinner.

WILLIAM BROWNE (1591–1643)

Fishing

Fishing, if I, a fisher, may protest,
Of pleasures is the sweetest, of sports the best,
Of exercises the most excellent;
Of recreations the most innocent;
But now the sport is marde, and wott ye why?
Fishes decrease, and fishers multiply.

THOMAS BASTARD (1566–1618)

The Angler's Song

As inward love breeds outward talk,
The hound some praise, and some the hawk,
Some, better pleas'd with private sport,
Use tennis, some a mistress court;
But these delights I neither wish,
Nor envy, while I freely fish.

Who hunts, doth oft in danger ride;
Who hawks, lures oft both far and wide;
Who uses games shall often prove
A loser; but who falls in love,
Is fetter'd in fond Cupid's snare;
My angle breeds me no such care.

Of recreation there is none
So free as fishing is alone;
All other pastimes do no less
Than mind and body both possess:
My hand alone my work can do,
So I can fish and study too.

I care not, I, to fish in seas,
Fresh rivers best my mind do please,
Whose sweet calm course I contemplate,
And seek in life to imitate:
In civil bounds I fain would keep,
And for my past offences weep.

And when the timorous Trout I wait
To take, and he devours my bait,
How poor a thing, sometimes I find,
Will captivate a greedy mind:
  And when none bite, I praise the wise
  Whom vain allurements ne'er surprise.

But yet, though while I fish, I fast,
I make good fortune my repast;
And thereunto my friend invite,
In whom I more than that delight:
  Who is more welcome to my dish
  Than to my angle was my fish.

WILLIAM BASSE (1602–53)

From *Upon Appleton House*

For now the waves are fall'n and dried,
And now the meadows fresher dyed,
Whose grass, with moister colour dashed,
Seems as green silks but newly washed.
No serpent new nor crocodile
Remains behind our little Nile,
Unless itself you will mistake,
Among these meads the only snake.

See in what wanton harmless folds
It everywhere the meadow holds;
And its yet muddy back doth lick,
Till as a crystal mirror slick,
Where all things gaze themselves, and doubt
If they be in it or without.
And for his shade which therein shines,
Narcissus-like, the sun too pines.

Oh what a pleasure 'tis to hedge
My temples here with heavy sedge,
Abandoning my lazy side,
Stretched as a bank unto the tide,
Or to suspend my sliding foot
On th' osier's underminèd root,
And in its branches tough to hang,
While at my lines the fishes twang!

ANDREW MARVELL (1621–78)

Directions for making of a Line, and for the colouring of both Rod and Line.

P*isc.* Well, Scholar, I have held you too long about these Cadis, and smaller *fish*, and *rivers*, and *Fish-ponds*, and my spirits are almost spent, and so I doubt is your patience; but being we are now almost at *Tottenham*, where I first met you, and where we are to part, I will lose no time, but give you a little direction how to make and order your Lines, and to colour the hair of which you make your Lines, for that is very needful to be known of an Angler; and also how to paint your Rod; especially your top, for a right grown top is a choice Commodity, and should be preserved from the water soaking into it, which makes it in wet weather to be heavy, and fish ill favouredly, and not true, and also it rots quickly for want of painting: and I think a good top is worth preserving, or I had not taken care to keep a top above twenty years.

But first for your line.

First, note, That you are to take care, that your hair be round and clear, and free from galls or scabs, or frets; for a well-chosen, even, clear, round hair, of a kind of glass-colour, will prove as strong as three uneven, scabby hairs, that are ill chosen, and full of galls or unevenness. You shall seldom find a black hair but it is round, but many white are flat and uneven, therefore, if you get a lock of right, round, clear, glass-colour hair make much of it.

And for making your *Line*, observe this rule, First let your hair be clean washt 'ere you go about to twist it: and then chuse not only the clearest hair for it, but hairs that be of an equal bigness, for such do usually stretch all together, and break altogether, which hairs of an unequal bigness never do, but break singly, and so deceive the Angler that trusts to them.

When you have twisted your links, lay them in water for a quarter of an hour, at least, and then twist them over again before you tie them into a Line: for those that do not so, shall usually find their Line to have a hair or two shrink, and be shorter than the rest at the first fishing with it, which is so much of the strength of the Line lost for want of first watering it, and then re-twisting it; and this is most visible in a seven-hair line, one of those which hath always a black hair in the middle.

And for dying of your hairs do it thus:

Take a pint of strong Ale, half a pound of soot, and a little quantity of the juice of *Walnut*-tree leaves, and an equal quantity of Allom, put these together into a pot, pan, or pipkin, and boil them half an hour, and having so done, let it cool; and being cold, put your hair into it, and there let it lie; it will turn your hair to be a kind of water or glass colour, or greenish, and the longer you let it lie, the deeper coloured it will be; you might be taught to make many other colours, but it is to little purpose; for doubtless the water-colour or glass-coloured hair is the most choice and most useful for an *Angler*; but let it not be too green.

But if you desire to colour hair greener; then do it thus: Take a quart of small Ale, half a pound of Allom, then put these into a pan or pipkin; and your hair into it with them; then put it upon a fire, and let it boil softly for half an hour, and then take out your hair, and let it dry, and having so done, then take a pottle of water, and put into it two handful of Marygolds, and cover it with a tile (or what you think fit) and set it again on the Fire, where it is to boil again softly for half an hour, about which time the scum will turn yellow, then put into it half a pound of Copperas beaten small, and with it the hair that you intend to colour, then let the hair be boiled softly till half the liquor be wasted, and then let it cool three or four hours with your hair in it: and you are to observe, that the more Copperas you put into it, the greener it will be, but doubtless the pale green is best; But if you desire yellow hair, (which is only good when the weeds rot) then put in the more *Mary-golds*, and abate most of the Copperas, or leave it quite out, and take a little Verdigrease instead of it.

This for colouring your hair. And as for painting your Rod, which must be in Oil, you must first make a size with glue and water, boiled together, until the glue be dissolved, and the size of a Lie-colour; then strike your size upon the wood with a Bristle, or a Brush, or Pencil, whilst it is hot: that being quite dry, take white Lead, and a little red lead, and a little cole-black, so much as altogether will make an ash-colour; grind these all together with Linseed Oil, let it be thick, and lay it thin upon the wood with a Brush or Pensil, this do for the ground of any colour to lie upon wood.

IZAAK WALTON (1593–1683) *The Compleat Angler*

To my dear Friend, Mr Iz. Walton, *in praise of Angling, which we both love.*

Down by this smooth streams wandering side,
Adorn'd & perfum'd with the pride
Of *Flora*'s Wardrobe, where the shrill
Aerial Quire express their skill,
First in alternate melody,
And, then, in chorus all agree.
Whilst the charm'd fish, as extasi'd
With sounds, to his own throat deni'd,
Scorns his dull Element, and springs
I' th' air, as if his Fins were wings.
'Tis here that pleasures sweet and high
Prostrate to our embraces lye:
Such as to Body, Soul, or Fame
Create no sickness, sin, or shame:

Roses not fenc'd with pricks grow here,
No sting to th' Hony-bag is near.
But (what's perhaps their prejudice)
They difficulty want and price.
An obvious rod, a twist of hair,
With hook hid in an insect, are
Engines of sport, would fit the wish
O' th' Epicure, and fill his dish.
In this clear stream let fall a *Grub*;
And straight take up a *Dace* or *Chub*.
Ith' mud your worm provokes a *Snig*,
Which being fast, if it prove big
The *Gotham* folly will be found
Discreet, e're ta'ne she must be drown'd.
The *Tench* (Physician of the Brook)
In yon dead hole expects your hook;
Which having first your pastime been,
Serves then for meat or medicine.
Ambush'd behind that root doth stay
A *Pike*, to catch, and be a prey.
The treacherous Quill in this slow stream
Betrays the hunger of a *Bream*.
An at that nimbler Ford, (no doubt)
Your false flie cheats a speckled *Trout*.
When you these creatures wisely chuse
To practise on, which to your use
Owe their creation, and when
Fish from your arts do rescue men;
To plot, delude, and circumvent,
Ensnare and spoil, is innocent.
Here by these crystal streams you may
Preserve a Conscience clear as they;
And when by sullen thoughts you find
Your harassed, not busied, mind
In sable melancholy clad,
Distemper'd, serious, turning sad;
Hence fetch your cure, cast in your bait,
All anxious thoughts and cares will straight
Fly with such speed, they'l seem to be
Possest with the *Hydrophobie*.
The waters calmness in your breast,
And smoothness on your brow shall rest.
Away with sports of charge and noise,
And give me cheap and silent joys,
Such as *Actaeon's* game pursue,
Their fate oft makes the tale seem true.

The sick or sullen *Hawk*, to day,
Flyes not; tomorrow, quite away.
Patience and Purse to Cards and Dice
Too oft are made a sacrifice:
The Daughters dower, th' inheritance
O' th' son, depend on one mad chance.
The harms and mischiefs which th' abuse
Of wine doth every day produce,
Make good the Doctrine of the *Turks*,
That in each grape a devil lurks.
And by yon fading sapless tree,
Bout which the *Ivy* twin'd you see,
His fate's foretold, who fondly places
His bliss in woman's soft embraces.
All pleasures, but the Angler's, bring
I' th' tail repentance like a sting.
  Then on these banks let me sit down,
Free from the toilsom Sword and Gown,
And pity those that do affect
To conquer Nations and protect.
My Reed affords such true content,
Delights so sweet and innocent,
As seldom fall unto the lot
Of Scepters, though they'r *justly got.*

THOMAS WEAVER (1616–63)

To My Dear and Most Worthy Friend, Mr Izaak Walton

Whilst in this cold and blust'ring clime,
  Where bleak winds howl, and tempests roar,
We pass away the roughest time
  Has been of many years before;

Whilst from the most tempest'ous nooks
  The chillest blasts our peace invade,
And by great rains our smallest brooks
  Are almost navigable made;

Whilst all the ills are so improv'd
  Of this dead quarter of the year,
That even you, so much belov'd,
  We would not now wish with us here;

In this estate, I say, it is
  Some comfort to us to suppose,
That in a better clime than this
  You our dear friend have more repose;

And some delight to me the while,
  Though nature now does weep in rain,
To think that I have seen her smile,
  And haply may I do again.

If the all-ruling Power please
  We live to see another May,
We'll recompense an age of these
  Foul days in one fine fishing day:

We then shall have a day or two,
  Perhaps a week, wherein to try,
What the best master's hand can do
  With the most deadly killing fly;

A day without too bright a beam,
  A warm, but not a scorching sun,
A southern gale to curl the stream,
  And (master) half our work is done.

There whilst behind some bush we wait
  The scaly people to betray,
We'll prove it just with treach'rous bait
  To make the preying trout our prey;

And think ourselves in such an hour
  Happier than those, though not so high,
Who, like Leviathans, devour
  Of meaner men the smaller fry.

This (my best friend) at my poor home
  Shall be our pastime and our theme,
But then should you not deign to come
  You make all this a flatt'ring dream.

CHARLES COTTON (1630–87)

From *Sir Roger and Will Wimble*

Gratis anhelans, multa agendo nihil agens.

PHAEDR. *Fab.* v. 2.

As I was yesterday morning walking with Sir Roger before his house, a country fellow brought him a huge fish, which, he told him, Mr Will Wimble had caught that morning; and that he presented it with his service to him, and intended to come and dine with him. At the same time he delivered a letter, which my friend read to me as soon as the messenger left him.

'SIR ROGER,

'I desire you to accept of a jack, which is the best I have caught this season. I intend to come and stay with you a week, and see how the perch bite in the Black River. I observed with some concern, the last time I saw you upon the bowling-green, that your whip wanted a lash to it; I will bring half-a-dozen with me that I twisted last week, which I hope will serve you all the time you are in the country. I have not been out of the saddle for six days past, having been at Eton with Sir John's eldest son. He takes to his learning hugely.—I am, Sir, your humble servant, WILL WIMBLE.'

This extraordinary letter, and message that accompanied it, made me very curious to know the character and quality of the gentleman who sent them; which I found to be as follows. Will Wimble is younger brother to a baronet, and descended of the ancient family of the Wimbles. He is now between forty and fifty: but being bred to no business, and born to no estate, he generally lives with his elder brother as superintendent of his game. He hunts a pack of dogs better than any man in the country, and is very famous for finding out a hare. He is extremely well versed in all the little handicrafts of an idle man: he makes a May-fly to a miracle; and furnishes the whole country with angle rods. As he is a good-natured officious fellow, and very much esteemed upon account of his family, he is a welcome guest at every house, and keeps up a good correspondence among all the gentlemen about him. He carries a tulip-root in his pocket from one to another, or exchanges a puppy between a couple of friends that live perhaps in the opposite sides of the county. Will is a particular favourite of all the young heirs, whom he frequently obliges with a net that he has weaved, or a setting dog that he has made himself. He now and then presents a pair of garters of his own knitting to their mothers or sisters; and raises a great deal of mirth among them, by inquiring as often as he meets them, how they wear? These gentleman-like manufactures and obliging little humours make Will the darling of the country.

JOSEPH ADDISON, *Essays*

From *Spring*

When with his lively ray the potent sun
Has pierced the streams and roused the finny race,
Then, issuing cheerful, to thy sport repair;
Chief should the western breezes curling play,
And light o'er ether bear the shadowy clouds.
High to their fount, this day, amid the hills
And woodlands warbling round, trace up the brooks;
The next, pursue their rocky-channelled maze,
Down to the river, in whose ample wave
Their little naiads love to sport at large.
Just in the dubious point where with the pool
Is mixed the trembling stream, or where it boils
Around the stone, or from the hollowed bank
Reverted plays in undulating flow,
There throw, nice-judging, the delusive fly;
And, as you lead it round in artful curve,
With eye attentive mark the springing game.
Straight as above the surface of the flood
They wanton rise, or urged by hunger leap,
Then fix with gentle twitch the barbèd hook—
Some lightly tossing to the grassy bank,
And to the shelving shore slow-dragging some,
With various hand proportioned to their force.
If, yet too young and easily deceived,
A worthless prey scarce bends your pliant rod,
Him, piteous of his youth and the short space
He has enjoyed the vital light of heaven,
Soft disengage, and back into the stream
The speckled infant throw. But, should you lure
From his dark haunt beneath the tangled roots
Of pendent trees the monarch of the brook,
Behoves you then to ply your finest art.
Long time he, following cautious, scans the fly,
And oft attempts to seize it, but as oft
The dimpled water speaks his jealous fear.
At last, while haply o'er the shaded sun
Passes a cloud, he desperate takes the death
With sullen plunge. At once he darts along,
Deep-struck, and runs out all the lengthened line;
Then seeks the farthest ooze, the sheltering weed,
The caverned bank, his old secure abode;
And flies aloft, and flounces round the pool,
Indignant of the guile. With yielding hand,
That feels him still, yet to his furious course

Gives way, you, now retiring, following now
Across the stream, exhaust his idle rage;
Till floating broad upon his breathless side,
And to his fate abandoned, to the shore
You gaily drag your unresisting prize.

JAMES THOMSON, *The Seasons*

The Old Fisher's Challenge

Oh! let it be in April-tide,
But one of April's best,
A mornin' that seems made o' May,
In dews and sunshine drest;
Frae off the Crags o' *Simonside*,
Let the fresh breezes blow,
And let auld *Cheviot's* side be green,
Albeit his head be snow.

Let the stream glitter i' the sun,
The curl be on the pool,
The rash gale rufflin' aye its face
Aneath the Alder's cool:
Or if the Spring will have her clouds,
Then let them pass me soon;
Or if they take a thought and stay,
Then let it be at noon.

Oh! freshly from his mountain holds
Comes down the rapid *Tyne*;
But *Coquet's* still the stream of streams;
So let her still be mine;
There's many a sawmon lies in *Tweed*,
An' many a trout in *Till*;
But *Coquet—Coquet* aye for me,
If I may have my will.

Let it be 'stream an' stream about,'
Or if that mayna be,
Take off old *Coquet* where ye like
From *Thirlmore* to the sea;

But leave to me the streams I love,
The streams that know my hand,
An' 'weight to weight' with the best be
That's in *Northumberland.*

Let me begin at *Brinkburn's* stream,
Fast by the Ruins gray,
An' end at bonny *Eeely-haugh*,
Just wi' the endin' day.
My foremost *flee*, the *heckle* red,
My tried Rod springin' free,
An' 'creel to creel'—wi' ony man
In a' the *North Countrie.*'

THOMAS DOUBLEDAY (1780–1870)

'Leven-Water'

The Clyde we left a little on our left-hand at Dunbritton, where it widens into an æstuary or frith, being augmented by the influx of the Leven. On this spot stands the castle formerly called Alcluyd, washed by these two rivers on all sides, except a narrow isthmus, which at every spring-tide is overflowed. The whole is a great curiosity, from the quality and form of the rock, as well as from the nature of its situation.—We now crossed the water of Leven, which, though nothing near so considerable as the Clyde, is much more transparent, pastoral, and delightful. This charming stream is the outlet of Lough-Lomond, and through a tract of four miles pursues its winding course, murmuring over a bed of pebbles, till it joins the Frith at Dunbritton. A very little above its source, on the lake, stands the house of Cameron, belonging to Mr Smollett, so embosomed in an oak wood, that we did not see it till we were within fifty yards of the door. I have seen the Lago di Garda, Albano, De Vico, Bolsena, and Geneva, and, upon my honour, I prefer Lough-Lomond to them all; a preference which is certainly owing to the verdant islands that seem to float upon its surface, affording the most enchanting objects of repose to the excursive view. Nor are the banks destitute of beauties, which even partake of the sublime. On this side they display a sweet variety of woodland, corn-field, and pasture, with several agreeable villas emerging as it were out of the lake, till, at some distance, the prospect terminates in huge mountains covered with heath, which being in bloom, affords a very rich covering of purple. Every thing here is romantic beyond imagination. This country is justly styled the Arcadia of Scotland; and I don't doubt but it may vie with Arcadia in every thing but climate.—I am sure it excels it in verdure, wood, and water.—What say you to a natural bason of pure water, near thirty miles long, and in some places seven miles broad, and in many above a hundred fathom deep, having four and twenty habitable islands, some of them stocked with deer, and all of them covered with wood; containing immense quantities of delicious fish, salmon, pike, trout, perch, flounders, eels, and powans, the last a delicate kind of fresh-water herring peculiar to this lake; and finally communicating with the sea, by sending off the Leven, through which all those species (except the powan) make their exit and entrance occasionally?

Inclosed I send you the copy of a little ode to this river, by Dr Smollett, who was born on the banks of it, within two miles of the place where I am now writing.—It is at least picturesque and accurately descriptive, if it has no other merit.—There is an idea of truth in an agreeable landscape taken from nature, which pleases me more than the gayest fiction which the most luxuriant fancy can display.

I have other remarks to make; but as my paper is full, I must reserve them till the next occasion. I shall only observe at present, that I am determined to penetrate at least forty miles into the Highlands, which now appear like a vast fantastic vision in the clouds, inviting the approach of,

Yours always,
Cameron, Aug. 28. MATT. BRAMBLE

ODE TO LEVEN-WATER

On Leven's banks, while free to rove,
And tune the rural pipe to love;
I envied not the happiest swain
That ever trod th' Arcadian plain.

Pure stream! in whose transparent wave
My youthful limbs I wont to lave;
No torrents stain thy limpid source;
No rocks impede thy dimpling course,

That sweetly warbles o'er its bed,
With white, round, polish'd pebbles spread;
While, lightly pois'd, the scaly brood
In myriads cleave thy crystal flood;
The springing trout in speckled pride;
The salmon, monarch of the tide;
The ruthless pike, intent on war;
The silver eel, and motled par

par] a small fish, not unlike the smelt, which it rivals in delicacy and flavour

Devolving from thy parent lake,
A charming maze thy waters make,
By bow'rs of birch, and groves of pine,
And edges flow'r'd with eglantine.

Still on thy banks so gaily green,
May num'rous herds and flocks be seen,
And lasses chanting o'er the pail,
And shepherd's piping in the dale,
And ancient faith that knows no guile,
And industry imbrown'd with toil,
And hearts resolv'd, and hands prepar'd,
The blessing they enjoy to guard.

TOBIAS SMOLLETT (1721–71),
The Expedition of Humphry Clinker

Rustic Fishing

On sunday mornings freed from hard employ
How oft I mark the young mischevous boy
With anxious haste his poles and lines provide
For make shifts oft crookd pins to threadings ty'd
And delve his knife with wishes ever warm
In rotten dunghills for the grub and worm
The harmless treachery of his hooks to bait
Tracking the dewy grass wi many a mate
To seek the brook that down the meadows glide
Where the grey willow shadows by its side
Were flag and reed in wild disorder spread
And bending bulrush bows its taper head
And just above the surface of the floods
Where water lileys mount their snowy buds
On whose broad swimming leaves of glossy green
The shining dragon flye is often seen
And hanging thorns whose roots washd bare appear
That shields the morehens nest from year to year
While crowding osiers mingling wild among
Prove snug asylums to her brood when young
Who when suppris'd by foes approaching near
Plunge neath the weeping boughs and dissapear
There far from terrors that the parson brings
Or church bell hearing when the summons rings
Half hid in meadow sweet and kecks high flowers
In lonly sports they spend the sunday hours

Tho ill supplyd for fishing seems the brook
That breaks the mead in many a stinted crook
Oft choakd in weeds and foild to find a road
The choice retirement of the snake and toad
Then lost in shallows dimpling restlessly
In fluttering struggles murmuring to be free
Oer gravel stones its depth can scarcly hide
It runs the remnant of its broken tide
Till seemly weary of each choaked controul
It rests collected in some gulled hole
Scoopd by the sudden floods when winters snow
Melts in confusion by a hasty thaw
There bent in hopfull musings on the brink
They watch their floating corks that seldom sink
Save when a warey roach or silver bream
Nibbles the worm as passing up the stream
Just urging expectations hopes astray
To view the dodging cork then slink away
Still hopes keep burning with untird delight
Till wobbling curves keep waving like a bite
If but the breezy wind their floats shoud spring
And move the water with a troubling ring
A captive fish still fills the anxious eyes
And willow wicks lie ready for the prize
Till evening gales awaken damp and chill
And nip the hopes that morning suns instill
When resting flyes have tired their gauzy wing
Nor longer tempt the watching fish to spring
Who at the worm nor nibbles more repeat
But lunge from night in sheltering flag retreat
Then dissapointed in their days employ
They seek amusment in a feebler joy
Short is the sigh for fancys provd untrue
With humbler hopes still pleasure they pursue
Where the rude oak bridge scales the narrow pass
Half hid in rustling reeds and scrambling grass
Or stepping stones stride oer the narrow sloughs
Which maidens daily cross to milk their cows
There they in artless glee for minnows run
And wade and dabble past the setting sun
Chasing the struttle oer the shallow tide
And flat stones turning up were gudgeons hide
Hopes visions with success here runneth high
And on a rush they string the little frye
All former hopes their ill success delayd
In this new change they fancy well repayd

And thus they wade and chatter oer their joys
Till night unlookd for your success destroys
Drives home the sons of solitude and streams
And stops uncloyd hopes ever freshning dreams
Who then like school boys that at truant play
In sloomy fear lounge on their homward way
And inly trembling as they gain the town
To meet chastisment from a parents frown
Where hazel twigs in readiness prepard
For their long abscence brings a mete reward

JOHN CLARE

Angling

Angling has pleasures that are much enjoyed
By tasteful minds of nature never cloyed
In pleasant solitudes where winding floods
Pass level meadows and oerhanging woods
Verged with tall reeds that rustle in the wind
A soothing music in the anglers mind
And rush right complasant that ever bows
Obesceience to the stream that laughs below
He feels delighted into quiet praise
And sweet the pictures that the mind essays
While gentle whispers on the southern wind
Brings health and quiet to the anglers mind
Smooth as the gentle river whirls along
And sweet as memory of some happy song

The morn is still and balmy all that moves
The trees are south gales which the angler loves
That stirs the waveing grass in idle whirls
And flush the cheeks and fan the jetty curls
Of milking maidens at their morns employ
Who sing and wake the dewy fields to joy
The sun just rising large and round and dim
Keeps creeping up oer the flat meadows brim

As rising from the ground to run its race
Till up it mounts and shows a ruddy face
Now is the time the angler leaves his dreams
In anxious movements for the silent streams
Frighting the heron from its morning toil
First at the river watching after coil

Now with the rivers brink he winds his way
For a choice place to spend the quiet day
Marking its banks how varied things appear
Now cloathed in trees and bushes and now clear
While steep the bank climbs from the waters edge
Then almost choaked with rushes flags and sedge
Then flat and level to the very brink
Tracked deep by cattle running there to drink
At length he finds a spot half shade half sun
That scarcely curves to show the waters run
Still clear and smooth quick he his line unlaps
While fish leap up and loud the water claps
Which fills his mind with pleasures of supprise
That in the deep hole some old monster lies

Right cautious now his strongest line to take
Lest some hugh monster should his tackle break
Then half impatient with a cautious throw
He swings his line into the depths below
The water rat hid in the shivering reeds
That feeds upon the slime and water weeds
Nibbling their grassy leaves with crizzling sound
Plunges below and makes his fancys bound
With expectations joy—down goes the book
In which glad leisure might for pleasure look
And up he grasps the angle in his hand
In readiness the expected prize to land
While tip toe hope gives expectations dream
Sweet as the sunshine sleeping on the stream

None but true anglers feel that gush of joy
That flushes in the patient minds employ
While expectation upon tip toe sees
The float just wave it cannot be a breeze
For not a waver oer the waters pass
Warm with the joyous day and smooth as glass
Now stronger moved it dances round then stops
Then bobs again and in a moment drops
Beneath the water—he with joys elate
Pulls and his rod bends double with the weight
True was his skill in hopes expecting dream
And up he draws a flat and curving bream
That scarcely landed from the tackle drops
And on the bank half thronged in sedges stops

Now sport the waterflyes with tiny wings
A dancing crowd imprinting little rings
And the rich lights the suns young splendours throw
Is by the very pebbles caught below
Behind the leaning tree he stoops to lean
And soon the stirring float again is seen
A larger yet from out its ambush shoots
Hid underneath the old trees cranking roots
The float now shakes and quickens his delight
Then bobs a moment and is out of sight
While scarce secured—down goes the cork again
And still a finer pants upon the plain
And bounds and flounces mid the new mown hay
And luck but ceases with the closing day

JOHN CLARE

An Angler's Rambles

I've angled far and angled wide,
On Fannich drear, by Luichart's side,
  Across dark Conan's current;
Have haunted Beauly's silver stream,
Where glimmering thro' the forest Dream
  Hangs its eternal torrent;

Among the rocks of wild Maree,
O'er whose blue billow ever free
  The daring eagles hover,
And where, at Glomach's ruffian steep,
The dark steam holds its angered leap,
  Many a fathom over;

By Lochy sad, and Laggan lake,
Where Spey uncoils his glittering snake
  Among the hills of thunder;
And I have swept my fatal fly
Where swarthy Findhorn hurries by
  The olden forest under;

On Tummel's solitary bed,
And where wild Tilt and Garry wed;
  In Athol's heathery valleys,
On Earn by green, Duneira's bower,
Below Breadalbane's Tay-washed tower,
  And Scone's once regal palace.

There have I swept the slender line,
And where the broad Awe braves the brine,
  Have watched the grey gilse gambol,
By nameless stream and tarn remote,
With light flies in the breeze afloat;
  Holding my careless ramble.

But dearer than all these to me
Is sylvan Tweed; each tower and tree
  That in its vale rejoices!
Dearer the streamlets one and all,
That blend with its Æolian brawl
  Their own enamouring voices!

THOMAS TOD STODDART (1810–80)

The Angler's Vindication

Say not our hands are cruel;
  What deeds invite the blame?
Content our golden jewel,
  No blemish on our name:
    Creation's lords
    We need no swords
  To win a withering fame.

Say not in gore and guile
  We waste the livelong day;
Let those alone revile
  Who feel our subtile sway,
    When fancy-led
    The sward we tread
  And while the morn away.

Oh! not in camp or court
  Our best delights we find,
But in the far resort
  With water, wood, and wind,
    Where Nature works
    And beauty lurks
  In all her craft enshrined.

There captive to her will
  Yet, 'mid our fetters free,
We seek by singing rill
  The broad and shady tree,
    And lisp our lay
    To flower and fay,
  Or mock the linnet's glee.

Thus glides the golden hour,
  Under the chimes to toil
Recall from brook and bower:
  Then laden with our spoil,
    Slowly we part
    With heavy heart
  And leave the haunted soil.

THOMAS TOD STODDART

Wednesday, 29 March 1871

Went down the meadows to Mrs Tudor's. Handsome Tudor was working in his garden. By the door lay a salmon rod on the ground, so I knew the Squire was having luncheon in the cottage. I went round and there he was with old Harry Pritchard. He brought out his telescope and we had a look at Crichton and Mrs Nicholl both wading in the river and fishing under the red cliff. I crossed the ditch, climbed the bank and went along the beautiful cliff walk on the edge of the cliff looking over the edge at Mrs Nicholl standing on a rock fishing far below till I came to a steep path leading down the rocks to where Crichton was fishing. 'Henry,' called Mrs Nicholl's voice faintly down the river. 'She has got a good fish,' said Crichton, winding up his line after looking at her a moment. We scrambled over the rocks to her, but she had landed her fish before we reached her. I was amazed to see Mrs Nicholl coolly wading more than ankle deep in the river with her ordinary lady's boots on. She walked about in the river as if she were on dry land, jumped from rock to rock, slipped off the rocks into the river, scrambled out again, splashed about like a fish. March water is cold. Mrs Nicholl must be an uncommonly plucky woman. Crichton says she rides to hounds and nothing stops her. She does not care what she does. He hooked a salmon the other day and his boy was clumsy in landing the fish, so Mrs Nicholl plunged into the water on the edge of a deep hole, embraced the great fish round the body, and carried him out in her arms.

FRANCIS KILVERT

'The Sacrifice to Trout'

How much the breeding of pheasants has told upon the existence of other creatures in fur and feathers I have already shown; and much the same thing is true of the preservation of trout. There is this difference, however: that while the pheasant has now produced its utmost effect, the alterations due to trout are increasing. Trout are now so highly and so widely preserved that the effect cannot but be felt. Their preservation in the numbers now considered necessary entails the destruction of some and the banishment of other creatures. The most important of these is the otter. Guns, dogs, traps set under water so as not to be scented; all modes of attack are pressed into the service, and it is not often that he escapes. When traces of an otter were found, a little while since, in the Kennet—he had left his mark on the back of a trout—the fact was recorded with as much anxiety as if a veritable wolf had appeared. With such animosity has the otter been hunted that he is becoming one of the rarest of wild animals here in the south. He is practically extinct on the majority of southern streams, and has been almost beaten off the Thames itself. But the otter is not likely to be exterminated in the sense that the wolf has been. Otters will be found elsewhere in England long after the last of them has disappeared from the south. Next the pike must be ousted from trout-streams. Special nets have been invented by which pike can be routed from their strongholds. Much hunting about quickens the intelligence of the pike to such a degree that he cannot be secured in the ordinary manner; he baffles the net by keeping close to the bank, behind stones, or by retiring to holes under roots. Perch have to go as well as pike; and then comes the turn of birds.

Herons, kingfishers, moorhens, coots, grebes, ducks, teal, various divers, are all proscribed on behalf of trout. Herons are regarded as most injurious to a fishery. As was observed a century ago, a single heron will soon empty a pond or a stretch of brook. As their long necks give them easy command of a wide radius in spying round them, it is rather difficult to shoot them with a shot-gun; but with the small-bore rifles now made no heron is safe. They are generally shot early in the morning. Were it not for the fact that herons nest like rooks, and that heronries are valued appurtenances in parks, they would soon become scarce. Kingfishers prey on smaller fish, but are believed to eat almost as many as herons. Kingfishers resort in numbers to trout nurseries, which are as traps for them: and there they are more than decimated. Owls are known to take fish occasionally, and are therefore shot. The greatest loss sustained in fisheries takes place in the spawning season, and again when the fry are about. Some students of fish-life believe that almost all wild-fowl will swallow the ova and fry of trout. It must be understood that I am not here entering into the question whether all these are really so injurious; I am merely giving a list of the 'dogs with a bad name'. Moorhens and coots are especially disliked because they are on or near the water day and night, and can clear off large quantities of fry. Grebes (di-dappers or dabchicks) are similar in habit, but less destructive because fewer. Ducks are ravenous devourers; teal are equally hated. The various divers which occasionally visit the streams are also guilty. Lastly, the swan is a well-known trout-pirate. Besides these, the two kinds of rat—land and water—have a black mark against them. Otter, pike, perch, heron, kingfisher, owl, moorhen, coot, grebe, diver, wild-duck, swan, teal, dipper, land-rat, and water-rat—altogether sixteen creatures— are killed in order that one may flourish. Although none of these, even in the south of England—except the otter—has yet been excluded, the majority of them are so thinned down as to be rarely seen unless carefully sought.

To go through the list: otters are practically excluded; the pike is banished from trout streams but is plentiful in others; so too with perch; herons, much reduced in numbers; owls, reduced; kingfishers, growing scarce; coots, much less numerous because not permitted to nest; grebes, reduced; wild-duck, seldom seen in summer, because not permitted to nest; teal, same; swan, not permitted on fisheries unless ancient rights protect it; divers, never numerous, now scarcer; moorhens, still fairly plentiful because their ranks are constantly supplied from moats and ponds where they breed under semi-domestic conditions. The draining of marsh-lands and levels began the exile of wild-fowl; and now the increasing preservation of trout adds to the difficulties under which these birds strive to retain a hold upon inland waters. The Thames is too long and wide for complete exclusion; but it is surprising how few moorhens even are to be seen along the river. Lesser rivers are still more empty, as it were, of life. The great osier-beds still give shelter to some, but not nearly so many as formerly. Up towards the spring-heads, where the feeders are mere runlets, the scarcity of wild-fowl has long been noticed. Hardly a wild-duck is now seen; one or two moorhens or a dabchick seem all. Coots have quite disappeared in some places: they are shot on ponds, having an ill reputation for the destruction of the fry of coarse or pond fish, as well as of trout. Not all these changes, indeed, are attributable to trout alone; but the trout holds a sort of official position and leads the van. Our southern rivers, with the exception of the Thames, are for the most part easily preserved.

They run through cultivated country, with meadows or cornfields, woods or copses, and rarely far through open, unenclosed land. A stranger, and without permission, would often find it difficult to walk half a mile along the bank of such a stream as this. Consequently, if it is desired to preserve it, the riparian owners can do so to the utmost, and the water-fowl considered injurious to fish can as easily be kept down. It is different in the north, for instance, where the streams have a background of moors, mountains, tarns, and lakes. In these their fastnesses birds find some security. From the coast they are also recruited; while on our southern coasts it is a source of lament that wild-fowl are not nearly so plentiful as formerly. Of course in winter it often happens that a flock of wild-fowl alight in passing; but how long do they stay? The real question is, how many breed? Where trout are carefully preserved, very few indeed; so that it is evident trout are making as much difference as the pheasants. Trout preservation has become much more extended since the fish has been studied and found to be easily bred. Advertisements are even put forward recommending people to keep trout instead of poultry, since they can be managed with certainty. It seems reasonable, therefore, to suppose that the influence of trout on wild creatures will continue to extend for some time yet. Already where trout preservation has been carefully carried out it has produced a visible impression upon their ranks. In ten years, if it were abandoned, most of these creatures would be plentiful again on the waters from which they have been driven; I should myself be very glad to see many of them back again.

But if preservation has excluded many creatures, it has also saved many. Badgers, in all probability, would be extinct—really extinct, like the wolf—were it not for the seclusion of covers. Without the protection which hunting affords them, foxes would certainly have disappeared. The stag and fallow-deer are other examples; so, too, the wild white cattle maintained in a few parks. In a measure the rook owes its existence to protection; for although naturalists have pointed out its usefulness, the rook is no favourite with agriculturists. Woodcocks, again, are protected, and are said to have increased, though it is open to question if their increased numbers may not be due to other causes. Cultivation banishes wild geese and snipe, but adds to the numbers of small birds, I fancy, and very probably to the number of mice. When the country was three-fourths champaign—open, unenclosed, and uncultivated—it cannot be supposed that so many grain-eating birds found sustenance as now. The subject is capable of much development. Enough, however, has been said to show that Nature at present is under artificial restraints; but her excluded creatures are for the most part ready to return if ever those restraints are removed.

RICHARD JEFFERIES, *The Life of the Fields*

From *There is a Hill*

A rushy island guards the sacred bower,
And hides it from the meadow, where in peace
The lazy cows wrench many a scented flower,
Robbing the golden market of the bees:
  And laden barges float
  By banks of myosote;
And scented flag and golden flower-de-lys
  Delay the loitering boat.

And on this side the island, where the pool
Eddies away, are tangled mass on mass
The water-weeds, that net the fishes cool,
And scarce allow a narrow stream to pass;
  Where spreading crowfoot mars
  The drowning nenuphars,
Waving the tassels of her silken grass
  Below her silver stars.

But in the purple pool there nothing grows,
Not the white water-lily spoked with gold;
Though best she loves the hollows, and well knows
On quiet streams her broad shields to unfold:
  Yet should her roots but try
  Within these deeps to lie,
Not her long-reaching stalk could ever hold
  Her waxen head so high.

Sometimes an angler comes, and drops his hook
Within its hidden depths, and 'gainst a tree
Leaning his rod, reads in some pleasant book,
Forgetting soon his pride of fishery;
  And dreams, or falls asleep,
  While curious fishes peep
About his nibbled bait, or scornfully
  Dart off and rise and leap.

ROBERT BRIDGES (1844–1930)

The Fisherman

Although I can see him still,
The freckled man who goes
To a grey place on a hill
In grey Connemara clothes
At dawn to cast his flies,
It's long since I began
To call up to the eyes
This wise and simple man.
All day I'd looked in the face
What I had hoped 'twould be
To write for my own race
And the reality;

The living men that I hate,
The dead man that I loved,
The craven man in his seat,
The insolent unreproved,
And no knave brought to book
Who has won a drunken cheer,
The witty man and his joke
Aimed at the commonest ear,
The clever man who cries
The catch-cries of the clown,
The beating down of the wise
And great Art beaten down.

Maybe a twelvemonth since
Suddenly I began,
In scorn of this audience,
Imagining a man,
And his sun-freckled face,
And grey Connemara cloth,
Climbing up to a place
Where stone is dark under froth,
And the down-turn of his wrist
When the flies drop in the stream;
A man who does not exist;
A man who is but a dream;
And cried, 'Before I am old
I shall have written him one
Poem maybe as cold
And passionate as the dawn.'

W. B. YEATS

The Old Angler

Twilight leaned mirrored in a pool
  Where willow boughs swept green and hoar,
Silk-clear the water, calm and cool,
  Silent and weedy shore:

There in abstracted, brooding mood
  One fishing sate. His painted float
Motionless as a planet stood;
  Motionless his boat.

A melancholy soul was this,
With lantern jaw, gnarled hand, vague eye;
Huddled in pensive solitariness
He had fished existence by.

Empty his creel; stolen his bait—
Impassively he angled on,
Though mist now showed the evening late
And daylight wellnigh gone.

Suddenly, like a tongueless bell,
Downward his gaudy cork did glide;
A deep, low-gathering, gentle swell
Spread slowly far and wide.

Wheeped out his tackle from noiseless winch,
And furtive as a thief, his thumb,
With nerve intense, wound inch by inch
A line no longer numb.

What fabulous spoil could this unplayed
Gape upward to a mortal air?—
He stoops engrossed; his tanned cheek greyed;
His heart stood still: for there,

Wondrously fairing, beneath the skin
Of secretly bubbling water seen,
Swims, not the silver of scale and fin—
But gold inmixt with green.

Deeply astir in oozy bed,
The darkening mirror ripples and rocks:
And lo—a wan-pale, lovely head,
Hook tangled in its locks!

Cold from her haunt—a Naiad slim.
Shoulder and cheek gleamed ivory white;
Though how faint stars stood over him,
The hour hard on night.

Her green eyes gazed like one half-blind
In sudden radiance; her breast
Breathed the sweet air, while gently twined,
'Gainst the cold water pressed,

Her lean webbed hands. She floated there,
  Light as a scentless petalled flower,
Water-drops dewing from her hair
  In tinkling beadlike shower.

So circling sidelong, her tender throat
  Uttered a grieving, desolate wail;
Shrill o'er the dark pool lapsed its note,
  Piteous as nightingale.

Ceased Echo. And he?—a life's remorse
  Welled to a tongue unapt to charm,
But never a word broke harsh and hoarse
  To quiet her alarm.

With infinite stealth his twitching thumb
  Tugged softly at the tautened gut,
Bubble-light, fair, her lips now dumb,
  She moved, and struggled not;

But with set, wild, unearthly eyes
  Pale-gleaming, fixed as if in fear,
She couched in the water, with quickening sighs,
  And floated near.

In hollow heaven the stars were at play;
  Wan glow-worms greened the pool-side grass;
Dipped the wide-bellied boat. His prey
  Gazed on; nor breathed. Alas!—

Long sterile years had come and gone;
  Youth, like a distant dream, was sped;
Heart, hope, and eyes had hungered on. . . .
  He turned a shaking head,

And clumsily groped amid the gold,
  Sleek with night dews, of that tangling hair,
Till pricked his finger keen and cold
  The barb imbedded there.

Teeth clenched, he drew his knife—'Snip, snip,'—
  Groaned, and sate shivering back; and she,
Treading the water with birdlike dip,
  Shook her sweet shoulders free:

Drew backward, smiling, infatuate fair,
His life's disasters in her eyes,
All longing and folly, grief, despair,
Daydreams and mysteries.

She stooped her brow; laid low her cheek,
And, steering on that silk-tressed craft,
Out from the listening, leaf-hung creek,
Tossed up her chin, and laughed—

A mocking, icy, inhuman note.
One instant flashed that crystal breast,
Leaned, and was gone. Dead-still the boat:
And the deep dark at rest.

Flits moth to flower. A water-rat
Noses the placid ripple. And lo!
Streams a lost meteor. Night is late,
And daybreak zephyrs flow. . . .

And he—the cheated? Dusk till morn,
Insensate, even of hope forsook,
He muttering squats, aloof, forlorn,
Dangling a baitless hook.

WALTER DE LA MARE (1873–1956)

The Fish

I caught a tremendous fish
and held him beside the boat
half out of water, with my hook
fast in a corner of his mouth.
He didn't fight.
He hadn't fought at all.
He hung a grunting weight,
battered and venerable
and homely. Here and there
his brown skin hung in strips
like ancient wallpaper,
and its pattern of darker brown
was like wallpaper:
shapes like full-blown roses
stained and lost through age.

He was speckled with barnacles,
fine rosettes of lime,
and infested
with tiny white sea-lice,
and underneath two or three
rags of green weed hung down.
While his gills were breathing in
the terrible oxygen
—the frightening gills,
fresh and crisp with blood,
that can cut so badly—
I thought of the coarse white flesh
packed in like feathers,
the big bones and the little bones,
the dramatic reds and blacks
of his shiny entrails,
and the pink swim-bladder
like a big peony.
I looked into his eyes
which were far larger than mine
but shallower, and yellowed,
the irises backed and packed
with tarnished tinfoil
seen through the lenses
of old scratched isinglass.
They shifted a little, but not
to return my stare.
—It was more like the tipping
of an object toward the light.
I admired his sullen face,
the mechanism of his jaw,
and then I saw
that from his lower lip
—if you could call it a lip—
grim, wet, and weaponlike,
hung five old pieces of fish-line,
or four and a wire leader
with the swivel still attached,
with all their five big hooks
grown firmly in his mouth.
A green line, frayed at the end
where he broke it, two heavier lines,
and a fine black thread
still crimped from the strain and snap
when it broke and he got away.
Like medals with their ribbons

frayed and wavering,
a five-haired beard of wisdom
trailing from his aching jaw.
I stared and stared
and victory filled up
the little rented boat,
from the pool of bilge
where oil had spread a rainbow
around the rusted engine
to the bailer rusted orange,
the sun-cracked thwarts,
the oarlocks on their strings,
the gunnels—until everything
was rainbow, rainbow, rainbow!
And I let the fish go.

ELIZABETH BISHOP (1911–79)

IV

At the Races

Likenesses of the Winners

The likenesses of the winners of the Derby, Leger, and Oaks, from paintings by that prince of artists in this particular line, Mr Herring, Sen., must all command an interest with the Sporting World that perhaps no other prints can call forth. Animals that have brought fortunes to some, wealth to many, heavy loss to some, and ruin to others, must ever be objects of paramount interest to thousands. Many, no doubt, in bitterness of heart anathematise the hour they first saw the originals; but, perhaps, as many hail the likeness of the noble animal who has brought wealth and happiness to their very door. A Derby or a Leger is not what a race was in former days, a *pastime:* no; it has now become a business, an event comprehending the interests of thousands; an event that raises many to the pinnacle of happiness, or drives them to the lowest depths of despair. Oh, how tumultuously throb those hearts whose possessors have turned from the warning voice of prudence, and staked their *all* on the efforts of *one* animal—a noble one it is true, and one whose generous nature disposes him to strain every nerve to obey the will of far less generous man! But then to the *initiated* comes the appalling doubt, will those generous efforts be permitted to avail? or have they not been rendered all but nugatory by rascality? Oh, it is a fearful thing to know we lean but on a fragile reed when we are aware the yawning gulf of despair awaits if that one feeble support deceives us! Watch but the countenances of those so deeply interested on seeing the object of their every hope stripped for the important, the all-engrossing contest: how rise or fall their hopes on seeing him pass in his preliminary canter! That face flushed and fevered by anxiety and hope, and that pallid with fear and fast receding confidence, show the internal struggle is doing its fearful work within.

They are at the starting-post waiting the dropping flag: hundreds scarcely feel they breathe: they wait with the same feeling of apprehension they would experience if expecting some great convulsion of nature. They're off: thousands of eyes take one and the same direction: every change in the race causes the blood to rush tumultuously to the heart, or scarcely to creep on its wonted course. The eventful turn is made: 'Here they come!'—'By George it's a fast race!'—'The crack is beat! the Duke, the Duke wins all the way!'—'No, no, the mare, the mare!'—'By Heavens!

Lord George has taken up the running. Robinson is shaking his mare; Day is setting to with his horse; both are whipping!'—'The mare, the mare!'—'No, no, the colt for a thousand.'—'A dead heat.'—'No, the mare wins by G—d! Hurrah!'—Ay, hurrah to the fortunate; but mark that man—that hurrah has struck the dagger to his heart: each muscle of that face is working with despair: its death-like hue tells the sad tale; its wretched owner pulls his hat over his drooping brow: he seeks, yet fears to seek, his once happy home; and yet he must—for what? to tell his wife and children they are houseless, and he a beggar!

May no such result ever happen to the true Sportsman! Thank God! it rarely does; for he neither allows his imprudence or his greediness of gain to lead him to such extremities. Let us turn, then, to the more cheering contemplation of him who has fairly and honourably won his thousands by the superior excellence of his favourite horse. If there is one brighter moment than another in a man's sporting career, it is the moment when he receives the congratulations of his friends at his success; and cordially and sincerely that man is ever congratulated of whom it is known he *always* 'runs to win'. To a man thus situated, what price could be too great for a faithful likeness of his winning horse! With what honest pride does he see that likeness decorating the walls of so many of the true lovers of our national sports! Whatever we may do that is laudable in itself would lose half its charm if the celebrity of it was as transient as its achievement. Whilst pride is one of the attributes of the human heart, the having our little triumphs chronicled and perpetuated gives them a ten-fold value in our eyes, and encourages us to fresh efforts; for though Mr Coriolanus might pretend to be angered at hearing his 'nothings monstered', that gentleman being defunct, we may fairly allow a little proper praise, and eke a little well-timed flattery is not always absolutely disagreeable.

That there are numberless men connected with the turf who feel no further interest in the horses than mere pecuniary gain or loss creates, is *true*, pity 'tis 'tis true; but there are many who glory in the triumph of their horse as evidence of good judgment in their favourite pursuit. Such are the men to whom the turf is largely indebted, and it is but a proper compliment paid to them in perpetuating their triumphs.

The rather large gentleman in bronze erected in Hyde Park, with a fig-leaf doing duty for a pair of unmentionables, is not merely a token of a nation's gratitude to the memory of thousands of fine fellows who bled or fell in their country's cause; for though thousands of names of heroes as great in soul as their more fortunate commanders, have never individually met the public eye, the *sons* of such men may look with pride on the trophy and say, 'But for such humble names as mine you never had been there.'—We thus perpetuate a race of heroes.

Whether it be battles on which depend the fate of nations, or a race on which depends the wealth or poverty of individuals, let the meed of praise be given to those to whom praise is due. We may praise by writing, it is true; but the representation of a hero or an event makes a more lasting impression on the mind, and perpetuates the memory of that event with greater force than all the written descriptions that could be penned. The historian describes, the printer or engraver lays the man or the event before our eyes: one panorama brings the field of Waterloo more faithfully to our senses, than all the writers in Christendom could do if they wrote to eternity.

Though we might describe a Bloomsbury, a Harkaway, or any other celebrated animal for ever, we should form but a very vague idea of him at last. Mr Herring's talent and the publisher's encouragement lay the object at once before us, and his form will be as familiar to our posterity as to ourselves. We know from records in print what race-horses have done in former days (that is, what a very few have done), and if the animal painter had been as much encouraged formerly as he is now, we should have been able to trace the form of the race-horse correctly from the time when the Beacon Course was first established. Our posterity will in this particular have an advantage over us, doubtless an advantage it will be to them, and a great one.

CHARLES BRINDLEY, *Stable Talk and Table Talk* (1846)

The Turf

In the reign of James I, private matches between gentlemen, *then their own jockeys*, became very common in England; and the first public race meetings appear at Garterley, in Yorkshire; Croydon, in Surrey; and Theobald's, on Enfield Chace; the prize being a golden bell. The art of training also may be said now to have commenced; strict attention was paid to the food and exercise of the horses, but the effect of weight was not taken into consideration, ten stone being generally, we have reason to believe, both the maximum and minimum of what the horses carried. James patronised racing; he gave five hundred pounds—a vast price in those days—for an Arabian, which, according to the Duke of Newcastle, was of little value, having been beaten easily by our native horses. Prince Henry had a strong attachment to racing as well as hunting, but he was cut off at an early age. Charles I was well inclined towards such sports, and excelled in horsemanship, but the distractions of his reign prevented his following these peaceful pastimes. According to Boucher, however, in his 'Survey of the Town of Stamford', the first valuable public prize was run for at that place in Charles the First's time, viz., a silver and gilt cup and cover, of the estimated value of eight pounds, provided by the care of the aldermen for the time being; and Sir Edward Harwood laments the scarcity of able horses in the kingdom, 'not more than two thousand being to be found equal to the like number of French horses'; for which he blames principally racing. In 1640, races were held in Newmarket; also in Hyde Park, as appears from a comedy called the 'Merry Beggars, or Jovial Crew', 1641:—'Shall we make a fling to London, and see how the spring appears there in Spring Gardens, and in *Hyde Park, to see the races, horse and foot?*'

The wily Cromwell was not altogether indifferent to the breed of running-horses, and with one of the stallions in his stud—Place's White Turk—do the oldest of our pedigrees end. He had also a famous brood-mare, called the Coffin mare, from the circumstance of her being concealed in a vault during the search for his effects at the time of the Restoration. Mr Place, stud-groom to Cromwell, was a conspicuous character of those days; and, according to some, the White Turk was his individual property. Charles II was a great patron of the race-course. He frequently honoured this pastime with his presence, and appointed races to be run in Datchet Mead, as also at Newmarket, where his horses were entered in his own name, and where he rebuilt the decayed palace of his grandfather James I. He also visited other places at which races were instituted, Burford Downs in particular—(since known as Bibury race-course, so often frequented by George IV when regent)—as witness the doggrel of old Baskerville:—

'Next for the glory of the place,
Here has been rode many a race.
King Charles the Second I saw here;
But I've forgotten in what year.
The Duke of Monmouth here also
Made his horse to sweat and blow,' &c.

At this time it appears that prizes run for became more valuable than they formerly had been; amongst them were bowls, and various other pieces of plate, usually estimated at the value of one hundred guineas; and from the inscriptions on these trophies of victory, much interesting information might be obtained. This facetious monarch was likewise a breeder of race-horses, having imported mares from Barbary, and other parts, selected by his Master of the Horse, sent abroad for the purpose, and called Royal Mares—appearing as such in the stud-book to this day. One of these mares was the dam of Dodsworth, bred by the King, and said to be the earliest race-horse we have on record, whose pedigree can be properly authenticated.

NIMROD (Charles James Apperley), (1777–1843),
The Chace, The Turf and The Road

The Death of Fred Archer

It was just three weeks before his tragic end in November, 1886, that Archer and myself went over to Ireland together. We were accompanied by Captain De Vere Smith, 'Garry' Moore, James Henry Smith ('Jim the

Penman'), and George Haughton. Archer crossed the St George's Channel to ride 'Cambusmore' for Lord Londonderry, who was then the Lord-Lieutenant, and I went over to act as starter at the October Meeting at the Curragh. We arrived in Dublin on Tuesday morning, October 19, by the mail train, and after breakfasting and looking round the city, we journeyed off to the Curragh.

Archer had nothing to ride that day, but went down as a spectator. A busy time he had, too, as he couldn't stir without a crowd of the 'bhoys' almost mobbing him in admiration. As he had not been riding for a few days, and had been indulging a bit, he was rather anxious to know his weight, and asked me to go to the weighing-room with him, as he knew I had been over there before. We went together, and I put him in the scales with his jacket and waistcoat off, and he weighed 9 st. 4 lb. He had only a thin pair of trousers and thin boots on, so I said:

'Why, you could only just about strip your saddle.'

He said: 'That is just what I could do; but never mind, my old horse has only 9 st. 3 lb. on, so I have only to get 1 lb. off.'

I looked at the list, and said:

'Your horse "Cambusmore" has only 9 st. on.'

He answered: 'What nonsense!'

So I bet him half a crown I was correct, and when he read the conditions over two or three times, he found out he was wrong. They had mixed them up in a real Irish fashion, hence Fred's mistake. I believe these were the conditions of the race: The Lord-Lieutenant's Plate, one and a half miles, for two-year-olds, 7 st.; three-year-olds, 8 st. 10 lb.; four years and upwards, 9 st.; 3 lb. allowed for mares and geldings. In England it is the rule to put it: 'Mares and geldings allowed 3 lb.'; but unless anyone read it right through, and looked carefully into it, they might easily make the same mistake as Archer, and think the weight for a five-year-old colt would be 9 st. 3 lb. We went back to Dublin that night, and a note came to Archer from Mr Michael Gunn, the proprietor, asking him as a particular favour to honour the theatre with his presence, and bring his friends. The royal box was reserved for him, and we all went to see 'The Mikado'. After the performance was over we walked out of the theatre, and were met by a most demonstrative crowd of over three hundred, who followed us all the way to the Shelbourne Hotel, shouting and 'Whoo-roo-ing' for the 'Great Mr Archer'. The next day, being Wednesday, he had nothing to ride, so he said he would not go down to the Curragh, but have a Turkish bath and get ready to ride 'Cambusmore'. He was also asked to ride Mr C. J. Blake's 'Isidore', who was thought to be a good thing at 8 st. 12 lb., in the race afterwards, a Sweepstakes for two-year-olds. He said he would try to do the weight, and he did it without walking two miles. A rather amusing thing occurred at this part of the visit. Mr G. Haughton was staying at the Shelbourne, and, wanting some medicine after his sea-voyage, Archer said to him:

'Will you have some of my mixture? I am just going to take some.'

He said: 'Yes; how much ought I to take?'

Fred said directly: 'You don't want to waste so much as I do'; and he gave him a tablespoonful, and took nearly a sherry-glass full himself.

The result was poor Haughton did 'walking exercise' all night, and couldn't go to the races the next day. I quote this to show the state poor Fred's stomach had got to with continual physicing. As mentioned in the earlier part of this story, he couldn't ride an ounce under 9 st. 4 lb. on the Tuesday afternoon, and on the Thursday he rode 8 st. 12 lb. This would not be considered anything to a man who walked with sweaters to get his weight off, but quite a different thing to a man who wasted himself on Turkish baths and physic.

When Archer came to the post on 'Cambusmore'—this was the first race he rode in Ireland; he thought he would like to win the first for the Lord-Lieutenant, and on mounting he had received such an ovation as is seldom heard on a racecourse—it wanted five minutes to starting-time, so we had a chat. I said:

'Well, Fred, I don't know if it is the excitement from the ovation they gave you, or the wasting you have done, but I never saw you look half so bad as you do now.'

He turned round laughing, and said:

'Well, if I look bad now, how shall I look next Wednesday, when I ride "St Mirin" at 8 st. 6 lb. in the Cambridgeshire?'

Nothing more was said, as the time was up. I started them, and he won. Archer was also successful in the next race, riding 8 st. 12 lb., but was beaten into third place on 'Black Rose' in the last race, the Welter Handicap, by Tom Beasley on 'Spahi' and Mr Cullen on 'Lord Chatham'. I need hardly tell you Mr Beasley had a most jovial reception on his return to the weighing-room.

On board the mail steamer on our way back, I said to Archer:

'You don't mean to say you are going to ride 8 st. 6 lb. next week?'

He answered me:

'Cus, I am sure to ride "St Mirin" 8 st. 6 lb., or at most 8 st. 7 lb. I shall win the Cambridgeshire, and then be able to come down into your country and enjoy myself this winter.'

We talked over the best place for him to stop at for the hunting season, but I begged of him not to try to ride so light as he talked about. I told him I had seen so many jockeys who wasted on physic, especially at the back end of the year, go out like the snuff of a candle. He said:

'Never mind if I go out or not, I shall do it.'

He asked me to call and see him at Newmarket when I got there for the Houghton Meeting, and I did so on the Wednesday morning. This was the Cambridgeshire day. I saw his sister, Mrs Coleman, who said Fred was in his Turkish bath, so I didn't meet him until he got on the course, and then I thought I had never seen him looking so bad before. However, he seemed cheerful enough, and laughed about our visit to Ireland. It was the last time I ever saw the poor fellow. When I read of his illness at Lewes, I said to my wife: 'Fred Archer will never get over this.'

Naturally, I was very much grieved, not to say shocked, to read of his sad end.

HENRY CUSTANCE (1842–1908), *Riding Recollections and Turf Stories* (1894)

The Real People

Having cleared the course, so to speak, without the assistance of the police, it may be as well for us to proceed forthwith to the heart of our subject. As an institution which is more firmly established among Englishmen than almost any other, and an institution seemingly of the highest credit, racing, one would imagine, should bear examination in the personal sense. Its patrons as a body are, to say the least, numerous, and that they are also powerful is indicated by the extraordinary influence they are always able to exert when the racing interest is in any way threatened by Parliament. With regard to the question of numbers it would be rash to hazard a strict estimate. Roughly, however, the male population of Britain may be divided into two classes, namely, Nonconformists, and persons who in one way or another support racing. And I shall not take it upon myself to assert that the first class—Nonconformists, to wit—have not amongst them a sufficient sprinkling of black and white sheep who are properly alive to the difference between a horse and handsaw, and think it no evil to have a trifling and surreptitious flutter on more or less classic events. It goes without saying, however, that class number two, that is to say the people who are not Nonconformists, stand in vigorous majority, and range from the King himself, down to some of the least savoury frequenters of his Majesty's prisons. The social scale involved, therefore, is of the very widest, and the facts about it most diversified. At the top you have a select côterie of fashionable and, one supposes, entirely blameless and honourable people. So closely on the steps of these as to be almost indistinguishable from them, follows a much bigger côterie of persons a little less fashionable and a little less blameless and scrupulous. Then come the sturdy, race-going middle-classes, honest in the main, and in the main lovers of sport for sport's sake.

It is at this point, I am afraid, that we must part company with what is on the whole fairly reputable. For there shall now step up a vast horde of professional race-frequenters, vulgar, under-bred, heavy-jawed, unscrupulous, rapacious dullards, almost to a man, and their grimy following of runners, touts, tic-tack men, ticket-snatchers, welshers, and tellers of the tale. And behind this monstrous regiment again you have uncountable congregations of the common people, some of whom make up what is called the public at our race-meetings throughout the country, but the vast majority of whom do their racing, not on the course, but in their homes and workshops, with the assistance of the daily papers and the starting-price bookmaker. When one surveys this motley assemblage in all its forces, and considers it in its true social meaning, one can scarcely pretend to be edified.

It is all very well for sporting journalists and punting members of Parliament to blare and babble for us on the nobility, beauty, and utility of the sporting instinct, and of the moral and financial advantages which accrue to the country through the sporting proclivities of the aforesaid mobs. Racing *per se* is no doubt a pretty and exciting matter. A fine horse always looks fine. A number of fine horses, racing finely, and ridden by fine horsemen in variegated silks will always please the eye. The enclosures and stands, at the better sort of race-meeting, are not without their picturesque qualities. And going to the races, and not to say coming back again, is by no means an unpleasant or unexhilarating business. The whole spirit and atmosphere of a racing function comes delectably on the senses. But as for the people without whom such functions appear to be an impossibility—faugh! They reek. They sweat. They shout. They yell. There is a glare in their eyes. They are out for some purpose, which is not holy. Ostensibly they have come to see a horse-race. Practically they have come for no such thing; they are here simply and solely to rage and chaffer and scramble over money. If you wish to see the devil snapping out of human eyes in his ugliest and most fiendish temper, you need only betake yourself to the next English race-meeting, whether on the flat or otherwise. If you want to rub shoulders with the off-scourings of the country, with the rogues and sharps and swindlers and bullies and blackguards and habitual criminals, against which society is constrained to protect itself at enormous expense, you must go to the same place.

T. W. H. Crosland (1869–1924), *Who Goes Racing*

'Bocock's Mare'

We gained the inner room at last, a cheerless apartment, adorned with sacred pictures, a sewing-machine, and an array of supplementary tumblers and wineglasses; but, at all events, we had it so far to ourselves. At intervals during the next half-hour Mary Kate burst in with cups and plates, cast them on the table and disappeared, but of food there was no sign. After a further period of starvation and of listening to the noise in the shop, Flurry made a sortie, and, after lengthy and unknown adventures, reappeared carrying a huge brown teapot, and driving before him Mary Kate with the remainder of the repast. The bread tasted of mice, the butter of turf-smoke, the tea of brown paper, but we had got past the critical stage. I had entered upon my third round of bread and butter when the door was flung open, and my valued acquaintance, Slipper, slightly advanced in liquor, presented himself to our gaze. His bandy legs sprawled consequentially, his nose was redder than a coal of fire, his prominent eyes rolled crookedly upon us, and his left hand swept behind him the attempt of Mary Kate to frustrate his entrance.

'Good evening to my vinerable friend, Mr Flurry Knox!' he began, in the voice of a town crier, 'and to the Honourable Major Yeates, and the English gintleman!'

This impressive opening immediately attracted an audience from the shop, and the doorway filled with grinning faces as Slipper advanced farther into the room.

'Why weren't ye at the races, Mr Flurry?' he went on, his roving eye taking a grip of us all at the same time; 'sure the Miss Bennetts and all the ladies was asking where were ye.'

'It'd take some time to tell them that,' said Flurry, with his mouth full; 'but what about the races, Slipper? Had you good sport?'

'Sport is it? Divil so pleasant an afthernoon ever you seen,' replied Slipper. He leaned against a side table, and all the glasses on it jingled. 'Does your honour know O'Driscoll?' he went on irrelevantly. 'Sure you do. He was in your honour's stable. It's what we were all sayin'; it was a great pity your honour was not there, for the likin' you had to Driscoll.'

'That's thrue,' said a voice at the door.

'There wasn't one in the Barony but was gethered in it, through and fro,' continued Slipper, with a quelling glance at the interrupter; 'and there was tints for sellin' porther, and whisky as pliable as new milk, and boys goin' round the tints outside, feeling for heads with the big ends of their blackthorns, and all kinds of recreations, and the Sons of Liberty's piffler and dhrum band from Skebawn; though faith! there was more of thim runnin' to look at the races than what was playin' in it; not to mintion different occasions that the bandmasther was atin' his lunch within in the whisky tint.'

'But what about Driscoll?' said Flurry.

'Sure it's about him I'm tellin' ye,' replied Slipper, with the practised orator's watchful eye on his growing audience. ''Twas within in the same whisky tint meself was, with the bandmasther and a few of the lads, an' we buyin' a ha'porth o' crackers, when I seen me brave Driscoll landin' into the tint, and a pair o' thim long boots on him; him that hadn't a shoe nor a stocking to his foot when your honour had him picking grass out o' the stones behind in your yard. "Well," says I to meself, "we'll knock some spoort out of Driscoll."

' "Come here to me, acushla!" says I to him; "I suppose it's some way wake in the legs y'are," says I, "an' the docthor put them on ye the way the people wouldn't thrample ye!"

' "May the divil choke ye!" says he, pleasant enough, but I knew by the blush he had he was vexed.

' "Then I suppose 'tis a left-tenant colonel y'are," says I; "yer mother must be proud out o' ye!" says I, "an' maybe ye'll lend her a loan o' thim waders when she's rinsin' your bauneen in the river!" says I.

' "There'll be work out o' this!" says he, lookin' at me both sour and bitther.

' "Well indeed, I was thinkin' you were blue-moulded for want of a batin'," says I. He was for fightin' us then, but afther we had him pacificated with about a quarther of a naggin o' sperrits, he told us he was goin' ridin' in a race.

' "An' what'll ye ride?" says I.

' "Owld Bocock's mare," says he.

' "Knipes!" says I, sayin' a great curse; "is it that little staggeen from the mountains; sure she's somethin' about the one age with meself," says I. "Many's the time Jamesy Geoghegan and meself used to be dhrivin' her to Macroom with pigs an' all soorts," says I; "an' is it leppin' stone walls ye want her to go now?"

' "Faith, there's walls and every vari'ty of obstackle in it," says he.

' "It'll be the best o' your play, so," says I, "to get it away home out o' this."

' "An' who'll ride her, so?" says he.

' "Let the divil ride her," says I.'

Leigh Kelway, who had been leaning back seemingly half asleep, obeyed the hypnotism of Slipper's gaze, and opened his eyes.

'That was now all the conversation that passed between himself and meself,' resumed Slipper, "and there was no great delay afther that till they said there was a race startin' and the dickens a one at all was goin' to ride only two, Driscoll, and one Clancy. With that then I seen Mr Kinahane, the Petty Sessions clerk, goin round clearin' the coorse, an' I gethered a few o' the neighbours, an' we walked the fields hither and over till we seen the most of th' obstackles.

' "Stand aisy now by the plantation," says I; "if they get to come as far as this, believe me ye'll see spoort," says I, "an' 'twill be a convanient spot to encourage the mare if she's anyway wake in herself," says I, cuttin' somethin' about five foot of an ash sapling out o' the plantation.

' "That's yer sort!" says Owld Bocock, that was thravellin' the race-coorse, peggin' a bit o' paper down with a thorn in front of every lep, the way Driscoll'd know the handiest place to face her at it.

'Well, I hadn't barely thrimmed the ash plant—'

'Have you any jam, Mary Kate?' interrupted Flurry, whose meal had been in no way interfered with by either the story or the highly scented crowd who had come to listen to it.

'We have no jam, only thraycle, sir,' replied the invisible Mary Kate.

'I hadn't the switch barely thrimmed,' repeated Slipper firmly, 'when I heard the people screechin', an' I seen Driscoll an' Clancy comin' in, leppin' all before them, an' Owld Bocock's mare bellusin' an' powderin' along, an' bedad! whatever obstackle wouldn't throw *her* down, faith, she'd throw *it* down, an' there's the thraffic they had in it.

' "I declare to me sowl," says I, "if they continue on this way there's a great chance some one o' thim'll win," says I.

' "Ye lie!" says the bandmasther, bein' a thrifle fulsome after his luncheon.

' "I do not," says I, "in regard of seein' how soople them two boys is. Ye might observe," says I, "that if they have no convanient way to sit on the saddle, they'll ride the neck o' the horse till such time as they gets an occasion to lave it," says I.

' "Arrah, shut yer mouth!" says the bandmasther; "they're puckin' out this way now, an' may the divil admire me!" says he, "but Clancy has the other bet out, and the divil such leatherin' and beltin' of Owld Bocock's mare ever you seen as what's in it!" says he.

'Well, when I seen them comin' to me, and Driscoll about the length of the plantation behind Clancy, I let a couple of bawls.

' "Skelp her, ye big brute!" says I. "What good's in ye that ye aren't able to skelp her?" '

The yell and the histrionic flourish of his stick with which Slipper delivered this incident brought down the house. Leigh Kelway was sufficiently moved to ask me in an undertone if 'skelp' was a local term.

'Well, Mr Flurry, and gintlemen,' recommenced Slipper, 'I declare to ye when Owld Bocock's mare heard thim roars she sthretched out her neck like a gandher, and when she passed me out she give a couple of grunts, and looked at me as ugly as a Christian.

' "Hah!" says I, givin' her a couple o' dhraws o' th' ash plant across the butt o' the tail, the way I wouldn't blind her; "I'll make ye grunt!" says I, "I'll nourish ye!"

'I knew well she was very frightful of th' ash plant since the winter Tommeen Sullivan had her under a sidecar. But now, in place of havin' any obligations to me, ye'd be surprised if ye heard the blaspheemious expressions of that young boy that was ridin' her; and whether it was over-anxious he was, turnin' around the way I'd hear him cursin', or whether it was some slither or slide came to Owld Bocock's mare, I dunno, but she was bet up agin the last obstackle but two, and before ye could say "Shnipes", she was standin' on her two ears beyond in th' other field! I declare to ye, on the vartue of me oath, she stood that way till she reconnoithered what side would Driscoll fall, an' she turned about then and rolled on him as cosy as if he was meadow grass!'

Slipper stopped short; the people in the doorway groaned appreciatively; Mary Kate murmured 'The Lord save us!'

'The blood was dhruv out through his nose and ears,' continued Slipper, with a voice that indicated the cream of the narration, 'and you'd hear his bones crackin' on the ground! You'd have pitied the poor boy.'

'Good heavens!' said Leigh Kelway, sitting up very straight in his chair.

'Was he hurt, Slipper?' asked Flurry casually.

'Hurt is it?' echoed Slipper in high scorn; 'killed on the spot!' He paused to relish the effect of the *dénouement* on Leigh Kelway. 'Oh, divil so pleasant an afthernoon ever you seen; and indeed, Mr Flurry, it's what we were all sayin', it was a great pity your honour was not there for the likin' you had for Driscoll.'

As he spoke the last word there was an outburst of singing and cheering from a carload of people who had just pulled up at the door. Flurry listened, leaned back in his chair, and began to laugh.

'It scarcely strikes one as a comic incident,' said Leigh Kelway, very coldly to me; 'in fact, it seems to me that the police ought—'

'Show me Slipper!' bawled a voice in the shop; 'show me that dirty little undherlooper till I have his blood! Hadn't I the race won only for he souring the mare on me! What's that you say? I tell ye he did! He left seven slaps on her with a handle of a hay-rake—'

There was in the room in which we were sitting a second door, leading to the back yard, a door consecrated to the unobtrusive visits of so-called 'Sunday travellers'. Through it Slipper faded away like a dream, and, simultaneously, a tall young man, with a face like a red-hot potato tied up in a bandage, squeezed his way from the shop into the room.

'Well, Driscoll,' said Flurry, 'since it wasn't the teeth of the rake he left on the mare, you needn't be talking!'

Leigh Kelway looked from one to the other with a wilder expression in his eye than I had thought it capable of. I read in it a resolve to abandon Ireland to her fate.

EDITH SOMERVILLE (1858–1949) and MARTIN ROSS (1862–1915),
The Complete Irish R.M.

At Galway Races

There where the course is,
Delight makes all of the one mind,
The riders upon the galloping horses,
The crowd that closes in behind:
We, too, had good attendance once,
Hearers and hearteners of the work;
Aye, horsemen for companions,
Before the merchant and the clerk
Breathed on the world with timid breath.
Sing on: somewhere at some new moon,
We'll learn that sleeping is not death,
Hearing the whole earth change its tune,
Its flesh being wild, and it again
Crying aloud as the racecourse is,
And we find hearteners among men
That ride upon horses.

W. B. YEATS

'Finishing Fourth'

In the previous December I had bought my eight-year-old horse Cockbird from a hard-riding youth whose father had been a hunting-field crony of my mother's. For the time being all other interests were out-weighed by my anxious ambition to win a point-to-point. Our groom Richardson had complete confidence in him. The only uncertainty in his mind—and my own—was whether I was a strong enough rider to hold him together and keep him up to his fences. It is also conceivable that we shared a horrid doubt whether I should be in the saddle at all by the end of a race. Cockbird, by the way, had only one imperfection, though I wasn't aware of it until I had ridden him in several races. But I must begin by enumerating his merits. He was extremely good-looking, and possessed all the points which go to make a first-rate hunter. His beautiful sloping shoulders were in themselves a guarantee that he would give one a comfortable ride, and his action was so smooth that one scarcely felt him moving while he galloped. When he came to a fence he shortened his stride and slipped over it, always jumping very big and getting away with unfaltering fluency after he landed. Besides being a natural jumper he had a perfect mouth, going well into his bridle without ever seeming to catch hold. He was, in fact, a 'patent safety', and had a fine constitution which enabled him to do a long day's hunting without ever seeming tired or being any the worse for it afterwards. His one weak point was that he didn't finish well in a race. He had apparently come to the conclusion that when he had jumped the last fence there was no further need to hurry. What did it matter, thought Cockbird—who gave one an impression of being a somewhat museful character—whether someone else passed the winning-post in front of him? He had completed the course in his usual artistic style, so why need he take it out of himself any more? In other words he lacked the competitive spirit, and preferred cantering in with dignity to hurrooshing home in a mad rush for victory. I must add that toward the end of his point-to-point racing career he took to trying to run out left-handed into the crowd after sailing over the last obstacle, and more than once I came up the straight with all my weight on the right rein! Had he been a really high-couraged horse we should have won more races than we did. But as things were he was what I needed—a thoroughly easy animal to ride—and I can never be too grateful for the vicarious credit which he earned me. Altogether I rode him in eleven races, of which he won four, was once second, and three times third. And in four hunting seasons he only gave me two falls, one at a big fence where he had a glare of evening sun in his eyes, and the other when he landed over a hairy hedge on to the stump of a willow. All of which proves conclusively that it was a lucky day for me when I got him for fifty pounds owing to a vet having asserted that he was a slight whistler—an accusation which turned out to be unfounded. And now, having given my old quad a good 'write up', I must ask the reader to accompany me to the saddling-enclosure where Richardson is strenuously tightening the girths, while I do my utmost to look pleased at being about to make my début, in the Open Race at the Ashford Valley Harriers Meeting.

The feel of it all comes back to me as though it had happened only yesterday. . . . The mild grey afternoon with its low sagging clouds; the smell of trampled grass, and the clamour of bookies bawling the odds; the yawning intestinal trepidation; and the ebbing aplomb with which I entered the weighing-tent to be jostled by the good humoured robustness of more experienced riders. And the background of being among a crowd of people none of whom took more than a casual interest in me as they consulted their race-cards and passed on to have a look at the favourite. An epitome of a young man's existence, one might moralize. Remembering it, I wish that it might happen all over again, just for a glimpse of the suppressed anxiety and restrained satisfaction on Richardson's keen-featured countenance, just for a taste of the excitement and uncertainty which can never be the same after one has ridden away from one's youth. Of the actual race not much need be written. There were eight runners, four of whom were previous winners, so I was in quite good company. As detailed in my hunting diary the course was a fairly easy one, though the going was heavy after much recent rain. 'Was well with them until half way round and then eased him a bit; got fifty yards behind the first three and couldn't catch them up again. Finished fourth.' Such was my way of describing the event; but it would have been more accurate to say that by half way round I was out of breath and very numb in the arms, and thereafter allowed Cockbird to canter along at his ease—my main object being to complete the course without mishap. Richardson, however, appeared to be quite satisfied with the result, and remarked that the old chap would be a stone better for the gallop. And my own sensations might be summarized as a state of enraptured relief at having got round without actually making a fool of myself. By an unavoidable coincidence it happened to be my mother's birthday—unavoidable being the right word, because she would obviously have preferred not to be spending the afternoon on tenterhooks of anxiety. Anyhow I returned to Ashford—the only poet in a bus-load of bookmakers—and the train took me home feeling that I might have done very much worse. My mother was delighted to hear that I'd 'come in fourth'—and even more delighted, I suspect, that I'd come back without any broken bones.

SIEGFRIED SASSOON (1886–1967), *The Weald of Youth*

A Note Left on the Mantelpiece
(*for his wife*)

Attracted by their winning names I chose
Little Yid and *Welsh Bard*; years later backed
the swanky jockeys, and still thought I lacked
inspiration, the uncommon touch, not
mere expertise. Each way, I paid in prose.

Always the colours and stadiums beckoned
till, on the nose, at Goodwood, the high gods
jinxed the favourite despite the odds.
Addict that I was, live fool and dead cert.
His velvet nostrils lagged a useless second.

A poet should have studied style not form
(sweet, I regret the scarcity of roses)
but by Moses and by the nine Muses
I'll no more. Each cruising nag is a beast
so other shirts can keep the centaur warm.

Adieu, you fading furlongs of boozing,
hoarse voices at Brighton, white rails, green course.
Conclusion? Why, not only the damned horse
but whom it's running against matters.
By the way, apologies for losing.

DANNIE ABSE (b. 1923)

At Grass

The eye can hardly pick them out
From the cold shade they shelter in,
Till wind distresses tail and mane;
Then one crops grass, and moves about
—The other seeming to look on—
And stands anonymous again.

Yet fifteen years ago, perhaps
Two dozen distances sufficed
To fable them: faint afternoons
Of Cups and Stakes and Handicaps,
Whereby their names were artificed
To inlay faded, classic Junes—

Silks at the start: against the sky
Numbers and parasols: outside,
Squadrons of empty cars, and heat,
And littered grass: then the long cry
Hanging unhushed till it subside
To stop-press columns on the street.

Do memories plague their ears like flies?
They shake their heads. Dusk brims the shadows.
Summer by summer all stone away,
The starting-gates, the crowds and cries—
All but the unmolesting meadows.
Almanacked, their names live; they

Have slipped their names, and stand at ease,
Or gallop for what must be joy,
And not a fieldglass sees them home,
Or curious stop-watch prophesies:
Only the groom, and the groom's boy,
With bridles in the evening come.

PHILIP LARKIN (1922–85)

The Old Racehorse

after Petronius

Learn from my fate how ill the end may be
of Pegasus in his own Thessaly.
There was no race at any festival,
even the Olympic, but I won them all,
and now, a horse forgotten and forlorn,
I drag the mill-stone to grind out the corn.

HUMBERT WOLFE (1886–1940), translated from an anonymous poem

V

In the Ring

'Lawn before the Duke's Palace'

Enter Le Beau [to Rosalind, Celia, and Touchstone]

Cel. Bon jour, Monsieur Le Beau; what's the news?

Le Beau. Fair princess, you have lost much good sport.

Cel. Sport! of what colour?

Le Beau. What colour, madam! how shall I answer you?

Ros. As wit and fortune will.

Touch. Or as the Destinies decree.

Cel. Well said: that was laid on with a trowel.

Touch. Nay, if I keep not my rank,—

Ros. Thou losest thy old smell.

Le Beau. You amaze me, ladies: I would have told you of good wrestling, which you have lost the sight of.

Ros. Yet tell us the manner of the wrestling.

Le Beau. I will tell you the beginning; and, if it please your ladyships, you may see the end; for the best is yet to do; and here, where you are, they are coming to perform it.

Cel. Well, the beginning, that is dead and buried.

Le Beau. There comes an old man and his three sons,—

Cel. I could match this beginning with an old tale.

Le Beau. Three proper young men, of excellent growth and presence.

Ros. With bills on their necks, 'Be it known unto all men by these presents.'

Le Beau. The eldest of the three wrestled with Charles, the Duke's wrestler; which Charles in a moment threw him, and broke three of his ribs, that there is little hope of life in him: so he served the second, and so the third. Yonder they lie; the poor old man, their father, making such pitiful dole over them that all the beholders take his part with weeping.

Ros. Alas!

Touch. But what is the sport, monsieur, that the ladies have lost?

Le Beau. Why, this that I speak of.

Touch. Thus men may grow wiser every day: it is the first time that ever I heard breaking of ribs was sport for ladies.

Cel. Or I, I promise thee.

Ros. But is there any else longs to see this broken music in his sides? is there yet another dotes upon rib-breaking? Shall we see this wrestling, cousin?

Le Beau. You must, if you stay here; for here is the place appointed for the wrestling, and they are ready to perform it.

Cel. Yonder, sure, they are coming: let us now stay and see it.

Flourish. Enter Duke Frederick, Lords, Orlando, Charles, and Attendants.

Duke F. Come on: since the youth will not be entreated, his own peril on his forwardness.

Ros. Is yonder the man?

Le Beau. Even he, madam.

Cel. Alas, he is too young! yet he looks successfully.

Duke F. How now, daughter and cousin! are you crept hither to see the wrestling?

Ros. Ay, my liege, so please you give us leave.

Duke F. You will take little delight in it, I can tell you, there is such odds in the man. In pity of the challenger's youth I would fain dissuade him, but he will not be entreated. Speak to him, ladies; see if you can move him.

Cel. Call him hither, good Monsieur Le Beau.

Duke F. Do so: I'll not be by.

Le Beau. Monsieur the challenger, the princess calls for you.

Orl. I attend them with all respect and duty.

Ros. Young man, have you challenged Charles the wrestler?

Orl. No, fair princess; he is the general challenger; I come but in, as others do, to try with him the strength of my youth.

Cel. Young gentleman, your spirits are too bold for your years. You have seen cruel proof of this man's strength: if you saw yourself with your eyes, or knew yourself with your judgement, the fear of your adventure would counsel you to a more equal enterprise. We pray you, for your own sake, to embrace your own safety, and give over this attempt.

Ros. Do, young sir; your reputation shall not therefore be misprised: we will make it our suit to the Duke that the wrestling might not go forward.

Orl. I beseech you, punish me not with your hard thoughts; wherein I confess me much guilty, to deny so fair and excellent ladies any thing. But let your fair eyes and gentle wishes go with me to my trial: wherein if I be foiled, there is but one shamed that was never gracious; if killed, but one dead that is willing to be so: I shall do my friends no wrong, for I have none to lament me; the world no injury, for in it I have nothing: only in the world I fill up a place, which may be better supplied when I have made it empty.

Ros. The little strength that I have, I would it were with you.

Cel. And mine, to eke out hers.

Ros. Fare you well: pray heaven I be deceived in you!

Cel. Your heart's desires be with you!

Cha. Come, where is this young gallant that is so desirous to lie with his mother earth?
Orl. Ready, sir; but his will hath in it a more modest working.
Duke F. You shall try but one fall.
Cha. No, I warrant your Grace, you shall not entreat him to a second, that have so mightily persuaded him from a first.
Orl. You mean to mock me after; you should not have mocked me before: but come your ways.
Ros. Now Hercules be thy speed, young man!
Cel. I would I were invisible, to catch the strong fellow by the leg.
[*They wrestle.*
Ros. O excellent young man!
Cel. If I had a thunderbolt in mine eye, I can tell who should down.
[*Shout. Charles is thrown.*
Duke F. No more, no more.
Orl. Yes, I beseech your Grace: I am not yet well breathed.
Duke F. How dost thou, Charles?
Le Beau. He cannot speak, my lord.
Duke F. Bear him away. What is thy name, young man?
Orl. Orlando, my liege; the youngest son of Sir Rowland de Boys.

WILLIAM SHAKESPEARE, *As You Like It*

'Wrestling Match'

Now, clear the ring! for, hand to hand,
The manly wrestlers take their stand.
Two o'er the rest superior rose,
And proud demanded mightier foes,
Nor call'd in vain; for Douglas came.
—For life is Hugh of Larbert lame;
Scarce better John of Alloa's fare,
Whom senseless home his comrades bear.
Prize of the wrestling match, the King
To Douglas gave a golden ring,
While coldly glanced his eye of blue,
As frozen drop of wintry dew.
Douglas would speak, but in his breast
His struggling soul his words suppress'd;
Indignant then he turn'd him where
Their arms the brawny yeomen bare,
To hurl the massive bar in air.
When each his utmost strength had shown,
The Douglas rent an earth-fast stone

From its deep bed, then heaved it high,
And sent the fragment through the sky
A rood beyond the farthest mark.
And still in Stirling's royal park,
The grey-hair'd sires, who know the past,
To strangers point the Douglas-cast,
And moralize on the decay
Of Scottish strength in modern day.

SIR WALTER SCOTT, from *The Lady of the Lake*

27 May 1665

Abroad, and stopped at Bear-garden stairs, there to see a prize fought. But the house so full there was no getting in there, so forced to go through an ale-house into the pit, where the bears are baited; and upon a stool did see them fight, which they did very furiously, a butcher and a waterman. The former had the better all along, till by and by the latter dropped his sword out of his hand, and the butcher, whether not seeing his sword dropped I know not, but did give him a cut over the wrist, so as he was disabled to fight any longer. But, Lord! to see how in a minute the whole stage was full of watermen to revenge the foul play, and the butchers to defend their fellow, though most blamed him; and there they all fell to it to knocking down and cutting many on each side. It was pleasant to see, but that I stood in the pit, and feared that in the tumult I might get some hurt. At last the battle broke up, and so I away.

SAMUEL PEPYS (1633–1703), *Diary*

A Prize Fight

Being a Person of insatiable Curiosity, I could not forbear going on *Wednesday* last to a Place of no small Renown for the Gallantry of the lower Order of *Britons*, namely, to the Bear-Garden at *Hockley in the Hole*; where (as a whitish brown Paper, put into my Hands in the Street, inform'd me) there was to be a Tryal of Skill to be exhibited between two Masters of the Noble Science of Defence, at two of the Clock precisely. I was not a little charm'd with the Solemnity of the Challenge, which ran thus:

'*I* James Miller, *Serjeant*, (*lately come from the Frontiers of* Portugal) *Master of the Noble Science of Defence, hearing in most Places where I have been of the great Fame of* Timothy Buck *of* London, *Master of the said Science, do invite him to meet me, and exercise at the several Weapons following,* viz.

Back-Sword,	*Single Falchon,*
Sword and Dagger,	*Case of Falchons,*
Sword and Buckler,	*Quarter-Staff.*'

If the generous Ardour in *James Miller* to dispute the Reputation of *Timothy Buck*, had something resembling the old Heroes of Romance, *Timothy Buck* return'd Answer in the same Paper with the like Spirit, adding a little Indignation at being challenged, and seeming to condescend to fight *James Miller*, not in regard to *Miller* himself, but in that, as the Fame went out, he had fought *Parkes* of *Coventry*. The Acceptance of the Combat ran in these Words:

'*I* Timothy Buck *of* Clare-Market, *Master of the Noble Science of Defence, hearing he did fight Mr* Parkes *of* Coventry, *will not fail (God willing) to meet this fair Inviter at the Time and Place appointed, desiring a clear Stage and no Favour.*

Vivat Regina.'

I shall not here look back on the Spectacles of the *Greeks* and *Romans* of this Kind, but must believe this Custom took its Rise from the Ages of Knight-Errantry; from those who lov'd one Woman so well, that they hated all Men and Women else; from those who would fight you, whether you were or were not of their Mind; from those who demanded the Combat of their Contemporaries, both for admiring their Mistress or discommending her. I cannot therefore but lament, that the terrible Part of the ancient Fight is preserved, when the amorous Side of it is forgotten. We have retained the Barbarity, but lost the Gallantry of the old Combatants. I could wish, methinks, these Gentlemen had consulted me in the Promulgation of the Conflict. I was obliged by a fair young Maid whom I understood to be called *Elizabeth Preston,* Daughter of the Keeper of the Garden, with a Glass of Water; whom I imagined might have been, for Form's sake, the general Representative of the Lady fought for, and from her Beauty the proper *Amarillis* on these Occasions. It would have ran better in the Challenge; *I* James Miller, *Serjeant, who have travelled Parts abroad, and came last from the Frontiers of* Portugal, *for the Love of* Elizabeth Preston, *do assert, That the said* Elizabeth is the Fairest of Women. Then the Answer; *I* Timothy Buck, *who have stay'd in* Great Britain *during all the War in Foreign Parts for the Sake of* Susanna Page, *do deny that* Elizabeth Preston *is so fair as the said* Susanna Page. Let *Susanna Page* look on, and I desire of *James Miller* no Favour.

This would give the Battel quite another Turn; and a proper Station for the Ladies, whose Complexion was disputed by the Sword, would animate the Disputants with a more gallant Incentive than the Expectation of Mony from the Spectators; though I would not have that neglected, but thrown to that Fair One whose Lover was approved by the Donor.

Yet, considering the Thing wants such Amendments, it was carried with great Order. *James Miller* came on first; preceded by two disabled Drummers, to shew, I suppose, that the Prospect of maimed Bodies did not in the least deter him. There ascended with the daring *Miller* a Gentleman, whose Name I could not learn, with a dogged Air, as unsatisfied that he was not Principal. This Son of Anger lowred at the whole Assembly, and weighing himself as he march'd around from Side to Side, with a stiff Knee and Shoulder, he gave Intimations of the Purpose he smothered till he saw the Issue of this Encounter. *Miller* had a blue Ribbond tyed round the Sword Arm; which Ornament I conceive to be the Remain of that Custom of wearing a Mistress's Favour on such Occasions of old.

Miller is a Man of six Foot eight Inches Height, of a kind but bold Aspect, well-fashioned, and ready of his Limbs; and such Readiness as spoke his Ease in them, was obtained from a Habit of Motion in Military Exercise.

The Expectation of the Spectators was now almost at its Height, and the Crowd pressing in, several active Persons thought they were placed rather according to their Fortune than their Merit, and took it in their Heads to prefer themselves from the open Area, or Pit, to the Galleries. This Dispute between Desert and Property brought many to the Ground, and raised others in proportion to the highest Seats by Turns for the Space of ten Minutes, till *Timothy Buck* came on, and the whole Assembly giving up their Disputes, turned their Eyes upon the Champions. Then it was that every Man's Affection turned to one or the other irresistibly. A judicious Gentleman near me said, *I could, methinks, be* Miller*'s Second, but I had rather have* Buck *for mine. Miller* had an audacious Look, that took the Eye; *Buck* a perfect Composure, that engaged the Judgment. *Buck* came on in a plain Coat, and kept all his Air till the Instant of Engaging; at which Time he undress'd to his Shirt, his Arm adorned with a Bandage of red Ribband. No one can describe the sudden Concern in the whole Assembly; the most tumultuous Crowd in Nature was as still and as much engaged, as if all their Lives depended on the first blow. The Combatants met in the Middle of the Stage, and shaking Hands as removing all Malice, they retired with much Grace to the Extremities of it; from whence they immediately faced about, and approached each other. *Miller* with an Heart full of Resolution, *Buck* with a watchful untroubled Countenance; *Buck* regarding principally his own Defence, *Miller* chiefly thoughtful of annoying his Opponent. It is not easie to describe the many Escapes and imperceptible Defences between two Men of quick Eyes and ready Limbs; but *Miller's* Heat laid him open to the Rebuke of the calm *Buck*, by a large Cut on the Forehead. Much Effusion of Blood covered his Eyes in a Moment, and the Huzzas of the Crowd undoubtedly quickened the Anguish. The Assembly was divided into Parties upon their different ways of Fighting; while a poor Nymph in one of the Galleries apparently suffered for *Miller*, and burst into a Flood of Tears. As soon as his Wound was wrapped up, he came on again with a little Rage, which still disabled him further. But what brave Man can be wounded into more Patience and Caution? The next was a warm eager Onset which ended in a decisive Stroke on the left Leg of *Miller*. The Lady in the Gallery, during this second Strife, covered her Face; and for my Part, I could not keep my Thoughts from being mostly employed on the Consideration of her unhappy Circumstance that Moment, hearing the Clash of Swords, and apprehending Life or Victory concerned her Lover in every Blow, but not daring to satisfie herself on whom they fell. The Wound was exposed to the View of all who could delight in it, and sewed up on the Stage. The surly Second of *Miller* declared at this Time, that he would that Day Fortnight fight Mr *Buck* at the same Weapons, declaring himself the Master of the renowned *Gorman*; but *Buck* denied him the Honour of that courageous Disciple, and asserting that he himself had taught that Champion, accepted the Challenge.

SIR RICHARD STEELE (1672–1729)

A Survey of the Amphitheatre

On, Pegasus! Why, whither turn ye?
What! lag, ere I've begun my journey?
If you so soon your speed diminish,
You'll grow quite crippled ere we finish.
My riddle by degrees unravels:
Good gentlemen, I'm on my travels.
You're journ'ing too, as I presume;
I warrant you, designed for Rome.
Shall we join chat? You'll quickly be-at-her;
I'm going to the Amphitheatre.
   Bless us, what's here? What hodge-podge ruin!
Is this that famous pile we're viewing,
So cracked up in our schools—and taverns?
This heap of stones and awkward caverns?
Vile place! more fit for brutes than men!
Rome? Phaugh! I think 'tis Daniel's den.
   Stop, let's observe. How vast the building!
In troth, I think they've walled a field in.
Look, tow'rd the centre have you seen-a
Rough pavement? That was their Arena,
The stage where combatants, I wist,
Of old went at it hand to fist.
There, in the fencing-science taught,
Their desp'rate gladiators fought,
Or beasts engaged (like cater-cousins)
Let loose to eat 'em up by dozens.

There, out of all those ugly nooks,
They issued: tigers, bears—adzooks!
While senators, on upper benches,
Sat safely cuddling of their wenches,
And ranged plebeian crowds, unmoved,
The horrid spectacle approved,
Heedless what mischief in the show
Befell poor fighting rogues below.
Some wounded, those by monsters fed on,
This a nose off, that ne'er a head on:
The common fate of gladiators.
Fine shows, where monarchs were spectators!
　Here, from these pipes by time decayed,
Observe, their currents were conveyed;
Which served, when former sports were spent,
Their water-fights to represent,
By authors named—(a pesters take ye!
Why what, ye Muses!)—their Naumachia;
Where soldiers armed made dreadful charges
From broadside hulks and leaky barges,
Brought through this arch, and this, and this through,
Holes, now, a dog could scarcely piss through.
Hang this queer, gloomy, dirty station;
I'm weary of the speculation.
　Let me from scenes so dread repair
Back to my country's milder air:
There visit famed bear-garden heroes,
From whose sham fights ne'er cause of fear rose,
Or trip to view some valiant Hibern
At Sutton's, neighb'ring seat to Tyburn,
Where gentle butchers oft resort,
That brotherhood's peculiar sport.
Here may I sit and fear no slaying,
Mid those meek masters of sword-playing;
Lay wagers, laugh at Figg and Stokes,
And all our harmless fighting folks.
Rome's fencing sparks, say what you please,
In wit fell vastly short of these;
Those met to kill, or to be killed,
But ours to have their pockets filled.
Shame of their boasted Roman sense!
To wisdom they've the best pretence,
Who ne'er in those encounters fight
To die—but get their living by't.

MOSES BROWNE (1704–87)

'A Bloody Victory'

As when two monarchs of the brindled breed
Dispute the proud dominion of the mead,
They fight, they foam, then wearied in the fray,
Aloof retreat, and low'ring stand at bay:
So stood the heroes, and indignant glared,
While grim with blood their rueful fronts were smeared,
Till with returning strength new rage returns,
Again their arms are steeled, again each bosom burns.
  Incessant now their hollow sides they pound,
Loud on each breast the bounding bangs resound;
Their flying fists around the temples glow,
And the jaws crackle with the massy blow.
The raging combat ev'ry eye appals,
Strokes following strokes and falls succeeding falls.
Now drooped the youth yet, urging all his might,
With feeble arm still vindicates the fight:
Till on the part where heaved the panting breath,
A fatal blow impressed the seal of death.
Down dropped the hero, welt'ring in his gore,
And his stretched limbs lay quiv'ring on the floor.
So when a falcon skims the airy way,
Stoops from the clouds and pounces on his prey,
Dashed on the earth the feathered victim lies,
Expands its feeble wings and, flutt'ring, dies.
His faithful friends their dying hero reared,
O'er his broad shoulders dangling hung his head;
Dragging its limbs, they bear the body forth,
Mashed teeth and clotted blood came issuing from his mouth.
  Thus then the victor—'O celestial pow'r!
Who gave this arm to boast one triumph more,
Now grey in glory, let my labours cease,
My blood-stained laurel wed the branch of peace;
Lured by the lustre of the golden prize,
No more in combat this proud crest shall rise;
To future heroes future deeds belong,
Be mine the theme of some immortal song.'
  This said—he seized the prize, while round the ring
High soared applause on acclamation's wing.

PAUL WHITEHEAD (1710–74) from *The Gymnasiad, or Boxing Match*, III

'On the Art of Defence'

After supper he said, 'I am sorry that prize-fighting is gone out; every art should be preserved, and the art of defence is surely important. It is absurd that our soldiers should have swords, and not be taught the use of them. Prize-fighting made people accustomed not to be alarmed at seeing their own blood, or feeling a little pain from a wound. I think the heavy glaymore was an ill-contrived weapon. A man could only strike once with it. It employed both his hands, and he must of course be soon fatigued with wielding it; so that if his antagonist could only keep playing a while, he was sure of him. I would fight with a dirk against Rorie More's sword. I could ward off a blow with a dirk, and then run in upon my enemy. When within that heavy sword, I have him; he is quite helpless, and I could stab him at my leisure, like a calf.'

JAMES BOSWELL (1740–95), *A Tour in the Hebrides with Dr Johnson*

Lines on the Fight between Randall and Turner

All hail to the Cove, see his doxies have crowned him,
With gin-dripping shamrocks just plucked from the plain,
See the Captain and Caleb are chuckling around him,
As he offers to scuttle a nob o'er again.

Ah! Erin be proud of the boy you have got,
And toast his sweet name in the water of life;
Drink joy to his double-ups, strength to his shot,
And a laurel each time he embarks in the strife.

Oh, the leek that beamed gaily on Turner's clear brow,
Glitters still in the wind both purely and bright,
Though the fast-springing buds are close clipped on it now,
Yet the leek is but robbed of the glare of its light.

Say, thou Shakespeare of Fancy men, who could resist
The Fibber, the Touter, the tight Bit of Stuff,
The man who knew head-work, and whose mutton fist
Could have tipped e'en a young rampant bullock enough.

Let feather bed whelps, without any discerning,
In fashion's gay round pass the best of their days;
Let students and poets, in bowers of learning,
Drawl out their existence, and sing their soft lays:

Be ours the wild pleasure, be ours the bright hopes,
Which e'en when devoid of our day-lights we see,
The chance of but flinging our man on the ropes,
Or of boring a customer down on his knee.

We're just like the flowers that bloom in that clime,
Where all sorts of sun-shining sweet-meats are eaten,
Blushing on, blooming on, through the whole summer-time,
And whose value's not known till most soundly they're beaten.

'Tis then that their soft rosey fragrance glows,
And expands with delight as their strength dies away,
And we, when the claret bright, torrent-like flows,
Prove our worth by our nobs being board-like and gay.

PIERCE EGAN (1772–1849)

'The Manly Art of Pugilism'

It is one of the greatest failings of human nature, incident to men in every station in society, that while in prosperity and a long run of good luck, few are provident enough to provide against a rainy day; much more from those who are in a line of life where a great deal depends upon chance, and an unlucky throw may reduce them considerably worse than their first outset in life; a memorable instance is to be remarked towards strengthening this argument, respecting the late Tom Johnson, of pugilistic celebrity, who, by his extraordinary success in fighting, it is said had realized the astonishing sum of near 5,000 pounds, and might, after contending for the championship of England in about sixteen fights, have retired from the scene of battles bravely fought and hardly won, into the vale of ease, become respectable, and have ended his days in peace and happiness. But by want of conduct he lost his property and his home; necessity compelled him to fight another battle; and, flattered that the chance was still in his favour whereby he might recruit his exhausted finances, he entered the field with all the gaiety of an adventurer; but alas, capricious fortune turned her back on him, and he (Tom Johnson) the hero of the tale, who had always been borne off upon the shoulders of his friends amid the shouts of victory, was now doomed, O dire reverse! by the desperate conflict he sustained, to give in, beat almost lifeless; the laurel torn from his veteran brow, and death the ultimate consequence from the severe blows he had received. Tom's reputation being gone as a pugilist in London, he strolled from race-grounds to fairs, endeavouring to pick up a crust as a gambler, but that proving a queer lay, he resorted to teaching the art of defence in Ireland, where he made his grand exit; proving the absolute necessity to men, in such an uncertain way of life, before they are completely done up, of making hay while the sun shines.

Boxing, at any rate, has been patronized for upwards of seventy years in England; and among its numerous leaders several of the Blood Royal have stood conspicuous towards its support, independent of Dukes, Lords, Honourables, etc. etc., besides, at one period, having an amphitheatre established, the amusements of which were publicly advertised whenever they took place, and money paid for admission. Under the direction of a regular manager, a variety of scenes of course were produced, both of the serious and comic cast, and a number of striking situations witnessed from the celebrity of the actors in the drama; and if the language did not rise to the sublimity of Shakespeare, or the bards of old, in making an impression upon the finer sympathies of the mind, the auditors, doubtless, were frequently awakened by the ballet of action, to touches of the most feeling sort. And from the best authorities that can be obtained, it appears that the audiences then were not only extremely respectable, but highly delighted, with the entertainments catered for them; the theatre, in general, was crowded upon these occasions, and the bill of fare given out for the next performance with all the regularity of the most refined place of amusement.

But what of that! Have not our classic theatres, within the last five and twenty years, possessing all the advantages of authors the most exalted and refined, actors the most inimitable and chaste, either to extort the tear or provoke the laugh, music the most ravishing, scenes and decorations, in point of magnificence and splendour, unparalleled, invited pugilism to their boards, and the names of some of the first rate boxers enriched their play-bills; and the audiences (of whom no doubt can attach to their respectability) testified their approbation by loud plaudits at the liberality of the managers in thus publicly displaying the principles of pugilism! And it is mentioned upon good authority that the most fashionable daily newspaper [*The World*] of that period, under the direction of an amateur captain, had a rapid increase of sale in respect to its containing the genuine correspondence between those celebrated heroes of the fist—Humphries and Mendoza.

In 1791, pugilism was in such high repute, and so strongly patronized, that Dan Mendoza was induced to open the small theatre at the Lyceum, in the Strand, for the express purpose of public exhibitions of sparring; and in his managerial capacity assured the public, by a very neat and appropriate address, that the manly art of boxing would be displayed, divested of all ferocity, rendered equally as neat and elegant as fencing; perfectly as useful, and might be as gracefully acquired. Several imitations would be given of celebrated ancient and modern pugilists; eminent performers were engaged to portray the science; and the whole conducted with the utmost propriety and decorum, that the female part of the creation might attend, without their feelings being infringed upon, or experiencing any unpleasant sensations.

We have long witnessed the good effects of this manly spirit in England; and, we trust, it will never be extinguished. Prejudice does much in favour of our native soil; but upon a dispassionate review of those countries where pugilism is unknown, we find that upon the most trifling misunderstanding, the life of the individual is in danger. In Holland the long knife decides too frequently; scarcely any person in Italy is without the stiletto; and France and Germany are not particular in using stones, sticks, etc. to gratify revenge; but in England, the fist only is used, where malice is not suffered to engender and poison the composition and induce the inhabitants to the commission of deeds which their souls abhor and shudder at, but an immediate appeal of boxing, the by-standers make a ring, and where no unfair advantage is suffered to be taken of each other. The fight done, the hand is given in token of peace; resentment vanishes; and the cause generally buried in oblivion. This generous mode of conduct is not owing to any particular rule laid down by education, it is an inherent principle, the impulse of the moment, acted upon by the most ignorant and inferior ranks of the people. Foreigners may sneer at us for our rudeness of customs and barbarity of manners; but, we trust, that Englishmen will ever wish to be admired more for their genuine honesty and rough sincerity, than for an assumed and affected politeness.

Having thus far cursorily expressed our opinions in favour of this manly art, we shall now proceed to shew some of its most powerful knock-down arguments.

PIERCE EGAN, from *Boxiana: Cursory Remarks on the Origin, Rise and Progress of Pugilism in England*

From *The Fight*

Reader, have you ever seen a fight? If not, you have a pleasure to come, at least if it is a fight like that between the Gasman and Bill Neate. The crowd was very great when we arrived on the spot; open carriages were coming up, with streamers flying and music playing, and the country-people were pouring in over hedge and ditch in all directions, to see their hero beat or be beaten. The odds were still on Gas, but only about five to four. Gully had been down to try Neate, and had backed him considerably, which was a damper to the sanguine confidence of the adverse party. The day, as I have said, was fine for a December morning. The grass was wet, and the ground miry, and ploughed up with multitudinous feet, except that, within the ring itself, there was a spot of virgin-green, closed in and unprofaned by vulgar tread, that shone with dazzling brightness in the mid-day sun. For it was now noon, and we had an hour to wait. This is the trying time. It is then the heart sickens, as you think what the two champions are about, and how short a time will determine their fate. After the first blow is struck, there is no opportunity for nervous apprehensions; you are swallowed up in the immediate interest of the scene—but

> *'Between the acting of a dreadful thing*
> *And the first motion, all the interim is*
> *Like a phantasma, or a hideous dream.'*

I found it so as I felt the sun's rays clinging to my back, and saw the white wintry clouds sink below the verge of the horizon. 'So,' I thought, 'my fairest hopes have faded from my sight!—so will the Gasman's glory, or that of his adversary, vanish in an hour.' The *swells* were parading in their white box-coats, the outer ring was cleared with some bruises on the heads and shins of the rustic assembly (for the *cockneys* had been distanced by the sixty-six miles); the time drew near; I had got a good stand; a bustle, a buzz, ran through the crowd; and from the opposite side entered Neate, between his second and bottle-holder. He rolled along, swathed in his loose greatcoat, his knock knees bending under his huge bulk; and, with a modest, cheerful air, threw his hat into the ring. He then just looked round, and begun quietly to undress; when from the other side there was a similar rush and an opening made, and the Gasman came forward with a conscious air of anticipated triumph, too much like the cock-of-the-walk. He strutted about more than became a hero, sucked oranges with a supercilious air, and threw away the skin with a toss of this head, and went up and looked at Neate, which was an act of supererogation. The only sensible thing he did was, as he strode away from the modern Ajax, to fling out his arms, as if he wanted to try whether they would do their work that day. By this time they had stripped, and presented a strong contrast in appearance. If Neate was like Ajax, 'with Atlantean shoulders, fit to bear' the pugilistic reputation of all Bristol, Hickman might be compared to Diomed, light, vigorous, elastic, and his back glistened in the sun, as he moved about, like a panther's hide. There was now a dead pause—attention was awe-struck. Who at that moment, big with a great event, did not draw his breath short—did not feel his heart throb? All was ready. They tossed up for the sun, and the Gasman won. They were led up to the *scratch*—shook hands, and went at it.

In the first round every one thought it was all over. After making play a short time, the Gasman flew at his adversary like a tiger, struck five blows in as many seconds, three first, and then following him as he staggered back, two more, right and left, and down he fell, a mighty ruin. There was a shout, and I said, 'There is no standing this.' Neate seemed like a lifeless lump of flesh and bone, round which the Gasman's blows played with the rapidity of electricity or lightning, and you imagined he would only be lifted up to be knocked down again. It was as if Hickman held a sword or a fire in that right hand of his, and directed it against an unarmed body. They met again, and Neate seemed, not cowed, but particularly cautious. I saw his teeth clenched together and his brows knit close against the sun. He held out both his arms at full length straight before him, like two sledge hammers, and raised his left an inch or two higher. The Gasman could not get over this guard—they struck mutually and fell, but without advantage on either side. It was the same in the next round; but the balance of power was thus restored—the fate of the battle was suspended. No one could tell how it would end. This was the only moment in which opinion was divided; for, in the next, the Gasman aiming a mortal blow at his adversary's neck, with his right hand, and failing from the length he had to reach, the other returned it with his left at full swing, planted a tremendous blow on his cheek-bone and eyebrow, and made a red ruin of that side of his face. The Gasman went down, and there was another shout—a roar of triumph as the waves of fortune rolled tumultuously from side to side. This was a settler. Hickman got up, and 'grinned horrible a ghastly smile,' yet he was evidently dashed in his opinion of himself; it was the first time he had ever been so punished; all one side of his face was perfect scarlet, and his right eye was closed in dingy blackness, as he advanced to the fight, less confident, but still determined. After one or two rounds, not receiving another such remembrancer, he rallied and went at it with his former impetuosity. But in vain. His strength had been weakened—his blows could not tell at such a distance—he was obliged to fling himself at his adversary, and could not strike from his feet; and almost as regularly as he flew at him with his right hand, Neate warded the blow, or drew back out of its reach, and felled him with the return of his left. There was little cautious sparring—no half-hits—no tapping and trifling, none of the *petit-maitreship* of the art—they were almost all knock-down blows:—the fight was a good stand-up fight. The wonder was the half-minute time. If there had been a minute or more allowed between each round, it would have been intelligible how they should by degrees recover strength and resolution; but to see two men smashed to the ground, smeared with gore, stunned, senseless, the breath beaten out of their bodies; and then, before you recover from the shock, to see them rise up with new strength and courage, stand ready to inflict or receive mortal offence, and rush upon each other 'like two clouds over the Caspian'—this is the most astonishing thing of all:—this is the high and heroic state of man! From this time forward the event became more certain every round; and about the twelfth it seemed as if it must have been over. Hickman generally stood with his back to me; but in the scuffle, he had changed positions, and Neate just then made a tremendous lunge at him, and hit him full in the face. It was doubtful whether he would fall backwards or forwards; he hung suspended for a minute or two, and then fell back, throwing his hands in the air, and with his face lifted up to the sky. I never saw anything more terrific than his aspect just before he fell. All traces of life, of natural expression, were gone from him. His face was like a human skull, a death's head spouting blood. The eyes were filled with blood, the nose streamed with blood, the mouth gaped blood. He was not like an actual man, but like a preternatural, spectral appearance, or like one of the figures in Dante's *Inferno*. Yet he fought on after this for several rounds, still striking the first desperate blow, and Neate standing on the defensive, and using the same cautious guard to the last, as if he had still all his work to do; and it was not till the Gasman was so stunned in the seventeenth or eighteenth round, that his senses forsook him, and he could not come to time, that the battle was declared over. Ye who despise the Fancy, do something to show as much *pluck*, or as much self-possession as this, before you assume a superiority which you have never given a single proof of by any one action in the whole course of your lives!—When the Gasman came to himself, the first words he uttered were, 'Where am I? What is the matter?' 'Nothing is the matter, Tom,—you have lost the battle, but you are the bravest man alive.' And Jackson whispered to him, 'I am collecting a purse for you, Tom.'—Vain sounds, and unheard at that moment! Neate instantly went up and shook him cordially by the hand, and seeing some old acquaintance, began to flourish with his fists, calling out, 'Ah! you always said I couldn't fight—what do you think now?' But all in good-humour, and without any appearance of arrogance; only it was evident Bill Neate was pleased that he had won the fight. When it was over, I asked Cribb if he did not think it was a good one? He said '*Pretty well!*' The carrier-pigeons now mounted into the air, and one of them flew with the news of her husband's victory to the bosom of Mrs Neate. Alas for Mrs Hickman!

WILLIAM HAZLITT (1778–1830)

Wednesday, 24 November 1813

12, Mezza Notte

Just returned from dinner with Jackson (the Emperor of Pugilism) and another of the select, at Crib's, the champion's. I drank more than I like, and have brought away some three bottles of very fair claret—for I have no headach. We had Tom Crib up after dinner;—very facetious, though somewhat prolix. He don't like his situation—wants to fight again—pray Pollux (or Castor, if he was the *miller*) he may! Tom has been a sailor—a coal-heaver—and some other genteel profession, before he took to the cestus. Tom has been in action at sea, and is now only three-and-thirty. A great man! has a wife and a mistress, and conversations well—bating some sad omissions and misapplications of the aspirate. Tom is an old friend of

battle was declared over] Scroggins said of the Gasman, that he thought he was a man of that courage, that if his hands were cut off he would still fight on with the stumps—like that of Widdrington—

'In doleful dumps,
Who, when his legs were smitten off,
Still fought upon his stumps.'

mine; I have seen some of his best battles in my nonage. He is now a publican, and, I fear, a sinner;—for Mrs Crib is on alimony, and Tom's daughter lives with the champion. *This* Tom told me,—Tom, having an opinion of my morals, passed her off as a legal spouse. Talking of her, he said, 'she was the truest of women'—from which I immediately inferred she could *not* be his wife, and so it turned out.

These panegyrics don't belong to matrimony;—for, if 'true', a man don't think it necessary to say so; and if not, the less he says the better. Crib is the only man except ——, I ever heard harangue upon his wife's virtue; and I listened to both with great credence and patience, and stuffed my handkerchief into my mouth, when I found yawning irresistible—By the by, I am yawning now—so, good night to thee.—*Νωαίρων*.

LORD BYRON, *Journal*

Thursday, 17 March 1814

I have been sparring with Jackson for exercise this morning; and mean to continue and renew my acquaintance with the muffles. My chest, and arms, and wind are in very good plight, and I am not in flesh. I used to be a hard hitter, and my arms are very long for my height (5 feet 8½ inches). At any rate, exercise is good, and this the severest of all; fencing and the broad-sword never fatigued me half so much.

LORD BYRON, *Journal*

England's Bruisers

Let no one sneer at the bruisers of England—what were the gladiators of Rome, or the bullfighters of Spain, in its palmiest days, compared to England's bruisers? Pity that ever corruption should have crept in amongst them—but of that I wish not to talk; let us still hope that a spark of the old religion, of which they were the priests, still lingers in the breasts of Englishmen. There they come, the bruisers, from far London, or from wherever else they might chance to be at the time, to the great rendezvous in the old city; some came one way, some another: some of tip-top reputation came with peers in their chariots, for glory and fame are such fair things that even peers are proud to have those invested therewith by their sides; others came in their own gigs, driving their own bits of blood, and I heard one say: 'I have driven through at a heat the whole hundred and eleven miles, and only stopped to bait twice.' Oh, the blood-horses of Old England! but they, too, have had their day—for everything beneath the sun there is a season and a time.

So the bruisers of England are come to be present at the grand fight speedily coming off; there they are met in the precincts of the old town, near the field of the chapel, planted with tender saplings at the restoration of sporting Charles, which are now become venerable elms, as high as many a steeple; there they are met at a fitting rendezvous, where a retired coachman, with one leg, keeps an hotel and a bowling-green. I think I now see them upon the bowling-green, the men of renown, amidst hundreds of people with no renown at all, who gaze upon them with timid wonder. Fame, after all, is a glorious thing, though it lasts only for a day. There's Cribb, the champion of England, and perhaps the best man in England; there he is, with his huge massive figure, and face wonderfully like that of a lion. There is Belcher, the younger, not the mighty one, who is gone to his place, but the Teucer Belcher, the most scientific pugilist that ever entered a ring, only wanting strength to be, I won't say what. He appears to walk before me now, as he did that evening, with his white hat, white greatcoat, thin genteel figure, springy step, and keen, determined eye. Crosses him, what a contrast! grim, savage, Shelton, who has a civil word for nobody, and a hard blow for anybody—hard! one blow, given with the proper play of his athletic arm, will unsense a giant. Yonder individual, who strolls about with his hands behind him, supporting his brown coat lappets, under-sized, and who looks anything but what he is, is the king of the light weights, so called—Randall! the terrible Randall, who has Irish blood in his veins; not the better for that, nor the worse; and not far from him is his last antagonist, Ned Turner, who, though beaten by him, still thinks himself as good a man, in which he is, perhaps, right, for it was a near thing; and 'a better shentleman', in which he is quite right, for he is a Welshman. But how shall I name them all? they were there by dozens, and all tremendous in their way. There was Bulldog Hudson, and fearless Scroggins, who beat the conqueror of Sam the Jew. There was Black Richmond—no, he was not there, but I knew him well; he was the most dangerous of blacks, even with a broken thigh. There was Purcell, who could never conquer till all seemed over with him. There was—what! shall I name thee last? ay, why not? I believe that thou art the last of all that strong family still above the sod, where mayst thou long continue—true piece of English stuff, Tom of Bedford—sharp as Winter, kind as Spring.

Hail to thee, Tom of Bedford, or by whatever name it may please thee to be called, Spring or Winter. Hail to thee, six-foot Englishman of the brown eye, worthy to have carried a six foot bow at Flodden, where England's yeomen triumphed over Scotland's king, his clans and chivalry. Hail to thee, last of England's bruisers, after all the many victories which thou hast achieved—true English victories, unbought by yellow gold; need I recount them? nay, nay! they are already well known to fame—sufficient to say that Bristol's Bull and Ireland's Champion were vanquished by thee, and one mightier still, gold itself, thou didst overcome; for gold itself strove in vain to deaden the power of thy arm; and thus thou didst proceed till men left off challenging thee, the unvanquishable, the incorruptible.

'Tis a treat to see thee, Tom of Bedford, in thy 'public' in Holborn way, whither thou hast retired with thy well-earned bays. 'Tis Friday night, and nine by Holborn clock. There sits the yeoman at the end of his long room, surrounded by his friends; glasses are filled, and a song is the cry, and a song is sung well suited to the place; it finds an echo in every heart—fists are clenched, arms are waved, and the portraits of the mighty fighting men of yore, Broughton, and Slack, and Ben, which adorn the walls, appear to smile grim approbation, whilst many a manly voice joins in the chorus.

GEORGE BORROW (1803–81), *Lavengro*

From *The Romany Rye*

Amongst the coachmen who frequented the inn was one who was called 'the bang-up coachman'. He drove to our inn, in the fore part of every day, one of what were called the fast coaches, and afterwards took back the corresponding vehicle. He stayed at our house about twenty minutes, during which time the passengers of the coach which he was to return with dined; those at least who were inclined for dinner, and could pay for it. He derived his sobriquet of 'the bang-up coachman' partly from his being dressed in the extremity of coach dandyism, and partly from the peculiar insolence of his manner, and the unmerciful fashion in which he was in the habit of lashing on the poor horses committed to his charge. He was a large, tall fellow of about thirty, with a face which, had it not been bloated by excess, and insolence, and cruelty stamped most visibly upon it, might have been called good-looking. His insolence indeed was so great that he was hated by all the minor fry connected with coaches along the road upon which he drove, especially the ostlers, whom he was continually abusing or finding fault with. Many was the hearty curse which he received when his back was turned; but the generality of people were much afraid of him, for he was a swinging strong fellow, and had the reputation of being a fighter, and in one or two instances had beaten in a barbarous manner individuals who had quarrelled with him.

I was nearly having a fracas with this worthy. One day, after he had been drinking sherry with a sprig, he swaggered into the yard, where I happened to be standing; just then a waiter came by carrying upon a tray part of a splendid Cheshire cheese, with a knife, plate, and napkin. Stopping the waiter, the coachman cut with the knife a tolerably large lump out of the very middle of the cheese, stuck it on the end of the knife, and putting it to his mouth nibbled a slight piece off it, and then, tossing the rest away with disdain, flung the knife down upon the tray, motioning the waiter to proceed: 'I wish,' said I, 'you may not want before you die what you have just flung away,' whereupon the fellow turned furiously towards me; just then, however, his coach being standing at the door, there was a cry for coachman, so that he was forced to depart, contenting himself for the present with shaking his fist at me, and threatening to serve me out on the first opportunity; before, however, the opportunity occurred he himself got served out in a most unexpected manner.

The day after this incident he drove his coach to the inn, and after having dismounted and received the contributions of the generality of the passengers, he strutted up, with a cigar in his mouth, to an individual who had come with him, and who had just asked me a question with respect to the direction of a village about three miles off, to which he was going. 'Remember the coachman,' said the knight of the box to this individual, who was a thin person of about sixty, with a white hat, rather shabby black coat, and buff-coloured trousers, and who held an umbrella and a small bundle in his hand. 'If you expect me to give you anything,' said he to the coachman, 'you are mistaken; I will give you nothing. You have been very insolent to me as I rode behind you on the coach, and have encouraged two or three trumpery fellows, who rode along with you, to cut scurvy jokes at my expense, and now you come to me for money: I am not so poor but I could have given you a shilling had you been civil; as it is, I will give you nothing.' 'Oh! you won't, won't you?' said the coachman; 'dear me! I hope I shan't starve because you won't give me anything—a shilling! why, I could afford to give you twenty if I thought fit, you pauper! civil to you, indeed! things are come to a fine pass if I need be civil to you! Do you know who you are speaking to? why the best lords in the country are proud to speak to me. Why, it was only the other day that the Marquis of—— said to me——' and then he went on to say what the Marquis said to him; after which, flinging down his cigar, he strutted up the road, swearing to himself about paupers.

'You say it is three miles to ——,' said the individual to me; 'I think I shall light my pipe, and smoke it as I go along.' Thereupon he took out from a side-pocket a tobacco-box and short meerschaum pipe, and implements for striking a light, filled his pipe, lighted it, and commenced smoking. Presently the coachman drew near, I saw at once that there was mischief in his eye; the man smoking was standing with his back towards him, and he came so nigh to him, seemingly purposely, that as he passed a puff of smoke came of necessity against his face. 'What do you mean by smoking in my face?' said he, striking the pipe of the elderly individual out of his mouth. The other, without manifesting much surprise, said, 'I thank you; and if you will wait a minute, I will give you a receipt for that favour;' then gathering up his pipe, and taking off his coat and hat, he laid them on a stepping-block which stood near, and rubbing his hands together, he advanced towards the coachman in an attitude of defence, holding his hands crossed very near to his face. The coachman, who probably expected anything but such a movement from a person of the age and appearance of the individual whom he had insulted, stood for a moment motionless with surprise; but, recollecting himself, he pointed at him derisively with his finger; the next moment, however, the other was close upon him, had struck aside the extended hand with his left fist, and given him a severe blow on the nose with his right, which he immediately followed by a left-hand blow in the eye; then drawing his body slightly backward, with the velocity of lightning he struck the coachman full in the mouth, and the last blow was severest of all, for it cut the coachman's lips nearly through; blows so quickly and sharply dealt I had never seen. The coachman reeled like a fir-tree in a gale, and seemed nearly unsensed. 'Ho! what's this? a fight! a fight!' sounded from a dozen voices, and people came running from all directions to see what was going on. The coachman, coming somewhat to himself, disencumbered himself of his coat and hat; and, encouraged by two or three of his brothers of the whip, showed some symptoms of fighting, endeavouring to close with his foe, but the attempt was vain, his foe was not to be closed with; he did not shift or dodge about, but warded off the blows of his opponent with the greatest *sang-froid*, always using the guard which I have already described, and putting in, in return, short chopping blows with the swiftness of lightning. In a few minutes the countenance of the coachman was literally cut to pieces, and several of his teeth were dislodged; at length he gave in; stung with mortification, however, he repented, and asked for another round; it was granted, to his own complete demolition. The coachman did not drive his coach back that day, he did not appear on the box again for a week; but he never held up his head afterwards. Before I quitted the inn, he had disappeared from the road, going no one knew where.

The coachman, as I have said before, was very much disliked upon the road, but there was an *esprit de corps* amongst the coachmen, and those who stood by did not like to see their brother chastised in such tremendous fashion. 'I never saw such a fight before,' said one. 'Fight! why, I don't call it a fight at all, this chap here ha'n't got a scratch, whereas Tom is cut to pieces; it is all along of that guard of his: if Tom could have got within his guard he would have soon served the old chap out.' 'So he would,' said another, 'it was all owing to that guard. However, I think I see into it, and if I had not to drive this afternoon, I would have a turn with the old fellow and soon serve him out.' 'I will fight him now for a guinea,' said the other coachman, half taking off his coat; observing, however, that the elderly individual made a motion towards him, he hitched it upon his shoulder again, and added, 'that is, if he had not been fighting already, but as it is, I am above taking an advantage, especially of such a poor old creature as that.' And when he had said this, he looked around him, and there was a feeble titter of approbation from two or three of the craven crew, who were in the habit of currying favour with the coachmen. The elderly individual looked for a moment at these last, and then said, 'To such fellows as you I have nothing to say;' then turning to the coachmen, 'and as for you,' he said, 'ye cowardly bullies, I have but one word, which is, that your reign upon the roads is nearly over, and that a time is coming when ye will be no longer wanted or employed in your present capacity, when ye will either have to drive dung-carts, assist as ostlers at village ale-houses, or rot in the workhouse.' Then putting on his coat and hat, and taking up his bundle, not forgetting his meerschaum and the rest of his smoking apparatus, he departed on his way. Filled with curiosity, I followed him.

'I am quite astonished that you should be able to use your hands in the way you have done,' said I, as I walked with this individual in the direction in which he was bound.

'I will tell you how I became able to do so,' said the elderly individual, proceeding to fill and light his pipe as he walked along. 'My father was a journeyman engraver, who lived in a very riotous neighbourhood in the outskirts of London. Wishing to give me something of an education, he sent me to a day-school, two or three streets distant from where we lived, and there, being a rather puny boy, I suffered much persecution from my schoolfellows, who were a very blackguard set. One day, as I was running home, with one of my tormentors pursuing me, old Sergeant Broughton, the retired fighting man, seized me by the arm——'

'Dear me,' said I, 'has it ever been your luck to be acquainted with Sergeant Broughton?'

'You may well call it luck,' said the elderly individual; 'but for him I should never have been able to make my way through the world. He lived only four doors from our house; so, as I was running along the street, with my tyrant behind me, Sergeant Broughton seized me by the arm. "Stop, my boy," said he; "I have frequently seen that scamp ill-treating you; now I will teach you how to send him home with a bloody nose; down with your bag of books; and now, my game chick," whispered he to me, placing himself between me and my adversary, so that he could not observe his motions, "clench your fist in this manner, and hold your arms in this, and when he strikes at you, move them as I now show you, and he can't hurt you; now, don't be afraid, but go at him." I confess that I was somewhat afraid, but I considered myself in some degree under the protection of the famous Sergeant, and, clenching my fist, I went at my foe, using the guard which my ally recommended. The result corresponded to a certain degree with the predictions of the Sergeant; I gave my foe a bloody nose and a black eye, though, notwithstanding my recent lesson in the art of self-defence, he contrived to give me two or three clumsy blows. From that moment I was the especial favourite of the Sergeant, who gave me further lessons, so that in a little time I became a very fair boxer, beating everybody of my own size who attacked me. The old gentleman, however, made me promise never to be quarrelsome, nor to turn his instructions to account, except in self-defence. I have always borne in mind my promise, and have made it a point of conscience never to fight unless absolutely compelled. Folks may rail against boxing if they please, but being able to box may sometimes stand a quiet man in good stead. How should I have fared to-day, but for the instruction of Sergeant Broughton? But for them, the brutal ruffian who insulted me must have passed unpunished. He will not soon forget the lesson which I have just given him—the only lesson he could understand. What would have been the use of reasoning with a fellow of that description? Brave old Broughton! I owe him much.'

GEORGE BORROW

Sayerius v. *Heenanus*

'Close round my chair, my children,
 And gather at my knee,
The while your mother poureth
 The Old Tom in my tea;
The while your father quaffeth
 His rot-gut Bordeaux wine—
'Twas not on such potations
 Were reared these thews o' mine.
Such drinks came in the very year
 —Methinks I mind it well—
That the great fight of HEENANUS
 With SAYERIUS befell.
These knuckles then were iron;
 This biceps like a cord;
This fist shot from the shoulder
 A bullock would have floored.

. . . . . .

Yet, in despite of all the jaw
 And gammon of the time,
That brands the art of self-defence
 —Old England's art—as crime,
From off mine ancient memories
 The rust of time I'll shake,
Your youthful bloods to quicken
 And your British pluck to wake.
I know it only slumbers;
 Let cant do what it will,
The British bull-dog *will* be
 The British bull-dog still.
Then gather to your grandsire's knee,
 The while his tale is told,
How SAYERIUS and HEENANUS
 Milled in the days of old.

The Beaks and Blues were watching,
 Agog to stop the Mill,
As we gathered to the station
 In the April morning chill.
By twos and threes, by fours and tens,
 To London Bridge we drew;
For we had had the office,
 That were good men and true;

And, saving such, the place of fight
  Was ne'er a man that knew.
From east and west, from north and south,
  The London Fancy poured,
Down to the sporting Cabman,
  Up to the sporting Lord.

. . . . . .

The stakes are pitched, the ropes are tied,
  The men have ta'en their stand;
HEENANUS wins the toss for place,
  And takes the eastward hand.
CUSICCIUS and MACDONALDUS
  Upon the Boy attend;
SAYERIUS owns BRUNTONUS,
  And JIM WELSHIUS for friend.
And each upon the other now
  A curious eye may throw,
As from the seconds' final rub
  In buff at length they show,
And from their corners to the scratch
  Move stalwartly and slow.

Then each his hand stretched forth to grasp,
His foeman's fives in friendly clasp;
Each felt his balance trim and true,
Each up to square his mauleys threw;
Each tried his best to draw his man—
The feint, the dodge, the opening plan,
Till left and right SAYERIUS tried;
HEENANUS' grin proclaimed him wide;
He shook his nit, a lead essayed,
Nor reached SAYERIUS' watchful head.
At length each left is sudden flung,
  We heard the ponderous thud,
And from each tongue the news was rung,
  SAYERIUS hath "First blood!"

Adown HEENANUS' Roman nose
Freely the tell-tale claret flows,
While stern SAYERIUS' forehead shows
That in the interchange of blows
  HEENANUS' aim was good!
Again each iron mauley swung,
And loud the counter-hitting rung,

Till breathless all, and wild with blows,
Fiercely they grappled for a close;
A moment in close hug they swing
Hither and thither, round the ring,
Then from HEENANUS' clinch of brass
SAYERIUS, smiling, slips to grass!

I trow mine ancient breath would fail
  To follow through the fight,
Each gallant round's still changing tale,
  Each feat of left and right.
How through two well-spent hours and more,
  Through bruise, and blow, and blood,
Like sturdy bulldogs, as they were,
  Those well-matched heroes stood.
How nine times in that desperate Mill
  HEENANUS, in his strength,
Knocked stout SAYERIUS off his pins,
  And laid him all at length;
But how in each succeeding round
  SAYERIUS smiling came,
With head as cool, and wind as sound,
As his first moment on the ground,
  Still confident, and game.
How, from HEENANUS' sledge-like fist,
Striving a smasher to resist,
SAYERIUS' stout right arm gave way,
Yet the maim'd hero still made play,
And when in-fighting threatened ill,
Was nimble in out-fighting still,
  Did still his own maintain—
In mourning put HEENANUS' glims;
Till blinded eyes and helpless limbs,
  The chances squared again.
How blind HEENANUS in despite
Of bleeding mug and waning sight
So gallantly kept up the fight,
  That not a man could say
Which of the two 'twere wise to back,
Or on which side some random crack
  Might not decide the day:
And leave us—whoso won the prize,—
Victor and vanquished, in all eyes,
  An equal need to pay.
Two hours and more the fight had sped,
  Near unto ten it drew,

But still opposed—one-armed to blind,—
They stood, the dauntless two.
Ah, me, that I have lived to hear
Such men as ruffians scorned,
Such deeds of valour brutal called,
Canted, preached down, and mourned!
Ah, that these old eyes ne'er again
A gallant Mill shall see!
No more behold the ropes and stakes,
With colours flying free!
But I forget the combat—
How shall I tell the close,
That left the Champion's Belt in doubt
Between those well-matched foes?
Fain would I shroud the tale in night,—
The meddling Blues that thrust in sight,—
The ring-keepers o'erthrown;—
The broken ring, the cumbered fight,
HEENANUS' sudden, blinded flight,—
SAYERIUS pausing, as he might,
Just when ten minutes used aright
Had made the fight his own!

Alas! e'en in those brighter days
We still had Beaks and Blues,—
Still, canting rogues, their mud to fling
On self-defence and on the Ring,
And fistic arts abuse!
And 'twas such varmint had the power
The Champion's fight to stay,
And leave unsettled to this hour
The honours of the day!

But had those honours rested
Divided, as was due,
SAYERIUS and HEENANUS
Had cut the belt in two.

And now my fists are feeble,
And my blood is thin and cold,
But 'tis better than Old Tom to me
To recall those days of old.'

WILLIAM MAKEPEACE THACKERAY (attr.) (1811–63)

The Meeting of Sayers and Heenan: 1860

I have no idea what kind of an animal Thomas Sayers may have really been in familiar and pacific life, but I had seen enough of him to recognise a remarkable simplicity and steadfastness, and the sight of his grave carried my thoughts back to a memorable spring morning some twenty years ago, and to a merry 'mill' in a Hampshire meadow, near a stream, not half a mile from Farnborough railway station.

In imagination I am again at the London Bridge terminus, with a 'there and back' ticket in my pocket. The hour is about four in the morning. There is a motley crowd, a huge gathering. There are butchers from Newgate Market; fish-porters from Billingsgate, bringing their vernacular with them; there are pugilists and poets, statesmen and publicans, dandies, men of letters, and even divines, elbowing each other in the semi-darkness.

We have taken our seats. There is considerable delay, but at last a bell rings, there is a snort, and then the monster train slides slowly out of the dimly lighted shed. Once beyond the station we quicken up. Away we tear in a gale of our own creation—a Faust flight on the devil's mantle, over the roofs of the houses, through market-gardens; and, leaving the steepled city behind us, we are soon hissing and snorting through the quiet country; then before very long we find ourselves in a willow-fringed and sunny little field.

For several months I had been confined to London pavements and the dead timber of the official desk. How well I remember the strange delightfulness of the green trees, the fresh grass, cool beneath my feet, and the gracious April air as it played upon my face! A lark is soaring and singing far above our heads, rejoicing in his glorious privacy of light; yokels and costermongers are clambering over fences and leaping dykes. And there, the observed of all observers, is the veteran Tom Oliver, superintending the erection of a twenty-four-foot arena.

Sayers was the first to make his appearance in the ring; but when his opponent, Heenan, threw his hat within the ropes, followed it, and stripped, there was a murmur of admiration. He was at once recognised as the most magnificent athlete that had ever been seen in such a place. He was five inches taller than Sayers—who, strictly speaking, was only a middle-weight—some two or three stone heavier, and (no small matter) he was eight years younger; while his length of reach was remarkable for even so tall a man.

Then, shall I ever forget the look of perfect self-possession and calm courage, mingled with curiosity, with which Sayers faced, gazed up, and smiled at his terrible antagonist? He had never set eyes on him before. Having lost the toss, he was obliged to accept the lower ground. But there he stood, his enormous shoulders shining in the sun, in his well-known and faultless attitude, tapping the ground lightly with his left foot, his arms

terminus] at that time the station at Farnborough [F.L.-L.]

well down, his head thrown back, ready for a shoot or a jump, and a smile of confidence on his open but not classical countenance.

Still—and no wonder—there was a pretty general opinion among outsiders, expressed in the flowery but forcible vernacular of the 'fancy', that the match was 'a horse to a hen'—that 'Heenan would knock Sayers into a cocked hat in ten minutes'; for how was Sayers to get at him? I could not but feel the force of this opinion, and that Bob Brettle's observation was an opposite one: 'Well, Tom may beat him, but may I, etc., if he can eat him!' However, as it turned out, Sayers had no difficulty in getting over Heenan's guard, for he punished him frightfully.

I recollect my strange tremor as the men stood up, advanced, shook hands, and took up their positions. The fight began about half-past seven, and finished soon after ten. I am not going to describe it. Has it not been already described in the racy columns of our revered old chronicler, *Bell's Life*? We have had enough of the 'rib-benders' and 'pile-drivers'. I will say, however, that never in the annals of the ring were courage, science, temper, judgment, and staying qualities combined and displayed in such a marvellous measure as by Tom Sayers on this memorable day. He fulfilled to the uttermost Livy's *facere et pati fortiter*. At the beginning of the encounter Heenan was both out-generalled and out-fought; but as early as the fourth round Sayers had his right arm completely disabled, and from that time he defended himself and attacked his gigantic adversary with only his left. The battle ended in a disgraceful scene of riot and blackguardism, especially among the backers of Sayers, who, as soon as they saw that their money was in extreme peril, broke into the ring. It ended by the umpire wisely deciding that it was a draw.

Volenti non fit injuria may be barbarous Latin, but it is sound sense. A boxing-match is a voluntary exhibition of pluck and endurance; there is no malice; and it proves to the uttermost the stuff of which a man is made. There was something in this great fight which the whole nation recognised, for it appealed to a very universal sympathy. It affected all classes, in a way that boys and men always will be affected when they hear of the exploits of a Peterborough or a Grenville. It was magnetic—and why should it not continue to move us? Though, when I recall this battle, and Heenan's face, out of which all that was human had been pommelled, I cry, 'Heaven forbid that the prize-ring should ever be revived in all its hideous and loathsome degradation!'

So long as manly sentiments and sheer English pluck are valued, so long shall the name of Thomas Sayers, the Polydeuces of our country, be held in honour.

Sayers had no difficulty . . .] He was remarkable as a fighter than as a sparrer. I have seen boxers quicker than Sayers. Nat Langham and Ned Donnelly were quicker, and so was Charlie Buller; but in force of hitting, either with right or left, and in his extraordinary skill of timing his man he had no equal. Like Entellus, he defended himself by the movement of his body. [F.L.-L.]

Dear reader, one of these days make a pilgrimage to Highgate, climb its steep ascent, and enter the rueful-looking, the lonely burial-ground. The custodian will be pleased to see you; he will greet you as he did me, and pilot you to the green resting-place of Michael Faraday, of whom a distinguished man of science well said, 'He was too good a man for me to estimate him, and he was too great a philosopher for me to understand him thoroughly.' Michael Faraday had the true spirit of a philosopher and a Christian. He was, indeed, one of England's worthiest sons, so it will do you no harm to muse awhile beside his grave.

Then, if by chance you should come upon another grave—a monument of mouldering stones, a forlorn *hic jacet* (it will not be far to seek; you will surely recognise it), you may at once pass on. You need not stay; but at least have a kindly thought for the plucky Englishman who lies buried there.

The grass on Tom's grave is also very green; and you will be as like to see the lark soaring, and to hear him rejoicing at Heaven's gate, from the one grave as from the other.

Alas, poor Tom! Like most of his calling, he died a young man. I happened to meet him on Hampstead Heath shortly after the battle, and not very long before his death. He was walking alone where John Keats had once liked to walk, in

> A melodious plot
> Of beechen green and shadows numberless.

We saluted as we passed, and I had the honour of grasping his hand—that fist which had so often administered his terrible blow, 'the auctioneer'.

Heenan died much about the same time as Sayers. There is a spice of romance in the story of the gallant Benicia Boy. He was the husband of Ada Menken, a handsome actress, with dark blue eyes—glorious eyes. She was the 'Infelicia' whose love poems Mr Dickens introduced to the reading public in 1868.

I remember seeing Ada at Astley's Amphitheatre in 'Mazeppa'; and, from what I have heard, I am inclined to think that, like some other splendid women, she may have been a handful as well as an armful.

FREDERICK LOCKER-LAMPSON, *My Confidences*

'A Sporting Bower'

Mr Toots, emancipated from the Blimber thraldom and coming into the possession of a certain portion of his wordly wealth, 'which', as he had been wont, during his last half-year's probation, to communicate to Mr Feeder every evening as a new discovery, 'the executors couldn't keep him out of,' had applied himself, with great diligence, to the science of Life. Fired with a noble emulation to pursue a brilliant and distinguished career, Mr Toots had furnished a choice set of apartments; had established among them a sporting bower, embellished with the portraits of winning horses, in which he took no particle of interest; and a divan, which made him poorly. In this delicious abode, Mr Toots devoted himself to the cultivation of those gentle arts which refine and humanize existence, his chief instructor in which was an interesting character called the Game Chicken, who was always to be heard of at the bar of the Black Badger, wore a shaggy white great-coat in the warmest weather, and knocked Mr Toots about the head three times a week, for the small consideration of ten and six per visit.

The Game Chicken, who was quite the Apollo of Mr Toots's Pantheon, had introduced to him a marker who taught billiards, a Life Guard who taught fencing, a jobmaster who taught riding, a Cornish gentleman who was up to anything in the athletic line, and two or three other friends connected no less intimately with the fine arts. Under whose auspices Mr Toots could hardly fail to improve apace, and under whose tuition he went to work.

CHARLES DICKENS, *Dombey and Son*

The Art of Boxing

The Art of Boxing has been practised more or less among the two great nations of antiquity. The Greeks and Romans held it in high respect, and even the Jews did not wholly eschew the art of smiting, while the descendants of the Tribes who settled in England have contributed many of the most brilliant boxers to the roll of fame. That every man who desires the development of the muscular powers of the human frame, the possession of quickness, decision, endurance, and courage should practise boxing is a matter of necessity, since by no other means can all these qualities be so thoroughly tested and cultivated. Every man should be able to use the weapons which nature has given him to the best of his ability:—not necessarily to oppress or injure others (since the best boxers are almost invariably the least quarrelsome and overbearing persons), but to be able to defend himself from attack or oppression on the part of others. The smallest and weakest man, by assiduous practice in boxing, may make himself an antagonist by no means to be despised; and well do we remember seeing a small, pale, slender-looking slip of a fellow, give a great hulking waterman, six or eight inches taller than himself, a very wholesome thrashing at Hampton Court once for attempting to bully him out of his fare. It was beautiful to see how the little man slipped away under the arms of the big one (who was weaving and wallopping them about like the sails of a windmill), propping him sharply here, there, and everywhere, until the bully, worn-out and bleeding, admitted that he had had enough, and the little one walked off without a mark, amid the cheers of the spectators. The big one was probably careful in future to deal more cautiously with his customers. Boxing has been called brutal. With persons who hold that view it is perhaps useless to argue; they look only at the worst aspect of the *means*, and entirely shut their eyes to the *object*, or better side of the question. But it may fairly be asked whether manners have improved since boxing was abolished by law; whether there is less brutality, less wife-beating and kicking, now than formerly; and whether the spectacle one so often sees, of two great hulking brutes blackguarding each other in the foulest and most filthy language, yet both afraid to hit one another from want of familiarity with the usages of combat, is an improving one? Is there less brutality, less criminal violence, often attended with fatal or nearly fatal results?—less ready use of un-English and unmanly weapons and means of offence than there was formerly? We say No, emphatically, and with certainty, *no*. In the old days, when boxing flourished, if a man had been seen ill-treating a weaker one or beating and kicking a woman, twenty men who could use their fists would have come forward promptly 'to help the weak', and the brute would soon have learnt at what a risk he indulged his propensities. Now twenty men will pass by on the other side, or scuttle off down a by-street to be out of the row.

Our great fatal mistake was made in putting down what was called 'prize-fighting'. It was *first* declared illegal, and then tolerated for many years. The professors of the art being thus placed under a social ban, and having to practise it in opposition to the law, the more respectable and better class of their patrons became gradually weeded out, and while the Tom Springs and Deaf Burkes, men of sterling worth, courage, and unimpeachable honesty, passed away, worse came in their places; and then, this, the natural result of such a course of treatment was pointed to as a reason for active interference and putting fighting down altogether. Yet the native love of seeing a well *stricken* field was never so strongly displayed as when Tom Sayers and Heenan fought their well contested fight, and the best blood in England stood by the ring side and looked on with breathless interest. Had such patronage always awaited the ring, had endeavours been made to raise its status and social condition instead of lowering it; had it been recognised as a national benefit that the youth of England should know how to protect itself, should know how to bear exertion and pain with unflinching courage and endurance; had it been admitted that a school for the encouragement and practice of the art in which the highest efficiency could be obtained was a national requisite, then indeed we should have had matters placed on a different footing, and the rowdyism and blackguardism one used to hear so much of and which were mainly due to the low parasites and hangers on of the Ring would not have been heard of at all, for the professors of the art, seeing themselves respected, would have put all this down with a strong hand. As it is, the school of boxing is rapidly dying out, and when the professors of the present day have passed away it will be hard to say where the new ones are to come from.

Unless, therefore, some strong step is taken to revive the fallen fortunes of the Ring, the school of British boxing will soon be a vision of the past, and Continental manners and practices of the worst type will find a home amongst us.

NED DONNELLY, from *Self Defence* (1879)

From *A Piece of Steak*

The gong struck and the two men advanced from their corners. Sandel came forward fully three-quarters of the distance, eager to begin again; but King was content to advance the shorter distance. It was in line with his policy of economy. He had not been well trained, and he had not had enough to eat, and every step counted. Besides, he had already walked two miles to the ringside. It was a repetition of the first round, with Sandel attacking like a whirlwind and with the audience indignantly demanding why King did not fight. Beyond feinting and several slowly delivered and ineffectual blows he did nothing save block and stall and clinch. Sandel wanted to make the pace fast, while King, out of his wisdom, refused to accommodate him. He grinned with a certain wistful pathos in his ring-battered countenance, and went on cherishing his strength with the jealousy of which only Age is capable. Sandel was Youth, and he threw his strength away with the munificent abandon of Youth. To King belonged the ring generalship, the wisdom bred of long, aching fights. He watched with cool eyes and head, moving slowly and waiting for Sandel's froth to foam away. To the majority of the onlookers it seemed as though King was hopelessly outclassed, and they voiced their opinion in offers of three to one on Sandel. But there were wise ones, a few, who knew King of old time, and who covered what they considered easy money.

The third round began as usual, one-sided, with Sandel doing all the leading, and delivering all the punishment. A half-minute had passed when Sandel, over-confident, left an opening. King's eyes and right arm flashed in the same instant. It was his first real blow—a hook, with the twisted arch of the arm to make it rigid, and with all the weight of the half-pivoted body behind it. It was like a sleepy-seeming lion suddenly thrusting out a lightning paw. Sandel, caught on the side of the jaw, was felled like a bullock. The audience gasped and murmured awe-stricken applause. The man was not muscle-bound, after all, and he could drive a blow like a trip-hammer.

Sandel was shaken. He rolled over and attempted to rise, but the sharp yells from his seconds to take the count restrained him. He knelt on one knee, ready to rise, and waited, while the referee stood over him, counting the seconds loudly in his ear. At the ninth he rose in fighting attitude, and Tom King, facing him, knew regret that the blow had not been an inch nearer the point of the jaw. That would have been a knock-out, and he could have carried the thirty quid home to the missus and the kiddies.

The round continued to the end of its three minutes, Sandel for the first time respectful of his opponent and King slow of movement and sleepy-eyed as ever. As the round neared its close, King, warned of the fact by sight of the seconds crouching outside ready for the spring in through the ropes, worked the fight around to his own corner. And when the gong struck, he sat down immediately on the waiting stool, while Sandel had to walk all the way across the diagonal of the square to his own corner. It was a little thing, but it was the sum of little things that counted. Sandel was compelled to walk that many more steps, to give up that much energy, and to lose a part of the precious minute of rest. At the beginning of every round King loafed slowly out from his corner, forcing his opponent to advance the greater distance. The end of every round found the fight manoeuvred by King into his own corner so that he could immediately sit down.

Two more rounds went by, in which King was parsimonious of effort and Sandel prodigal. The latter's attempt to force a fast pace made King uncomfortable, for a fair percentage of the multitudinous blows showered upon him went home. Yet King persisted in his dogged slowness, despite the crying of the young hot-heads for him to go in and fight. Again, in the sixth round, Sandel was careless, again Tom King's fearful right flashed out to the jaw, and again Sandel took the nine seconds' count.

By the seventh round Sandel's pink of condition was gone and he settled down to what he knew was to be the hardest fight in his experience. Tom King was an old un, but a better old un than he had ever encountered—an old un who never lost his head, who was remarkably able at defence, whose blows had the impact of a knotted club, and who had a knock-out in either hand. Nevertheless, Tom King dared not hit often. He never forgot his battered knuckles, and knew that every hit must count if the knuckles were to last out the fight. As he sat in his corner, glancing across at his opponent, the thought came to him that the sum of his wisdom and Sandel's youth would constitute a world's champion heavy-weight. But that was the trouble, Sandel would never become a world champion. He lacked the wisdom, and the only way for him to get it was to buy it with Youth; and when wisdom was his, Youth would have been spent in buying it.

King took every advantage he knew. He never missed an opportunity to clinch, and in effecting most of the clinches his shoulder drove stiffly into the other's ribs. In the philosophy of the ring a shoulder was as good as a punch so far as damage was concerned, and a great deal better so far as concerned expenditure of effort. Also, in the clinches King rested his weight on his opponent, and was loath to let go. This compelled the interference of the referee, who tore them apart, always assisted by Sandel, who had not yet learned to rest. He could not refrain from using those glorious flying arms and writhing muscles of his, and when the other rushed into a clinch, striking shoulder against ribs, and with head resting under Sandel's left arm, Sandel almost invariably swung his right behind his own back and into the projecting face. It was a clever stroke, much admired by the audience, but it was not dangerous, and was, therefore, just that much wasted strength. But Sandel was tireless and unaware of limitations, and King grinned and doggedly endured.

Sandel developed a fierce right to the body which made it appear that King was taking an enormous amount of punishment, and it was only the old ringsters who appreciated the deft touch of King's left glove to the other's biceps just before the impact of the blow. It was true the blow landed each time; but each time it was robbed of its power by that touch on the biceps. In the ninth round, three times inside a minute, King's right hooked its twisted arch to the jaw; and three times Sandel's body, heavy as it was, was levelled to the mat. Each time he took the nine seconds allowed him and rose to his feet, shaken and jarred, but still strong. He had lost much of his speed, and he wasted less effort. He was fighting grimly; but he continued to draw upon his chief asset, which was Youth. King's chief asset was experience. As his vitality had dimmed and his vigour abated, he had replaced them with cunning, with wisdom born of the long fights and with a careful shepherding of strength. Not alone had he learned never to make a superfluous movement, but he had learned how to seduce an opponent into throwing his strength away. Again and again, by feint of foot and hand and body he continued to inveigle Sandel into leaping back ducking, or countering. King rested, but he never permitted Sandel to rest. It was the strategy of Age.

Early in the tenth round King began stopping the other's rushes with straight lefts to the face, and Sandel, grown wary, responded by drawing the left, then by ducking it and delivering his right in a swinging hook to the side of the head. It was too high up to be vitally effective; but when first it landed, King knew the old, familiar descent of the black veil of unconsciousness across his mind. For the instant, or for the slightest fraction of an instant, rather, he ceased. In the one moment he saw his opponent ducking out of his field of vision and the background of white, watching faces; in the next moment he again saw his opponent and the background of faces. It was as if he had slept for a time and just opened his eyes again, and yet the interval of unconsciousness was so microscopically short that there had been no time for him to fall. The audience saw him totter and his knees give, and then saw him recover and tuck his chin deeper into the shelter of his left shoulder.

Several times Sandel repeated the blow, keeping King partially dazed, and then the latter worked out his defence, which was also a counter. Feinting with his left he took a half-step backward, at the same time upper cutting with the whole strength of his right. So accurately was it timed that it landed squarely on Sandel's face in the full, downward sweep of the duck, and Sandel lifted in the air and curled backward, striking the mat on his head and shoulders. Twice King achieved this, then turned loose and hammered his opponent to the ropes. He gave Sandel no chance to rest or to set himself, but smashed blow in upon blow till the house rose to its feet and the air was filled with an unbroken roar of applause. But Sandel's strength and endurance were superb, and he continued to stay on his feet. A knock-out seemed certain, and a captain of police, appalled at the dreadful punishment, arose by the ringside to stop the fight. The gong struck for the end of the round and Sandel staggered to his corner, protesting to the captain that he was sound and strong. To prove it, he threw two back-air-springs and the police captain gave in.

Tom King, leaning back in his corner and breathing hard, was disappointed. If the fight had been stopped, the referee, perforce, would have rendered him the decision, and the purse would have been his. Unlike Sandel, he was not fighting for glory or career, but for thirty quid. And now Sandel would recuperate in the minute of rest.

Youth will be served—this saying flashed into King's mind, and he remembered the first time he had heard it, the night when he had put away Stowsher Bill. The toff who had bought him a drink after the fight and patted him on the shoulder had used those words. Youth will be served! The toff was right. And on that night in the long ago he had been Youth. To-night Youth sat in the opposite corner. As for himself, he had been fighting for half an hour now, and he was an old man. Had he fought like Sandel, he would not have lasted fifteen minutes. But the point was that he did not recuperate. Those upstanding arteries and that sorely tried heart would not enable him to gather strength in the intervals between the rounds. And he had not had sufficient strength in him to begin with. His legs were heavy under him and beginning to cramp. He should not have walked those two miles to the fight. And there was the steak which he had got up longing for that morning. A great and terrible hatred rose up in him for the butchers who had refused him credit. It was hard for an old man to go into a fight without enough to eat. And a piece of steak was such a little thing, a few pennies at best; yet it meant thirty quid to him.

With the gong that opened the eleventh round, Sandel rushed, making a show of freshness which he did not really possess. King knew it for what it was—a bluff as old as the game itself. He clinched to save himself, then going free, allowed Sandel to get set. This was what King desired. He feinted with his left, drew the answering duck and swinging upward hook, then made the half-step backward, delivered the upper cut full to the face and crumpled Sandel over to the mat. After that he never let him rest, receiving punishment himself, but inflicting far more, smashing Sandel to the ropes, hooking and driving all manner of blows into him, tearing away from his clinches or punching him out of attempted clinches, and ever when Sandel would have fallen, catching him with one uplifting hand and with the other immediately smashing him into the ropes where he could not fall.

The house by this time had gone mad, and it was his house, nearly every voice yelling: 'Go it, Tom!' 'Get 'im! Get 'im!' 'You've got 'im, Tom! You've got 'im!' It was to be a whirlwind finish, and that was what a ring-side audience paid to see.

And Tom King, who for half an hour had conserved his strength, now expended it prodigally in the one great effort he knew he had in him. It was his one chance—now or not at all. His strength was waning fast, and his hope was that before the last of it ebbed out of him he would have beaten his opponent down for the count. And as he continued to strike and force, coolly estimating the weight of his blows and the quality of the damage wrought, he realized how hard a man Sandel was to knock out. Stamina and endurance were his to an extreme degree, and they were the virgin stamina and endurance of youth. Sandel was certainly a coming man. He had it in him. Only out of such rugged fibre were successful fighters fashioned.

Sandel was reeling and staggering, but Tom King's legs were cramping and his knuckles going back on him. Yet he steeled himself to strike the fierce blows, every one of which brought anguish to his tortured hands. Though now he was receiving practically no punishment, he was weakening as rapidly as the other. His blows went home, but there was no longer the weight behind them, and each blow was the result of a severe effort of will. His legs were like lead, and they dragged visibly under him; while Sandel's backers, cheered by this symptom, began calling encouragement to their man.

King was spurred to a burst of effort. He delivered two blows in succession—a left, a trifle too high, to the solar plexus, and a right cross to the jaw. They were not heavy blows, yet so weak and dazed was Sandel that he went down and lay quivering. The referee stood over him, shouting the count of the fatal seconds in his ear. If before the tenth second was called, he did not rise, the fight was lost. The house stood in hushed silence. King rested on trembling legs. A mortal dizziness was upon him, and before his eyes the sea of faces sagged and swayed, while to his ears, as from a remote distance, came the count of the referee. Yet he looked upon the fight as his. It was impossible that a man so punished could rise.

Only youth could rise, and Sandel rose. At the fourth second he rolled over on his face and groped blindly for the ropes. By the seventh second he had dragged himself to his knee, where he rested, his head rolling groggily on his shoulders. As the referee cried 'Nine!' Sandel stood upright, in proper stalling position, his left arm wrapped about his face, his right wrapped about his stomach. Thus were his vital points guarded, while he lurched forward toward King in the hope of effecting a clinch and gaining more time.

At the instant Sandel arose, King was at him, but the two blows he delivered were muffled on the stalled arms. The next moment Sandel was in the clinch and holding on desperately while the referee strove to drag the two men apart. King helped to force himself free. He knew the rapidity with which Youth recovered, and he knew that Sandel was his if he could prevent that recovery. One stiff punch would do it. Sandel was his, indubitably his. He had out-generalled him, out-fought him, out-pointed him. Sandel reeled out of the clinch, balanced on the hair line between defeat and survival. One good blow would topple him over and down and out. And Tom King, in a flash of bitterness, remembered the piece of steak and wished that he had it then behind that necessary punch he must deliver. He nerved himself for the blow, but it was not heavy enough nor swift enough. Sandel swayed, but did not fall, staggering back to the ropes and holding on. King staggered after him, and, with a pang like that of dissolution, delivered another blow. But his body had deserted him. All that was left of him was a fighting intelligence that was dimmed and clouded from exhaustion. The blow that was aimed for the jaw struck no higher than the shoulder. He had willed the blow higher, but the tired muscles had not been able to obey. And, from the impact of the blow, Tom King himself reeled back and nearly fell. Once again he strove. This time his punch missed altogether, and, from absolute weakness, he fell against Sandel and clinched, holding on to him to save himself from sinking to the floor.

King did not attempt to free himself. He had shot his bolt. He was gone. And Youth had been served. Even in the clinch he could feel Sandel growing stronger against him. When the referee thrust them apart, there, before his eyes, he saw Youth recuperate. From instant to instant Sandel grew stronger. His punches, weak and futile at first, became stiff and accurate. Tom King's bleared eyes saw the gloved fist driving at his jaw, and he willed to guard it by interposing his arm. He saw the danger, willed the act; but the arm was too heavy. It seemed burdened with a hundredweight of lead. It would not lift itself, and he strove to lift it with his soul. Then the gloved fist landed home. He experienced a sharp snap that was like an electric spark, and, simultaneously, the veil of blackness enveloped him.

When he opened his eyes again he was in his corner, and he heard the yelling of the audience like the roar of the surf at Bondi Beach. A wet sponge was being pressed against the base of his brain, and Sid Sullivan was blowing cold water in a refreshing spray over his face and chest. His gloves had already been removed, and Sandel, bending over him, was shaking his hand. He bore no ill-will toward the man who had put him out, and he returned the grip with a heartiness that made his battered knuckles protest. Then Sandel stepped to the centre of the ring and the audience hushed its pandemonium to hear him accept young Pronto's challenge and offer to increase the side bet to one hundred pounds. King looked on apathetically while his seconds mopped the streaming water from him, dried his face, and prepared him to leave the ring. He felt hungry. It was not the ordinary, gnawing kind, but a great faintness, a palpitation at the pit of the stomach that communicated itself to all his body. He remembered back into the fight to the moment when he had Sandel swaying and tottering on the hair-line balance of defeat. Ah, that piece of steak would have done it! He had lacked just that for the decisive blow, and he had lost. It was all because of the piece of steak.

His seconds were half-supporting him as they helped him through the ropes. He tore free from them, ducked through the ropes unaided, and leaped heavily to the floor, following on their heels as they forced a passage for him down the crowded centre aisle. Leaving the dressing-room for the street, in the entrance to the hall, some young fellow spoke to him.

'W'y didn't yuh go in an' get 'im when yuh 'ad him?' the young fellow asked.

'Aw, go to hell!' said Tom King, and passed down the steps to the sidewalk.

The doors of the public-house at the corner were swinging wide, and he saw the lights and the smiling barmaids, heard the many voices discussing the fight and the prosperous chink of money on the bar. Somebody called to him to have a drink. He hesitated perceptibly, then refused and went on his way.

He had not a copper in his pocket, and the two-mile walk home seemed very long. He was certainly getting old. Crossing the Domain, he sat down suddenly on a bench, unnerved by the thought of the missus sitting up for him, waiting to learn the outcome of the fight. That was harder than any knockout, and it seemed almost impossible to face.

He felt weak and sore, and the pain of his smashed knuckles warned him that, even if he could find a job at navvy work, it would be a week before he could grip a pick handle or a shovel. The hunger palpitation at the pit of the stomach was sickening. His wretchedness overwhelmed him, and into his eyes came an unwonted moisture. He covered his face with his hands, and, as he cried, he remembered Stowsher Bill and how he had served him that night in the long ago. Poor old Stowsher Bill! He could understand now why Bill had cried in the dressing-room.

JACK LONDON (1876–1916)

'Eighteen Rounds'

From the beginning of the bout
My luck was gone, my hand was out.
Right from the start Bill called the play,
But I was quick and kept away
Till the fourth round, when work got mixed,
And then I knew Bill had me fixed.
My hand was out, why, Heaven knows;
Bill punched me when and where he chose.
Through two more rounds we quartered wide
And all the time my hands seemed tied;

Bill punched me when and where he pleased.
The cheering from my backers ceased,
But every punch I heard a yell
Of 'That's the style, Bill, give him hell.'
No one for me, but Jimmy's light
'Straight left! Straight left!' and 'Watch his right.'

I don't know how a boxer goes
When all his body hums from blows;
I know I seemed to rock and spin,
I don't know how I saved my chin;
I know I thought my only friend
Was that clinked flask at each round's end
When my two seconds, Ed and Jimmy,
Had sixty seconds help to gimme.
But in the ninth, with pain and knocks
I stopped: I couldn't fight nor box.
Bill missed his swing, the light was tricky,
But I went down, and stayed down, dicky.
'Get up,' cried Jim. I said, 'I will.'
Then all the gang yelled, 'Out him, Bill.
Out him.' Bill rushed . . . and Clink, Clink, Clink.
Time! and Jim's knee, and rum to drink.
And round the ring there ran a titter:
'Saved by the call, the bloody quitter.'

They drove (a dodge that never fails)
A pin beneath my finger nails.
They poured what seemed a running beck
Of cold spring water down my neck;
Jim with a lancet quick as flies
Lowered the swellings round my eyes.
They sluiced my legs and fanned my face
Through all that blessed minute's grace;
They gave my calves a thorough kneading,
They salved my cuts and stopped the bleeding.
A gulp of liquor dulled the pain,
And then the two flasks clinked again.
Time!

        There was Bill as grim as death.
He rushed, I clinched, to get more breath
And breath I got, though Billy bats
Some stinging short-arms in my slats.
And when we broke, as I foresaw,
He swung his right in for the jaw.

I stopped it on my shoulder bone,
And at the shock I heard Bill groan—
A little groan or moan or grunt
As though I'd his hit his wind a bunt.

And hit it hard, with all your power
On something hard for half an hour,
While someone thumps you black and blue,
And then you'll know what Billy knew.
Bill took that pain without a sound
Till half-way through the eighteenth round.
And then I sent him down and out,
And Silas said, 'Kane wins the bout.'

JOHN MASEFIELD, from *The Everlasting Mercy*

Driscoll's Last Fight

The night of October 21st, 1919, is still splendidly fresh in our memory. Then Jim Driscoll met Charles Ledoux over the championship distance. Seldom, if ever, has boxing produced a drama more thrilling. Here was an old man, as boxers go, for Driscoll was then in his fortieth year, who dared to get into the ring and gamble in his knowledge of ringcraft against a man twenty-seven years of age, who by common consent stood almost alone as a fighter, as distinct from a boxer, of his weight. Yet for fourteen and a half rounds, Driscoll—toothless, grey-headed, wrinkled-faced—did pretty well what he pleased. But he could not survive against irrepressible youth and viciousness as personified by Ledoux. Half way through the fifteenth round, the Frenchman hit Driscoll on the jaw and the body, and made him half stagger. Then, like a human hurricane, Ledoux battered the old champion in such a way as to reduce him to a hopeless condition. It was merciful that the gong sounded when it did, for one more blow would have stretched Driscoll on the floor. He came up for the sixteenth round, his knees sagging, his face telling of pain, and the light gone out of his eyes. By habit only did he strike a fighting attitude, and his chief second—Badger—threw a towel into the ring as a token of defeat.

No contest within recent years has gone so obviously in favour of one man as this did. It was Driscoll all the time. We often talk and write about the straight left, but we rarely see it as it was introduced and employed by Driscoll on this night. It was wonderful to behold. It was shot out like lightning; it stabbed and stung in a way that would have caused any man less sensitive and courageous than Ledoux to have imagined that he was up against all the fighters that ever were. But this little Frenchman never troubled about anything except to hammer his way to victory. He was no boxer, but he was indeed a glorious fighter, clean and chivalrous to a degree. He was cruel without intending to be cruel, but with all his tenacity of purpose there was Driscoll always making points by sheer matchless skill. It was any odds on Driscoll, until he was hit on the jaw. When Ledoux landed, you could almost hear Driscoll gasp. His legs gave to crossing, his arms became limp—age told its tale.

The defeat of Driscoll was a glorious one, but it hurt us all. He had spread out the magic of boxing; he only lost because he believed that he was young, when he was really old. With the gloves that had been his intimate companions during a long life in the ring, he brushed away tears that trickled down his deeply lined face. Driscoll should never have known the necessity of 'coming back'. Still, we were glad of his return, because so long as he was strong on his feet, his fighting brain clear and quick, and his eye ablaze with life, he showed us that which we had almost forgotten—that boxing is a wondrous and exacting science.

Ledoux, as he made his way to his dressing-room, one of his eyes terribly discoloured and big, said: 'I was losing all the time and yet I won. I was a baby, what you call a novice—Driscoll is great.'

We rose as one man to cheer Driscoll, and in the dining-room upstairs, in almost less time than it takes to record the fact, more than two thousand pounds had been given to establish a fund for the incomparable, peerless Jim.

Before he returned to France, Ledoux sent a five pound note to 'your marvellous Driscoll, who lost because he was forty years of age'. To the end of his days Ledoux will speak affectionately of Driscoll. Would that Jim could regain his youth! Such a man as he was in his prime not only lifts boxing out of a rut, but is a source of inspiration to every youngster who practises it. Is it not extraordinary that, when little short of forty and after having lived in retirement for a long time, when in fact we believed that he had given up entirely; he should come and dazzle us all by his un-exampled cleverness?

Driscoll did not agree to fight Ledoux without having weighed up all his chances. First, he studied the Frenchman from every point of view; he knew, as we all did, that Ledoux was an uncompromising fighter, that as cleverness went he was no wonder. When Driscoll, after having spent a long holiday at Harrogate, came to the club, he gave it out that he would at once go into training.

'I feel so good,' he declared, and those who were privileged to see him at work at Cardiff came away sure that the old champion had won back his first youth. It may not be common knowledge, but a day or two before the fight Driscoll strained his hand in tuning up a motor car; also he suffered from gastric ailment. Had he escaped these troubles, he might have been able to have lived twenty full rounds against Ledoux. But it is certain that whatever disabilities he suffered, he would have romped home had the contest been limited to fifteen rounds.

As a matter of fact, François Descamps, about as good a match maker as needs be, would not listen to Ledoux meeting Driscoll over anything but the championship distance. Said he 'Charles could never win by boxing, but he can win by his strength. For fifteen rounds Driscoll will be very good, very clever; he will then be winning, but after that, twenty-seven will beat forty. Eh, Mr Bettinson? If France had such a boxer as Driscoll, she would regard him as a national asset—she would have him teach her young men. If France had a Driscoll as her boxing master, she would become premier boxing nation of the world. Driscoll is the greatest living example of what a true boxer is.'

A. F. BETTINSON and B. BENNISON,
from *The Home of Boxing* (1922)

Peerless Jim Driscoll

I saw Jim Driscoll fight in nineteen ten.
That takes you back a bit. You don't see men
Like Driscoll any more. The breed's died out.
There's no one fit to lace his boots about.
All right son. Have your laugh. You know it all.
You think these mugs today that cuff and maul
Their way through ten or fifteen threes can fight:
They hardly know their left hand from their right.
But Jim, he knew; he never slapped or swung,
His left hand flickered like a cobra's tongue
And when he followed with the old one-two
Black lightning of those fists would dazzle you.
By Jesus he could hit. I've never seen
A sweeter puncher: every blow as clean
As silver. *Peerless Jim* the papers named him,
And yet he never swaggered, never bragged.
I saw him once when he got properly tagged—
A sucker punch from nowhere on the chin—
And he was hurt; but all he did was grin
And nod as if to say, 'I asked for that.'
No one was ever more worth looking at;
Up there beneath the ache of arc-lamps he
Was just like what we'd love our sons to be
Or like those gods you've heard about at school . . .
Well, yes, I'm old; and maybe I'm a fool.
I only saw him once outside the ring
And I admit I found it disappointing.
He looked just—I don't know—just ordinary,
And smaller, too, than what I thought he'd be:
An ordinary man in fact, like you or me.

VERNON SCANNELL (b. 1922)

Mastering the Craft

To make the big time you must learn
The basic moves: left jab and hook,
The fast one-two, right-cross; the block
And counter-punch; the way to turn
Opponents on the ropes; the feint
To head or body; uppercut;
To move inside the swing and set
Your man up for the kill. But don't
Think that this is all; a mere
Beginning only. It is through
Fighting often you will grow
Accomplished in manoeuvres more
Subtle than the text-books know:
How to change your style to meet
The unexpected move that might
Leave you open to the blow
That puts the lights out for the night.

The same with poets: they must train,
Practise metre's footwork, learn
The old iambic left and right,
To change the pace and how to hold
The big punch till the proper time,
Jab away with accurate rhyme;
Adapt the style or be knocked cold.
But first the groundwork must be done.
Those poets who have never learnt
The first moves of the game, they can't
Hope to win.
Yet here comes one,
No style at all, untrained and fat,
Who still contrives to knock you flat.

VERNON SCANNELL

Comeback

The wind is in a whipping mood tonight.
Whatever changes, these old noises don't.
My Grandad must have heard it much the same
And lain in bed and known that sleep had gone
To find a quieter place.

When I was twelve,
And that's a good half century ago,
I used to lie awake, not that the wind
Could scare sleep from my bed, but something could:
A sharp electric charge of restlessness
Would needle and excite for hours on end,
And, in imagination, I would touch
Each object of my shadow treasury—
An odd collection for a kid to love—
Not foreign stamps or hollow eggs in beds
Of cotton-wool, not model aeroplanes
Or rolling-stock, nor hoarded coins or cards,
But articles of apparatus, kit
And clothing of a special usefulness,
The paraphernalia of the fighter's craft.
It seems unlikely now that all that gear,
Which came to be the tackle and the tools
Of my life's trade, could thrill me in those days
As later only women's secrets could.
Yet that's the way it was, and even now
I catch a tiny tremor of the old
Excitement on the sagging wires of nerve
Recalling how I'd lay the objects out—
The black kid boots, white ankle-socks, the gloves
Like giant kidneys, skipping-rope and towel,
The glittering robe embroidered on the back
With my brave name; black satin trunks
With yellow stripes and wide band at the waist;
And no less sacred, no less magical,
The grim and necessary armour of
Gum-shield, jockstrap and protective cup.
Not that I really owned these things. Not then.
The only kit I had for training nights
Was my old sand-shoes, cotton football shorts
And winter vest. But one day I would wear
The finest stuff. I knew I'd make the big time,
And I did.

Listen to that wind.
It's strange how all its anger comforts you,
Maybe because it means I'm not alone;
We share the long hours of the night, the two
Of us, the old and tireless wind and me.
Does the wind have memories to shuffle through?
If so, they can't be very cheerful ones,
Judging by that sound.

Oh, yes, I knew
I'd get to be a champion one day,
Though that was not the most important thing.
Important, yes, but what meant more to me
Was making myself good enough to wear
The garb the great ones wore. And even more
Important was the pleasure in the game,
Though 'pleasure' seems too weak a word for that
Drench of power that filled you when you fought
And overcame with cunning, speed and skill
A tough opponent. Many times I've made
A perfect move, smooth as satin, quick as a cat,
The muscles thinking faster than a wink,
A double feint and counter, something you
Could never in a thousand lessons teach
An ordinary fighter to perform:
A miracle, a gift. Those moments make
Your life worthwhile.

The other stuff was muck:
I mean the silver trophies, medals, praise;
And later, fighting pro, the fancy belts,
The pictures on the sports page, interviews,
The youngsters scrambling for your scribbled name,
Even the big-time purses and the girls,
The bitches who would suck the virtue from you,
Press near your fame until the glitter dimmed,
They'd smear you with their artificial honey
And leave you spoiled and shamed.

I think it's strange
That when you've reached the top and won the crown
And every childish fantasy is fact,
It's strange how disappointing it all seems.
Success and fame, I've had the two and found
That both were fragile as those eggshell globes
They hang on Christmas trees. I used to think
The boys who'd never made the top, the ones
Who fought for peanuts in the shabby halls
And lost more often than they won, I thought
Them pitiable. Not now. They never knew
The failure of success, and they were real
Members of our craft, good workmen, proud
To wear the badges of the trade, a breed
That, if it dies, would surely mean the end
Of what I still believe the greatest game.

I won my first
Big title at the Albert Hall.
I fought a good old-timer from the North,
Birkenhead I think it was. He knew
The moves, was cagey as a monkey-house,
But he was past his best and in the seventh
I felt him weaken; as his strength seeped out
I seemed to suck it in like Dracula.
I put him down three times and in the ninth
He took a fast right-cross and folded up.
I knew he wouldn't rise. I did my dance
Above his fallen body, and the crowd
Bellowed their brainless worship of my feat.
I never thought that night my turn would come,
That eight years later in the selfsame ring
My nose would squash against the dust and resin
As I lay flat, I'd hear the same applause
But for the other man, new champion,
A youngster, strong, ambitious, arrogant.
By that time I had fought in Canada,
Twice at the Garden in New York, Berlin,
Milan and Paris, Rome, the Blackfriars Ring
And Stadium Club and places I've forgot.
I'd made and spent a fortune for those days,
And now they wrote me off. Another fool
Who once had been a fighter, now a ghost,
A fading name in yellowing papers, soon
Remembered only by a very few
And even they would get the details wrong
And, after too much booze, remember fights
I'd never had.

The wind is dying down
But still it makes its music, now less wild
But melancholy. It seems to sense my mood.
I doubt if I shall sleep tonight at all.
To tell the truth I have a taste for that
Sad sound of wind with darkness in its throat;
I like it when it snatches rain like seeds,
Throws handfuls at the window. But tonight
Is dry. No rain. No sleep. Only the wind
And memories.

After that defeat
I drank too much, I played the horses, too,
And lost the little capital I'd saved.

I was not old—a little over thirty—
Young enough in years, but I had fought
Two hundred contests as a pro, was tired.
But there was nothing else to do but fight.
It was my trade, the only one I knew.
And so I made my comeback, cut out booze,
Began to train with rope and heavy bag,
Run in the misty mornings through the park
And spar in the gym at night. I got a fight
In Leeds and put my man away in three.
I went back to the Club and showed them there
I still knew more about my business than
Those youngsters with their blasting energy
But little sense of what to do with it:
They sprayed their shots all round the field of fire;
I hoarded ammunition, only pressed
The trigger when I knew my shots would tell.
Once more my name appeared in fresh black ink,
My picture on a million breakfast tables.
They matched me for the title once again.
The fight was held in summer, out of doors,
White City was the place. The night was fine
And thousands came to see the veteran
Hand out a lesson to the cheeky boy
Who called himself the Champion. I knew
I'd win the title back. I'd seen him fight:
He was young and strong, with fair ability,
But I was master of a hundred tricks
He'd never heard about. I might be old
But I was also wise.

The fight began
At nine o'clock at night as dark came down.
The arc-lamps gushed white brilliance on the ring.
Beyond the ropes, the crowd, a factory
Of noise and appetites, was idling now
Though very soon I knew the huge machine
Would roar to tumult, hammer out acclaim,
And I would be the target of that praise.
The comeback would succeed, though history
Was littered with the names of those who'd failed.
I would not fail.

The first round proved to me
That my opponent was no better than
A score of fighters I had met before

And beaten easily. I jabbed and moved,
Slipping his leads and hurting him inside.
I took my time, collected points and foiled
His two attempts to trap me on the ropes.
The round was mine.

The second round began
With brisker action from us both; he swung
A left and followed with an uppercut
Slung hard towards my heart. I moved away,
Stepped in and jabbed and jolted back his head;
I saw my chance and threw a big right hand.
I felt the jar to elbow as my fist
Connected with his jaw. He should have gone.
Most would. He staggered back but did not fall.
The engines of applause were roaring wild.
He faded back. I knew I had him then.
I took my time, I was too old a hand
To crowd in, throwing leather at his head.
I stalked him to the ropes and measured him:
A feint downstairs, a jab—I saw his chin
And threw again the punch to douse the lights—
I never knew what happened. Something burst
Inside my head; my skull was opened up
And starless midnight flooded into it.
I'll never know what happened on that night,
Why my right fist did not connect and end
The fight with me as Champion. They said
He beat me to the punch. Maybe. It seemed
A thunderbolt had fallen from the skies,
A biblical defeat, the fall of Pride.
One thing was sure: I had not won the bout
Nor would I ever have another chance.
I'd never be a champion again.

I said that I'd retire,
Hang up the gloves for good, but very soon
I went into the ring, though now I knew
That I would never make the top again.
I fought in little halls and local baths,
Making a pound or two but taking some
Beatings from boys who five years earlier
Could not have laced my shoes. Sometimes I'd dream
That I would even yet surprise them all,
Come back and dazzle them with my old skill.

I nursed the dream till not so long ago
And then I gave myself a shake and said,
'Stop acting like a kid. You're grown up now.'
I got a job as trainer at a club
In Bermondsey. It's fine. I like it there.
I taught those boys some things they'd never learn
From amateurs. I still work there. It's good.
I like to see them in the ring. I like
The smell of rubbing oils, to hear the swish
And slap of skipping-rope, the thud of fist
On bag. I like it all. I don't complain.
I'm quite a lucky man.

The windows pale.
The wind itself seems tired now. I lie
Stretched out, but not to take the final count;
I have a round or two left in me yet.
My body is my own biography:
The scars, old fractures, ribs and nose, thick ear;
That's what I am, a score of ancient wounds
And in my head a few remembered scenes
And even those I'm not too sure about—
I've heard them say my brains are scrambled now—
I'm not too sure. Not sure of anything
Except I'm proud of what I've been—although
I would have liked another chance—sure, too,
I'll never make another comeback now
Unless the dead can make it, as some say.

VERNON SCANNELL

A Hungry Fighter

It is well known that I am a prize fighter by profession
. . . I am now writing a New Canto of Don Juan . . .
John Clare to Eliza Phillips (1841)

The headguard's padded pith
protects my father's face.
Juice erupts in tiny sacs
like smallpox through the vaseline.

He steams in the morning cold,
trailing clouds of glory
through the hard acoustic gym,
that spring of 1932.

High-handed, hinges of hair
in his streaming armpits,
he drubs this leather fig—
attentive to its anapaests

until the one includes the many.
A single giant salami
forms part of his diet;
the twelve-ounce gloves

are raw sienna curves
like parrot tongues,
bluntly repeating
again and again

a phrase book of grunts.
His mind translates
the tick of skipping ropes
until the big time fills his head.

He hears a Pentecostal wind.
Scales flinch under his feet:
this featherweight of whiteness
is all he has for sale.

After the southpaw Johnny Magorie,
a title fight with Micky McGuire:
they duck into the ring,
black bottom briefly

in the fuming trays of rosin,
then bumps-a-daisy, glove
on glove. The referee
patrols the bandaged ropes,

dapper in his black bow tie.
A cut begins to irrigate
above the champion's eye.
My father slips a lead

and flicks the cut,
his fluent fists
clenched question marks
to which there is no answer.

McGuire takes a count of six
then, breaking from a clinch,
he crosses with a right
that finds the throat.

Helpless as a naked girl,
my father covers up
then crawls like a baby
baring his gumshield.

His second threw the towel in—
a thick Turkish towel
like fleecy tripe,
left behind in the Albert Hall.

The gym is rubble now,
a bathos of bricks
by the railway line,
Russian salad out in the rain.

I will inherit his vest,
its English rose, one petal
darned, his boxing licence
with the rusty staples,

the silver-plated cup
presented by von Ribbentrop
which stands on the sideboard,
confidently arms akimbo

but worn away by Duraglit.
Touching their terror,
I gaze at them now,
longer than someone in love.

CRAIG RAINE (b. 1944)

VI

The Football War

Carved on a tombstone

Who ever hear on Sonday
Will practis playing at Ball
It may be before Monday
The Devil will Have you all.

ANONYMOUS. At Llanfair Church, Caerwent

'Games in Season'

Eche time and season hath his delite and joyes,
Loke in the stretes, beholde the little boyes;
Howe in fruite season for joy they sing and hop,
In Lent is eche one full busy with his top,
And nowe in winter, for all the greevous colde,
All rent and ragged, a man may them beholde;
They have great pleasour supposing well to dine;
When men be busied in killing of fat swine,
They get the bladder and blowe it great and thin,
With many beanes or peason put within;
It ratleth, soundeth, and shineth clere and fayre,
While it is throwen and caste up in the ayre;
Eche one contendeth and hath a great delite,
With foote and with hande the bladder for to smite;
If it fall to grounde, they lifte it up agayne;
This wise to labour, they count it for no payne;
Renning and leaping, they drive away the colde.
The sturdie plowmen lustie, strong and bolde,
Overcommeth the winter with driving the footeball,
Forgetting labour and many a grevous fall.

ALEXANDER BARCLAY (*c.* 1476–1552), from *Eglogue V*

Hugh of Lincoln

Four and twenty bonny boys
  Were playing at the ba,
And by it came him sweet Sir Hugh,
  And he played oer them a'.

He kicked the ba with his right foot,
  And catchd it wi his knee,
And throuch-and-thro the Jew's window
  He gard the bonny ba flee.

He's doen him to the Jew's castell,
  And walkd it round about;
And there he saw the Jew's daughter,
  At the window looking out.

'Throw down the ba, ye Jew's daughter,
  Throw down the ba to me!'
'Never a bit,' says the Jew's daughter,
  ''Till up to me come ye.'

'How will I come up? How can I come up?
  How can I come to thee?
For as ye did to my auld father,
  The same ye'll do to me.'

She's gane till her father's garden,
  And pu'd an apple red and green;
'Twas a' to wyle him sweet Sir Hugh,
  And to entice him in.

She's led him in through ae dark door,
  And sae has she thro nine;
She's laid him on a dressing-table,
  And stickit him like a swine.

And first came out the thick, thick blood,
  And syne came out the thin,
And syne came out the bonny heart's blood;
  There was nae mair within.

ANONYMOUS (?14th century)

'A Comparison'

Am I so round with you as you with me
That like a football you do spurn me thus?
You spurn me hence, and he will spurn me hither:
If I last in this service, you must case me in leather.

WILLIAM SHAKESPEARE, *The Comedy of Errors*

Friendlie Kinde of Fyghte

Lord, remove these exercises from the Sabaoth. Any exercise which withdraweth from godliness, either upon the Sabaoth or any other day, is wicked and to be forbiden. Now who is so grosly blinde that seeth not that these aforesaid exercises not only withdraw us from godlinesse and virtue, but also haile and allure us to wickednesse and sin? for as concerning football playing I protest unto you that it may rather be called a *friendlie kinde of fyghte* than a play or recreation—a bloody and murthering practice than a felowly sport or pastime. For dooth not everyone lye in waight for his adversarie, seeking to overthrow him and picke him on his nose, though it be on hard stones, on ditch or dale, on valley or hill, or whatever place soever it be he careth not, so he have him downe; and he that can serve the most of this fashion he is counted the only felow, and who but he?

So that by this means sometimes their necks are broken, sometimes their backs, sometimes their legs, sometimes their armes, sometimes their noses gush out with blood, sometimes their eyes start out, and sometimes hurte in one place, sometimes in another. But whosoever scapeth away the best goeth not scot free, but is either forewounded, craised, or bruised, so as he dyeth of it or else scapeth very hardlie; and no mervaile, for they have the sleights to meet one betwixt two, to dash him against the hart with their elbowes, to butt him under the short ribs with their griped fists, and with their knees to catch him on the hip and pick him on his neck, with a hundred such murthering devices.

And hereof groweth envy, rancour, and malice, and sometimes brawling, murther, homicide, and great effusion of blood, as experience daily teacheth. Is this murthering play now an exercise for the Sabaoth day?

PHILIP STUBBES (*fl.* 1583), *Anatomy of Abuses in the Realme of England*

'The Dangers of Foot-ball'

Where Covent-Garden's famous temple stands,
That boasts the work of Jones' immortal hands;
Columns with plain magnificence appear,
And graceful porches lead along the square:
Here oft' my course I bend, when lo! from far
I spy the furies of the foot-ball war:
The 'prentice quits his shop, to join the crew,
Encreasing crouds the flying game pursue.
Thus, as you roll the ball o'er snowy ground,
The gath'ring globe augments with ev'ry round.
But whither shall I run? the throng draws nigh,
The ball now skims the street, now soars on high;
The dext'rous glazier strong returns the bound,
And gingling sashes on the pent-house sound.

JOHN GAY, from *Trivia, or the Art of Walking the Streets of London*

'The School-house Match'

Three-quarters of an hour are gone; first winds are failing, and weight and numbers beginning to tell. Yard by yard the School-house have been driven back, contesting every inch of ground. The bull-dogs are the colour of mother earth from shoulder to ankle, except young Brooke who has a marvellous knack of keeping his legs. The School-house are being penned in their turn, and now the ball is behind their goal, under the Doctor's wall. The Doctor and some of his family are there looking on, and seem as anxious as any boy for the success of the School-house. We get a minute's breathing time before old Brooke kicks out, and he gives the word to play strongly for touch, by the three trees. Away goes the ball, and the bull-dogs after it, and in another minute there is shout of 'In touch!' 'Our ball!' Now's your time, old Brooke, while your men are still fresh. He stands with the ball in his hand, while the two sides form in deep lines opposite one another: he must strike it straight out between them. The lines are thickest close to him, but young Brooke and two or three of his men are shifting up further, where the opposite line is weak. Old Brooke strikes it out straight and strong, and it falls opposite his brother. Hurrah! that rush has taken it through the School line, and away past the three trees, far into their quarters, and young Brooke and the bull-dogs are close upon it. The School leaders rush back, shouting 'Look out in goal,' and strain every nerve to catch him, but they are after the fleetest foot in Rugby. There they go straight for the School goal-posts, quarters scattering before them. One after another the bull-dogs go down, but young Brooke holds on. 'He is down.' No! a long stagger, but the danger is past; that was the shock of Crew, the most dangerous of dodgers. And now he is close to the School goal, the ball not three yards before him. There is a hurried rush of the School fags to the spot, but no one throws himself on the ball, the only chance, and young Brooke has touched it right under the School goal posts.

The School leaders come up furious, and administer toco to the wretched fags nearest at hand; they may well be angry, for it is all Lombard-street to a china orange that the School-house kick a goal with the ball touched in such a good place. Old Brooke of course will kick it out, but who shall catch and place it? Call Crab Jones. Here he comes, sauntering along with a straw in his mouth, the queerest, coolest fish in Rugby: if he were tumbled into the moon this minute, he would just pick himself up without taking his hands out of his pockets or turning a hair. But it is a moment when the boldest charger's heart beats quick. Old Brooke stands with the ball under his arm motioning the School back; he will not kick-out till they are all in goal, behind the posts; they are all edging forwards, inch by inch, to get nearer for the rush at Crab Jones, who stands there in front of old Brooke to catch the ball. If they can reach and destroy him before he catches, the danger is over; and with one and the same rush they will carry it right away to the School-house goal. Fond hope! it is kicked out and caught beautifully. Crab strikes his heel into the ground, to mark the spot where the ball was caught, beyond which the School line may not advance; but there they stand, five deep, ready to rush the moment the ball touches the ground. Take plenty of room! don't give the rush a chance of reaching you! place it true and steady! Trust Crab Jones—he has made a small hole with his heel for the ball to lie on, by which he is resting on one knee, with his eye on old Brooke. 'Now!' Crab places the ball at the word, old Brooke kicks, and it rises slowly and truly as the School rush forward.

Then a moment's pause, while both sides look up at the spinning ball. There it flies, straight between the two posts, some five feet above the cross-bar, an unquestioned goal; and a shout of real genuine joy rings out from the School-house players-up, and a faint echo of it comes over the close from the goal-keepers under the Doctor's wall. A goal in the first hour—such a thing hadn't been done in the School-house match these five years.

'Over!' is the cry: the two sides change goals, and the School-house goal-keepers come threading their way across through the masses of the School; the most openly triumphant of them, amongst whom is Tom, a School-house boy of two hours' standing, getting their ears boxed in the transit. Tom indeed is excited beyond measure, and it is all the sixth form boy, kindest and safest of goal-keepers, has been able to do to keep him from rushing out whenever the ball has been near their goal. So he holds him by his side, and instructs him in the science of touching.

At this moment Griffith, the itinerant vendor of oranges from Hill Morton, enters the close with his heavy baskets; there is a rush of small boys upon the little pale-faced man, the two sides mingling together, subdued by the great Goddess Thirst, like the English and French by the streams of the Pyrenees. The leaders are past oranges and apples, but some of them visit their coats, and apply innocent-looking ginger-beer bottles to their mouths. It is no ginger-beer though, I fear, and will do you no good. One short mad rush, and then a stitch in the side, and no more honest play; that's what comes of those bottles.

But now Griffith's baskets are empty, the ball is placed again midway, and the School are going to kick off. Their leaders have sent their lumber into goal, and rated the rest soundly, and one hundred and twenty picked players-up are there, bent on retrieving the game. They are to keep the ball in front of the School-house goal, and then to drive it in by sheer strength and weight. They mean heavy play and no mistake, and so old Brooke sees; and places Crab Jones in quarters just before the goal, with four or five picked players, who are to keep the ball away to the sides, where a try at goal, if obtained, will be less dangerous than in front. He himself, and Warner and Hedge, who have saved themselves till now, will lead the charges.

'Are you ready?' 'Yes.' And away comes the ball kicked high in the air, to give the School time to rush on and catch it as it falls. And here they are amongst us. Meet them like Englishmen, you School-house boys, and charge them home. Now is the time to show what mettle is in you—and there shall be a warm seat by the hall fire, and honour, and lots of bottled beer to-night, for him who does his duty in the next half-hour. And they are all well met. Again and again the cloud of their players-up gathers before our goal, and comes threatening on, and Warner or Hedge, with young Brooke and the relics of the bull-dogs, break through and carry the ball back; and old Brooke ranges the field like Job's war-horse: the thickest scrummage parts asunder before his rush, like the waves before a clipper's bows; his cheery voice rings over the field, and his eye is everywhere. And if these miss the ball, and it rolls dangerously in front of our goal, Crab Jones and his men have seized it and sent it away towards the sides with the unerring drop-kick. This is worth living for; the whole sum of school-boy existence gathered up into one straining, struggling half-hour worth a year of common life.

The quarter to five has struck, and the play slackens for a minute before goal; but there is Crew, the artful dodger, driving the ball in behind our goal, on the island side, where our quarters are weakest. Is there no one to meet him? Yes! look at little East! the ball is just at equal distances between the two, and they rush together, the young man of seventeen and the boy of twelve, and kick it at the same moment. Crew passes on without a stagger; East is hurled forward by the shock, and plunges on his shoulder, as if he would bury himself in the ground; but the ball rises straight into the air, and falls behind Crew's back, while the 'bravos' of the School-house attest the pluckiest charge of all that hard-fought day. Warner picks East up lame and half stunned, and he hobbles back into goal, conscious of having played the man.

And now the last minutes are come, and the School gather for their last rush, every boy of the hundred and twenty who has a run left in him. Reckless of the defence of their own goal, on they come across the level big-side ground, the ball well down amongst them, straight for our goal, like the column of the Old Guard up the slope at Waterloo. All former charges have been child's play to this. Warner and Hedge have met them, but still on they come. The bull-dogs rush in for the last time; they are hurled over or carried back, striving hand, foot, and eyelids. Old Brooke comes sweeping round the skirts of the play, and turning short round picks out the very heart of the scrummage, and plunges in. It wavers for a moment—he has the ball! No, it has passed him, and his voice rings out clear over the advancing tide, 'Look out in goal.' Crab Jones catches it for a moment; but before he can kick, the rush is upon him and passes over him; and he picks himself up behind them with his straw in his mouth, a little dirtier, but as cool as ever.

The ball rolls slowly in behind the School-house goal not three yards in front of a dozen of the biggest School players-up.

There stands the School house præpostor, safest of goal-keepers, and Tom Brown by his side, who has learned his trade by this time. Now is your time, Tom. The blood of all the Browns is up, and the two rush in together, and throw themselves on the ball, under the very feet of the advancing column; the præpostor on his hands and knees arching his back, and Tom all along on his face. Over them topple the leaders of the rush, shooting over the back of the præpostor; but falling flat on Tom, and knocking all the wind out of his small carcase.

'Our ball,' says the præpostor, rising with his prize; 'but get up there, there's a little fellow under you.' They are hauled and roll off him, and Tom is discovered a motionless body.

Old Brooke picks him up. 'Stand back, give him air,' he says; and then feeling his limbs, adds, 'No bones broken. How do you feel, young un?'

'Hah-hah,' gasps Tom as his wind comes back, 'pretty well, thank you—all right.'

'Who is he?' says Brooke.

'Oh, it's Brown, he's a new boy; I know him,' says East, coming up.

'Well, he is a plucky youngster, and will make a player,' says Brooke.

And five o'clock strikes. 'No side' is called, and the first day of the School-house match is over.

THOMAS HUGHES (1822–96), *Tom Brown's Schooldays*

4 February 1873

John Hatherell said that old Langley Common was once a great play place on Sunday, and on Sunday afternoons football and hockey and other games went on all over the common. The Revd. Samuel Ashe, then Rector of Langley Burrell, used to come round quietly under the trees and bide his time till the football came near him when he would catch up the ball and pierce the bladder with a pin. But some of the young fellows would be even with the parson for they would bring a spare bladder, blow it, and soon have the football flying again.

FRANCIS KILVERT, *Diary*

Sonnet: A Footballer

If I could paint you, friend, as you stand there,
Guard of the goal, defensive, open-eyed,
Watching the tortured bladder slide and glide
Under the twinkling feet; arms bare, head bare,
The breeze a-tremble through crow-tufts of hair;
Red-brown in face, and ruddier having spied
A wily foeman breaking from the side,
Aware of him,—of all else unaware:
If I could limn you, as you leap and fling
Your weight against his passage, like a wall;
Clutch him and collar him, and rudely cling
For one brief moment till he falls—you fall:
My sketch would have what Art can never give,
Sinew and breath and body; it would live.

EDWARD CRACROFT LEFROY (1855–91)

On Early Football in Wales

In South Cardiganshire it seems that about eighty years ago the population, rich and poor, male and female, of opposing parishes, turned out on Christmas Day and indulged in the game of football with such vigour that it became little short of a serious fight. The parishioners of Celland and Pencarreg were particularly bitter in their conflicts; men threw off their coats and waistcoats, and women their gowns, and sometimes their petticoats. At Llanwennog, an extensive parish below Lampeter, the inhabitants for football purposes were divided into the Bros and Blaenaus. My informant, a man over eighty, now an inmate of Lampeter Workhouse, gives the following particulars: In North Wales the Ball was called the Bel Troed, and was made with a bladder covered with a Cwd Tarw. In South Wales it was called the Bel Ddu, and was usually made by the shoemaker of the parish, who appeared on the ground on Christmas Day with the ball under his arm, and, said my informant, he took good care not to give it up until he got his money for making it. The Bros, it should be stated, occupied the high ground of the parish. They were nick-named 'Paddy-Bros' from a tradition that they were descendants from Irish people who settled on the hills in days long gone by. The Blaenaus occupied the lowlands, and, it may be presumed, were pure-bred Brythons. The more devout of the Bros and Blaenaus joined in the service in the parish church on Christmas morning. At any rate, the match did not begin until about midday, when the service was finished. Then the whole of the Bros and Blaenaus, rich and poor, male and female, assembled on the turnpike road which divided the highland from the lowlands. The ball having been redeemed from the crydd, it was thrown high in the air by a strong man, and when it fell Bros and Blaenaus scrambled for its possession, and a quarter of an hour frequently elapsed before the ball was got out from the struggling heap of human beings. Then if the Bros, by hook or by crook, could succeed in taking the ball up the mountain to their hamlet of Rhyddlan they won the day; while the Blaenaus were successful if they got the ball to their end of the parish at New Court. The whole parish was the field of operations, and sometimes it would be dark before either party scored a victory. In the meantime many kicks would be given and taken, so that on the following day some of the competitors would be unable to walk, and sometimes a kick on the shins would lead to the two men concerned to abandon the game until they had decided which was the better pugilist. There do not appear to have been any rules for the regulation of the game; and the art of football playing in the olden time seems to have been to reach the goal. When once the goal was reached, the victory was celebrated by loud hurrahs and the firing of guns, and was not disturbed until the following Christmas Day. Victory on Christmas Day, added the old man, was so highly esteemed by the whole country-side that a Bro or a Blaenau would as soon lose a cow from his cowhouse, as the football from his portion of the parish.

Oswestry Observer, 2 March 1887

Association Football in the 19th Century

A man attending the first F.A. Cup Final on the Oval cricket ground in London in March 1872 between the Wanderers and the Royal Engineers would probably have been a gentleman. Certainly the twenty-two players and the officials were. He would have seen a field with flags marking the boundaries and a tape eight feet above the ground stretching between two flimsy looking goalposts twenty-four feet apart. There were no other markings on the pitch. Most of the players probably wore long trousers and fancy caps in addition to their team shirts and rather formidable looking boots. The game probably started late.

As to the play itself, dribbling with the ball by individuals past opponents was its central feature. Individual players hung on to the ball as long as they could and other members of their team backed them up in the hope of gaining possession when the man on the ball lost it. 'Rushes' down the field by one side or the other probably provided some of the game's more exciting moments. Passing, or combination, was not yet in vogue although by the following year the Royal Engineers were noted for it. They did not use the new method in this game, however, or if they did, it did not help them much because they lost 1–0. Most players were attackers and both sides played with a goalkeeper, two backs, one half-back and seven forwards. The long kicking of the backs, selected for their strength and solidity rather than their ball skill or speed, would also have been prominent, as would the heavy shoulder charging by all players. There was little heading. The goalkeepers, when called upon, did a lot of punching out and kicking rather than catching. The main reason for that was that they could be charged over even when not in possession of the ball. Indeed an unsubtle but fiendishly effective tactic was for one attacker to charge the goalkeeper to the ground while another tried to steer the ball between the posts. Many goals were scored from 'scrimmages' following such incidents or from individual efforts like the one which resulted in Lord Kinnaird scoring for the Wanderers in their 2–1 Cup Final victory over Oxford University in 1873. *Bell's Life* described how

> Kinnaird got the ball to himself at the lower side of the play and brought it toward the Oxford goal in such splendid style that, despite the strenuous exertions of some of the fastest of the Oxonians to overhaul him, he eluded their efforts and the goalkeeper's (who should have charged him instead of remaining at home) also.

When the ball went out of play on either side of the pitch it was thrown in one-handed and at right angles to the playing area, by whichever player from either side reached it first. Free kicks for handling the ball or for foul play were very few as were appeals by the players to the two umpires and referee although that was the accepted method of drawing the attention of those officials to a particular incident. The spectacle was vigorous and robust in the main although some of the dribblers were very good.

TONY MASON, *Association Football and English Society 1863–1915*

From *A Shropshire Lad*

Twice a week the winter thorough
  Here stood I to keep the goal:
Football then was fighting sorrow
  For the young man's soul.

Now in Maytime to the wicket
  Out I march with bat and pad:
See the son of grief at cricket
  Trying to be glad.

Try I will; no harm in trying:
  Wonder 'tis how little mirth
Keeps the bones of man from lying
  On the bed of earth.

A. E. HOUSMAN (1859–1936)

'New Blood'

No one showed a desire to invest in second debentures of the Bursley F.C. Ltd.

Still, speakers kept harping on the necessity of new blood in the team, and then others, bolder, harped on the necessity of new blood on the board.

'Shares on sale!' cried the Councillor. 'Any buyers? Or,' he added, 'do you want something for nothing—as usual?'

At length a gentleman rose at the back of the hall.

'I don't pretend to be an expert on football,' said he, 'though I think it's a great game, but I should like to say a few words as to this question of new blood.'

The audience craned its neck.

'Will Mr Councillor Machin kindly step up to the platform?' the Mayor suggested.

And up Denry stepped.

The thought in every mind was: 'What's he going to do? What's he got up his sleeve—this time?'

'Three cheers for Machin!' people chanted gaily.

'Order!' said the Mayor.

Denry faced the audience. He was now accustomed to audiences. He said:

'If I'm not mistaken, one of the greatest modern footballers is a native of this town.'

And scores of voices yelled, 'Ay! Callear! Callear! Greatest centre forward in England!'

'Yes,' said Denry. 'Callear is the man I mean. Callear left the district, unfortunately for the district, at the age of nineteen for Liverpool. And it was not till after he left that his astonishing abilities were perceived. It isn't too much to say that he made the fortune of Liverpool City. And I believe it is the fact that he scored more goals in three seasons than any other player has done in the League. Then, York County, which was in a tight place last year, bought him from Liverpool for a high price, and, as all the world knows, Callear had his leg broken in the first match he played for his new club. That just happened to be the ruin of the York Club, which is now quite suddenly in bankruptcy (which happily we are not), and which is disposing of its players. Gentlemen, I say that Callear ought to come back to his native town. He is fitter than ever he was, and his proper place is in his native town.'

Loud cheers.

'As captain and centre forward of the club of the mother of the Five Towns, he would be an immense acquisition and attraction, and he would lead us to victory.'

Renewed cheers.

'And how,' demanded Councillor Barlow, jumping up angrily, 'are we to get him back to his precious native town? Councillor Machin admits that he is not an expert on football. It will probably be news to him that Aston Villa have offered £700 to York for the transfer of Callear, and Blackburn Rovers have offered £750, and they're fighting it out between 'em. Any gentleman willing to put down £800 to buy Callear for Bursley?' he sneered. 'I don't mind telling you that steam-engines and the King himself couldn't get Callear into our club.'

'Quite finished?' Denry inquired, still standing.

Laughter, overtopped by Councillor Barlow's snort as he sat down.

Denry lifted his voice.

'Mr Callear, will you be good enough to step forward and let us all have a look at you?'

The effect of these apparently simple words surpassed any effect previously obtained by the most complex flights of oratory in that hall. A young, blushing, clumsy, long-limbed, small-bodied giant stumbled along the central aisle and climbed the steps to the platform, where Denry pointed him to a seat. He was recognized by all the true votaries of the game. And everybody said to everybody: 'By Gosh! It's him, right enough. It's Callear!' And a vast astonishment and expectation of good fortune filled the hall. Applause burst forth, and though no one knew what the appearance of Callear signified, the applause continued and waxed.

'Good old Callear!' the hoarse shouts succeeded each other. 'Good old Machin!'

'Anyhow,' said Denry, when the storm was stilled, 'we've got him here, without either steam-engines or His Majesty. Will the directors of the club accept him?'

'And what about the transfer?' Councillor Barlow demanded.

'Would you accept him and try another season if you could get him free?' Denry retorted.

Councillor Barlow always knew his mind, and was never afraid to let other people share that knowledge.

'Yes,' he said.

'Then I will see that you have the transfer free.'

'But what about York?'

'I have settled with York provisionally,' said Denry. 'That is my affair. I have returned from York today. Leave all that to me. This town has had many benefactors far more important than myself. But I shall be able to claim this originality: I'm the first to make a present of a live man to the town. Gentlemen—Mr Mayor—I venture to call for three cheers for the greatest centre forward in England, our fellow-townsman.'

The scene, as the *Signal* said, was unique.

And at the Sports Club and the other clubs afterwards, men said to each other: 'No one but him would have thought of bringing Callear over specially and showing him on the platform. . . . That's cost him above twopence, that has!'

Two days later a letter appeared in the *Signal* (signed 'Fiat Justitia'), suggesting that Denry, as some reward for his public spirit, ought to be the next mayor of Bursley, in place of Alderman Bloor deceased. The letter urged that he would make an admirable mayor, the sort of mayor the old town wanted in order to wake it up. And also it pointed out that Denry would be the youngest mayor that Bursley had ever had, and probably the youngest mayor in England that year. The sentiment in the last idea appealed to the town. The town decided that it would positively *like* to have the youngest mayor it had ever had, and probably the youngest mayor in England that year. The *Signal* printed dozens of letters on the subject. When the Council met, more informally than formally, to choose a chief magistrate in place of the dead alderman, several councillors urged that what Bursley wanted was a young and *popular* mayor. And, in fine, Councillor Barlow was shelved for a year. On the choice being published the entire town said: 'Now we *shall* have a mayoralty—and don't you forget it!'

And Denry said to Nellie: 'You'll be mayoress to the youngest mayor, etc., my child. And it's cost me, including hotel and travelling expenses, eight hundred and eleven pounds six and sevenpence.'

The rightness of the Council in selecting Denry as mayor was confirmed in a singular manner by the behaviour of the football and of Callear at the opening match of the season.

It was a philanthropic match, between Bursley and Axe, for the benefit of a county orphanage, and, according to the custom of such matches, the ball was formally kicked off by a celebrity, a pillar of society. The ceremony of kicking off has no sporting significance; the celebrity merely with gentleness propels the ball out of the white circle and then flies for his life from the *mêlée*; but it is supposed to add to the moral splendour of the game. In the present instance the posters said: 'Kick-off at 3-45 by Councillor E. H. Machin, Mayor-designate'. And, indeed, no other celebrity could have been decently selected. On the fine afternoon of the match Denry therefore discovered himself with a new football at his toes, a silk hat on his head, and twenty-two Herculean players menacing him in attitudes expressive of an intention to murder him. Bursley had lost the toss, and hence Denry had to kick towards the Bursley goal. As the *Signal* said, he 'despatched the sphere' straight into the keeping of Callear, who as centre forward was facing him, and Callear was dodging down the field with it before the Axe players had finished admiring Denry's effrontery. Every reader will remember with a thrill the historic match in which the immortal Jimmy Brown, on the last occasion when he captained Blackburn Rovers, dribbled the ball himself down the length of the field, scored a goal, and went home with the English Cup under his arm. Callear evidently intended to imitate the feat. He was entirely wrong. Dribbling tactics had been killed forever, years before, by Preston North End, who invented the 'passing' game. Yet Callear went on, and good luck seemed to float over him like a cherub. Finally he shot; a wild, high shot; but there was an adverse wind which dragged the ball down, swept it round, and blew it into the net. The first goal had been scored in twenty seconds! (It was also the last in the match.) Callear's reputation was established. Useless for solemn experts to point out that he had simply been larking for the gallery, and that the result was a shocking fluke—Callear's reputation was established. He became at once the idol of the populace. As Denry walked gingerly off the field to the grandstand, he, too, was loudly cheered, and he could not help feeling that, somehow, it was he who had scored that goal. And although nobody uttered the precise thought, most people did secretly think, as they gazed at the triumphant Denry, that a man who triumphed like that, because he triumphed like that, was the right sort of man to be mayor, the kind of man they needed.

ARNOLD BENNETT (1867–1931), *The Card*

'An Unwelcome Game'

There was, in those days, a private school at Westgate kept by a burly, red-faced clergyman called Mr Bull, with whom my father had some slight acquaintance. The sight of Mr Bull's boys playing football on the other side of some iron railings put into my father's head the bright idea which cost me so much. Without consulting me, he called upon Mr Bull, reminded him of a meeting many years ago at Cambridge or Schwalbach or wherever else, and asked him whether his lonely Eton boy might join Mr Bull's boys for a game of football. Mr Bull said he might; let the boy report to the Games Master on the football field the following afternoon.

My father returned to our lodging in high feather, and told me the good news. I was horrified. I had never played football in my life, nor even kicked a football since childhood days. I, too, had looked through those iron railings, and watched the intricate manœuvring, the curious waiting about combined with sudden darts and gyrations of soccer-players, and saw at a glance that it would be impossible for me, wholly uninstructed, to walk on to that field and 'play football'. I protested, pleading that I did not know how to play football. 'Not play football? A strong, active boy like you! Of course you can play football.'

My father swept all my objections aside. He had no intention of allowing his own bright idea, and his old friend Bull's 'kindness', to go for nothing. I had only to do as the other boys did. I should enjoy it enormously. Nothing of the parson about Bull. He couldn't have been nicer. Shorts? Only little boys wear shorts. Had I not my knickerbockers and a jersey? Brown boots would do perfectly.

Had I been a little older, I might have reminded my father of his habit of deriding both private schools and organised games. Had my mother not been so grief-stricken, I might have called in aid an ally to whom my father invariably gave in. As it was, spiritless and panic-stricken, I lived over in imagination the dreadful hour that was to come.

On the following day I put on my grey flannel knickerbockers, my white jersey and my brown walking-boots with slightly pointed toes, and walked down to the school. The little boys were already gathering into groups on the beastly field. They all wore shorts, stockings with coloured tops, and football-boots with square toes and strips of leather across the soles to prevent slipping. As I walked towards them across the grass I realised for the first time that I was a giant, towering above a race of pygmies, but an awkward stick of a giant. My knickerbockers among all those bare knees gave me a curious feeling of being slightly effeminate, such as a young priest might have when first walking in a cassock among a crowd of men in trousers. My smooth soles felt insecure on the wet grass, speckled with worm-casts.

The Games Master, with a ball under one arm and a whistle round his neck, was reading out names from a piece of paper. He was the first games master I had seen; he wore a Norfolk jacket and an enormous woollen scarf and looked healthier than seemed quite human. He appeared to be surprised as I approached him; it was clear that Mr Bull had forgotten to tell him about me; and my ordeal was aggravated at the very start by the unforeseen necessity of explaining myself. The pygmies stared, with small upturned faces. The Games Master, unsmilingly, asked me at what position I usually played. I told him I had never played. It took him some time to take this in, and I murmured something about being at Eton, in the despairing hope, I suppose, that he might think I was all right at the Eton game. In the end he decided to put me in Bunny's side as an extra half-back. I had no idea what a half-back might be.

I have made, in later life, a friend called Bunny, to whom I am grateful, among much else, for his having finally exorcised the nightmare association with which that trivial nickname had been, for most of my life, made odious to me. Not that there was anything hateful about Bunny himself. He was a very short, stocky little boy with a freckled face and two little peeping front teeth which must have earned him his soubriquet. As captain of my side he took no notice of me whatsoever. But if ever I have been humiliated beyond bearing it was by Bunny. For Bunny was a prodigy of skill at soccer. One of the smallest boys in the game, he dominated it. 'Well done, Bunny!' 'Well kicked, Bunny!' 'Shoot, Bunny!' and Bunny shot, and into the goal went the ball. I, in contrast to Bunny, was staggering about in hopeless confusion. On the few occasions when the ball came to me, I kicked it as hard as I could in the direction of the opposing goal, thereby upsetting any plan that was afoot. I could not recognise friend from foe. I knew nothing of passing. I was always getting in the way. And round me, and across me, and behind me, Bunny darted and leapt, intercepting, dodging, tackling, dribbling, passing and shooting, with the Games Master shouting approval and praise. I seemed to get taller and taller, more and more conspicuous, as I blundered about. I felt a fool and knew I must be looking one. If only someone had laughed at me, so that I could have laughed with him; if only the Games Master had suggested that I should drop out and try to learn something from the side-line! But football was clearly no laughing matter at Bull's; I was surrounded with serious, intent and contemptuous little faces. It was hellish, and it went on for an hour.

I have no recollection of saying goodbye to Bunny or the Games Master, or of thanking them for my nice game, but I suppose I must have said something. Nor do I remember making any report to my father. If I did so, I probably said it was 'quite fun'. Humiliation was the very last thing I should ever have confessed to. But my father did not suggest another game. Perhaps Mr Bull gave him a hint.

L. E. Jones (1885–1969), *I Forgot to Tell You*

Alnwick Football Song

Now from the castle came the ball,
Out from the porch it flew, man,
Cheered the heart of every soul,
Each to his courage drew, man;
In Bailiffgate they kicked her fast,
And Narrowgate stood the hard blast,
The folk in Pottergate were fast,
The crowd like horse did smash, man.

The ball then to the market flew,
The crowd they followed fast, man,
The kicks it made her black and blue,
Her very ribs were smashed, man;
They kicked her then up Bondgate street,
Just like a flock of highland sheep,
Some skinned their shins, some lamed their feet,
They ran so swift and fleet, man.

They kicked it then around the town,
Just like a butterfly, man,
For every skelp was like a drum,
It really was a spree, man;
Each ran at her to get a bat,
Another's trip would gar him stot,
Then down he'd come like any snot,
And tumbled like a block, man.

Each trade was active in its part,
The blacksmiths and the nailers,
Both millwrights and joiner lads,
The cobblers and the tailors;
The blacksmiths they did run with glee,
The nailers followed up the spree,
The cobbler says, 'It is for me,
For cunning and for sly, man'.

The slater and the ostler lads,
Look to be very keen, man,
The mason and the tailor lads
Were plodding to the e'en, man;
The ball then says, 'I'll have a drink,
Because the cobbler gave the wink';
The tailor cries, 'O Lord I'll sink,
My very heart plays clink, man'.

The mason he came creeping out,
Just like a half-drowned cat, man,
The water made him blubber up,
Just like a water rat, man;
'O Lord' he cried, 'I've had bad luck,
For in the water like a duck,
I oft went down but ay came up,
And now I've got ashore, man.'

skelp] hit gar him stot] make him stagger snot] fool
e'en] eyes plays clink] beats fast

At Alnwick ball some tore their coat,
And others peeled their shins, man,
Some shoes was torn off their feet,
And some had patched skins, man;
Some strained their arms and others legs,
Some on the ground got filthy pegs,
Were just a havoc like Mons Megs,
The ball went with such force, man.

Up Barney-side the ball took flight,
Tom ran just like a hare, man,
The dirt flew from his heels that night,
A full half mile and mair, man;
The gardeners of him got a sight,
Which put them all to running flight,
But Tommy bade them all good night,
He was so quick at flight, man.

Tom has got home into the town,
Let's give him a huzza, man,
And drink a pint of good stout brown,
On the strength of the foot ball, man;
Here is a health unto his grace,
Landlords and Tenants of this place,
And every honest sonsy face,
Next year shall kick the ball, man.

ANONYMOUS

The Pleasures of Rugby

When first I played I nearly died,
 The bitter memory still rankles—
They formed a scrum with ME inside!
 Some kicked the ball and some my ankles,
I did not like the game at all,
 Yet, after all the harm they'd done me,
Whenever I came near the ball
 They knocked me down and stood upon me.

RUPERT BROOKE (1887–1915), in *Rugby School Magazine* 1904

pegs] legs Mons Megs] cannon at Edinburgh Castle mair] more
sonsy] cheerful

R.W.P.P. Killed in the Trenches

Rugby, Oxford University, Harlequins, England

Ronald is dead; and we shall watch no more
His swerving swallow-flight adown the field
Amid eluded enemies, who yield
Room for his easy passage, to the roar
Of multitudes enraptured, who acclaim
Their country's captain slipping toward his goal,
Instant of foot, deliberate of soul—
'All's well with England; Poulton's on his game.'

Aye, all is well: our orchard smiling fair;
Our Oxford not a wilderness that weeps;
Our boys tumultuously merry where
Amongst old elms his comrade spirit keeps
Vigil of love, All's well. And over there,
Amid his peers, a happy warrior sleeps.

ALFRED OLLIVANT (1874–1927)

The Rugger Match

Oxford and Cambridge—Queen's—December
To Hugh Brooks

I

The walls make a funnel, packed full; the distant gate
Bars us from inaccessible light and peace.
Far over necks and ears and hats, I see
Policemen's helmets and cards hung on the ironwork:
'One shilling', 'No change given', 'Ticket-holders only';
Oh Lord! What an awful crush! There are faces pale
And strained, and faces with animal grins advancing,
Stuck fast around mine. We move, we pause again
For an age, then a forward wave and another stop.
The pressure might squeeze one flat. Dig heels into ground
For this white and terrified woman whose male insists
Upon room to get back. Why didn't I come here at one?
Why come here at all? What strange little creatures we are,
Wedged and shoving under the contemptuous sky!

All things have stopped; the time will never go by;
We shall never get in! . . . Yet through the standing glass
The sand imperceptible drops, the inexorable laws
Of number work also here. They are passing and passing,
I can hear the tick of the turnstiles, tick, tick, tick,
A man, a woman, a man, shreds of the crowd,
A man, a man, till the vortex sucks me in
And, squeezed between strangers hurting the flat of my arms,
I am jetted forth, and pay my shilling, and pass
To freedom and space, and a cool for the matted brows.
But we cannot rest yet. Fast from the gates we issue,
Spread conelike out, a crowd of loosening tissue.
All jigging on, and making as we travel
'Pod, pod' of feet on earth, 'chix, chix' on gravel.
Heads forward, striding eagerly, we keep
Round to the left in semi-circular sweep
By the back of a stand, excluded, noting the row
Of heads that speck the top, and, caverned below,
The raw, rough, timber back of the new-made mound.
Quicker! The place is swarming! Around, around
Till the edge is reached, and we see a patch of green,
Two masts with a crossbar, tapering, white and clean,
And confluent rows of people that merge and die
In a flutter of faces where the grand-stand blocks the sky.
We hurry along, past ragged files of faces,
Flushing and quick, peering for empty places.
I see one above me, I step and prise and climb,
And stand and turn and breathe and look at the time,
Survey the field, and note with superior glance,
The anxious bobbing fools who still advance.

II

Ah! They are coming still. It is filling up.
It is full. They come. There is almost an hour to go,
Yet all find room, the dribbles of black disappear
In the solid piles around that empty green,
We are packed and ready now. They might as well start,
But two-forty-five was their time, and its only ten past,
And its got to be lived through. I haven't a newspaper,
I wish I could steal that little parson's book.
I count three minutes slowly; they seem like an hour;
And then I change feet and loosen the brim of my hat,
And curse the crawling of time. Oh body, body!
Why did I order you here, to stand and feel tired,
To ache and ache when the time will never pass,

In this buzzing crowd, before all those laden housetops,
Around this turf, under the lid of the sky?
I fumble my watch again: it is two-twenty:
Twenty-five minutes to wait. One, two, three, four,
Five, six, seven, eight: what is the good of counting?
It won't be here any quicker, aching hips,
Bored brain, unquiet heart, you are doomed to wait.
Why did I make you come? We have been before,
Struggling with time, fatigued and dull and alone
In all this tumultuous, chattering, happy crowd
That never knew pain and never questions its acts. . . .
Never questions? Do not deceive yourself.
Look at the faces around you, active and gay,
They are lined, there are brains behind them, breasts beneath them,
They have only escaped for an hour, and even now
Many, like you, have not escaped; and away
Across the field those faces ascending in tiers,
Each face is a story, a tragedy and a doubt;
And the teams where they wait, in the sacred place to the right,
Are bewildered souls, who have heard of and brooded on death,
And thought about God. But this is a football match;
And anyhow I don't feel equal to thinking,
And I'm certain the teams don't; they've something better to do.
It is half-past two, and, thank Heaven, a minute over.
We are all here now. The laggards have all booked seats
And stroll in lordly leisure along the front.
What a man! Six foot, silk hat, brown face, moustache!
What a fat complacent parson, snuggling down
In the chair there, among all his cackling ladies!
I have seen that youth before. My neighbour now
On my left shouts out to a college friend below us,
'Tommy! Hallo! Do you think we are going to beat 'em?'
My watch. Twenty-to-three. That lot went quickly;
Five minutes more is nothing; I'm lively now
And fit for a five-mile run. One, two, three, four. . . .
It isn't worth bothering now, it's all but here,
Here, here; a rustle, a murmur, a ready silence,
A billowing cheer—why, here they come, running and passing,
The challenging team! By God, what magnificent fellows!
They have dropped the ball, they pause, they sweep onward again,
And so to the end. Here are the rest of them,
Swinging up the field and back as they came,
With cheers swelling and swelling. They disappear,
And out, like wind upon water, come their rivals,
With cheers swelling and swelling, to run and turn
And vanish; and now they are all come out together,

Two teams walking, touch-judges and referee.
And they all line up, dotted about like chessmen,
And the multitude holds its breath, and awaits the start.

III

Whistle! A kick! A rush, a scramble, a scrum,
The forwards are busy already, the halves hover round,
The three-quarters stand in backwards diverging lines,
Eagerly bent, atoe, with elbows back,
And hands that would grasp at a ball, trembling to start,
While the solid backs vigilant stray about
And the crowd gives out a steady resolute roar,
Like the roar of a sea; a scrum, a whistle, a scrum;
A burst, a whistle, a scrum, a kick into touch;
All in the middle of the field. He is tossing it in,
They have got it and downed it, and whurry, oh, here they come,
Streaming like a waterfall, oh, he has knocked it on,
Right at our feet, and the scrum is formed again,
And everything seems to stop while they pack and go crooked.
The scrum-half beats them straight with a rough smack
While he holds the ball, debonair. . . . How it all comes back,
As the steam goes up of their breath and their sweating trunks!
The head low down, the eyes that swim to the ground,
The mesh of ownerless knees, the patch of dark earth,
The ball that comes in, and wedges and jerks, and is caught
And sticks, the dense intoxicant smell of sweat,
The grip on the moisture of jerseys, the sickening urge
That seems powerless to help; the desperate final shove
That somehow is timed with a general effort, the sweep
Onward, while enemies reel, and the whole scrum turns
And we torrent away with the ball. Oh, I know it all. . . .
I know it. . . . Where are they?. . . . Far on the opposite line,
Aimlessly kicking while the forwards stand gaping about,
Deprived of their work. Convergence. They are coming again,
They are scrumming again below, red hair, black cap,
And a horde of dark colourless heads, and straining backs;
A voice rasps up through the howl of the crowd around
(Triumphant now in possession over all the rest
Of crowds who have lost the moving treasure to us)—
'Push, you devils!' They push, and push, and push;
The opponents yield, the fortress wall does down,
The ram goes through, an irresistible rush
Crosses the last white line, and tumbles down,
And the ball is there. A try! A try! A try!
The shout from the host we are assaults the sky.

Deep silence. Line up by the goal-posts. A man lying down,
Poising the pointed ball, slanted away,
And another who stands, and hesitates, and runs
And lunges out with his foot, and the ball soars up,
While the opposite forwards rush below it in vain,
And curves to the posts, and passes them just outside.
The touch-judge's flag hangs still. It was only a try!
Three points to us. The roar is continuous now,
The game swings to and fro like a pendulum
Struck by a violent hand. But the impetus wanes,
The forwards are getting tired and all the outsides
Run weakly, pass loosely; there are one or two penalty kicks,
And a feeble attempt from a mark. The ball goes out
Over the heads of the crowd, comes wearily back;
And, lingering about in mid-field, the tedious game
Seems for a while a thing interminable.
And nothing happens, till all of a sudden a shrill
Blast from the whistle flies out and arrests the game.
Half-time. . . .Unlocking. . . . The players are all erect,
Easy and friendly, standing about in groups,
Figures in sculpture, better for mud-stained clothes;
Couples from either side chatting and laughing,
And chewing lemons, and throwing the rinds away.

IV

The pause is over. They part from each other, sift out;
The backs trot out to their stations, the forwards spread;
The captains beckon with hands, and the ball goes off
To volleys and answering volleys of harsher cheers;
For the top of the hill is past, we course to the close.
We've a three-point lead. Can we keep it? It isn't enough.
We have always heard their three-quarters are better than ours,
If they once get the ball. They have got it, he runs, he passes,
The centre dodges, is tackled, passes in time
To the other centre who goes like a bird to the left
And flings it out to the wing. The goal is open;
He has only to run as he can. No, the back is across,
He has missed him; he has him; they topple, head over heels,
And the ball bumps along into touch. They are stuck on our line;
Scrum after scrum, with those dangerous threes standing waiting,
Threat after threat forced back; a save, a return;
And the same thing over again, till the ball goes out
Almost unnoticed, and before we can see what is done,
That centre has kicked, he has thought of the four points,
The ball soars, slackens, keeps upright with effort,

Then floats between posts and falls, ignored, to the ground,
Its grandeur gone, while the touch-judge flaps his flag,
And the multitude becomes an enormous din
Which dies as the game resumes, and then rises again,
As battle of cry of triumph and counter-cry,
Defiant, like great waves surging against each other.
They work to the other corner, they stay there long;
They push and wheel, there are runs that come to nothing,
Till the noise wanes, and a curious silence comes.
They lead by a point, their crowd is sobered now,
Anxious still lest a sudden chance should come,
Or a sudden resource of power in mysterious foes
Which may dash them again from their new precarious peak,
Whilst we in our hearts are aware of the chilling touch
Of loss, of a fatal thing irrevocable,
Feel the time fly to the dreaded last wail of the whistle,
And see our team as desperate waves that dash
Against a wall of rock, to be scattered in spray.
Yet fervour comes back, for the players have no thought for the past
Except as a goad to new effort, not they will be chilled:
Fiercer and faster they fight, a grimness comes
Into shoving and running and tackling and handing off.
We are heeling the ball now cleanly, time after time
One half picks it up and instantly jabs it away,
And the beautiful swift diagonal quarter-line
Tips it across for the wing to go like a stag
Till he's cornered and falls and the gate swings shut again.
Thirty fighting devils, ten thousand throats,
Thundering joy at each pass and tackle and punt,
Yet the consciousness grows that the time approaches the end,
The threat of conclusion grows like a spreading tree
And casts its shadow on all the anxious people,
And is fully known when they stop as a man's knocked out
And limps from the field with his arms round two comrades' necks.
The gradual time seems to have suddenly leapt. . .
And all this while the unheeded winter sky
Has faded, and the air gone bluer and mistier.
The players, when they drift away to a corner
Distant from us, seem to have left our world.
We see the struggling forms, tangling and tumbling,
We hear the noise from the featureless mass around them,
But the dusk divides. Finality seems to have come.
Nothing can happen now. The attention drifts.
There's a pause; I become a separate thing again,
Almost forget the game, forget my neighbours,
And the noise fades in my ears to a dim rumour.

I watch the lines and colours of field and buildings,
So simple and soft and few in the vapoury air,
I am held by the brightening orange lights of the matches
Perpetually pricking the haze across the ground,
And the scene is tinged with a quiet melancholy,
The harmonious sadness of twilight in willowed waters,
Still avenues or harbours seen from the sea.
Yet a louder shout recalls me, I wake again,
Find there are two minutes left, and its nearly over,
See a few weaklings already walking out,
Caring more to avoid a crush with the crowd
Than to give the last stroke to a ritual of courtesy
And a work of intangible art. But we're all getting ready,
Hope gone, and fear, except in the battling teams.
Regret. . . a quick movement of hazy forms,
O quiet, O look, there is something happening,
Sudden one phantom form on the other wing
Emerges from nothingness, is singled out,
Curving in a long sweep like a flying gull,
Through the thick fog, swifter as borne by wind,
Swerves at the place where the corner-flag must be,
And runs, by Heaven he's over! and runs, and runs,
And our hearts leap, and our sticks go up in the air
And our hats whirl, and we lose ourselves in a yell
For a try behind the posts. We have beaten them!

V

Outside; and a mob hailing cabs, besieging the station,
Sticks, overcoats, scarves, bowler hats, intensified faces,
Rushes, apologies, voices: 'Simpson's at seven,'
'Hallo, Jim,' 'See you next term,' 'I've just seen old Peter.'
They go to their homes, to catch trains, all over the city,
All over England; or, many, to make a good night of it,
Eat oysters, drink more than usual, dispute of the match.
For the match is all over, and what, being done, does it matter?
What happened last year? I was here; I should know, but I don't.
Next year there will be another, with another result,
Just such another crowd, just as excited.
And after next year, for a year and a year and a year,
Till customs have changed and things crumbled and all this strife
Is a dim word from the past. Why, even to-night,
When the last door has been locked, the last groundsman will go,
Leaving that field which was conquered and full of men,
With darkened houses around, void and awake,
Silently talking to the silent travelling moon:

'The day passed. They have gone again. They will die.'
To-night in the moon the neighbouring roofs will lie
Lonely and still, all of their dwellers in bed;
The phantom stands will glisten, the goal-posts rise
Slanting their shadows across the grass, as calm
As though they had never challenged an eager swarm,
Or any ball had made their crossbars quiver.
Clouds will pass, and the city's murmur fade,
And the open field await its destiny
Of transient invaders coming and going.
What was the point of it? Why did the heart leap high
Putting reason back, to watch that fugitive play?
Why not? We must all distract ourselves with toys.
Not a brick nor a heap remains, the more durable product
Of all that effort and pain. Yet, sooner or later,
As much may be said of any human game,
War, politics, art, building, planting and ploughing,
The explorer's freezing, the astronomer's searching of stars,
The philosopher's fight through the thickening webs of thought,
And the writing of poems; a hand, a stir and a sinking.
As so, no more, of the general game of the Race,
That cannot know of its origin or its end,
But strives, for their own sake, its courage and skill
To increase, till Frost or a Flying Flame calls 'Time!'
I have seen this day men in the beauty of movement,
A gallant jaw set, the form of a hero that flew,
Cunning, a selfless flinging of self in the fray,
Strength, compassion, control, the obeying of laws,
Victory, and a struggle against defeat.
I think that the Power that gave us the bodies we have,
Can only be praised by our use of the things He gave,
That we are not here to turn our backs to the sun,
Or to scorn the delight of our limbs. And for those who have eyes
The beauty of this is the same as the beauty of flowers,
And of eagles and lions and mountains and oceans and stars,
And I care not, but rather am glad that the thought will recur
That in Egypt the muscles moved under the shining skins
As here, and in Greece where Olympian champions died,
And in isles long ago, where never a record was kept.
And now I'll go home, and open a bottle of port,
And think upon beauty and God and the wonder of love,
That laughs at the shadow of Death, and my vanished youth,
And the throbbing heart that beats its own drum to the grave,
Returning absurdly again to the fact that we won,
Content to let darkness deepen, and stars shine.

SIR JOHN SQUIRE (1884–1958)

The Great Day

'Lowe has yet to receive a pass in International football'—The Press passim.

I can recollect it clearly,
Every detail pretty nearly,
  Though it happened many, many years ago.
Yes, my children, I, your grand-dad
A reserved seat in the stand had
On the afternoon when someone passed to Lowe.

There he stood, poor little chappie,
Looking lonely and unhappy,
  While the other players frolicked with the ball.
For he knew he could not mingle
In the fun with Coates and Dingle;
  He could simply go on tackling—that was all.
I had stooped to light my briar,
For the wind was getting higher,
  When a thousand voices screamed a startled 'Oh!'
I looked up. A try or something?
Then sat gaping like a dumb thing.
  My children, somebody had passed to Lowe!

I remember how he trembled
(For to him the thing resembled
  A miracle), then gave a little cry;
And spectators who were near him
Were too overcome to cheer him;
  There were sympathetic tears in every eye.
His astonishment was utter.
He was heard to gulp, and mutter,
  'What on earth has happened now, I'd like to know?'
And incredulous reporters
Shouted out to the three-quarters;
  'Do we dream? Or did you really pass to Lowe?'

There was sweat upon his forehead
And his stare was simply horrid:
  He stood and goggled feebly at the ball.
It was plain he suffered badly,
For the crowd, now cheering madly,
  Saw him shudder, start to run, then limply fall.
Then a doctor, who was handy,
Fanned his face and gave him brandy;
  And at last, though his recovery was slow,

He regained his health and reason
By the middle of next season;
But the shock came very near to killing Lowe.

P. G. WODEHOUSE (1881–1975)

Stanley Matthews

Not often *con brio*, but *andante*, *andante*
horseless, though jockey-like and jaunty
Straddling the touchline, live margin
not out of the game, nor quite in,
Made by him green and magnetic, stroller
Indifferent as a cat dissembling, rolling
A little as on deck, till the mouse, the ball,
slides palely to him,
And shyly almost, with deprecatory cough, he is off.

Head of a Perugino, with faint flare
Of the nostrils, as though, Lipizzaner-like,
he sniffed at the air,
Finding it good beneath him, he draws
Defenders towards him, the ball a bait
They refuse like a poisoned chocolate,
retreating, till he slows his gait
To a walk, inviting the tackle, inciting it

Till, unrefusable, dangling the ball at the instep
He is charged—and stiffening so slowly
It is barely perceptible, he executes with a squirm
Of the hips, a twist more suggestive than apparent,
that lazily disdainful move *toreros* term
a Veronica—it's enough.
Only emptiness following him, pursuing some scent
Of his own, he weaves in towards,
not away from, fresh tacklers,
Who, turning about to gain time, are by him
harried, pursued not pursuers.

Now gathers speed, nursing the ball as he cruises,
Eyes judging distance, noting the gaps, the spaces
Vital for colleagues to move to, slowing a trace,
As from Vivaldi to Dibdin, pausing,
and leisurely, leisurely, swings

To the left upright his centre, on hips
His hands, observing the goalkeeper spring,
  heads rising vainly to the ball's curve
Just as it's plucked from them; and dispassionately
Back to his mark he trots, whistling through closed lips.

Trim as a yacht, with similar lightness
  —of keel, of reaction to surface—with salt air
Tanned, this incomparable player, in decline fair
  to look at, nor in decline either,
Improving like wine with age, has come far—
  born to one, a barber, who boxed
Not with such filial magnificence, but well.
'The greatest of all time', *meraviglioso* Matthews—
  Stoke City, Blackpool, and England.
Expressionless enchanter, weaving as on strings
  Conceptual patterns to a private music, heard
Only by him, to whose slowly emerging theme
  He rehearses steps, soloist in compulsions of a dream.

ALAN ROSS (b. 1922)

The Game

Follow the crowds to where the turnstiles click.
The terraces fill. *Hoompa*, blares the brassy band.
Saturday afternoon has come to Ninian Park
and, beyond the goalposts, in the Canton Stand
between black spaces, a hundred matches spark.

Waiting, we recall records, legendary scores:
Fred Keenor, Hardy, in a royal blue shirt.
The very names, sad as the old songs, open doors
before our time where someone else was hurt.
Now, like an injured beast, the great crowd roars.

The coin is spun. Here all is simplified
and we are partisan who cheer the Good,
hiss at passing Evil. Was Lucifer offside?
A wing falls down when cherubs howl for blood.
Demons have agents: the Referee is bribed.

The white ball smacks the crossbar. Satan rose
higher than the others in the smoked brown gloom
to sink on grass in a ballet dancer's pose.
Again, it seems, we hear a familiar tune
not quite identifiable. A distant whistle blows.

Memory of faded games, the discarded years;
talk of Aston Villa, Orient, and the Swans.
Half-time, the band played the same military airs
as when the Bluebirds once were champions.
Round touchlines, the same cripples in their chairs.

Mephistopheles had his joke. The honest team
dribbles ineffectually, no one can be blamed.
Infernal backs tackle, inside forwards scheme,
and if they foul us need we be ashamed?
Heads up! Oh for a Ted Drake, a Dixie Dean.

'Saved' or else, discontents, we are transferred
long decades back, like Faust must pay that fee.
The Night is early. Great phantoms in us stir
as coloured jerseys hover, move diagonally
on the damp turf, and our eidetic visions blur.

God sign our souls! Because the obscure Staff
of Hell rules this world, jugular fans guessed
the result half way through the second half
and those who know the score just seem depressed.
Small boys swarm the field for an autograph.

Silent the Stadium. The crowds have all filed out.
Only the pigeons beneath the roofs remain.
The clean programmes are trampled underfoot,
and natural the dark, appropriate the rain,
whilst, under lampposts, threatening newsboys shout.

DANNY ABSE

From *This Sporting Life*

I followed Frank into the tunnel. A body like his made for some security. A few officials touched his back, then my back, as we turned into the tunnel and broke into a trot. A tremendous roar coincided with the daylight, and grew as we streamed on to the field. The loudspeakers blared the 'Entrance of the Gladiators'.

In spite of the drizzle and the cold, the terraces were black with people. We stood clean and neat in a circle in the middle of the field, passing the ball, conspicuous against the greenery in red and blue arrowed jerseys and white shorts.

A plume of steam, brilliant against the greyness of the sky, detached itself from the lip of the cooling tower and drifted slowly over the field. A man in a white jersey with red horizontal configurations broke from the tunnel mouth. A second roar—rattles, bells, trumpet blasts—a stream of red and white flooded the darker greenery of the lower field. I looked for numbers two and five and at the size of their forwards. They were young.

Frank was standing with the ref and the other captain—bow-legged, small, not unlike Maurice. They shook hands, tossed a coin, and Frank indicated we'd play the way we were already facing.

A fresh burst from the crowd encouraged the line up. Maurice ran up like he'd done a thousand times before and kicked off. The six forwards ran down the field. I carried on a straight course, knowing I could give the impression of strong attack without having to do anything—the player gathering the ball would run obliquely to the centre of the field and pass to one of the half-backs.

This he did, giving a fast convenient pass to the little captain who'd scarcely collected the ball than he was nearly killed by a short-arm from Maurice coming up in anticipation. The man lay still, covered in mud, his short legs splayed over the grass. The ref went over with a warning glance at Maurice to see how dead the man was. 'That's the way, Maurice,' Frank said.

We made a scrum over the spot, the short piston limbs interlocking, then straining. A movement began across the field and young Arnie ran in with an ankle tap and the player crumbled. The ball rolled free and the boy scooped it up alertly with one hand and side-stepping started to run down the field. He found Frank with a long pass coming up laboriously in support. The great bulk of Frank, his lessened speed, drew the opposing forwards magnetically. They leapt wildly at his slow procession through them. Before he fell under their simultaneous attacks he flicked the ball expertly into the gap he'd deliberately created. Maurice, waiting in receipt, didn't hear the oppressive noise that came from Frank as he hit the ground; he took the ball one-handed and with short precise steps cut his way through to the full-back, and was almost on the line when the winger, coming across with a greater and more famous speed, knocked him over like a stalk.

The two teams shot into positions in the thick din of excitement. Frank stood behind Maurice and took the ball as it came between the scrum-half 's legs. I started running up from behind, Frank held the ball, then slipped it to me as I passed in full stride. I hit the wall of waiting men like a rock. For a second they yielded, drew together, and held. A dull pain shot from the top of my skull. I struggled into a position I knew would ease the impact and give me more chance with any excited fist. I heard through compressed ears the screams and groans of the crowd, almost the individual voices of agony, before I was flung down.

I rose with the same motion and played the ball. Young Arnie had it. I'd never realized how popular he was with the crowd. When, with an apparently casual blow, he was banged down, I was vaguely satisfied at his indiscretion. I took the ball as he played it and sent it to the centres. It passed straight to the super-protected wingman. He gathered cleanly and bustled up the field only to be shoved into touch. The crowd disapproved.

We folded down to the scrum, panting with the first breathlessness, steam rising from the straining 'backs. I saw the damp shape roll between my legs and Maurice snatched it up impatiently. With an extravagant dummy he shot by the still dazed captain and was caught by the winger. He kicked out, lashed out, contorted, and threw himself over the line.

The crowd screamed and surged like penned animals, like a suddenly disturbed pool. Whistles, bells, and trumpets crashed and soared on the animal roar. I ran to him, banged his back, and we walked back in pleased groups.

The full-back failed at goal. A slight breeze moved across the ground, spraying the drizzle. A spurt of vivid steam swirled over the pitch and drifed in slow ascent. I stared down at the bare patch of earth at my feet, soft and muddy. I bent down and touched it reassuringly, and as the flurry of rain changed direction looked up at the similarly worn patch at the centre. The ball wasn't there. A tiger was running across the spot just after kicking. I narrowed my eyes, and in the thick air, against the dark prominence of the cooling towers, saw the slim oval shape.

'Yours, Art!' Maurice shouted behind me. The wet leather smacked into my crooked arms and I twisted instinctively into the grip of the surrounding men. I fell comfortably and was pressed to the ground. I stopped to watch the ball move from hand to hand across the field.

'Come on, Arthur lad,' somebody shouted either behind me or from the crowd. I followed the ball mechanically, attached to it by an invisible string. Perhaps I didn't need a car now. It was getting too old, too knocked about, and I'd never afford another.

I took the ball and burst down the middle of the field. I avoided two men and passed. The movement petered out.

I took some trouble to stay on the blind side during the play-the-ball. I rested nervously, scarcely tired, slightly puzzled. My ankles ached: I'd bound them too tightly. The drug I'd taken seemed to have been absorbed. My chest was constricted. The dampness went through to the bone, numbing. Black, unknown faces, streaked with skin or blood, slow black limbs, moving continually past, interlocking, swaying, beating, followed by the steam, seeping from the skin, polluted by the mud, vaporizing in the cold air.

I ran in close to a play-the-ball and took the pass. I broke into the oblique long-paced run popular with the crowd.

I chose the right wing, a stretch of field more familiar and where the winger was of a slighter build. He waited for me cautiously, feet astride, nervously crouched, encouraging me to run between him and the touch. I checked my stride and began to run on the outside of my feet, and moved straight towards him. He moved sideways again, still urging me to pass him between the touchline. I hated his mean scheming. I ran at him and shoved out my left fist. I saw his flash of fear, the two arms pushed out protectively, the silly stagger backwards, the two wounds torn in the turf by his sliding heels. I sensed the shape of the full-back running diagonally to intercept. I brought my knees up higher and concentrated on the line.

There was Arnie's boyish supporting shout. I'd only to give it to him for a score. I shoved my hand at the full-back's head as he came in, and felt the slackening of his arms. I threw myself forward, and hit somebody hard. I fell over sideways into touch.

The smell of the earth, and grass—Arnie pulling me to my feet. A brown liquid running down my nose, over my lip, and seeping into my mouth. Arnie watched it with sickened fascination.

'That's great, Art! . . . great!' Maurice was telling me. I leaned down in the scrum, watched the ball come in, go out. I stood up. The whistle went. Half-time.

The men sprawled and collapsed on to the massage table and the bench. Belching and groaning. There was no gas left. 'Blind that bastard when he comes round the loose head. You go for his legs. Have you got that? Leave the frog's head to me.'

'Did you see how he belted Morgan?'

'Nay, but bloody hell, fair's fair.'

'I got more money playing Union in Wales than I've ever done up here . . . and I tell you, if. . . .'

They calmed down. The warmth, the smell of the hot bath, and Dai's single persistent voice guided the resentment. Frank brought over a bottle of water and rested his steaming carcass beside mine. He tipped the bottle to his lips, swilled his mouth, and spat. When I took the bottle from him I saw the blood oozing from his hair. It dried with the mud over his forehead, round his eyes, and over his swollen nose. 'You all right?' he said. 'I'm stuffed. I'm an arse for wukking last night.'

The room was a stall of steaming cattle. Dai was going at it hard, telling how everything was going wrong. I crunched an ammonia phial in my fingers and shoved it up Frank's nose. He shuddered, choked, and coughed to life.

We walked back on to the field slowly. A milder, impatient cheer met our second appearance, a tired trumpet. We stood and waited in the rain for the other team. With the weather thickening and the light fading early the crowd had thinned slightly either end of the ground. The better part of it was now stuffed in the main stand and in the covered stand opposite. Somewhere amongst the dark mass was my father. And Johnson. 'We're on the radio now,' Maurice said as he ran by. 'Keep your hair parted.'

'See you.'

'That's it, kid.'

The game entered its long drag. With Frank half-dazed I ran about encouraging the side. Everybody wanted a good run with the ball to make sure their names went over the air on the Northern Service. In the scrum I leaned heavily against Arnie, feeling a bated reassurance in holding his back. I began to take advantage of planning the game by not taking part in it. When I actually held the ball and peered out, rain-blinded, at those dim circulating shapes I felt unsure and sent the ball away with a careful movement of the wrists. At one point I turned too slowly and unbalanced, and heard it credited with a noise from the crowd as a dark shape passed me, shooting up mud either side. A roar drew a curtain round the ground. We lined up behind the posts. Overhead, in the low cloud, an aircraft thundered.

'Bad luck, Arthur,' young Arnie said deliberately. I watched the placing of the ball carefully, the meticulous run of the kicker, the swing through of his leg, the small shape spinning silently through the rain and curving between the posts. A crisp eruption by the crowd.

I began to resent the activity around me. An old way of escape. I looked to the life that wasn't absorbed in the futility of the game—to the tall chimney and the two flowering cylinders of the power station, half hidden by cloud, the tops of the buses passing the end of the ground, the lights turned on inside the upper decks, the people sitting uncommitted behind the windows. The houses were lit too, in their slow descent to the valley. I moved back to the centre, imitating the figures whose activity suddenly tired me. I was ashamed of being no longer young.

We were pressed back to our line. Maurice stole the ball and flicked it back to Frank. He stormed into the wall of men and was thrown down in a cloud of dirty steam and spray. Arnie was treated the same. They ran a yard, two yards, from the line and were thrown back as much. Frank tried again, pumping his huge body forward and concealing his grunt of pain as he was flung down. He had another go, and with a cry of frustration and rage, he was seized, lifted, and turned over before being dropped on his head and shoulders. He wheezed like a beaten machine as his skull drove into the earth.

The indignity brought a mixed cry of wonder and amusement from the crowd. I hoped Kenny wasn't there. 'There's nothing on that field that can take punishment like Frank Miles,' George often said to visiting chairmen. 'And I'm including the ball as well.'

To my left the tiger captain watched the struggle of his forwards. 'The ball! The ball!' he was shouting. 'Leave the man. . . . Get the bleeding ball!' He beat himself with impatience.

The leather smacked into my outstretched hands. I ran straight at the man. 'Go on Art! Go on Art!' Maurice screamed behind me. I ran into him, over him. Trampled him and broke free into a gap. A pain thudded in my head in echo to my feet. An arm gripped my waist, slipped, caught again, and a fist sank into my neck. I carried him along. Then another caught me round the nose and eyes, the fingers explored for pain, forcing me to my knees. Arnie took the ball and with his boy's shout of triumph threw himself into the confusion of mud and men, his body searching, like a tentacle, for an opening. He ran ten yards to a scream from the crowd, then fell into the sea of limbs.

I was still kneeling, absorbed in an odd resigned feeling. My back teeth chattered as I pulled myself up, my hands shook with cold, and I despised myself for not feeling hate for the man who'd torn my nostril. I was used to everything now. Ten years of this, ten years of the crowd—I could make one mistake, one slight mistake only, and the whole tragedy of living, of being alive, would come into the crowd's throat and roar its pain like a maimed animal. The cry, the rage of the crowd echoed over and filled the valley—a shape came towards me in the gloom.

I glimpsed the fierce and brilliant whiteness of its eyes and clenched teeth through its mask of mud, flashing with a useless hostility. It avoided my preparations to delay it, veering past out of reach. I put my foot out, and as the man stumbled took a swing with my fist. I missed, and fell down with a huge sound from the crowd. The man recovered and went on running. He ran between the posts. Frank picked me up, the mud covering my tears. Where's the bleeding full-back? I wanted to shout. But I could only stare unbelievingly at my legs which had betrayed me.

DAVID STOREY (b. 1933)

VII

Bat and Pad

From *Cricket. An Heroic Poem*

When the returning sun begins to smile,
And shed its glories round this sea-girt isle;
When newborn nature, decked in vivid green,
Chases dull winter from the charming scene;
High-panting with delight, the jovial swain
Trips it exulting o'er the flow'r-strewed plain.
Thy pleasures, Cricket! all his heart control;
Thy eager transports dwell upon his soul.
He weighs the well-turned bat's experienced force
And guides the rapid ball's impetuous course;
His supple limbs with nimble labour plies,
Nor bends the grass beneath him as he flies.
The joyous conquests of the late-flown year,
In fancy's paint, with all their charms appear,
And now again he views the long-wished season near.
O thou, sublime inspirer of my song,
What matchless trophies to thy worth belong!
Look round the globe, inclined to mirth, and see
What daring sport can claim the prize from thee!
   Not puny Billiards where, with sluggish pace,
The dull ball trails before the feeble mace;
Where no triumphant shouts, no clamours, dare
Pierce through the vaulted roof and wound the air,
But stiff spectators quite inactive stand,
Speechless attending to the striker's hand;
Where nothing can your languid spirits move,
Save where the marker bellows out 'Six-love!',
Or when the ball, close-cushioned, slides askew,
And to the op'ning pocket runs, a *cou*!
Nor yet that happier game, where the smooth Bowl
In circling mazes wanders to the goal;

cou] *coup*; pocketing the ball without first striking another

Where, much divided between fear and glee,
The youth cries 'Rub!—O flee, you ling'rer, flee!'
  Not Tennis' self, thy sister sport, can charm,
Or with thy fierce delights our bosoms warm:
Though full of life, at ease alone dismayed,
She calls each swelling sinew to her aid,
Her echoing courts confess the sprightly sound,
While from the racket the brisk balls rebound,
Yet, to small space confined, ev'n she must yield
To nobler Cricket the disputed field.
  O parent Britain, minion of renown!
Whose far-extended fame all nations own,
Of sloth-promoting sports, forewarned, beware!
Nor think thy pleasures are thy meanest care.
Shun with disdain the squeaking masquerade,
Where fainting Vice calls Folly to her aid;
Leave the dissolving song, the baby dance,
To soothe the slaves of Italy and France.
While the firm limb and strong-braced nerve are thine,
Scorn eunuch sports, to manlier games incline,
Feed on the joys that health and vigour give;
Where Freedom reigns, 'tis worth the while to live.
  Nursed on thy plains, first Cricket learned to please,
And taught thy sons to slight inglorious ease:
And see where busy counties strive for fame,
Each greatly potent at this mighty game!
Fierce Kent, ambitious of the first applause,
Against the world combined asserts her cause;
Gay Sussex sometimes triumphs o'er the field,
And fruitful Surrey cannot brook to yield;
While London, queen of cities! proudly vies,
And often grasps the well-disputed prize.

JAMES DANCE (1722–74)

The Song of Tilly Lally

O, I say, you Joe,
Throw us the ball!
I've a good mind to go
And leave you all.
I never saw such a bowler
To bowl the ball in a tansy
And clean it with my hankercher
Without saying a word.

That Bill's a foolish fellow;
He has given me a black eye.
He does not know how to handle a bat
Any more than a dog or a cat;
He has knock'd down the wicket,
And broke the stumps,
And runs without shoes to save his pumps.

WILLIAM BLAKE (1757–1827)

John Small (1737–1826)

Here lies, bowled out by Death's unerring ball,
A Cricketer renowned, by name John Small,
But though his name was Small, yet great his fame,
For nobly did he play the noble game;
His life was like his innings, long and good,
Full ninety summers he had death withstood.

At length the ninetieth winter came, when (fate
Not leaving him one solitary mate)
This last of Hambledonians, Old John Small,
Gave up his bat and ball, his leather, wax and all.

PIERCE EGAN

Cricket at Harrow

High, through those elms, with hoary branches crown'd,
Fair Ida's bower adorns the landscape round;
There Science, from her favour'd seat, surveys
The vale where rural Nature claims her praise;
To her awhile resigns her youthful train,
Who move in joy, and dance along the plain;
In scatt'd groups each favour'd haunt pursue:
Repeat old pastimes, and discover new;
Flush'd with his rays, beneath the noontide sun,
In rival bands, between the wickets run,
Drive o'er the sward the ball with active force,
Or chase with nimble feet its rapid course.

Alonzo! best and dearest of my friends. . . .
. . . when confinement's lingering hour was done,
Our sport, our studies, and our souls were one:
Together we impell'd the flying ball;
Together waited in our tutor's hall;
Together join'd in cricket's manly toil.

LORD BYRON

Village Cricket

I doubt if there be any scene in the world more animating or delightful than a cricket match—I do not mean a set match at Lord's ground for money, hard money, between a certain number of gentlemen and players, as they are called—people who make a trade of that noble sport, and degrade it into an affair of bettings, and hedgings, and cheatings, it may be, like boxing or horse-racing; nor do I mean a pretty fête in a gentleman's park, where one club of cricketing dandies encounters another such club, and where they show off in graceful costume to a gay marquee of admiring belles, who condescend so to purchase admiration, and while away a long summer morning in partaking cold collations, conversing occasionally, and seeming to understand the game—the whole being conducted according to ball-room etiquette, so as to be exceedingly elegant and exceedingly dull.

No! the cricket that I mean is a real solid old-fashioned match between neighbouring parishes, where each attacks the other for honour and a supper, glory and half a crown a man. If there be any gentlemen amongst them, it is well—if not, it is so much the better. Your gentleman cricketer is in general rather an anomalous character. Elderly gentlemen are obviously good for nothing; and young beaux are, for the most part, hampered and trammelled by dress and habit: the stiff cravat, the pinched-in waist, the dandy-walk—oh, they will never do for cricket! Now, our country lads, accustomed to the flail or the hammer (your blacksmiths are capital hitters), have the free use of their arms; they know how to move their shoulders; and they can move their feet too—they can run; then they are so much better made, so much more athletic, and yet so much lissomer—to use a Hampshire phrase, which deserves at least to be good English. Here and there, indeed, one meets with an old Etonian, who retains his boyish love for that game which formed so considerable a branch of his education: some even preserve their boyish proficiency, but in general it wears away like the Greek, quite as certainly, and almost as fast; a few years of Oxford, or Cambridge, or the Continent, are sufficient to annihilate both the power and the inclination. No! a village match is the thing—where our highest officer, our conductor (to borrow a musical term), is but a little farmer's second son; where a day-labourer is our bowler, and a blacksmith our long-stop; where the spectators consist of the retired cricketers, the veterans of the green, the careful mothers, the girls, and all the boys of two parishes, together with a few amateurs, little above them in rank, and not at all in pretension; where laughing and shouting, and the very ecstasy of merriment and good humour, prevail.

MARY R. MITFORD (1787–1855)

From *'The Pickwick Club'*

The wickets were pitched, and so were a couple of marquees for the rest and refreshment of the contending parties. The game had not yet commenced. Two or three Dingley Dellers, and All-Muggletonians, were amusing themselves with a majestic air by throwing the ball carelessly from hand to hand; and several other gentlemen dressed like them, in straw hats, flannel jackets, and white trousers—a costume in which they looked very much like amateur stone-masons—were sprinkled about the tents, towards one of which Mr Wardle conducted the party.

Several dozen of 'How-are-you's?' hailed the old gentleman's arrival; and a general raising of the straw hats, and bending forward of the flannel jackets, followed his introduction of his guests as gentlemen from London, who were extremely anxious to witness the proceedings of the day, with which, he had no doubt, they would be greatly delighted.

'You had better step into the marquee, I think, sir,' said one very stout gentleman, whose body and legs looked like half a gigantic roll of flannel, elevated on a couple of inflated pillow-cases.

'You'll find it much pleasanter, sir,' urged another stout gentleman, who strongly resembled the other half of the roll of flannel aforesaid.

'You're very good,' said Mr Pickwick.

'This way,' said the first speaker; 'they notch in here—it's the best place in the whole field;' and the cricketer, panting on before, preceded them to the tent.

'Capital game—smart sport—fine exercise—very,' were the words which fell upon Mr Pickwick's ear as he entered the tent; and the first object that met his eyes was his green-coated friend of the Rochester coach, holding forth, to the no small delight and edification of a select circle of the chosen of All-Muggleton. His dress was slightly improved, and he wore boots; but there was no mistaking him.

The stranger recognised his friends immediately: and, darting forward and seizing Mr Pickwick by the hand, dragged him to a seat with his usual impetuosity, talking all the while as if the whole of the arrangements were under his especial patronage and direction.

'This way—this way—capital fun—lots of beer—hogsheads; rounds of beef—bullocks; mustard—cart loads; glorious day—down with you—make yourself at home—glad to see you—very.'

Mr Pickwick sat down as he was bid, and Mr Winkle and Mr Snodgrass also complied with the directions of their mysterious friend. Mr Wardle looked on, in silent wonder.

'Mr Wardle—a friend of mine,' said Mr Pickwick.

'Friend of yours!—My dear sir, how are you?—Friend of *my* friend's—give me your hand, sir'—and the stranger grasped Mr Wardle's hand with all the fervour of a close intimacy of many years, and then stepped back a pace or two as if to take a full survey of his face and figure, and then shook hands with him again, if possible, more warmly than before.

'Well; and how came you here?' said Mr Pickwick, with a smile in which benevolence struggled with surprise.

'Come,' replied the stranger—'stopping at Crown—Crown at Muggleton—met a party—flannel jackets—white trousers—anchovy sandwiches—devilled kidneys—splendid fellows—glorious.'

Mr Pickwick was sufficiently versed in the stranger's system of stenography to infer from this rapid and disjointed communication that he had, somehow or other, contracted an acquaintance with the All-Muggletons, which he had converted, by a process peculiar to himself, into that extent of good fellowship on which a general invitation may be easily founded. His curiosity was therefore satisfied, and putting on his spectacles he prepared himself to watch the play which was just commencing.

All-Muggleton had the first innings; and the interest became intense when Mr Dumkins and Mr Podder, two of the most renowned members of that most distinguished club, walked, bat in hand, to their respective wickets. Mr Luffey, the highest ornament of Dingley Dell, was pitched to bowl against the redoubtable Dumkins, and Mr Struggles was selected to do the same kind office for the hitherto unconquered Podder. Several players were stationed, to 'look out,' in different parts of the field, and each fixed himself into the proper attitude by placing one hand on each knee, and stooping very much as if he were 'making a back' for some beginner at leap-frog. All the regular players do this sort of thing;—indeed it's generally supposed that it is quite impossible to look out properly in any other position.

The umpires were stationed behind the wickets; the scorers were prepared to notch the runs; a breathless silence ensued. Mr Luffey retired a few paces behind the wicket of the passive Podder, and applied the ball to his right eye for several seconds. Dumkins confidently awaited its coming with his eyes fixed on the motions of Luffey.

'Play!' suddenly cried the bowler. The ball flew from his hand straight and swift towards the centre stump of the wicket. The wary Dumkins was on the alert; it fell upon the tip of the bat, and bounded far away over the heads of the scouts, who had just stooped low enough to let it fly over them.

'Run—run—another.—Now, then, throw her up—up with her—stop there—another—no—yes—no—throw her up, throw her up!'—Such were the shouts which followed the stroke; and, at the conclusion of which All-Muggleton had scored two. Nor was Podder behindhand in earning laurels wherewith to garnish himself and Muggleton. He blocked the doubtful balls, missed the bad ones, took the good ones, and sent them flying to all parts of the field. The scouts were hot and tired; the bowlers were changed and bowled till their arms ached; but Dumkins and Podder remained unconquered. Did an elderly gentleman essay to stop the progress of the ball, it rolled between his legs or slipped between his fingers. Did a slim gentleman try to catch it, it struck him on the nose, and bounded pleasantly off with redoubled violence, while the slim gentleman's eye filled with water, and his form writhed with anguish. Was it thrown straight up to the wicket, Dumkins had reached it before the ball. In short, when Dumkins was caught out, and Podder stumped out, All-Muggleton had notched some fifty-four, while the score of Dingley Dellers was as blank as their faces. The advantage was too great to be recovered. In vain did the eager Luffey, and the enthusiastic Struggles, do all that skill and experience could suggest, to regain the ground Dingley Dell had lost in the contest;—it was of no avail; and in an early period of the winning game Dingley Dell gave in, and allowed the superior prowess of All-Muggleton.

CHARLES DICKENS, *Pickwick Papers*

Tom Brown's Last Match

Another two years have passed, and it is again the end of the summer half-year at Rugby; in fact, the School has broken up. The fifth-form examinations were over last week, and upon them have followed the speeches, and the sixth-form examinations for exhibitions; and they too are over now. The boys have gone to all the winds of heaven, except the town boys and the eleven, and the few enthusiasts besides who had asked leave to stay in their houses to see the result of the cricket matches. For this year the Wellesburn return match and the Marylebone match were played at Rugby, to the great delight of the town and neighbourhood, and the sorrow of those aspiring young cricketers who have been reckoning for the last three months on showing off at Lords' ground.

The Doctor started for the Lakes yesterday morning, after an interview with the Captain of the eleven, in the presence of Thomas, at which he arranged in what school the cricket dinners were to be, and all other matters necessary for the satisfactory carrying out of the festivities; and warned them as to keeping all spirituous liquors out of the close, and having the gates closed by nine o'clock.

The Wellesburn match was played out with great success, the School winning by three wickets; and to-day the great event of the cricketing year, the Marylebone match, is being played. What a match it has been!

The London eleven came down by an afternoon train yesterday, in time to see the end of the Wellesburn match; and as soon as it was over, their leading men and umpire inspected the ground, criticizing it rather unmercifully.

The Captain of the School eleven, and one or two others, who had played the Lords' match before, and knew old Mr Aislabie and several of the Lord's men, accompanied them: while the rest of the eleven looked on from under the Three Trees with admiring eyes, and asked one another the names of the illustrious strangers, and recounted how many runs each of them had made in the late matches in *Bell's Life*. They looked such hard-bitten, wiry, whiskered fellows, that their young adversaries felt rather desponding as to the result of the morrow's match.

The ground was at last chosen, and two men set to work upon it to water and roll: and then, there being yet some half-hour of daylight, some one had suggested a dance on the turf. The close was half-full of citizens and their families, and the idea was hailed with enthusiasm. The cornopean-player was still on the ground; in five minutes the eleven and half a dozen of the Wellesburn and Marylebone men got partners somehow or another, and a merry country-dance was going on, to which every one flocked, and new couples joined in every minute, till there were a hundred of them going down the middle and up again—and the long line of school buildings looked gravely down on them, every window glowing with the last rays of the western sun, and the rooks clanged about in the tops of the old elms, greatly excited, and resolved on having their country dance too, and the great flag flapped lazily in the gentle western breeze.

Altogether it was a sight which would have made glad the heart of our brave old founder, Lawrence Sheriff, if he were half as good a fellow as I take him to have been.

It was a cheerful sight to see: but what made it so valuable in the sight of the Captain of the School eleven was, that he there saw his young hands shaking off their shyness and awe of the Lords' men, as they crossed hands and capered about on the grass together; for the strangers entered into it all, and threw away their cigars, and danced and shouted like boys; while old Mr Aislabie stood by looking on in his white hat, leaning on a bat, in benevolent enjoyment. 'This hop will be worth thirty runs to us to-morrow, and will be the making of Raggles and Johnson,' thinks the young leader, as he revolves many things in his mind, standing by the side of Mr Aislabie, whom he will not leave for a minute, for he feels that the character of the School for courtesy is resting on his shoulders.

But when a quarter to nine struck, and he saw old Thomas beginning to fidget about with the keys in his hand, he thought of the Doctor's parting monition, and stopped the cornopean at once, notwithstanding the loud-voiced remonstrances from all sides; and the crowd scattered away from the close, the eleven all going into the School-house, where supper and beds were provided for them by the Doctor's orders.

Deep had been the consultations at supper as to the order of going in, who should bowl the first over, whether it would be best to play steady or freely; and the youngest hands declared that they shouldn't be a bit nervous, and praised their opponents as the jolliest fellows in the world, except perhaps their old friends the Wellesburn men. How far a little good-nature from their elders will go with the right sort of boys!

The morning had dawned bright and warm, to the intense relief of many an anxious youngster, up betimes to mark the signs of the weather. The eleven went down in a body before breakfast, for a plunge in the cold bath in the corner of the close. The ground was in splendid order, and soon after ten o'clock, before spectators had arrived, all was ready, and two of the Lords' men took their places at the wickets; the School, with the usual liberality of young hands, having put their adversaries in first. Old Bailey stepped up to the wicket, and called play, and the match has begun.

* * * * *

'Oh, well bowled! well bowled, Johnson,' cries the Captain, catching up the ball and sending it high above the rook trees, while the third Marylebone man walks away from the wicket, and old Bailey gravely sets up the middle stump again and puts the bails on.

'How many runs?' away scamper three boys to the scoring-table, and are back again in a minute amongst the rest of the eleven, who are collected together in a knot between wicket.

'Only eighteen runs, and three wickets down!'

'Huzza for old Rugby!' sings out Jack Raggles, the long-stop, toughest and burliest of boys, commonly called 'Swiper Jack'; and forthwith stands on his head, and brandishes his legs in the air in triumph, till the next boy catches hold of his heels, and throws him over on to his back.

'Steady there, don't be such an ass, Jack,' says the Captain; 'we haven't got the best wicket yet. Ah, look out now at cover-point,' adds he, as he sees a long-armed bare-headed, slashing-looking player coming to the wicket. 'And, Jack, mind your hits; he steals more runs than any man in England.'

And they all find that they have got their work to do now; the newcomer's off-hitting is tremendous, and his running is like a flash of lightning. He is never in his ground except when his wicket is down. Nothing in the whole game so trying to boys; he has stolen three byes in the first ten minutes, and Jack Raggles is furious, and begins throwing over savagely to the further wicket, until he is sternly stopped by the Captain. It is all that young gentleman can do to keep his team steady, but he knows that everything depends on it, and faces his work bravely. The score creeps up to fifty, the boys begin to look blank, and the spectators, who are now mustering strong, are very silent. The ball flies off his bat to all parts of the field, and he gives no rest and no catches to any one.

But cricket is full of glorious chances, and the goddess who presides over it loves to bring down the most skilful players. Johnson the young bowler is getting wild, and bowls a ball almost wide to the off; the batter steps out and cuts it beautifully to where cover-point is standing very deep, in fact almost off the ground. The ball comes skimming and twisting along about three feet from the ground; he rushes at it, and it sticks somehow or other in the fingers of his left hand, to the utter astonishment of himself and the whole field. Such a catch hasn't been made in the close for years, and the cheering is maddening.

'Pretty cricket,' says the Captain, throwing himself on the ground by the deserted wicket with a long breath: he feels that a crisis has passed.

I wish I had space to describe the match; how the Captain stumped the next man off a leg-shooter, and bowled small cobs to old Mr Aislabie, who came in for the last wicket. How the Lords' men were out by half-past twelve o'clock for ninety-eight runs. How the Captain of the School eleven went in first to give his men pluck, and scored twenty-five in beautiful style; how Rugby was only four behind in the first innings. What a glorious dinner they had in the fourth-form school, and how the cover-point hitter sang the most topping comic songs, and old Mr Aislabie made the best speeches that ever were heard, afterwards. But I haven't space, that's the fact, and so you must fancy it all, and carry yourselves on to half-past seven o'clock, when the School are again in, with five wickets down, and only thirty-two runs to make to win. The Marylebone men played carelessly in their second innings, but they are working like horses now to save the match.

There is much healthy, hearty, happy life scattered up and down the close; but the group to which I beg to call your especial attention is there, on the slope of the island, which looks towards the cricket ground. It consists of three figures; two are seated on a bench, and one on the ground at their feet. The first, a tall, slight, and rather gaunt man, with a bushy eyebrow, and a dry humorous smile, is evidently a clergyman. He is carelessly dressed, and looks rather used up, which isn't much to be wondered at, seeing that he has just finished six weeks of examination work; but there he basks, and spreads himself out in the evening sun, bent on enjoying life, though he doesn't quite know what to do with his arms and legs. Surely it is our friend the young Master, whom we have had glimpses of before, but his face has gained a great deal since we last came across him.

And by his side, in white flannel shirt and trousers, straw hat, the Captain's belt, and the untanned yellow cricket shoes which all the eleven wear, sits a strapping figure, near six feet high, with ruddy tanned face and whiskers, curly brown hair and a laughing dancing eye. He is leaning forward with his elbows resting on his knees, and dandling his favourite bat, with which he has made thirty or forty runs to-day, in his strong brown hands. It is Tom Brown, grown into a young man nineteen years old, a praepostor and Captain of the eleven, spending his last day as a Rugby boy, and let us hope as much wiser as he is bigger, since we last had the pleasure of coming across him.

THOMAS HUGHES, *Tom Brown's Schooldays*

The Deserted Parks

'Solitudinem faciunt: Parcum appellant'

Amidst thy bowers the tyrant's hand is seen,
The rude pavilions sadden all thy green;
One selfish pastime grasps the whole domain,
And half a faction swallows up the plain;
Adown thy glades, all sacrificed to cricket,
The hollow-sounding bat now guards the wicket;
Sunk are thy mounds in shapeless level all,
Lest aught impede the swiftly rolling ball;
And trembling, shrinking from the fatal blow,
Far, far away thy hapless children go.

The man of wealth and pride
Takes up a space that many poor supplied;
Space for the game, and all its instruments,
Space for pavilions and for scorers' tents;
The ball, that raps his shins in padding cased,
Has wore the verdure to an arid waste;
His Park, where these exclusive sports are seen,
Indignant spurns the rustic from the green;
While through the plain, consigned to silence all,
In barren splendour flits the russet ball.

LEWIS CARROLL (1832–98)

Ballade of Dead Cricketers

Ah, where be Beldham now, and Brett,
  Barker, and Hogsflesh, where be they?
Brett, of all bowlers fleetest yet
  That drove the bails in disarray?
And Small that would, like Orpheus, play
  Till wild bulls followed his minstrelsy?
Booker, and Quiddington, and May?
  Beneath the daisies, there they lie!

And where is Lambert, that would get
The stumps with balls that broke astray?
And Mann, whose balls would ricochet
In almost an unholy way
(So do baseballers 'pitch' today);
George Lear, that seldom let a bye,
And Richard Nyren, grave and gray?
Beneath the daisies, there they lie!

Tom Sueter, too, the ladies' pet,
Brown that would bravest hearts affray;
Walker, invincible when set,
(Tom, of the spider limbs and splay);
Think ye that we could match them, pray,
These heroes of Broad-halfpenny,
With Buck to hit, and Small to stay?
Beneath the daisies, there they lie!

Envoy

Prince, canst thou moralize the lay?
How all things change below the sky?
Of Fry and Hirst shall mortals say,
'Beneath the daisies, there they lie!'

ANDREW LANG (1844–1912)

A Cricket Bowler

Two minutes' rest till the next man goes in!
The tired arms lie with every sinew slack
On the mown grass. Unbent the supple back,
And elbows apt to make the leather spin
Up the slow bat and round the unwary shin,—
In knavish hands a most unkindly knack;
But no guile shelters under this boy's black
Crisp hair, frank eyes, and honest English skin.

Two minutes only. Conscious of a name,
The new man plants his weapon with profound
Long-practised skill that no mere trick may scare.
Not loth, the rested lad resumes the game:
The flung ball takes one madding tortuous bound,
And the mid-stump three somersaults in air.

EDWARD CRACROFT LEFROY

A Reminiscence of Cricket

Once in my heyday of cricket,
  Oh day I shall ever recall!
I captured that glorious wicket,
  The greatest, the grandest of all.

Before me he stands like a vision,
  Bearded and burly and brown,
A smile of good-humoured derision
  As he waits for the first to come down.

A statue from Thebes or from Cnossus,
  A Hercules shrouded in white,
Assyrian bull-like Colossus,
  He stands in his might.

With the beard of a Goth or a Vandal,
  His bat hanging ready and free,
His great hairy hands on the handle,
  And his menacing eyes upon me.

And I—I had tricks for the rabbits,
  The feeble of mind or of eye,
I could see all the duffer's bad habits
  And guess where his ruin might lie.

The capture of such might elate one,
  But it seemed like some horrible jest
That I should serve tosh to the great one,
  Who had broken the hearts of the best.

Well, here goes! Good Lord, what a rotter!
  Such a sitter as never was dreamt;
It was clay in the hands of the potter,
  But he tapped it with quiet contempt.

The second was better—a leetle;
  It was low, but was nearly long-hop;
As the housemaid comes down on the beetle
  So down came the bat with a chop.

He was sizing me up with some wonder,
My broken-kneed action and ways;
I could see the grim menace from under
The striped peak that shaded his gaze.

The third was a gift or it looked it—
A foot off the wicket or so;
His huge figure swooped as he hooked it,
His great body swung to the blow.

Still when my dreams are night-marish,
I picture that terrible smite,
It was meant for a neighbouring parish,
Or any old place out of sight.

But—yes, there's a but to the story—
The blade swished a trifle too low;
Oh wonder, and vision of glory!
It was up like a shaft from a bow.

Up, up, like the towering game-bird,
Up, up, to a speck in the blue,
And then coming down like the same bird,
Dead straight on the line that it flew.

Good Lord, was it mine! Such a soarer
Would call for a safe pair of hands;
None safer than Derbyshire Storer,
And there, face uplifted, he stands.

Wicket-keep Storer, the knowing,
Wary and steady of nerve,
Watching it falling and growing
Marking the pace and the curve.

I stood with my two eyes fixed on it,
Paralysed, helpless, inert;
There was 'plunk' as the gloves shut upon it,
And he cuddled it up to his shirt.

Out—beyond question or wrangle!
Homeward he lurched to his lunch!
His bat was tucked up at an angle,
His great shoulders curved to a hunch.

Walking he rumbled and grumbled,
   Scolding himself and not me;
One glove was off, and he fumbled,
   Twisting the other hand free.

Did I give Storer the credit
   The thanks he so splendidly earned?
It was mere empty talk if I said it,
   For Grace was already returned.

Sir Arthur Conan Doyle (1859–1930)

At Lord's

It is little I repair to the matches of the Southron folk,
   Though my own red roses there may blow;
It is little I repair to the matches of the Southron folk,
   Though the red roses crest the caps, I know.
For the field is full of shades as I near the shadowy coast,
And a ghostly batsman plays to the bowling of a ghost,
And I look through my tears on a soundless-clapping host
   As the run-stealers flicker to and fro,
      To and fro:
   O my Hornby and my Barlow long ago!

It is Glo'ster coming North, the irresistible,
   The Shire of the Graces, long ago!
It is Gloucestershire up North, the irresistible,
   And new-risen Lancashire the foe!
A Shire so young that has scarce impressed its traces,
Ah, how shall it stand before all-resistless Graces?
O, little red rose, their bats are as maces
   To beat thee down, this summer long ago!

This day of seventy-eight they are come up North against thee
   This day of seventy-eight, long ago!
The champion of the centuries, he cometh up against thee,
   With his brethren, every one a famous foe!
The long-whiskered Doctor, that laugheth rules to scorn,
While the bowler, pitched against him, bans the day that he was
      born;
And G.F. with his science makes the fairest length forlorn;
   They are come from the West to work thee woe!

It is little I repair to the matches of the Southron folk,
  Though my own red roses there may blow;
It is little I repair to the matches of the Southron folk,
  Though the red roses crest the caps, I know.
For the field is full of shades as I near the shadowy coast,
And a ghostly batsman plays to the bowling of a ghost,
And I look through my tears on a soundless-clapping host,
  As the run-stealers flicker to and fro,
    To and fro:
  O my Hornby and my Barlow long ago!

FRANCIS THOMPSON (1859–1907)

The Blues at Lord's

Near-neighboured by a blandly boisterous Dean
Who 'hasn't missed the match since '92',
Proposing to perpetuate the scene
I concentrate my eyesight on the cricket.
The game proceeds, as it is bound to do
Till tea-time or the fall of the next wicket.

Agreeable sunshine fosters greensward greener
Than College lawns in June. Tradition-true,
The stalwart teams, capped with contrasted blue,
Exert their skill; adorning the arena
With modest, manly, muscular demeanour—
Reviving memories in ex-athletes who
Are superannuated from agility—
And (while the five-ounce fetish they pursue)
Admired by gloved and virginal gentility.

My intellectual feet approach this function
With tolerance and Public-School compunction;
Aware that, whichsoever side bats best,
Their partisans are equally well-dressed.

For, though the Government has gone vermilion
And, as a whole, is weak in Greek and Latin,
The fogies harboured by the august Pavilion
Sit strangely similar to those who sat in
The edifice when first the Dean went pious—
For possible preferment sacrificed
His hedonistic and patrician bias,
And offered his complacency to Christ.

Meanwhile some Cantab slogs a fast half-volley
Against the ropes. 'Good shot, sir! O good shot!'
Ejaculates the Dean in accents jolly. . . .
Will Oxford win? Perhaps. Perhaps they'll not.
Can Cambridge lose? Who knows? One fact seems sure;
That, while the Church approves, Lord's will endure.

SIEGFRIED SASSOON

Vitai Lampada

There's a breathless hush in the Close to night—
  Ten to make and the match to win—
A bumping pitch and a blinding light,
  An hour to play and the last man in.
And it's not for the sake of a ribboned coat,
  Or the selfish hope of a season's fame,
But his Captain's hand on his shoulder smote:
  'Play up! play up! and play the game!'

The sand of the desert is sodden red,—
  Red with the wreck of a square that broke;—
The Gatling's jammed and the Colonel dead,
  And the regiment blind with dust and smoke.
The river of death has brimmed his banks,
  And England's far, and Honour a name,
But the voice of a schoolboy rallies the ranks:
  'Play up! play up! and play the game!'

This is the word that year by year,
  While in her place the School is set,
Every one of her sons must hear,
  And none that hears it dare forget.
This they all with a joyful mind
  Bear through life like a torch in flame,
And falling fling to the host behind—
  'Play up! play up! and play the game!'

SIR HENRY NEWBOLT (1862–1938)

Six and Out

The pitch was only smooth in parts;
  It sank at either crease,
And motor vans and bakers' carts
  At times disturbed the peace.

The bowler found it hard to hit
  The lamp-post's slender stem.
The broader wicket, opposite,
  Was cleared at 6 p.m.

It was a keen, determined school,
  Unorthodox and free;
Harsh circumstance oft made the rule,
  And not the M.C.C.

The scorer, seated by the wall,
  Kept up a fire of talk;
He was both umpires, crowd and all,
  And plied a busy chalk.

So, standing, musing on the scene,
  I let the moments pass:
How well he drove it to the screen . . .
  And then—the crash of glass!

I watched the players as they ran,
  And heard, while yet they fled,
The loud voice of an angry man,
  The law's majestic tread.

G. D. MARTINEAU (1835–1919)

W.G. Loquitur

Good sirs, who sit at home tonight,
And listen in the fading light
To voices floating on the air
From here, from there, from everywhere:
Imagine now that out of space
Comes the deep spirit voice of Grace—
Old W.G.—whose mighty frame
No more shall lumber through the game—
Old W.G.—whose burly beard
No more is seen, no more is feared:
Yet, from my corner in the sky,
When, not unenvious, I descry
Flannels in fashion down below—
When old familiar sounds I know
Float up—the heavy roller's sound
Clanking across the county ground—
The busy whirr no spring forgets
Of cricket balls in cricket nets—
The insect hum of shillings spun,
Silver and black, against the sun—
The call of the pavilion bell,
Tolling its matin summons—well,
Even an angel or two is stirred,
And when the umpire speaks the word,
The first word of the season—'Play!'—
It has my blessing every May.
Sweet May! ah, month beyond compare!
For now you taste the firstlings rare:
The first square cut, the first clean drive,
The first sharp-shooter you survive,
The first fine glance, the first fair guide,
The first good victory for your side:
Sweet May! once more I smell your oil
Smoothing my bat; and press your soil
Under my thumb; once more I feel
The good soft give of pine or deal
Beneath the nails that pierce the boards
In dressing rooms from Leeds to Lords:
Sweet May! you hold a thrill apart,
For now the batsman strains his art
To make the loveliest score of all—
A century to a cuckoo's call.
How many, many Mays have burst
Their buds, and spread their boughs, since first

I learned to watch the ball, to wait,
And always hold my bat up straight!
How many Mays, alas! since last
I let the ball at point go past!
No more! no more! above the crowds
Like a Jehovah in the clouds
I sit, *sans* bat or ball, and dream,
A captain now without a team:
Yet though I miss, I miss my May,
Happy that other men still play
The game all England flocked to see
When W.G. was W.G.
So then! to business! Now, my lads,
Up with the stumps! on with the pads!
Out with the cap! whose gaudy rings
Will mellow in a few more springs,
And, as the colours fade, proclaim
A real old master of the game.
Come! to the pitch! The field is set.
Caution, remember, till you get
Your eye in. 'Two leg, umpire, please.'
The wicket-keeper bends his knees;
The slips, with swinging arms, lean low,
Hawks for a swoop, three in a row;
Long-off, beside the boundary-track,
Stands with his hands behind his back,
Lolling; the bowler now has spaced
His run; he turns; his fingers taste
The seam, caress the stitch; he comes;
Through the bright air the new ball hums
A delicate, cleaving note; you sight
Against the screen its clear, red flight,
Tense in the sun; and as it spins,
The prologue ends, and play begins.

HERBERT FARJEON (1887–1945)

Cricket at Worcester, 1938

Dozing in deck-chair's gentle curve,
Through half-closed eyes I watched the cricket,
Knowing the sporting press would say
'Perks bowled well on a perfect wicket.'

Fierce mid-day sun upon the ground;
Through heat-haze came the hollow sound
Of wary bat on ball, to pound
The devil from it, quell its bound.

Sunburned fieldsmen, flannelled cream,
Looked, though urgent, scarce alive,
Swooped, like swallows of a dream,
On skimming fly, the hard-hit drive.

Beyond the score-box, through the trees
Gleamed Severn, blue and wide,
Where oarsmen 'feathered' with polished ease
And passed in gentle glide.

The back-cloth, setting off the setting,
Peter's cathedral soared,
Rich of shade and fine of fretting
Like cut and painted board.

To the cathedral, close for shelter,
Huddled houses, bent and slim,
Some tall, some short, all helter-skelter,
Like a sky-line drawn for Grimm.

This the fanciful engraver might
In his creative dream have seen,
Here, framed by summer's glaring light,
Grey stone, majestic over green.

Closer, the bowler's arm swept down,
The ball swung, swerved and darted,
Stump and bail flashed and flew;
The batsman pensively departed.

Like rattle of dry seeds in pods
The warm crowd faintly clapped,
The boys who came to watch their gods,
The tired old men who napped.

The members sat in their strong deck-chairs
And sometimes glanced at the play,
They smoked and talked of stocks and shares,
And the bar stayed open all day.

JOHN ARLOTT (b. 1914)

The Cricket Match

The scores were level and there were two wickets to fall. Silence fell. The gaffers, victims simultaneously of excitement and senility, could hardly raise their pint pots for it was past six o'clock, and the front door of the Three Horseshoes was now as wide open officially as the back door had been unofficially all afternoon.

Then the Major, his red face redder than ever and his chin sticking out almost as far as the Napoleonic Mr Ogilvy's, bowled a fast half-volley on the leg-stump. The sexton, a man of iron muscle from much digging, hit it fair and square in the middle of the bat, and it flashed like a thunderbolt, waist-high, straight at the youth in the blue jumper. With a shrill scream the youth sprang backwards out of its way and fell over on his back. Immediately behind him, so close were the fieldsmen clustered, stood the mighty Boone. There was no escape for him. Even if he had possessed the figure and the agility to perform back-somersaults, he would have lacked the time. He had been unsighted by the youth in the jumper. The thunderbolt struck him in the midriff like a red-hot cannonball upon a Spanish galleon and with the sound of a drumstick upon an insufficiently stretched drum. With a fearful oath, Boone clapped his hands to his outraged stomach and found that the ball was in the way. He looked at it for a moment in astonishment and then threw it down angrily and started to massage the injured spot while the field rang with applause at the brilliance of the catch.

Donald walked up and shyly added his congratulations. Boone scowled at him.

'I didn't want to catch the bloody thing,' he said sourly, massaging away like mad.

'But it may save the side,' ventured Donald.

'Blast the bloody side,' said Boone.

Donald went back to his place.

The scores were level and there was one wicket to fall. The last man in was the blacksmith, leaning heavily upon the shoulder of the baker, who was going to run for him, and limping as if in great pain. He took guard and looked round savagely. He was clearly still in a great rage.

The first ball he received he lashed at wildly and hit straight up in the air to an enormous height. It went up and up and up, until it became difficult to focus it properly against the deep, cloudless blue of the sky, and it carried with it the hopes and fears of an English village. Up and up it went, and then at the top it seemed to hang motionless in the air, poised like a hawk, fighting, as it were, an heroic but forlorn battle against the chief invention of Sir Isaac Newton, and then it began its slow descent.

In the meanwhile things were happening below, on the terrestrial sphere. Indeed, the situation was rapidly becoming what the French call *mouvementé*. In the first place, the blacksmith forgot his sprained ankle and set out at a capital rate for the other end, roaring in a great voice as he went, 'Come on, Joe!' The baker, who was running on behalf of the invalid, also set out, and he also roared, 'Come on, Joe!' and side by side, like a pair of high-stepping hackneys, the pair cantered along. From the other end Joe set out on his mission, and he roared, 'Come on, Bill!' So all three came on. And everything would have been all right, so far as the running was concerned, had it not been for the fact that Joe, very naturally, ran with his head thrown back and his eyes goggling at the hawk-like cricket ball. And this in itself would not have mattered if it had not been for the fact that the blacksmith and the baker, also very naturally, ran with their heads turned not only upwards but also backwards as well, so that they too gazed at the ball, with an alarming sort of squint and truly terrific kink in their necks. Half-way down the pitch the three met with a magnificent clang, reminiscent of early, happy days in the tournament-ring at Ashby-de-la-Zouch, and the hopes of the village fell with the resounding fall of their three champions.

But what of the fielding side? Things were not so well with them. If there was doubt and confusion among the warriors of Fordenden, there was also uncertainty and disorganization among the ranks of the invaders. Their main trouble was the excessive concentration of their forces in the neighbourhood of the wicket. Napoleon laid it down that it was impossible to have too many men upon a battlefield, and he used to do everything in his power to call up every available man for a battle. Mr Hodge, after a swift glance at the ascending ball and a swift glance at the disposition of his troops, disagreed profoundly with the Emperor's dictum. He had too many men, far too many. And all except the youth in the blue silk jumper, and the mighty Boone, were moving towards strategical positions underneath the ball, and not one of them appeared to be aware that any of the others existed. Boone had not moved because he was more or less in the right place, but then Boone was not likely to bring off the catch, especially after the episode of the last ball. Major Hawker, shouting 'Mine, mine!' in a magnificent self-confident voice, was coming up from the bowler's end like a battle-cruiser. Mr Harcourt had obviously lost sight of the ball altogether, if indeed he had ever seen it, for he was running round and round Boone and giggling foolishly. Livingstone and Southcott, the two cracks, were approaching competently. Either of them would catch it easily. Mr Hodge had only to choose between them, and, coming to a swift decision, he yelled above the din, 'Yours, Livingstone!' Southcott, disciplined cricketer, stopped dead. Then Mr Hodge made a fatal mistake. He remembered Livingstone's two missed sitters, and he reversed his decision and roared, 'Yours, Bobby!' Mr Southcott obediently started again while Livingstone, who had not heard the second order, went straight on. Captain Hodge had restored the *status quo*.

In the meantime the professor of ballistics had made a lightning calculation of angles, velocities, density of the air, barometer-readings and temperatures, and had arrived at the conclusion that the critical point, the spot which ought to be marked in the photographs with an X, was one yard to the north-east of Boone, and he proceeded to take up station there, colliding on the way with Donald and knocking him over. A moment later Bobby Southcott came racing up and tripped over the recumbent Donald and was shot head first into the Abraham-like bosom of Boone. Boone stepped back a yard under the impact and came down with his spiked boot, surmounted by a good eighteen stone of flesh and blood, upon the professor's toe. Almost simultaneously the portly wicketkeeper, whose movements were a positive triumph of the spirit over the body bumped the professor from behind. The learned man was thus neatly sandwiched between Tweedledum and Tweedledee, and the sandwich was instantly converted into a ragout by Livingstone, who made up for his lack of extra weight—for he was always in perfect training—by his extra momentum. And all the time Mr Shakespeare Pollock hovered alertly upon the outskirts like a rugby scrum-half, screaming American University cries in a piercingly high tenor voice.

At last the ball came down. To Mr Hodge it seemed a long time before the invention of Sir Isaac Newton finally triumphed. And it was a striking testimony to the mathematical and ballistical skill of the professor that the ball landed with a sharp report upon the top of his head. Thence it leapt up into the air a foot or so, cannoned on to Boone's head, and then trickled slowly down the colossal expanse of the wicketkeeper's back, bouncing slightly as it reached the massive lower portions. It was only a foot from the ground when Mr Shakespeare Pollock sprang into the vortex with a last ear-splitting howl of victory and grabbed it off the seat of the wicketkeeper's trousers. The match was a tie. And hardly anyone on the field knew it except Mr Hodge, the youth in the blue jumper, and Mr Pollock himself. For the two batsmen and the runner, undaunted to the last, had picked themselves up and were bent on completing the single that was to give Fordenden the crown of victory. Unfortunately, dazed with their falls, with excitement, and with the noise, they all three ran for the same wicket, simultaneously realized their error, and all three turned and ran for the other—the blacksmith, ankle and all, in the centre and leading by a yard, so that they looked like pictures of the Russian troika. But their effort was in vain, for Mr Pollock had grabbed the ball and the match was a tie.

And both teams spent the evening at the Three Horseshoes, and Mr Harcourt made a speech in Italian about the glories of England and afterwards fell asleep in a corner, and Donald got home to Royal Avenue at one o'clock in the morning, feeling that he had not learnt very much about the English from his experience of their national game.

A. G. MACDONELL (1895–1941), from *England, their England* (1933)

Wicket Maiden

It is a game for gentle men;
Entirely wrong that man's spare rib
Should learn the mysteries of spin.

Women should not be allowed
To study subtleties of flight;
They should bowl underarm and wide.

Or, better still, not bowl at all,
Sit elegant in summer chairs,
Flatter the quiet with pale applause.

It shouldn't happen, yet it did:
She bowled a wicked heartbreak—one,
That's all. God help the next man in.

VERNON SCANNELL

The Captain

I liked the Captain, all the seams
He fell apart at, going mad

Because he thought the shivered elms
Would fall upon his ashen head

And swifts would peck his eyes. Bad dreams
Can't take the quickness that he had

Who flighted slow leg-breaks that swung
In from the off, then looped away,

Or, lolled on August vapours, hung
And came through flat and how was that?

I liked the Captain, all his schemes
For harassing the right hand bat.

I liked the Captain, all his themes
And each strange learned word he said

Who read solely Victoriana
And had by heart half *Silas Marner*

Along with odd tunes in his head:
He thought the swifts would peck his eyes.

They shall not cut him down to size
Nor seek to break his flighted mind

In institutions. Nothing dead
But he shall be restored again.

Elms shall respect unshaven brain
And birds his wisdom. World needs him.

Come all, come any revolution,
The Captain is the man for spin.

KIT WRIGHT (b. 1944)

Packer's Circuit

Something about this game
eternally fades, to bring
the lost outfielders in,

those whited ruminants
under the layers of green
whom old men at the field-edge

dream, dead name by name,
that played the day with a weeping
willow for ashes, ashes,

till you could believe, by a thin
tide of shadow that washes
play to its close, the ball

swung most sharply in tear-gas,
the rotten grave took spin,
a ghost could make a hundred

with the board of a coffin lid
and Father Time himself
scythe off his balls and sing

for something about this game
eternally fades, to bring
the lost outfielders in.

KIT WRIGHT

Stagnant Pond

The grass has a Mohican cut
playing cricket for the Sunday Sinners
I steal a single with a baseball bunt—

in the pavilion
Denis shunts forward in my vacant seat
and on the flip side of my pencilled poem
like swansdown on a stagnant pond
doodles in beautiful italic script:

musicians on a cathedral crawl
Coventry Canterbury and Rome
anacreontic madrigals and Keats' nightingales
blowing out one last organ stop of sadness—
they look down on the marbled marquetry
and hear the strangest cry 'The Hyriads'—

I leg it back to the pavilion
marvel at the calligraphy
erase my HB poem
Denis defecting to the Saints
had vanished in a whiff of aftershave
leaving me his inspiration like a donor card.

MICHAEL HENRY (b. 1942)

Hutton, Hobbs and the Classical Style

The characteristics of the classical style in cricket, or in anything else, are precision of technique, conservation of energy, and power liberated proportionately so that the outlines of execution are clear and balanced. Hutton is the best example to be seen at the present time of the classical style of batsmanship. He is a model for the emulation of the young. We cannot say as much of, for instance, Worrell, who is the greatest stroke-player of the moment; it would be perilous if a novice tried to educate himself by faithfully observing the play of Worrell. A sudden snick through the slips by Worrell might cause us to lift an eyebrow, but we wouldn't think that something had gone wrong with the element in which Worrell naturally revels; for it is understood that Worrell and all cricketers of his kind live on the rim of their technical scope. A snick by a Jack Hobbs is a sort of disturbance of a cosmic orderliness. It is more than a disturbance; it is a solecism in fact, as though a great writer of prose were to fall into an untidy period, or actually commit bad grammar. The classical style admits of no venturings into the unknown, of no strayings from first principles. A dissonance is part and parcel of romantic excess and effort; all right in Strauss, impossible in Mozart, where not a star of a semi-quaver may fall. The exponent of the classical style observes, and is content to observe, the limitations imposed by law, restraint, taste. He finds his liberty within the confines of equipoise.

I suppose that the three or four exemplars of the truly classic style of batsmanship have been W. G. Grace, Arthur Shrewsbury, Hayward and Hobbs; I can't include Maclaren; for something of a disturbing rhetoric now and then entered into his generally noble and correct diction. Trumper was, of course, all styles, as C. B. Fry has said, from the lyrical to the dramatic. Maclaren once paid, in a conversation with me, the most generous tribute ever uttered by one great player to another. 'I was supposed to be something of a picture gallery myself,' said he. 'People talked of the "Grand Manner" of Maclaren. But compared with Victor I was as a cab-horse to a Derby winner. . . .'

In our own day, Hutton comes as near as anybody to the classical style, though there are moments when the definition of it, as expounded above, needs to be loosened to accommodate him. Dignity, and a certain lordliness, are the robes and very presence of classicism. Frankly, Hutton many times is obliged to wear the dress or 'overhauls' of utility; moreover, his resort to the passive 'dead bat', though shrewd and tactical, scarcely suggests grandeur or the sovereign attitude. The truth is that the classical style of batsmanship was the consequence of a classical style of bowling—bowling which also observed precision, clarity of outline, length, length, length! It is as difficult to adapt classical calm and dignity of poise to modern in-swingers and 'googlies' as it would be to translate Milton into Gertrude Stein, or Haydn into Tin-pan Alley.

But Hutton, in the present far from classical epoch, follows the line of Hobbs, and if all that we know today of batsmanship as a science were somehow taken from our consciousness, the grammar and alphabet could be deduced from the cricket of Hutton, and codified again; he is all the text-books in an omnibus edition. Compared with him Bradman, who has been accused of bloodless mechanical efficiency, was as a volcanic eruption threatening to destroy Pompeii.

We need to be careful of what we mean if we call Hutton a stylist, which, we have agreed, he is. Style is commonly but mistakenly supposed to be indicated by a flourish added to masterful skill, a spreading of peacock's feathers. (The peacock is efficiently enough created and marvellously beautiful without that.) Style with Hutton is not a vanity, not something deliberately cultivated. It is a bloom and finish, which have come unself-consciously from organized technique rendered by experience instinctive in its rhythmical and attuned movements. His drives to the off-side have a strength that is generated effortlessly from the physical dynamo, through nerve and muscle, so that we might almost persuade ourselves that the current of his energy, his life-force, is running electrically down the bat's handle into the blade, without a single short-circuit or fusing, thence into the ball, endowing it, as it speeds over the grass, with the momentum of no dead material object compact of leather, but of animate life.

His 'follow through' in his drives is full and unfettered. But the style is the man: there is no squandering in a Hutton innings. Bradman, to refer again to the cricketer known as an 'adding-machine' was a spendthrift compared to Hutton, who is economical always, counting every penny, every single, of his opulent income of runs. We shall understand, when we come to consider the way of life that produced him, his habitat, why with Hutton, the style is indeed the man himself.

Some of us are obliged to work hard for our places in the sun; others have greatness thrust upon them. A fortunate few walk along divinely appointed ways, the gift of prophecy marking their courses. Hutton was scarcely out of the cradle of the Yorkshire nursery nets when Sutcliffe foretold the master to come, not rolling the eye of fanaticism but simply in the manner of a shrewd surveyor of 'futures'. But Sutcliffe knew all the time that the apprenticeship of Hutton had been served in that world of vicissitude and distrust which are the most important factors forming the North of England character under the pressure of an outlook which thinks it's as well to 'take nowt on trust'—not even a fine morning. In his first trial for the Yorkshire Second XI, May 1933, he was dismissed for nothing against Cheshire. Four years after, when he was first invited to play for England, he also made nothing, bowled Cowie. Next innings he was 'slightly more successful'—'c. Vivian, b. Cowie 1'. Though he was only eighteen years old when he scored a hundred for Yorkshire in July 1934—the youngest Yorkshire cricketer to achieve such distinction—illness as well as the run of the luck of the game hindered his progress, dogged him with apparent malice. When he reappeared on the first-class scene again it was just in time to take part in that dreadful holocaust at Huddersfield, when Essex bowled Yorkshire out for 31 and 99. Hutton's portion was two noughts. In his very first match for Yorkshire at Fenners in 1934 J. G. W. Davies ran him out brilliantly—for nought. Until yesteryear, in fact, the Fates tried him. The accident to his left forearm, incurred while training in a Commando course, nearly put an end to his career as a cricketer altogether.

He has emerged from a hard school. It has never been with Hutton a case of roses all the way; he had to dig his cricket out of his bones; a bat and the Yorkshire and England colours didn't fall into his mouth like silver cutlery. According to the different threads or warp of our nature and being, a different texture is an inevitable consequence. There is no softness in Hutton's psychological or, therefore, in his technical make-up. And there are broadly two ways of getting things done in our limited world. We walk either by faith or by reason. There are, in other words, the born inexplicable geniuses and those we can account for in terms of the skill they have inherited. They are in a way the by-products of skill and experience accumulated and still pregnant in their formative years; their contribution is to develop the inheritance to a further, though rationally definable stage of excellence. But we know where they come from and how. Hutton is one of the greatest of these. But a Compton, or, better for our illustration, a Trumper seems to spring into being with all his gifts innate and in full bloom from the beginning. He improved in certainty of touch with experience, but as soon as he emerges from the chrysalis there is magic in his power, something that 'defies augury'; he is a law unto himself, therefore dangerous as a guide or example to others who are encased in mortal fallibility. But I am wandering from a contemplation of classicism and Hutton.

The unique or ineluctable genius isn't, of course, necessarily the great master. No cricketer has possessed, or rather been more possessed by genius, than Ranji; for his mastery was the most comprehensive known yet in all the evolution of the game. Hobbs summed-up in himself all that had gone before him in established doctrine of batsmanship. He was encyclopaedic; we could deduce from his cricket not only grammar but history. We could infer from any Hobbs innings the various forces that had produced and perfected his compendious technique over years which witnessed changes which were revolutionary as never before, ranging from the fast bowlers of the post-Grace period, in which Hobbs was nurtured, to the advent of the modern refinements and licences—swerve and 'googly' and all the rest. When Hobbs began his career the attack he faced day by day was much the same in essentials as the one familiar enough to W. G. But very soon Hobbs was confronted by bowling of the new order of disrule, which W. G. couldn't understand; and Hobbs was not only the first to show how the 'googly' should be detected and exposed and how swerve should be played in the middle of the blade; he taught others and led the way. Hobbs was the bridge over which classical cricket marched to the more complex epoch of the present. Hutton is the only cricketer living at the moment who remotely resembles Hobbs by possession of what I shall call here a thoroughly schooled or canonical method. He doesn't commit crudities. The 'wrong' stroke at times—yes, because of an error of judgment. But never an *uninstructed* stroke.

He is a quiet thoughtful Yorkshireman, with widely-spaced blue eyes that miss nothing. And his batting is quiet and thoughtful; even in his occasional punishing moods, when his strokes are animating as well as ennobling the field, he doesn't get noisy or rampagious. His stance at the wicket is a blend of easeful muscular organization and keen watchfulness.

The left shoulder points rather more to the direction of mid-on than would satisfy Tom Hayward; but here again is evidence that Hutton is a creature or rather a creation of his environment; that is to say, he is obliged to solve problems of spin and swerve not persistently put to Hayward day by day. With Hayward and his school, the left leg was the reconnoitring force, the cat's whisker, the pioneer that moved in advance to 'sight' the enemy. With Hutton it is the right leg that is the pivot, the springboard. But often he allowed it to change into an anchor which holds him back when he should be moving out on the full and changing tide of the game. He is perfect at using the 'dead' bat—rendering it passive, a blanket or a buffer, against which spin or sudden rise from the pitch come into contact as though with an anaesthetic. He plays so close to the ball, so much over it that he has acquired a sort of student's slope of the shoulders; at the sight of a fizzing off-break he is arched like a cat. Even when he drives through the covers, his head and eyes incline downwards, and the swing of the bat doesn't go past the front leg until the ball is struck. He can check the action of any stroke extremely late, and so much does he seem to see a delivery all the way that we are perplexed that so frequently he is clean-bowled by a length well up to him. From the back foot he can hit straight for four; and all his hits leave an impressive suggestion of power not entirely expended.

We shall remember, after we have relegated his 364 against Australia at Kennington Oval in 1938 to the museum of records in sport rather than to the things that belong to cricket, his innings at Sydney in the second Test match during the 1946–1947 rubber; only 37 but so dazzling in clean diamond-cut strokes that old men present babbled of Victor Trumper. He has even while playing for Yorkshire more than once caused some raising of the eyebrows. At Nottingham in 1948 he not only played, but played well, Miller, Johnston and Johnson as though for his own private and personal enjoyment. But usually he subdues his hand to what it works in—Yorkshire cricket. I have heard people say that he is not above 'playing for himself'. Well, seeing that he is Yorkshire to the bone's marrow, we should find ourselves metaphysically involved if we tried to argue that he is ever not playing for Yorkshire.

There is romance even in Yorkshire cricket, though they keep quiet about it. Romance has in fact visited the life and career of Hutton. In July 1930, the vast field of Headingley was a scene of moist, hot congestion with, apparently, only one cool, clean, well brushed individual present, name of Bradman, who during the five hours' traffic of the crease, made at will 300 runs, and a few more, before half-past six. He returned to the pavilion as though fresh from a band-box; the rest of us, players, umpires, crowd and scorers, especially the scorers, were exhausted; dirty, dusty and afflicted by a sense of the vanity of life. In all the heat and burden of this day at Leeds, more than twenty years ago, a boy of fourteen years was concealed amongst the boiling multitude; and so many of these thousands seethed and jostled that one of them, especially an infant in the eyes of the law, couldn't possibly (you might have sworn) have made the slightest difference to what we were all looking at, or to the irony of subsequent history. The solemn fact is that as Bradman compiled the 334 which was then the record individual score in a Test match, the boy hidden in the multitude was none other than the cricketer chosen already by the gods to break this record, if not Bradman's heart, eight years afterwards.

NEVILLE CARDUS (1889–1975), from *Cricket All The Year*

VIII

A Garland for Golfers

9 Feb. 1687

I rose at 7. I thought upon the method of pathologie and in playing the golve. I found that in all motions of your armes ye most contract your fingers verie strait and grip fast anything that is in them, for that doth command the motion exactly and keeps all the muscles of armes verie bent, I digested the rules of playing the golve into verse thus:

Gripe fast, stand with your left leg first not farr;
Incline your back and shoulders, but beware
You raise them not when back the club you bring;
Make all the motion with your bodie's swinge
And shoulders, holding still the muscles bent;
Play slowly first till you the way have learnt.
At such lenth hold the club as fitts your strenth,
The lighter head requires the longer lenth.
That circle wherein moves your club and hands
At forty-five degrees from the horizon stands
What at on stroak to effect not your dispaire
Seek only 'gainst the nixt it to prepare

I thought to digest the generall rules of motion into verse, which are these:

All motion with the strongest joynts performe
Lett the weaker second and perfect the same
The stronger joynt its motion first most end
Before the nixt to move in the least intend.
The muscles most with tonic motion move
For which the gripping fast great helpe doth prove.

THOMAS KINCAID (17th century), from *The Thoughts of Thomas Kincaid 1687–8*

'Victory on the Last Green'

To free the ball the chief now turns his mind,
Flies to the bank where lay the orb confined;
The pond'rous club upon the ball descends,
Involved in dust th' exulting orb ascends;
Their loud applause the pleased spectators raise;
The hollow bank resounds Castalio's praise.
  A mighty blow Pygmalion then lets fall;
Straight from th' impulsive engine starts the ball,
Answ'ring its master's just design, it hastes,
And from the hole scarce twice two clubs' length rests.
  Ah! what avails thy skill, since Fate decrees
Thy conqu'ring foe to bear away the prize?
  Full fifteen clubs' length from the hole he lay,
A wide cart-road before him crossed his way;
The deep cut tracks th' intrepid chief defies,
High o'er the road the ball triumphing flies,
Lights on the green, and scours into the hole;
Down it sinks depressed Pygmalion's soul.
Seized with surprise th' affrighted hero stands,
And feebly tips the ball with trembling hands;
The creeping ball its want of force complains,
A grassy tuft the loit'ring orb detains:
Surrounding crowds the victor's praise proclaim,
The echoing shore resounds Castalio's name.

THOMAS MATHISON (d. 1754), from *The Goff. An Heroi-Comical Poem*

In Praise of Gutta Percha

Sung at the meeting of the Innerleven Golf Club, 1st September, 1848

Of a' the changes that of late
Have shaken Europe's social state,
Let wondering politicians prate,
  And 'bout them make a wark a'.
A subject mair congenial here,
And dearer to a Golfer's ear
I sing—the change brought round this year
  By balls of GUTTA PERCHA!

Though Gouf be of our Games most rare,
Yet truth to speak, the tear and wear
O' balls were felt to be severe,
  And source o' great vexation.
When Gourlay's balls cost half-a-crown,
And Allan's not a farthing down,
The feck o's wad be harried soon
  In this era of taxation.

Raight fain we were to be content
Wi' used up balls new lickt wi' paint,
That ill concealed baith scar and rent—
  Balls scarcely fit for younkers.
And though our best wi' them we tried,
And nicely every club applied,
They whirred and fuffed, and dooked and shied,
  And sklentit into bunkers.

But times are changed—we dinna care
Though we may ne'er drive leather mair,
Be't stuffed wi' feathers or wi' hair—
  For noo we're independent.
At last a substance we hae got
Frae which, for scarce mair than a groat,
A ba' comes that can row and stot—
  A ba' the most transcendent.

They say it comes frae yont the sea,
The concrete juice o' some rare tree—
And hard and horny though it be,
  Just steep it in hot water—
As soft as potty soon 'twill grow,
Then 'tween your loofs a portion row—
When cool, a ba' ye'll get, I trow,
  That ye for years may batter.

Hail, GUTTA PERCHA, precious gum!
O'er Scotland's links lang may ye bum—
Some purse-proud billies haw and hum,
  And say ye're douf at fleein'.
But let them try ye fairly out
Wi' only balls for days about
Your merits they will loudly tout,
  And own they have been leein'.

'Tis true—at first ye seem to hing,
And try the air wi' timid wing—
But firmer grown, a sweep ye'll fling
Wi' ony ba' o' leather.
Ye're keen and certain at a put—
Nae weet your sides e'er open up—
And though for years your ribs they whup,
Ye'll never moutt a feather.

And should ony wild unchancy whack
Or cleek-stroke e'er gie ye a chack,
As wi' some Indian tomahawk,
Ye're mended unco easy.
How piteous e'er may be your plight,
The hot bath puts you a' to right;
Again you grow right smooth, and tight,
And fresh as ony daisy.

But noo that a' your praise is spent,
Ye'll listen to a friend's comment,
And kindlier tak on the paint—
Then wad ye be perfection.
And sure some scientific loon
On golfing will bestow a boon,
And brighten your complexion.

W. GRAHAM (18th century)

The Golfer's Garland

At Goff we contend without rancour or spleen,
And bloodless the laurels we reap on the green;
From vig'rous exertions our raptures arise,
And to crown our delights no poor fugitive dies.

From exercise keen, from strength active and bold,
We'll traverse the green, and forget we grow old;
Blue Devils, diseases, dull sorrow and care,
Knock'd down by our Balls as they whizz thro' the air.

Health, happiness, harmony, friendship, and fame,
Are the fruits and rewards of our favourite game.
A sport so distinguish'd the Fair must approve:
Then to Goff give the day, and the ev'ning to love.

Our first standing toast we'll to Goffing assign,
No other amusement's so truly divine;
It has charms for the aged, as well as the young,
Then as first of field sports let its praises be sung.

The next we shall drink to our friends far and near,
And the mem'ry of those who no longer appear;
Who have play'd their last round, and pass'd over that bourne
From which the best Goffer can never return.

Of rural diversions too long has the Chace
All the honours usurp'd, and assum'd the chief place;
But truth bids the Muse from henceforward proclaim,
That Goff, first of sports, shall stand foremost in fame.

O'er the Heath, see our heroes in uniform clad,
In parties well match'd, how they gracefully spread;
While with long strokes and short strokes they tend to the goal,
And with putt well directed plump into the hole.

ANONYMOUS (*c.* 1790)

The Golfiad

Arma virumque cano.—VIRGIL, *Æn.* i. l. 1.

Balls, clubs, and men I sing, who first, methinks,
Made sport and bustle on North Berwick Links,
Brought coin and fashion, betting, and renown,
Champagne and claret, to a country town,
And lords and ladies, knights and squires to ground
Where washerwomen erst and snobs were found!

Had I the pow'rs of him who sung of Troy—
Gem of the learned, bore of every boy—
Or him, the bard of Rome, who, later, told
How great Æneas roam'd and fought of old—
I then might shake the gazing world like them:
For, who denies I have as grand a theme?
Time-honour'd Golf !—I heard it whisper'd once
That he who could not play was held a dunce
On old Olympus, when it teem'd with gods.
O rare!—but it's a lie—I'll bet the odds!

No doubt these heathen gods, the very minute
They knew the game, would have delighted in it!
Wars, storms, and thunder—all would have been off !
Mars, Jove, and Neptune would have studied Golf,
And swiped—like Oliphant and Wood below—
Smack over Hell at one immortal go!
Had Mecca's Prophet known the noble game
Before he gave his paradise to fame,
He would have promis'd, in the land of light,
Golf all the day—and Houris all the night!
But this is speculation: we must come,
And work the subject rather nearer home;
Lest in attempting all too high to soar,
We fall, like Icarus, to rise no more.

The game is ancient—manly—and employs,
In its departments, women, men, and boys:
Men play the game, the boys the clubs convey,
And lovely woman gives the prize away,
When August brings the great, the medal day!
Nay, more: tho' some may doubt, and sneer, and scoff,
The female muse has sung the game of Golf,
And trac'd it down, with choicest skill and grace,
Thro' all its bearings, to the human race;
The tee, the start of youth—the game, our life—
The ball when fairly bunkered, man and wife.

Now, Muse, assist me while I strive to name
The varied skill and chances of the game.
Suppose we play a match: if all agree,
Let Clan and Saddell tackle Baird and me.
Reader, attend! and learn to play at Golf;
The lord of Saddell and myself strike off !
He strikes—he's in the ditch—this hole is ours;
Bang goes my ball—it's bunker'd, by the pow'rs.
But better play succeeds, these blunders past,
And in six strokes the hole is halved at last.

O hole! tho' small, and scarcely to be seen,
Till we are close upon thee, on the green;
And tho' when seen, save Golfers, few can prize,
The value, the delight, that in thee lies;
Yet, without thee, our tools were useless all—
The club, the spoon, the putter, and the ball:

Hell] a range of broken ground on St Andrews Links.

For all is done—each ball arranged on tee,
Each stroke directed—but to enter thee!
If—as each tree, and rock, and cave of old,
Had *its* presiding nymph, as we are told—
Thou hast *thy* nymph; I ask for nothing but
Her aid propitious when I come to putt.
Now for the second: And here Baird and Clan
In turn must prove which is the better man:
Sir David swipes sublime!—into the quarry!
Whiz goes the chief—a sneezer, by Old Harry!
'Now, lift the stones, but do not touch the ball,
The hole is lost if it but move at all:
Well play'd, my cock! you could not have done more;
'Tis bad, but still we may get home at four.'
Now, near the hole Sir David plays the odds;
Clan plays the like, and wins it, by the gods!
'A most disgusting *steal*; well, come away,
They're one ahead, but we have four to play.
We'll win it yet, if I can cross the ditch:
They're over, smack! come, there's another *sich*.'
Baird plays a trump—we hole at three—they stare,
And miss their putt—so now the match is square.

And here, who knows but, as old Homer sung,
The scales of fight on Jove's own finger hung?
Here Clan and Saddell; there swing Baird and I,—
Our merits, that's to say: for half an eye
Could tell, if *bodies* in the scales were laid,
Which must descend, and which must rise ahead.

If Jove were thus engaged, we did not see him,
But told our boys to clean the balls and tee 'em.
In this next hole the turf is most uneven;
We play like tailors—only in at seven,
And they at six; most miserable play!
But let them laugh who win. Hear Saddell say,
'Now, by the piper who the pibroch played
Before old Moses, we are one ahead,
And only two to play—a special *coup*!
Three five-pound notes to one!' 'Done, sir, with you.'
We start again; and in this dangerous hole
Full many a stroke is played with heart and soul:
'Give me the iron!' either party cries,
As in the quarry, track, or sand he lies.
We reach the green at last, at even strokes;
Some caddie chatters, *that* the chief provokes,

And makes him miss his putt; Baird holes the ball;
Thus, with but one to play, 'tis even all!
'Tis strange, and yet there cannot be a doubt,
That such a snob should put a chieftain out:
The noble lion, thus, in all his pride,
Stung by the gadfly, roars and starts aside;
Clan did *not* roar—*he* never makes a noise—
But said, 'They're very troublesome, these boys.'
His partner muttered something not so civil,
Particularly, 'scoundrels'—'at the devil!'
Now Baird and Clan in turn strike off and play
Two strokes, the best that have been seen today.
His spoon next Saddell takes, and plays a trump—
Mine should have been as good but for a bump
That turn'd it off. Baird plays the odds—it's all
But in!—at five yards, good, Clan holes the ball!
My partner, self, and song—all three are done!
We lose the match, and all the bets thereon!
Perhaps you think that, tho' I'm not a winner,
My muse should stay and celebrate the dinner;
The ample joints that travel up the stair,
To grace the table spread by Mrs. Blair;
The wine, the ale, the toasts, the jokes, the songs,
And all that to such revelry belongs:—
It may not be! 'twere fearful falling off
To sing such trifles after singing Golf
In most majestic strain; let others dwell
On such, and rack their carnal brains to tell
A tale of sensuality!—Farewell!

GEORGE FULLERTON CARNEGIE (1800–51)

Medal Day at St Andrews

This is the season of Congresses, and many have been in session lately, but few, we venture to think, have excited more enthusiasm among those who attended them than one that met last week at St Andrews—we suppose we must hardly say in session. On the last day of September the 'Royal and Ancient Golf Club' of that Royal and ancient burgh assembled by the shores of their sad-resounding sea, in the weather-beaten district known as the 'East Nuik of Fife', to hold their annual autumnal meeting. Students of Scottish history remember the decaying city of the Scottish patron saint as the seat of an archiepiscopal see whose metropolitans played a conspicuous part in the religious troubles that convulsed the kingdom. Archaeologists may have made pilgrimages to the ruins of its venerable shrines, or to the fragments of the famous castle that witnessed the burning of Wishart, the murder of the Cardinal who martyred him, and the fervid ministrations of the Scottish Apostle when the Reformers were being blockaded by the avengers of blood. But we fear that modern Scotchmen set but small store by those stirring memories, ecclesiastical or political. In Scotland St Andrews is best known as the capital and head-quarters of Golf, and golf is pre-eminently the national game. Curling alone can pretend to vie with it in popularity, but curling depends on the caprices of the weather. It can only be enjoyed in an iron frost, whereas you may indulge in golf any day or all days; and in point of antiquity even the venerable St Andrews itself, with its musty memories, need not be ashamed of its profitable foster child.

Golf has been played by the Scots literally from time immemorial, and we have little doubt that there were golf holes to be filled on the North Inch of Perth on the memorable day when the ground was cleared for the combat between the Clan Chattan and the Clan Quhele. We know, at all events, that His Majesty James II, nephew of that Earl of Rothsay who perished miserably in the tower of Falkland, found himself constrained to promulgate a statute against the game, setting forth that its too universal popularity interfered with the training for the national defence. The Scots of our own time are more peaceably disposed than their ancestors; but we venture to say that even a Liberal Ministry that advocated any such measure nowadays would have small chance in Scotch constituencies when they sent down candidates to contest the seats.

There are districts and burghs where every second inhabitant is a golfer. It is the game of the country gentry, of the busy professional men, of the *bourgeoisie* of flourishing centres of trade, of many of the artisans, and even of the tag-rag and bobtail. People who never took a golf club in their hands have a high regard for it as a game which is eminently respectable. It is the one amusement which any 'douce' man may pursue, irrespective of his calling, and risk neither respect nor social consideration. Read the list of the champions who paired off for the round of the course at last Thursday's contest, and we believe you will actually find gentlemen in Orders—and those, Scottish Orders—figuring among them. The fact speaks volumes to those who are familiar with local prejudices, for it is an unwritten canon of the Church that the consecrated caste of the Levites should avoid giving even a shadow of offence. This we know, that rising young barristers may take rank as golfers without resigning the hope of briefs, while they might as well sign a self-denying ordinance as go out fox-hunting even once in a way, or be detected indulging in the frivolity of dancing. On the other hand, the most ardent fox-hunters, salmon-fishers, deer-stalkers,—the men who are most devoted to the sports which make the pulses throb with the most irrepressible excitement, are among the very keenest patrons of the game. Once a golfer you are always a golfer; you find besides that *bon chien chasse de race* and the hereditary taste will break out in successive generations.

Wherever the golfer settles, or wherever he colonizes, he prospects the neighbourhood with both eyes wide open. One he naturally rivets on the main chance—on the farming, grazing, mining, or whatever may be his special object; but with the other he glances at the capabilities of the ground for his favourite game. We hear of golf in Canada, in Australia, in New Zealand, in all the colonies that are most affected by Scotchmen. There are towns in France where the Scotch settlers have inoculated the natives with the love of it; while in England it has been acclimatized from the bleak coasts of Northumberland to the sunny shores of Devon, and reports of matches are regularly forwarded to our sporting contemporaries from Crookham and Wimbledon, Blackheath and Westward Ho.

We own that at first sight it is difficult for the uninitiated looker-on to sympathise with the evident enthusiasm of the players. There does not seem to be anything very stimulating in grinding round a barren stretch of ground, impelling a gutta-percha ball before you, striving to land it in a succession of small holes in fewer strokes than your companion and opponent. But as to the reality of the excitement, you are soon compelled to take that for granted. You see gentlemen of all ages, often of the most self-indulgent or sedentary habits, turning out in every kind of weather, persevering to the dusk of a winter day, in spite of bitter wind and driving showers; or dragging about their cumbrous weight of flesh in hot defiance of the most sultry summer temperature. The truth is, that, appearances notwithstanding, experience proves it to be one of the most fascinating of pursuits; nor can there be any question that it is among the most invigorating. You play it on some stretch of ground by the sea, generally sheltered more or less by rows of hummocky sand-hills which break the force of the breeze without intercepting its freshness. You keep moving for the most part, although there is no need for moving faster than is necessary to set the blood in healthy circulation. In a tournament like that which ended on Wednesday at St Andrews you select your own partner. The deep-chested, strapping young fellows in their prime, with the reach of arm and strength of shoulder that make their swing so tremendous in driving the ball, pair off together. The obese and elderly gentlemen, touched in the wind by time, and doubtful subjects for insurance offices, may jog round placidly at their own pace. When the players are fairly handicapped as they ought to be, the excitement lasts from the beginning to the finish of the game—each separate stroke has its visible result; ill-luck may balk you when you least expect it, and a trivial mistake may land you in some fatal difficulty. Strength will tell no doubt, but it is skill that lands the winner. Be cautious as you will even when playing over the flat, it is seldom that your ball will be lying on the level, leaving you nothing to do but to take a free sweep at it with a sharp eye and a steady wrist. The variety of the clubs that your 'caddie' staggers under behind you is eloquent of the extreme niceties of the play. The club proper or the driver is a long shaft of seasoned hickory, tapering to a tough and narrow neck, before it swells into the broad flattened head, faced with horn or loaded with lead, which is intended to come in contact with the ball. But you have the shafts of others shortened to a variety of lengths, and the heads scooped out and bevelled away at all conceivable angles. This one is to be used when the ball lies embedded in a tuft of grass; that other when the ball must be 'skied' or lifted over some swell of the ground that looms awkwardly full in front of you. Then, again, there are clubs headed with iron instead of wood, with which you may lay on with less fear of breakages, when the ball has to be excavated by knack and force from some ugly pitfall it has chosen to settle into. Finally, there are the putting clubs, and in their judicious use is embodied the perfection of golfing science. It is comparatively easy getting your ball near to the hole; a combination of fair luck with average skill will carry most people over the long distances at a reasonable pace. But it is quite another thing succeeding in 'holing yourself'. Around each of the small circular orifices is a tolerably smooth bit of turf, termed the putting green, and once landed on the green or near to it, you settle down to a sort of lawn billiards. It is then the cool and wary old players have the advantage over their more athletic adversaries. It is then that nervousness will come out if you are any way given to it, and many a fine player will show himself flurried when a ring of scientific amateurs with money on the match are closing round and watching him breathlessly. He singles out the short stiff club he is to strike with, draws back and stoops to let his eye travel over the bit of round that lies between his ball and the hole. All may look pretty level in a bird's-eye view, but there are endless minute inequalities and obstacles; the stump of a green blade may divert the ball at the moderate pace at which he must set it rolling. Nothing but long experience and cool reflection will indicate the line the ball should be directed by, or train him to regulate the precise strength of his stroke. Let him lay on his hands half an ounce too heavily, and he sees the ball glide past the edge. Let him rest then a feather weight too lightly, and as it trickles down the imperceptible slope, it takes a faint bias to the side and balances itself tremblingly upon the lip instead of tumbling over the edge. There is exhilaration in the brisk walk round the links in the fresh sea air, but it is the culminating excitement of the critical moments on the putting greens which gives the national game its universal zest.

Not that you may not have had excitement in plenty, and in the way of play too, in the course of that same brisk round. The links, as we said, are stretches of short sandy grass by the sea shore, although occasionally they rise into steep downs, or sometimes, as with the Inches at Perth, are meadows on the banks of a river. Flat they are, and ought to be, in their general character, but if they were level like a lawn over all their surface, half the pleasures of Golf would be gone. The charm of the 'going' game lies in the excitement of the 'hazards'—a variety of malignant natural obstacles which are set like so many traps for the ball. Often skill may be trusted to clear these; sometimes skill will avail nothing, as when a sudden gust of wind curls your ball aside; not unfrequently a somewhat indifferent stroke will meet with punishment beyond its demerits. You meant to send your ball up the straight course, full in front of you, clearing the Scylla of a furze thicket on the one side, the Charybdis of a yawning sand-pit on the other. Your ball has made a turn to the right hand or to the left. In the former case it has fallen among the furze roots, and extrication is probably hopeless. You may as well lift it at once and submit to the penalty. In the latter you betake yourself to the most weighty of your irons, and labour to disengage yourself with more or less success. But hazards of the kind, though disagreeable, are indispensable, and on their quantity and character depend the merits of a golf ground. Thus the most famous gathering-places in Scotland, St Andrews—which claims precedence over all—and North Berwick, Prestwick, and Gullane, come very nearly to perfection in their several ways. But there are others nearly as good, although less notorious. Often, however, the hazards are wanting in a country where there is plenty of elbow-room with other conditions in your favour, and it is to that fact, coupled with ignorance, that we may attribute the comparatively circumscribed popularity of Golf. It certainly has the merit of being one of the healthiest, cheapest, and most innocent of recreations, and considering the ubiquity of Scotchmen who have delighted in it in their boyhood, it is a marvel that it has not been more generally acclimated all over the world.

The Times, 5 October 1874

Golf

Mabel Mulholland, the exquisite friend of my youth, married to a 'whole-time' player of games, used sometimes to wonder aloud whether God had intended His creature, Man, to spend its conscious hours in knocking a small white ball into a hole. I could see her point. The broad lawns that spread about Worlingham Hall were dotted with golfballs, that lay there, plentiful as mushrooms in a bumper year, to enable A.J.M. to practise his mashie-shots without the exertion of following up the ball. In his middle years he profoundly shocked me by enunciating the, to me, pernicious heresy that golf was a better sport than shooting. . . .

There had been nothing in my earlier years to incline me towards the game. As a very small boy indeed I had trudged round Hempton Common while my father and the bearded Mr Curtis, both wearing scarlet blazers to scare an imaginary public out of their way, knocked little white balls into gorse-bushes. And after the game they sat with two other men at a green-baize table in the wooden hut which served as club-house, and talked and talked, while I, insufferably bored, fidgeted in a corner. There was no tablecloth on the table, nor cups, nor plates; not a bun was in sight, only a bulging water-jug and two glasses. I felt as desolate as I had felt when awaking prematurely from my morning rest and peeping into the day-nursery, I saw no sign of dinner, only the nurses by the red table-cloth, busy with their work-baskets. There is an aridity, a dreariness about an unlaid table which I never could bear; and I think my enforced presence at a committee meeting of the Hempton Golf Club, unrefreshed by so much as a finger-biscuit, gave me an early prejudice against golf itself.

My first attempts to play the game, on the brand-new course at Valescure, were not such as to kindle ambition in me. The fairways, cut through the *maquis*, were narrow and stony; a few ancient warped clubs of my father's seemed to me most unhandy things with which to hit a ball, and, in spite of a few lessons from an English professional, I rarely managed to get the ball into the air. Nor had I at that time seen a golfer. My father and his friends were all hopeless rabbits, and there was nothing in our raw nine holes, except the exquisite views of mountain and sea between the stone pines, to attract good players. And when a school-friend, Julian Martin-Smith, came over for the day from Cannes, and displayed to my astonished eyes the ease and grace of a born golfer, I felt discouragement, not emulation. For if that was how a golf-ball should and could be hit, the game was clearly beyond me. I had my rowing to think about, and I did not persevere.

At Oxford I took against golf for quite other reasons. Accepting with heart and soul the stern traditions of the boat club that the things for which one rowed were the honour and renown of the college, I could envy, but never approve of, the men who went off with their clubs to enjoy themselves. It was all right for Archie Gordon, valuable oarsman as he might well have been, because he played golf for the University against Cambridge; besides, he was a Scot, for whom golf was less a game than a natural function. But when Eric Romilly and Compton-Bracebridge and a bunch of my familiars spent their afternoons having fun, and returned to eat crumpets without a tremor of conscience, I, who had been tubbing freshmen, felt that for all their charm they were essentially wasters. What good were they to the college? Men who were never in training!

But after going down from Oxford I began to soften towards golf. May it partly be that about this very time a new golf correspondent was beginning to write in *The Times* and in *Country Life?* A writer whose English was so impeccable, whose style so fluent, whose quotations so apt, that even those who cared nothing about the game found themselves irresistibly drawn to read him? How was it possible to side any longer with the 'hitting-a-little-ball-into-a-hole' school of thought when golf matches and tournaments were being reported in terms that Homer might have envied? When Tolley was always 'majestic', when Miss Wethered was the 'illustrious lady', when it could be written of a fine swinger of a golf-club that he must have had a beautiful tune running in his head, when even the tune could be identified as a hymn-tune:

> Happy birds that soar and fly,
> Round Thy altars, O Most High,

how could any reader continue to think of such a game, played by such lordly persons to the sound of such inward music, as anything but a noble one, made for heroes? I, for one, could not. Mr Bernard Darwin, making literature out of sport, did even more. He compelled us to believe that a golfer, fighting out the final of a championship in that most selfish of contests, a single at golf, was performing deeds that fell little short of heroic. I have no doubt whatever that, to be a great golfer, a man must have gifts of nerve, of temperament, of self-control, without which mere technical skill in hitting the little white ball would be of small avail. But it is not the high moral qualities of a Bobby Jones that Mr Darwin asks us to admire, nor his sheer skill either. In fact Mr Darwin asks us for nothing; rather he compels us to see Mr Bobby Jones as a paladin, a Roland, a gallant figure of romance, with his 'brave' putts, his 'daring' approaches, his 'intrepid' recoveries. The word 'glory' occurs as readily in Mr Darwin's reports of the contest for the President's Putter as in Napier's *History of the Peninsular War*. In short, Mr Darwin is a romantic, who has imagined a world of giants and splendour and, by the cunning of his pen, has made us believe in it too. His writing, call it what he may, is not reporting, it is creative. He has lifted a mere game to the level of chivalry, and made knightly tourneys out of stroke-competitions. And for his addicts there is no coming back to earth. His prose, readable to deceiving-point, sees to that. And how craftily he calls in aid the larks going up over Princes' at Sandwich, or the view of the Forth from Gullane Hill, to charm us into believing that the majestic Tolleys drew strength from their habitat! He weaves the landscape into the game, and all but credits a long, decisive putt to the sea-breezes of St Andrews. Or, like Milton, he intoxicates us with names, not of places or men but of holes and bunkers. Who, wherever English is spoken, has not heard of the Cardinal or the Principal's Nose? Who but Mr Darwin would venture to compare a solemn and silent contest between two courteous and self-controlled gentlemen to the snapping and worrying of curs? Yet 'dog-fight' is one of his favourite words for describing just such a contest. And we accept it and believe in it.

Mr Darwin's accomplishment must surely be unique. He has not only devoted his life to playing a game and to writing about it; he has managed to convince us that his life has been well spent. For he has endowed that game with so much humanity, nature, bravery, even poetry, that it appears, when seen through his eyes, to satisfy most of the requirements of a civilized and manly life and the life, into the bargain, of an artist. It is a remarkable performance.

It would be too much to say that, but for Mr Darwin, I should never have taken up golf. There were concurrent social pressures. I began to feel out of things at a gay party, for instance, with the Asquith family at Littlestone or Archerfield, when all the men and half the girls went off to the links, and I alone was incompetent to join them. So I took lessons; I got the ball into the air; I felt, now and then, the sensuous thrill of a well-timed stroke; and although I have, through natural ineptness, remained a rabbit for life, I count myself a golfer. By a golfer I mean a man who can walk on to the first tee of a strange course without feeling that he is being watched from every window in the club-house. (I do not include the first tee at Sandwich when White's Club is holding its annual competition. With Lewis Palmer I once found myself on that tee and on that occasion; it was just after lunch; the members of White's, in check tweeds, were drinking coffee on the balconies; they looked like the well-fed tigers they were; it was too much; I hit the ball with the toe of my driver, and it cannoned off the sand-box into a clump of marram-grass, and a roar of laughter went up behind me of which the memory makes me wince to this day.)

L. E. JONES, *I Forgot to Tell You*

Great Golfers

I have an immense field of choice, for I have seen them all from Willie Fernie (there was effortless beauty hard to beat), whom I watched nearly sixty years ago, to Henry Cotton, who must rank very high. I read an article the other day by Leonard Crawley, himself a very fine golfer, saying that if he were given the choice by Providence he would be Walter Hagen. It is no bad choice, for Hagen was most alluring, with his casualness and flamboyancy concealing a cold, shrewd, calculating brain, and above all with his powers of recovery. There was a certain shot chipped clean out of the cross-bunker in front of the 15th green at Sandwich when the championship hung by a hair—but I must refrain. I will choose two for the intense enjoyment I have had from them, J. H. Taylor and John Ball, very different in method and temperament, but alike in seductive greatness.

I have never wavered in my allegiance to J. H. since I first saw him in 1895. Especially in those 'gutty' days when the loose, long, slashing 'St Andrew's swing' was golfing youth's ideal, here was a player such as one had never seen before. There was no grand flourish of swing, but by comparison a quietness that was almost, not quite, stiffness. With his right foot well forward he seemed to be playing his full drives rather as other men played their mashie shots. He was so quick over it too and gave the ball what looked no more than a careless little switch. But how undeviatingly straight it went! Here was accuracy with a vengeance! It was only a little while before I first saw him that someone had coined the aphorism, apropos of his victory at Sandwich, that the only hazards for him were the guide flags. Good golf reduced to its simplest elements consists in doing the same thing over and over again. That was what he appeared to do and has been doing ever since. The charm of mechanical accuracy was there, but not that of suave and unmoved calm such as I have praised in other heroes. Outwardly J. H. can be dour and quiet enough, for that is part of his professional armour, but anyone who knows him is conscious that there are flames leaping up within. Some Scottish sage has declared of golf that it is 'aye fechtin' against ye' and J. H. always gave the impression of fighting, whether against himself, his enemy, the game or the elements. For that reason he has always been at his best, whether as a spectacle or a player, in the vilest weather, steady and immovable in the wind and rain, with his cap pulled down over his eyes, planted flat-footed and four-square. There was one cleek shot in a gale at Hoylake—but no, again I must control myself, and Hoylake brings me naturally to John Ball.

There are many people besides me, though not so many now as there once were, who are prepared to argue any golfing point with a reasonably open mind except that of beauty of style. As to that they will admit no question. There was only one John Ball. It may be that there were some things about his style not wholly beautiful, a certain rigidity of limb, for instance, in addressing the ball and a curious underhand grip of the right hand, but the swing itself was the perfection of that indefinable thing called rhythm; the upswing melted imperceptibly into the downswing in a way that belonged only to him. So at least thought his fanatical admirers, and I doubt whether any other golfer has had so many as John had in Hoylake, where the ordinary business of life seemed to come to an end if he were playing a big match and the whole population tramped prayerfully round behind him. He inspired this frantic hero-worship without in the smallest degree going out to seek it. When on one occasion of his winning a championship elsewhere all Hoylake was assembled at the station to welcome him, he got out of the train at the previous station and walked quietly home, alone and unsuspected across the links. He was reserved to the verge of shyness and said scarcely anything, except no doubt to the circle of his few intimates, but his sayings became famous, and he became a legend in his life-time.

Hoylake was inclined to regard him as uncanny, crediting him with mysterious powers of second sight and, if the stories are true, he was an inspired prophet about some of his own matches. Before his final at Westward Ho! against Abe Mitchell he said to Mr Janion, the Secretary at Hoylake and the most immobile of watchers, 'Do you remember having to come with me to the 37th at Prestwick?' Mr Janion admitted that he had so far bestirred himself. 'Well,' went on John, 'you'll have to go one hole further to-day'; and at the 38th hole Abe Mitchell topped his drive into a ditch and John Ball was champion for the eighth time.

Putting, in which John did not particularly excel, is the part of golf which can appear most magical, and by way of supplement, I must add a putter to my gallery. Here I have no doubt at all. He shall be Jerome Travers, once Open Champion and several times Amateur Champion of the United States. I saw him win one of those Amateur Championships at Garden City when he was reduced to driving with an iron and was in mortal terror of hitting his mashie shots off the socket; and yet he won comfortably and was never severely pressed. He just putted his way through with such precision of striking on the green as I have never seen. He had not the diabolical aspect of another great American putter, Walter Travis, heightened as it was by the familiar black cigar, but he was to my eyes more perfectly mechanical. The ball clicked off his club and into the hole as if he had been wound up by a penny in the slot.

BERNARD DARWIN (1876–1961), from *Unforgettable Days*

Scientific Golf

People are continually writing to the papers—or it may be one solitary enthusiast who writes under a number of pseudonyms—on the subject of sport, and the over-doing of the same by the modern young man. I recall one letter in which 'Efficiency' gave it as his opinion that if the Young Man played less golf and did more drill, he would be all the better for it. I propose to report my doings with the professor on the links at some length, in order to refute this absurd view. Everybody ought to play golf, and nobody can begin it too soon. There ought not to be a single able-bodied infant in the British Isles who has not foozled a drive. To take my case. Suppose I had employed in drilling the hours I had spent in learning to handle my clubs. I might have drilled before the professor by the week without softening his heart. I might have ported arms and grounded arms and presented arms, and generally behaved in the manner advocated by 'Efficiency', and what would have been the result? Indifference on his part, or—and if I overdid the thing—irritation. Whereas, by devoting a reasonable portion of my youth to learning the intricacies of golf I was enabled. . . .

It happened in this way.

To me, as I stood with Ukridge in the fowl-run on the morning following my maritime conversation with the professor, regarding a hen that had posed before us, obviously with a view to inspection, there appeared a man carrying an envelope. Ukridge, who by this time saw, as Calverley almost said, 'under every hat a dun', and imagined that no envelope could contain anything but a small account, softly and silently vanished away, leaving me to interview the enemy.

'Mr Garnet, sir?' said the foe.

I recognised him. He was Professor Derrick's gardener.

I opened the envelope. No. Father's blessings were absent. The letter was in the third person. Professor Derrick begged to inform Mr Garnet that, by defeating Mr Saul Potter, he had qualified for the final round of the Combe Regis Golf Tournament, in which, he understood, Mr Garnet was to be his opponent. If it would be convenient for Mr Garnet to play off the match on the present afternoon, Professor Derrick would be obliged if he would be at the Club House at half-past two. If this hour and day were unsuitable, would he kindly arrange others. The bearer would wait. . . .

I felt ruthless towards the professor. I cannot plead ignorance of the golfer's point of view as an excuse for my plottings. I knew that to one whose soul is in the game as the professor's was, the agony of being just beaten in an important match exceeds in bitterness all other agonies. I knew that, if I scraped through by the smallest possible margin, his appetite would be destroyed, his sleep o' nights broken. He would wake from fitful slumber moaning that if he had only used his iron instead of his mashie at the tenth, all would have been well; that, if he had putted more carefully on the seventh green, life would not be drear and blank; that a more judicious manipulation of his brassy throughout might have given him something to live for. All these things I knew.

And they did not touch me. I was adamant. The professor was waiting for me at the Club House, and greeted me with a cold and stately inclination of the head.

'Beautiful day for golf,' I observed in my gay, chatty manner. He bowed in silence.

'Very well,' I thought. 'Wait. Just wait.'

'Miss Derrick is well, I hope?' I added aloud.

That drew him. He started. His aspect became doubly forbidding.

'Miss Derrick is perfectly well, sir, I thank you.'

'And you? No bad effect, I hope, from your dip yesterday?'

'Mr Garnet, I came here for golf, not conversation,' he said.

We made it so. I drove off from the first tee. It was a splendid drive. I should not say so if there were anyone else to say so for me. Modesty would forbid. But, as there is no one, I must repeat the statement. It was one of the best drives of my experience. The ball flashed through the air, took the bunker with a dozen feet to spare, and rolled on to the green. I had felt all along that I should be in form. Unless my opponent was equally above himself, he was a lost man. I could toy with him.

The excellence of my drive had not been without its effect on the professor. I could see that he was not confident. He addressed his ball more strangely and at greater length than any one I had ever seen. He waggled his club over it as if he were going to perform a conjuring trick. Then he struck and topped it.

The ball rolled two yards.

He looked at it in silence. Then he looked at me—also in silence.

I was gazing seawards.

When I looked round he was getting to work with a brassy.

This time he hit the bunker, and rolled back. He repeated this manœuvre twice.

'Hard luck!' I murmured sympathetically on the third occasion, thereby going as near to being slain with a niblick as it has ever been my lot to go.

Your true golfer is easily roused in times of misfortune; and there was a red gleam in the eye of the professor turned to me.

'I shall pick my ball up,' he growled.

We walked on in silence to the second tee. He did the second hole in four, which was good. I did it in three, which—unfortunately for him—was better.

I won the third hole.

I won the fourth hole.

I won the fifth hole.

I glanced at my opponent out of the corner of my eyes. The man was suffering. Beads of perspiration stood out on his forehead.

His play had become wilder and wilder at each hole in arithmetical progression. If he had been a plough he could hardly have turned up more soil. The imagination recoiled from the thought of what he would be doing in another half-hour if he deteriorated at his present speed.

A feeling of calm and content stole over me. I was not sorry for him. All the viciousness of my nature was uppermost in me. Once, when he missed the ball clean at the fifth tee, his eye met mine, and we stood staring at each other for a full half-minute without moving. I believe, if I had smiled then, he would have attacked me without hesitation. There is a type of golfer who really almost ceases to be human under stress of the wild agony of a series of foozles.

The sixth hole involves the player in a somewhat tricky piece of cross-country work, owing to the fact that there is a nasty ditch to be negotiated some fifty yards from the green. It is a beast of a ditch, which, if you are out of luck, just catches your second shot. 'All hope abandon ye who enter here' might be written on a notice board over it.

The professor entered there. The unhappy man sent his second, as nice and clean a brassy shot as he had made all day, into its very jaws. And then madness seized him. A merciful local rule, framed by kindly men who have been in that ditch themselves, enacts that in such a case the player may take his ball and throw it over his shoulder, losing a stroke. But once, so the legend runs, a scratch man who found himself trapped, scorning to avail himself of this rule at the expense of its accompanying penalty, wrought so shrewdly with his niblick that he not only got out but actually laid his ball dead: and now optimists sometimes imitate his gallantry, though no one yet has been able to imitate his success.

The professor decided to take a chance: and he failed miserably. As I was on the green with my third, and, unless I putted extremely poorly, was morally certain to be down in five, which is bogey for the hole, there was not much practical use in his continuing to struggle. But he did in a spirit of pure vindictiveness, as if he were trying to take it out of the ball. It was a grisly sight to see him, head and shoulders above the ditch, hewing at his obstinate colonel. It was a similar spectacle that once induced a lay spectator of a golf match to observe that he considered hockey a silly game.

'*Sixteen!*' said the professor between his teeth. Then he picked up his ball.

I won the seventh hole.

I won the eighth hole.

The ninth we halved, for in the black depths of my soul I had formed a plan of fiendish subtlety. I intended to allow him to win—with extreme labour—eight holes in succession.

Then, when hope was once more strong in him, I would win the last, and he would go mad.

I watched him carefully as we trudged on. Emotions chased one another across his face. When he won the tenth hole he merely refrained from oaths. When he won the eleventh a sort of sullen pleasure showed in his face. It was at the thirteenth that I detected the first dawning of hope. From then onward it grew.

When, with a sequence of shocking shots, he took the seventeenth hole in seven, he was in a parlous condition. His run of success had engendered within him a desire for conversation. He wanted, as it were, to flap his wings and crow. I could see Dignity wrestling with Talkativeness. I gave him the lead.

'You have got back your form now,' I said.

Talkativeness had it. Dignity retired hurt. Speech came from him with a rush. When he brought off an excellent drive from the eighteenth tee, he seemed to forget everything.

'Me dear boy,'—he began; and stopped abruptly in some confusion. Silence once more brooded over us as we played ourselves up the fairway and on to the green.

He was on the green in four. I reached it in three. His sixth stroke took him out.

I putted carefully to the very mouth of the hole.

I walked up to my ball, and paused. I looked at the professor. He looked at me.

'Go on,' he said hoarsely.

Suddenly a wave of compassion flooded over me. What right had I to torture the man like this?

'Professor,' I said.

'Go on,' he repeated.

'That looks a simple shot,' I said, eyeing him steadily, 'but I might miss it.'

He started.

'And then you would win the Championship.'

He dabbed at his forehead with a wet ball of a handkerchief.

'It would be very pleasant for you after getting so near it the last two years.'

'Go on,' he said for the third time. But there was a note of hesitation in his voice.

'Sudden joy,' I said, 'would almost certainly make me miss it.'

We looked at each other. He had the golf fever in his eyes.

'If,' I said slowly, lifting my putter, 'you were to give your consent to my marriage with Phyllis—'

He looked from me to the ball, from the ball to me, and back again to the ball. It was very, very near the hole.

'Why not?' I said.

He looked up, and burst into a roar of laughter.

'You young devil,' said he, smiting his thigh, 'you young devil, you've beaten me.'

I swung my putter, and the ball trickled past the hole.

'On the contrary,' I said, 'you have beaten me.'

I left the professor at the Club House and raced back to the farm. I wanted to pour my joys into a sympathetic ear. Ukridge, I knew, would offer that same sympathetic ear. A good fellow, Ukridge. Always interested in what you had to tell him; never bored.

'Ukridge!' I shouted.

No answer.

I flung open the dining-room door. Nobody.

I went into the drawing-room. It was empty. I drew the garden, and his bedroom. He was not in either.

'He must have gone for a stroll,' I said.

I rang the bell.

The Hired Retainer appeared, calm and imperturbable as ever.

'Sir?'

'Oh, where is Mr Ukridge, Beale?'

'Mr Ukridge, sir,' said the Hired Retainer nonchalantly, 'has gone.'

'Gone!'

'Yes, sir. Mr Ukridge and Mrs Ukridge went away together by the three o'clock train.'

P. G. WODEHOUSE, *Love Among the Chickens*

Seaside Golf

How straight it flew, how long it flew,
  It clear'd the rutty track
And soaring, disappeared from view
  Beyond the bunker's back—
A glorious, sailing, bounding drive
That made me glad I was alive.

And down the fairway, far along
  It glowed a lonely white;
I played an iron sure and strong
  And clipp'd it out of sight,
And spite of grassy banks between
I knew I'd find it on the green.

And so I did. It lay content
  Two paces from the pin;
A steady putt and then it went
  Oh, most securely in.
The very turf rejoiced to see
That quite unprecedented three.

Ah! seaweed smells from sandy caves
  And thyme and mist in whiffs,
In-coming tide, Atlantic waves
  Slapping the sunny cliffs,
Lark song and sea sounds in the air
And splendour, splendour everywhere.

SIR JOHN BETJEMAN (1906–84)

'University Match of '35'

I drove Henry out to the trials in my own car—a 1928 Austin Seven. We discussed chances. There was one Freshman certain to get in, Laddie Lucas, the reigning boy champion—how many other brilliant new boys would there be? Having met Hugh I felt peculiarly nervous. It was no sedative to find myself paired with the great Lucas. I was glad it was only a question of marking cards, not a match, but I had not enough detachment not to play against him. The first hole is long, a bogey five. I started appallingly well with a three, and another three at the second where it is easy to take four. Laddie was left-handed. He had one of the most glorious golfing actions I have ever seen. A great left-hander is nothing like a right-hander in a mirror. He played golf as Frank Woolley played cricket, with a magnificent natural grace and panache. Hugh's secretary, who took our cards, still looking about seven feet high but no longer so fierce was Tony Law.

Invitations to play in matches came on C.U.G.C. postcards. Judging by the previous year I knew the most likely post. The first time it felt like the end of Sweeney as I sat in my digs:

> And you wait for a knock and the turning of a lock
> for you know the hangman's waiting for you.

He would be, if there were no knock. I kept clicking my watch open and shut in a futile way. The card asked me to be at King and Harper's at six-thirty a.m. All our away matches were played beyond London. We drove our own cars. Mine being slow was a reserve, but on occasions I made Surrey only a little astern of the Vauxhalls and Hillmans.

Match days, for me, began the evening before. I went back to my rooms usually directly from Mildenhall. I was always too excited to read. I played my gramophone. Oh desperate solitary drinking! I gave myself a glass of sherry—sometimes, even two. Sometimes I gave myself the finale of Beethoven No 7 with the second glass, but generally I preferred Ellington's slow gloomy Blues-tunes. My landlady brought me a boiled egg and bread and butter. About seven I went to bed. I wonder, now, if there was any stirring of the black cauldron of The Ferns. I lay and thought of tomorrow ('cras amet'). I wondered what the course would be like: all were strange to me. Who would I play against? Then, how would I play? There was no set pattern, but at some moment I was overcome with nerves. I lay physically trembling all over for lifetimes of blank minutes. I was powerless to combat this. Sometimes I was sick. These attacks lasted anything up to an hour. Then I slept, like the living, deep and lost until my landlady's daughter woke me with a jug of shaving water and a cup of tea at five-thirty. I was confidently nervous when I came to play. The day was in an envelope, like a love-letter. There were preordained generalities but would there be, in it, some positive message? You put it away into a pocket of delicious trepidation. Walking through Cambridge in the dawn twilight of autumn was like the chilling promises of a mermaid. In the dim watery air moved the shapeless forms of 'bedders' more antediluvian and undiscoverable than the undiscovered coelacanth. Else a vast silence reigned. The silence that emanates from stone is wholly different from brick-silence. We drove west into opening day. We ate an enormous breakfast at a pub in St Albans. By half-past nine we were changing to play at Sunningdale, say, or Woking. A serious innocence in golf in those beautiful birch and heather and emerald green gardens kept me straight. Caddies told me to aim left, or right, of the pitfalls of knowledge. I did. Worplesdon shone in autumn dew and dewy filaments and patterns of dew on fallen leaves and tiny wakes of dew behind your ball on the long putts though the greens had been 'swept'. I went round in seventy-one. By some kind of divination Hugh had paired Laddie and me as foursomes partners. I had complete faith in his powers to get me out of any trouble, consequently I seldom put him crooked. Never once were we at odds with each other—not even at the eighteenth at West Hill where my drive was a couple of feet in, on the fairway, to the right, just by a holly tree. Being left-handed he had to stand mostly in the tree. Like two actors do, who are *en rapport*, we produced and improved each other. I never had any doubt which was the star-player. I know that whatever gifts I have as a producer of poetry-readers have a deep root here.

Laddie and I were always likely to win. This gave me great confidence for the afternoon 'singles' matches. After tea, and possibly a drink, there was a tedious drive back to Cambridge, eastward into darkening night, sometimes against time, for cars had to be in by eight-thirty. It never seemed a long day.

Laddie, early and duly, got his Blue. There came a home match at Mildenhall, in which for the first and only time our partnership was beaten. I went on for the second act in a curious and cussed frame of mind, both resilient and resentful. I thought, damn Laddie for letting me down, damn me for letting him down, if I don't win this afternoon it's no use. I was playing against Henry Longhurst. Already amongst golfing journalists who were doubtable, he was known to be redoubtable, like Bernard Darwin. I had no reason to doubt or re-doubt Henry's golf. In the gathering gloom we walked up to the last tee. We were all square. I needed a four for a seventy-two. As I walked towards my drive which I had prudently, or fearfully, placed up left, I saw Hugh and Tony slip from the clubhouse. I would have seen an ant. The hours, days, months, concentrated upon this. I knew exactly how to play this shot. I had no qualms at all. I took my mashie-niblick and put my ball a yard from the hole. Henry's second was at the back of the green. His putt was inside where my ball lay. He too had seen Hugh and Tony. He too had captained Cambridge. I conceived he might give me my putt. For the first time for two-and-a-half hours, Henry stopped talking. The silence lay heavy between my ball and the hole. I think I held my putter about an inch from the head, shut my eyes, and shovelled. I can hear the ball drop. I shall never see it. Then I heard Hugh ask in his soft diffident voice: 'Would you care to play against Oxford?' as if, really, I might have something better to do. I said I would. I read Yeats almost all night for sheer joy and relief and to convince myself that this had really happened. I understood why Henry did not give me the putt, and blessed him.

The University match of 1935 was at Burnham and Berrow in Somerset. During the season the Neilson Strolling Players had not had very good notices. The Oxford National Theatre had played to full houses. One felt a mere sort of Gielgud, who could not regularly break seventy, was not considered. Our chances were not favoured by the Press.

Not long before the match Hugh had decided on a switch. He and Laddie were to play top foursomes; Paddy Gold and I were to play bottom. This exchange was to me no more than a delightful change of rhyme. I had had four years of three compulsory team-games. I had no inkling of what a true team was until these months. We 'trained' very happily at the Grand Atlantic Hotel, Weston-super-Mare. Pimm's No 1 Cup was one-and-six a half pint, an expensive relaxation.

The weather was 'blue March days'. Rumours, I have said, are supersonic round golf courses to spectators. The worst comes twice as fast to players. Almost before we had started, some happy ape, no doubt a double first at Oxford, told us 'Neilson and Lucas seven down at the ninth' but before we had finished the morning a sober mathematical genius, no doubt with an ordinary degree at Cambridge, told us that Neilson and Lucas had done the last nine in two over threes and got five back. Something like that had happened: I think none of us wanted to know exactly what. It meant anything was possible. Paddy and I stood on the thirty-fifth tee one up, for the first time all day. This was a short hole. I cut mine a shade. I heard Bernard Darwin groan as deep as the bunker we were in. Kenneth Scott—the name one, but how far, above mine at Lytham—middled his. All square. I and Ken walked forward to where the drives would land. Oxford first, left in the rough. Gold, pure gold, clang down the middle. Ken chose to do precisely what I would have done, he took out a spoon, and my heart warmed to him. It was a wild risk. When he hit the ball two yards my heart did not exactly bleed for him, but I knew how he felt. Oxford passed us in three, but all I had to do was hit the ball on to the green. It got nicely near and Paddy whose drive won us the match was appropriately not asked to putt. 'By a miracle,' wrote Darwin, 'the day was even.' I don't think any of us felt the score of two-and-a-half matches all was miraculous: what we did feel was that Hugh and Laddie had showed us that we could win. The next day was warmer and bluer. I played in a cricket shirt. At lunch time on the second day, knowing elder-statesmen 'know'. I heard one say that although he was not exactly walking away with it, as expected, Duncan was sure to beat Neilson. Class would tell. But class is a delphic oracle. Hugh's defeat of Duncan was the measure both of skill and a personal courage none of us doubted. No one match 'wins' a team match. As far as is possible this did. News filtered back to me, playing seventh out of ten: 'Hugh's beaten Tony Duncan.' Whatever the news brought to Aix it was nothing to this. My own personal crisis was over and past. My opponent had stabbed himself to the heart three times on the twenty-eighth green, and his body grew lighter and ligher as I carried him in. Oxford elders were forced to admit that if Gold won, in the last match. . . .

At this moment Mama materialised from a sand-hill. It is the fate of most parents to watch the University match in acute discomfort, their sons having demanded invisibility. She was still almost bent double from watching through people's legs. My brother Bill had driven her down. He appeared too and we all three hurried back towards the fifteenth (thirty-third) green. We were in time to see the hole gobble up Paddy's ball and hear Bernard give a great whooping noise. I was glad I had heard both. Bill had a brand new overcoat. Thinking I was getting cold in my cricket shirt he made me put it on. It was the first time I wore a coat I still wear now, but he has

> made of earth and sea
> His overcoat for ever,
> And wears the turning globe.

PATRIC DICKINSON (b. 1914), *The Good Minute*

IX

Bowls and Tennis

A Parallel betwixt Bowling and Preferment

Preferment, like a game at boules,
  To feede our hope hath divers play:
Heere quick it runns, there soft it roules,
  The betters make and shew the way
On upper ground, so great allies
  Doe many *cast* on their desire;
Some up are thrust and forc'd to rise,
  When those are stopt that would aspire.

Some, whose heate and zeal exceed,
  Thrive well by *rubbs* that curb their haste,
And some that languish in their speed
  Are cherished by some favour's blaste;
Some rest in other's *cutting out*
  The fame by whom themselves are made;
Some fetch a *compass* farr about,
  And secretly the marke invade.

Some get by *knocks*, and so advance
  Their fortune by a boysterous aime:
And some, who have the sweetest chance,
  Their en'mies *hit*, and win the game.
The fairest *casts* are those that owe
  No thanks to fortune's giddy sway;
Such honest men good *bowlers* are
  Whose own true *bias cutts* the way.

WILLIAM STROAD (1602–45), from Justin Paggit's *Memorandum Book*

The Bowling Green

This poem was originally written by Addison in Latin, intended as an imitation of, and tribute to, Virgil's *Georgics*. Nicholas Amhurst translated it and subsequently published it in *Poems on Several Occasions* (1719).

Where smooth and level as the Summer Main,
A spacious Area opens on the Plain;
While with descending Dews the Herbage sweats,
Nor feels the rising Sun's intenser Heats,
The sharpen'd Scythe prevents the grassy Height,
And reaps the scanty Harvest of the Night:
The rolling Stone renews its Morning Round,
To crush the springing Turf, and sink the knotty Ground.
And now the polish'd Globes, a num'rous Band,
Prepar'd for Motion by the Artist's Hand;
Glitt'ring with Oil, and splendid to the Sight,
O'er the soft, verdant Surface speed their Flight.
But least some Bowler should his Cast disown,
By diff'rent Marks the diff'rent Orbs are known:
For Gamesters vary; some prefer the Bowl
That byas'd wheels obliquely to the Goal:
While others will a diff'rent Choice approve
Of those which in a Line directly move.
The chosen Numbers part on either side,
As, or Consent, or doubtful Lots divide;
Each Chief assumes his Arms; when now behold
The Jack exulting o'er the Surface roll'd;
At which their missive Orbs the Bowlers aim,
And who arrives the nearest, wins the Game.
The Leader poises in his Hand the Bowl,
And gently launches to the distant Goal:
The current Orb prolongs its circling Course,
Till by Degrees it loses all its Force.
When now another o'er the Level bounds,
And Orb succeeding Orb the Block surrounds:
Scatter'd they lie, and barricade the Green,
That scarce a single Bowl can pass between.
When now, with better Skill, and nicer Care,
The dext'rous Youth renews the Wooden War,
Beyond the rest his winding Timber flies,
And works insinuating, and wins the Prize.
But if perchance he sees, with Madness stung,
The lagging Wood move impotent along;
If its faint Motion languish on the way,
And, short of Length, it press the verdant Lay:

Nimbly he strides behind a-cross the Grass,
And bending hovers o'er the rolling Mass;
Least foul Disgrace should on his Arm redound,
He blames the Rising-Rub and guilty Ground.

What sudden Laughter echoes o'er the Green,
When some unlucky, artless Cast is seen;
When the too pond'rous Lead with stubborn Force
Allures the Globe from its appointed Course!
The Bowler chafes, and fruitless Rage ensues,
His Body to a Thousand Postures screws:
He blames he knows not what, with angry Blood,
He frets, he stamps, and damns th'erroneous Wood:
Th'erroneous Wood his fruitless Rage disdains,
And still its former, wayward Course maintains.

But if a Bowl, dismiss'd with equal Strength,
Obtains exactly the intended Length,
And, nicely passing thro' the crouding Balls,
Prone on the passive Jack incumbent falls:
With loud Applause the splitting Heav'ns they rend,
And all the Caster and the Cast commend.
When now the adverse Foe projects around
His careful Eyes, and marks the ambient Ground:
And studious the contiguous Globes to part,
He summons all his Strength and all his Art;
Th'extended Vigour of his Nerves applies,
And rapid from his Arm the brandish'd Engine flies.
Scarce half so swiftly to the Elëian Goal
With rival Speed the whirling Chariots roll;
While the fleet Axle mocks the flagging Wind,
And leaves the flying Village far behind.

When, if the Wooden Guards, immure the Foe,
And break the Vengeance of the whirling Blow;
If the conflicting Orbs are driv'n around,
And, loosely scatter'd, strew th' Olympic Ground:
He chides his Fate, his fervid Spleen boils high,
Calls the Gods false, and Damns the guilty Sky.

But if his Bowl with easy Passage slide,
And with a Clash the wedded Orbs divide;
His Partners shout, the Croud espouse his Cause,
And the wide Plain re-murmurs with Applause.

Mean while the Dog-Star burns with sultry Heat,
And ev'ry Limb is drown'd in briny Sweat:
They court the shady Breeze, and cool of Day,
And from their Temples wipe the trickling Drops away.

JOSEPH ADDISON and NICHOLAS AMHURST
(1697–1742)

From *The Bowling-Green*

Where fair Sabrina's wand'ring currents flow,
A large smooth plain extends its verdant brow;
Here ev'ry morn, while fruitful vapours feed
The swelling blade and bless the smoking mead,
A cruel tyrant reigns: like Time, the swain
Whets his unrighteous scythe, and shaves the plain.
Beneath each stroke the peeping flow'rs decay,
And all th' unripened crop is swept away.
The heavy roller next he tugs along,
Whiffs his short pipe, or rears a rural song;
With curious eye then the pressed turf he views,
And ev'ry rising prominence subdues.
Now when each craving stomach was well stored,
And 'Church and King' had travelled round the board,
Hither at Fortune's shrine to pay their court,
With eager hopes the motley tribe resort:
Attorneys spruce in their plate-buttoned frocks,
And rosy parsons, fat and orthodox;
Of ev'ry sect, Whigs, Papists and High-fliers,
Cornuted aldermen, and hen-pecked squires;
Foxhunters, quacks, scribblers in verse and prose,
And half-pay captains, and half-witted beaux.
On the green cirque the ready racers stand,
Disposed in pairs, and tempt the bowler's hand;
Each polished sphere does his round brother own,
The twins distinguished by their marks are known.
As the strong rein guides the well-managed horse,
Here weighty lead infused directs their course.
These in the ready road drive on with speed,
But those in crooked paths more artfully succeed.
So the tall ship, that makes some dang'rous bay,
With a side wind obliquely slopes her way.
Lo! there the silver tumbler fixed on high,
The victor's prize, inviting every eye!

The champions or consent or chance divide,
While each man thinks his own the surer side,
And the jack leads, the skilful bowler's guide.
   Bendo stripped first; from foreign coasts he brought
A chaos of receipts, and anarchy of thought,
Where the tumultuous whims, to faction prone,
Still justled monarch Reason from her throne:
More dang'rous than the porcupine's his quill,
Inured to slaughter, and secure to kill.
Let loose, just heav'n, each virulent disease,
But save us from such murderers as these;
Might Bendo live but half a patriarch's age,
Th' unpeopled world would sink beneath his rage;
Nor need t' appease the just Creator's ire
A second deluge, or consuming fire.
He winks one eye, and knits his brow severe,
Then from his hand launches the flying sphere;
Out of the green the guiltless wood he hurled,
Swift as his patients from this nether world:
Then grinned malignant, but the jocund crowd
Deride his senseless rage, and shout aloud.
   Next, Zadoc, 'tis thy turn, imperious priest!
Still late at church, but early at a feast.
No turkey-cock appears with better grace,
His garments black, vermilion paints his face;
His wattles hang upon his stiffened band,
His platter feet upon the trigger stand,
He grasps the bowl in his rough brawny hand.
Then squatting down, with his grey goggle-eyes
He takes his aim, and at the mark it flies.
Zadoc pursues, and wobbles o'er the plain,
But shakes his strutting paunch and ambles on in vain;
For oh! wide-erring to the left it glides,
The inmate lead the lighter wood misguides.
He sharp reproofs with kind entreaties joins,
Then on the counter side with pain reclines;
As if he meant to regulate its course
By pow'r attractive and magnetic force.
Now almost in despair, he raves, he storms,
Writhes his unwieldy trunk in various forms:
Unhappy Proteus! still in vain he tries
A thousand shapes, the bowl erroneous flies,
Deaf to his pray'rs, regardless of his cries.
His puffing cheeks with rising rage inflame,
And all his sparkling rubies glow with shame.

Bendo's proud heart, proof against Fortune's frown,
Resolves once more to make the prize his own;
Cautious he plods, surveying all the green,
And measures with his eye the space between.
But as on him 'twas a peculiar curse
To fall from one extreme into a worse,
Conscious of too much vigour, now for fear
He should exceed, at hand he checks the sphere.
Soon as he found its languid force decay,
And the too weak impression die away,
Quick after it he scuds, urges behind
Step after step, and now, with anxious mind,
Hangs o'er the bowl slow-creeping on the plain,
And chides its faint efforts, and bawls amain.
Then on the guiltless green the blame to lay,
Curses the mountains that obstruct his way;
Brazens it out with an audacious face,
His insolence improving with disgrace.
Zadoc, who now with three black mugs had cheered
His drooping heart, and his sunk spirits reared,
Advances to the trig with solemn pace,
And ruddy hope sits blooming on his face.
The bowl he poised, with pain his hams he bends,
On well-chose ground unto the mark it tends:
Each adverse heart pants with unusual fear,
With joy he follows the propitious sphere.
Alas! how frail is ev'ry mortal scheme!
We build on sand, our happiness a dream.
Bendo's short bowl stops the proud victor's course,
Purloins his fame, and deadens all its force.
At Bendo from each corner of his eyes
He darts malignant rays, then mutt'ring flies
Into the bow'r; there, panting and half-dead,
In thick mundungus clouds he hides his head.

WILLIAM SOMERVILLE

Tennis Fashionable in England

We have undoubted authority to prove that Henry VII was a tennis player. In a MS. register of his expenditures made in the thirteenth year of his reign, and preserved in the Remembrancer's Office, this entry occurs: 'Item, for the king's loss at tennis, twelvepence; for the loss of balls, threepence.' Hence one may infer, that the game was played abroad, for the loss of the balls would hardly have happened in a tennis-court. His son Henry, who succeeded him, in the early part of his reign was much attached to this diversion; which propensity, as Hall assures us, being perceived by certayne craftie persons about him, they brought in Frenchmen and Lombards to make wagers with hym, and so he lost muche money; but when he perceyved theyr crafte, he eschued the company and let them go.' He did not however give up the amusement, for we find him, according to the same historian, in the thirteenth year of his reign, playing at tennis with the emperor Maximilian for his partner, against the prince of Orange and the marquis of Brandenborow: 'the earl of Devonshire stopped on the prince's side, and the lord Edmond on the other side; and they departed even handes on both sides, after eleven games fully played.' Among the additions that king Henry VIII made to Whitehall, if Stowe be correct, were 'divers fair tennis-courts, bowling-allies, and a cockpit.'

James I, if not himself a tennis player, speaks of the pastime with commendation, and recommends it to his son as a species of exercise becoming a prince. Charles II frequently diverted himself with playing at tennis, and had particular kind of dresses made for that purpose. So had Henry VIII. In the wardrobe rolls we meet with tenes-cotes for the king, also tennis-drawers and tennis-slippers.

JOSEPH STRUTT (1749–82)

'Royal Tennis'

2 *September*, 1667. I went to see a great match at tennis, between Prince Rupert and one Captain Cooke against Bab. May and the elder Chichly, where the King was and Court; and it seems they are the best players at tennis in the nation. But this puts me in mind of what I observed in the morning, that the King, playing at tennis, had a steele-yard carried to him; and I was told it was to weigh him after he had done playing; and at noon Mr Ashburnham told me that it is only the King's curiosity, which he usually hath of weighing himself before and after his play, to see how much he loses in weight by playing; and this day he lost $4\frac{1}{2}$ lbs.

SAMUEL PEPYS, *Diary*

Tea and Tennis

We proceeded to the tennis-court. I played with the sun in my eyes. I might, if I chose, emphasise that fact, and attribute my subsequent rout to it, adding, by way of solidifying the excuse, that I was playing in a strange court with a borrowed racquet, and that my mind was preoccupied—

firstly, with *l'affaire* Hawk, secondly, and chiefly, with the gloomy thought that Phyllis and my opponent seemed to be on friendly terms with each other. Their manner at tea had been almost that of an engaged couple. There was a thorough understanding between them. I will not, however, take refuge behind excuses. I admit, without qualifying the statement, that Mr Chase was too good for me. I had always been under the impression that lieutenants in the Royal Navy were not brilliant at tennis. I had met them at various houses, but they had never shone conspicuously. They had played an earnest, unobtrusive game, and generally seemed glad when it was over. Mr Chase was not of this sort. His service was bottled lightning. His returns behaved like jumping crackers. He won the first game in precisely six strokes. He served. Only once did I take the service with the full face of the racquet, and then I seemed to be stopping a bullet. I returned it into the net. The last of the series struck the wooden edge of my racquet, and soared over the back net into the shrubbery, after the manner of a snick to long slip off a fast bowler.

'Game,' said Mr Chase, 'we'll look for that afterwards.'

I felt a worm and no man. Phyllis, I thought, would probably judge my entire character from this exhibition. A man, she would reflect, who could be so feeble and miserable a failure at tennis could not be good for much in any department of life. She would compare me instinctively with my opponent, and contrast his dash and brilliance with my own inefficiency. Somehow the massacre was beginning to have a bad effect on my character. All my self-respect was ebbing. A little more of this, and I should become crushed—a mere human jelly. It was my turn to serve. Service is my strong point at tennis. I am inaccurate, but vigorous, and occasionally send in a quite unplayable shot. One or two of these, even at the expense of a fault or so, and I might be permitted to retain at least a portion of my self-respect.

I opened with a couple of faults. The sight of Phyllis, sitting calm and cool in her chair under the cedar, unnerved me. I served another fault. And yet another.

'Here, I say, Garnet,' observed Mr Chase plaintively, 'do put me out of this hideous suspense. I'm becoming a mere bundle of quivering ganglions.'

I loathe facetiousness in moments of stress. I frowned austerely, made no reply, and served another fault, my fifth.

Matters had reached a crisis. Even if I had to lob it underhand, I must send the ball over the net with the next stroke.

I restrained myself this time, eschewing the careless vigour which had marked my previous efforts. The ball flew in a slow semi-circle, and pitched inside the correct court. At least, I told myself, I had not served a fault.

What happened then I cannot exactly say. I saw my opponent spring forward like a panther and whirl his racquet. The next moment the back net was shaking violently, and the ball was rolling swiftly along the ground on a return journey to the other court.

'Love-forty,' said Mr Chase. 'Phyllis!'

'Yes?'

'That was the Tilden Slosh.'

'I thought it must be,' said Phyllis.

In the third game I managed to score fifteen. By the merest chance I returned one of his red-hot serves, and—probably through surprise—he failed to send it back again.

In the fourth and fifth games I omitted to score. Phyllis had left the cedar now, and was picking flowers from the beds behind the court.

We began the sixth game. And now for some reason I played really well. I struck a little vein of brilliance. I was serving, and this time a proportion of my serves went over the net instead of trying to get through. The score went from fifteen all to forty-fifteen. Hope began to surge through my veins. If I could keep this up, I might win yet.

The Tilden Slosh diminished my lead by fifteen. The Johnson Slam brought the score to Deuce. Then I got in a really fine serve, which beat him. 'Vantage In. Another Slosh. Deuce. Another Slam. 'Vantage out. It was an awesome moment. There is a tide in the affairs of men, which, taken by the flood—. I served. Fault. I served again—a beauty. He returned it like a flash into the corner of the court. With a supreme effort I got to it. We rallied. I was playing like a professor. Then whizz—!

The Slosh had beaten me on the post.

'Game *and*—' said Mr Chase, tossing his racquet into the air and catching it by the handle. 'Good game that last one.'

I turned to see what Phyllis thought of it.

At the eleventh hour I had shown her of what stuff I was made.

She had disappeared.

'Looking for Miss Derrick?' said Chase, jumping the net, and joining me in my court, 'she's gone into the house.'

'When did she go?'

'At the end of the fifth game,' said Chase.

'Gone to dress for dinner, I suppose,' he continued. 'It must be getting late. I think I ought to be going, too, if you don't mind. The professor gets a little restive if I keep him waiting for his daily bread. Great Scott, that watch can't be right! What do you make it? Yes, so do I. I really think I must run. You won't mind. Good night, then. See you to-morrow, I hope.'

I walked slowly out across the fields. That same star, in which I had confided on a former occasion, was at its post. It looked placid and cheerful. *It* never got beaten by six games to love under the very eyes of a lady-star. *It* was never cut out ignominiously by infernally capable lieutenants in His Majesty's Navy. No wonder it was cheerful.

P. G. WODEHOUSE, *Love Among the Chickens*

Pot Pourri from a Surrey Garden

Miles of pram in the wind and Pam in the gorse track,
  Coco-nut smell of the broom, and a packet of Weights
Press'd in the sand. The thud of a hoof on a horse-track—
    A horse-riding horse for a horse-track—
    Conifer county of Surrey approached
  Through remarkable wrought-iron gates.

Over your boundary now, I wash my face in a bird-bath,
  Then which path shall I take? that over there by the pram?
Down by the pond! or—yes, I will take the slippery third path,
    Trodden away with gym shoes,
    Beautiful fir-dry alley that leads
  To the bountiful body of Pam.

Pam, I adore you, Pam, you great big mountainous sports girl,
  Whizzing them over the net, full of the strength of five:
That old Malvernian brother, you zephyr and khaki shorts girl,
    Although he's playing for Woking,
    Can't stand up
  To your wonderful backhand drive.

See the strength of her arm, as firm and hairy as Hendren's;
  See the size of her thighs, the pout of her lips as, cross,
And full of a pent-up strength, she swipes at the rhododendrons,
    Lucky the rhododendrons,
    And flings her arrogant love-lock
  Back with a petulant toss.

Over the redolent pinewoods, in at the bathroom casement,
  One fine Saturday, Windlesham bells shall call:
Up the Butterfield aisle rich with Gothic enlacement,
    Licensed now for embracement,
    Pam and I, as the organ
  Thunders over you all.

SIR JOHN BETJEMAN

Golden Dawn

A backhand slice is but a paltry shot,
no backbone in it, *sauve qui peut*, unless
hit to the corner baseline, asymptote
plus malice, Pinterishly-primed duress
allowing one to charge in, tête-à-tête,
and do a hotshot number at the net.

When I was young and skinny, I'd not weight
enough to terrorise the baldest ball.
Now that I'm thick, and wise, and roseate
and compact of the waist chimerical
the drop-shot wounds me, and the high lob pains.
Either the body's lacking, or the brains,

it's never damn well right. And that's a shame.
O sages in your manuals, Kenny, Fred
come be the singing-masters of my game,
that ace-tormented serve, weak overhead!
Iron out my faults. Let these joints thrive
and put some bottle in my cross-court drive.

Once in the rankings I shall never smoke
or swear, raise hell at discos, quarrel, swank.
If I can have a swimming pool, and clock
odd starlets on the brink, own my own bank,
I'll bow out gracefully, by fame paroled,
and sit up in the stands as good as gold.

WILLIAM SCAMMELL (b. 1939)

Park Tennis

The women concern themselves with being
feminine, walking like models and tossing
back their loose hair. Their play resembles
beach jokari, that muddle of elastic, and
when they run skirts and crucifixes become
wild. Ball gathering is a coy technique;
like nymphs stooping to low flowers. Later

the men arrive carrying travelling bags
and hurrying as if for a flight. They wear
coloured socks, rehearse exotic air shots
with the racquet in fashion and, between
points, hold it to the body like a mace.
They leave talking of injuries and osteopaths.
Each day I watch, seated and absorbed.

DAVID JACOBS (b. 1949)

X

In and On the Water

Swimming

Swimming is an exercise of great antiquity; and, no doubt, familiar to the inhabitants of this country, at all times. The heroes of the middle ages are sometimes praised for their skill in swimming: it is said of Olaf Fryggeson, a king of Norway, that he had no equal in his art. Peacham, describing the requisites for a complete gentleman, mentions swimming as one; and particularly recommends it to such as were inclined to follow a military profession. In this he seems to have followed an old poetical writer, who speaks in this manner:—

> To swymme, is eke to lerne in sommer leson.
> Men fynde not a bridge, so often as a flood,
> Swymmyng to voyde; and chase an hoste wil eson.
> Eke after rayne the rivers goeth wood,
> That every man in t'host can swymme, is good:
> Knyght, squyer, footman, cook, and cosynere.
> And grome, and page, in swymmyng is to lere.

Meaning thereby, that the art of swimming ought to be learned by every class of persons belonging to an army: and, perhaps, it may not be improper to add, by every other person also.

Swimming and diving are mentioned by the author of the Visions of Pierce Ploughman, in the following manner:—

> Take two strong men and in Temese cast them,
> And both naked as a needle, ther non sikerer than other;
> The one hath cunnynge and can swymme and dyve,
> The other is lewed of that laboure, lerned never to swym,
> With trowest of these two in Temese is most in dred,
> He that never dived ne nought can of swymmyng,
> Or the swymmer that is safe if he himself lyke?

Boys in the country usually learn to swim with bundles of bullrushes, and with corks where the rushes cannot readily be procured; particularly in the neighbourhood of London, where we are told, two centuries back, there were men who could teach the art of swimming well, and, says the author, 'for commoditie of river and water for that purpose, there is no where better.'

I am sorry to add, that swimming is by no means so generally practised with us in the present day as it used to be in former times. We have several treatises on the art of swimming and diving, and in the Encyclopaedia Britannica are many excellent directions relating to it, under the article Swimming.

JOSEPH STRUTT

Written after Swimming from Sestos to Abydos

9 May 1810

If, in the month of dark December,
  Leander, who was nightly wont
(What maid will not the tale remember?)
  To cross thy stream, broad Hellespont!

If, when the wintry tempest roared,
  He sped to Hero, nothing loth,
And thus of old thy current poured,
  Fair Venus! how I pity both!

For *me*, degenerate modern wretch,
  Though in the genial month of May,
My dripping limbs I faintly stretch,
  And think I've done a feat today.

But since he crossed the rapid tide,
  According to the doubtful story,
To woo,—and—Lord knows what beside,
  And swam for Love, as I for Glory;

'Twere hard to say who fared the best:
  Sad mortals! thus the Gods still plague you!
He lost his labour, I my jest;
  For he was drowned, and I've the ague.

LORD BYRON

The Swimmer

Who would linger idle,
Dallying would lie,
When wind and wave, a bridal
Celebrating, fly?
Let him plunge among them,
Who hath woo'd enough,
Flirted with them, sung them!
In the salt sea-trough
He may win them, onward
On a buoyant crest,
Far to seaward, sunward,
Ocean-borne to rest!
Wild wind will sing over him,
And the free foam cover him,
Swimming seaward, sunward,
On a blithe sea-breast!
  On a blithe sea-bosom
Swims another too,
Swims a live sea-blossom,
A grey-wing'd seamew!
Grape-green all the waves are,
By whose hurrying line
Half of ships and caves are
Buried under brine;
Supple, shifting ranges
Lucent at the crest,
With pearly surface-changes
Never laid to rest:
Now a dripping gunwale
Momently he sees,
Now a fuming funnel,
Or red flag in the breeze.
Arms flung open wide,
Lip the laughing sea:
For playfellow, for bride,
Claim her impetuously!

THE HON. RODEN NOEL (1834–94)

From *The Bothie of Tober-na-Vuolich*

There is a stream (I name not its name, lest inquisitive tourist
Hunt it, and make it a lion, and get it at last into guide-books),
Springing far off from a loch unexplored in the folds of great
mountains,
Falling two miles through rowan and stunted alder, enveloped
Then for four more in a forest of pine, where broad and ample
Spreads, to convey it, the glen with heathery slopes on both sides:
Broad and fair the stream, with occasional falls and narrows;
But, where the glen of its course approaches the vale of the river,
Met and blocked by a huge interposing mass of granite,
Scarce by a channel deep-cut, raging up, and raging onward,
Forces its flood through a passage so narrow a lady would step it.
There, across the great rocky wharves, a wooden bridge goes,
Carrying a path to the forest; below, three hundred yards, say,
Lower in level some twenty-five feet, through flats of shingle,
Stepping-stones and a cart-track cross in the open valley.
But in the interval here the boiling pent-up water
Frees itself by a final descent, attaining a basin,
Ten feet wide and eighteen long, with whiteness and fury
Occupied partly, but mostly pellucid, pure, a mirror;
Beautiful there for the colour derived from green rocks under;
Beautiful, most of all, where beads of foam uprising
Mingle their clouds of white with the delicate hue of the stillness,
Cliff over cliff for its sides, with rowan and pendent birch boughs,
Here it lies, unthought of above at the bridge and pathway,
Still more enclosed from below by wood and rocky projection.
You are shut in, left alone with yourself and perfection of water,
Hid on all sides, left alone with yourself and the goddess of bathing.
Here, the pride of the plunger, you stride the fall and clear it;
Here, the delight of the bather, you roll in beaded sparklings,
Here into pure green depth drop down from lofty ledges.

ARTHUR HUGH CLOUGH (1819–61)

On a Spring-board

The light falls gently from the dormer-panes,
And sleeps upon the water sleeping too,—
Such water as the fond Boeotian knew
When in the liquid fount he view'd the stains

Of his own love-looks. What sweet idlesse reigns
From gleam to gleam, and makes the soul in view
Of long'd-for bliss a longer path pursue,
And still be hoping while she still refrains?
Now see me work a deed exceeding rash!
There sinks my pocket-wealth of hoarded cash
Through the green floor. So did the Samian king,
Blest overmuch, engulph the fateful ring;
But here are no fat fish to bolt and bring
My treasure back from limbo, therefore—splash!

EDWARD CRACROFT LEFROY

The Swimmers

The cove's a shining plate of blue and green,
With darker belts between
The trough and crest of the lazily rising swell,
And the great rocks throw purple shadows down
Where transient sun-sparks wink and burst and drown,

And the distant glimmering floor of pebble and shell
Is bright or hidden as the shadow wavers,
And everywhere the restless sun-steeped air
Trembles and quavers,
As though it were
More saturate with light than it could bear.

Now come the swimmers from slow-dripping caves,
Where the shy fern creeps under the veined roof,
And wading out meet with glad breast the waves.
One holds aloof,
And climbs alone the reef with shrinking feet
That scarce endure the jagged stone's dull heat,
Till on the edge he poises
And flies towards the water, vanishing
In wreaths of white, with echoing liquid noises,
And swims beneath, a vague, distorted thing.

Now all the other swimmers leave behind
The crystal shallow and the foam-wet shore,
And sliding into deeper waters find
A living coolness in the lifting flood:
Then through their bodies leaps the sparkling blood,
So that they feel the faint earth's drought no more.

There now they float, heads raised above the green,
White bodies cloudily seen,
Further and further from the brazen rock
On which the hot air shakes, on which the tide
Vainly throws with soundless shock
The cool and lagging wave. Out, out they go,
And now upon a mirrored cloud they ride,
Or turning over, with soft strokes and slow,
Slide on like shadows in a tranquil sky.
Behind them, on the tall parched cliff, the dry
And dusty grasses grow
In shallow ledges of the arid stone,
Starving for coolness and the touch of rain.
But, though to earth they must return again,
Here come the soft sea airs to meet them blown
Over the surface of the outer deep,
Scarce moving, staying, falling, straying, gone,
Light and delightful as the touch of sleep . . .

One wakes and splashes round,
And magically all the others wake
From their sea-dream, and now with rippling sound
Their arms the silence break.
And now again the crystal shallows take
The dripping bodies whose cool hour is done:
They pause upon the beach, they pause and sigh,
And vanish in the caverns one by one.

Soon the wet footmarks on the stones are dry:
The cove sleeps on beneath the unwavering sun.

EDWARD SHANKS (1892–1953)

East Anglian Bathe

Oh when the early morning at the seaside
  Took us with hurrying steps from Horsey Mere
To see the whistling bent-grass on the leeside
  And then the tumbled breaker-line appear,
On high, the clouds with mighty adumbration
  Sailed over us to seaward fast and clear
And jellyfish in quivering isolation
  Lay silted in the dry sand of the breeze

And we, along the table-land of beach blown
  Went gooseflesh from our shoulders to our knees
And ran to catch the football, each to each thrown,
  In the soft and swirling music of the seas.

There splashed about our ankles as we waded
  Those intersecting wavelets morning-cold,
And sudden dark a patch of sea was shaded,
  And sudden light, another patch would hold
The warmth of whirling atoms in a sun-shot
  And underwater sandstorm green and gold.
So in we dived and louder than a gunshot
  Sea-water broke in fountains down the ear.
How cold the bathe, how chattering cold the drying.
  How welcoming the inland reeds appear,
The wood-smoke and the breakfast and the frying,
  And your warm freshwater ripples, Horsey Mere.

SIR JOHN BETJEMAN

Captain Webb's Channel Swim

At 3.22 a.m. he declined any refreshment, and half an hour later there was light enough to dowse lanterns . . . The breeze [then] produced a nasty bobble, but as the tide was at present setting to leeward it was not so bad as it might have been . . . Two bells found it very hazy over the land, but he still seemed in as good spirits as ever, and even had a little personal chaff with us. He did not seem strong enough, however, to make much way across the tide, and . . . it was a touch-and-go matter whether he would not be drifted too far to the eastward, and have to await another tide to fetch in . . . Some beef tea and a top-up of brandy were called for at 5.25 a.m., when his voice seemed faltering a bit. By four bells the lop had become really serious, but he declined to wear his spectacles. All hope of fetching in off Sangatte had to be abandoned. For the next hour he made literally no in-shore progress, although both the row boats were kept on his weather side, to ward off the sea as much as possible . . . at 7.25 the poor fellow complained bitterly of the sea, which of course increased greatly in crossing the broken water of the Ridens. It was cruel to think that this might be the cause of defeat when within actual hail of port, and nothing but unflinching bulldog pluck now kept the man going . . . At eight bells we sounded in ten fathoms, and had all but opened the entrance to Calais harbour. Luckily, however, the tide had by this time eased considerably, and he was enabled to get almost slack water and make a little headway for the shore instead of getting drifted to the eastward of Calais.

At 8.23 a.m. he took some brandy, and said he was 'as right as a bird, bar the sea.' He was swimming a quicker but shorter stroke of twenty-two to the minute . . . At 9.20 a.m. Capt. Dane was sighted coming out of Calais harbour in his gig, with all possible speed; and this was the best bit of luck we had met with since the same gallant skipper had left us at sea just before midnight. By 9.25 a.m. he had placed his gig in a capital position on Webb's weather side, where such a large craft made a far more effectual breakwater than our own two cockleshells of row boats. At 9.34 he seemed quite lively when Capt. Dane told him there was a grand reception waiting him ashore. Now, however, the S.W. stream had begun to make and the tide was going aweather, which further increased the brave swimmer's difficulties. At 9.40 a.m. we timed him at twenty-six strokes to the minute but they were short indeed compared to those of the first eighteen hours or so. However, the gig mended matters, somewhat, and her crew cheered him repeatedly in true British Jack Tar fashion . . . At 10.30 he laughingly hoped that 'the Frenchmen would give him some good grub ashore.' As a proof of how keen his intellect had remained throughout, he promptly requested us by name to immediately take in two or three feet of rope which had accidentally got overboard as he wished to take no unfair advantage. After a few more strokes the brave Matthew Webb stood upright in five feet of water on Calais sands abreast of the bathing establishment and half a mile to the westward of Calais pier at 10.40.15 a.m. English time on Wednesday, 25 August 1875, after having been in the water twenty-one hours forty-four minutes and fifty-five seconds without touching artificial support of any kind, and having swum as nearly as possible over thirty-nine miles and a half of ground.

Capt. Webb was assisted into a trap, driven to the Hotel de Paris, and at once put to bed, a medical man being in attendance. His pulse was at 72, and after three hours' sleep he woke up all right, bar weakness and hunger. At 10 p.m. he again turned in and slept soundly for twelve hours.

From *The Country Gentleman's Newspaper* (1875)

Skating

Skating is by no means a recent pastime, and probably the invention proceeded rather from necessity than the desire of amusement.

It is the boast of a northern chieftain, that he could traverse the snow upon skates of wood. I cannot by any means ascertain at what time skating made its first appearance in England, but we find some traces of such an exercise in the thirteenth century, at which period, according to Fitzstephen, it was customary in the winter, when the ice would bear them, for the young citizens of London to fasten the leg bones of animals under the soles of their feet by tying them round their ancles, and then taking a pole shod with iron into their hands, they pushed themselves forward by striking it against the ice, and moved with celerity equal, says the author, to a bird flying through the air, or an arrow from a cross-bow; but some allowance, I presume, must be made for the poetical figure: he then adds, 'at times, two of them thus furnished agree to start opposite one to another, at a great distance; they meet, elevate their poles, attack, and strike each other, when one or both of them fall, and not without some bodily hurt; and, even after their fall, are carried a great distance from each other, by the rapidity of the motion, and whatever part of the head comes upon the ice, it is sure to be laid bare.'

The wooden skates shod with iron or steel, which are bound about the feet and ancles like the talares of the Greeks and Romans, were most probably brought into England from the Low Countries, where they are said to have originated, and where it is well known they are almost universally used by persons of both sexes when the season permits. In Hoole's translation of the Vocabulary by Comenius, called Orbis Sensualium Pictus, the skates are called scrick-shoes from the German, and in the print at the head of the section, in that work, they are represented longer than those of the present day, and the irons are turned up much higher in the front.

JOSEPH STRUTT

'And in the Frosty Season'

And in the frosty season, when the sun
Was set, and visible for many a mile
The cottage windows blazed through twilight gloom,
I heeded not their summons: happy time
It was indeed for all of us—for me
It was a time of rapture! Clear and loud
The village clock tolled six,—I wheeled about,
Proud and exulting like an untired horse
That cares not for his home. All shod with steel.
We hissed along the polished ice in games
Confederate, imitative of the chase
And woodland pleasures,—the resounding horn,
The pack loud chiming, and the hunted hare.
So through the darkness and the cold we flew,
And not a voice was idle; with the din
Smitten, the precipices rang aloud;
The leafless trees and every icy crag
Tinkled like iron; while far distant hills
Into the tumult sent an alien sound

Of melancholy not unnoticed, while the stars
Eastward were sparkling clear, and in the west
The orange sky of evening died away.
Not seldom from the uproar I retired
Into a silent bay, or sportively
Glanced sideway, leaving the tumultuous throng,
To cut across the reflex of a star
That fled, and, flying still before me, gleamed
Upon the glassy plain; and oftentimes,
When we had given our bodies to the wind,
And all the shadowy banks on either side
Came sweeping through the darkness, spinning still
The rapid line of motion, then at once
Have I, reclining back upon my heels,
Stopped short; yet still the solitary cliffs
Wheeled by me—even as if the earth had rolled
With visible motion her diurnal round!
Behind me did they stretch in solemn train,
Feebler and feebler, and I stood and watched
Till all was tranquil as a dreamless sleep.

WILLIAM WORDSWORTH, *The Prelude*

Elfin Skates

I

They wheel'd me up the snow-clear'd garden way,
 And left me where the dazzling heaps were thrown;
 And as I mused on winter sports once known,
Up came a tiny man to where I lay.
He was six inches high; his beard was grey
 As silver frost; his coat and cap were brown,
 Of mouse's fur; while two wee skates hung down
From his wee belt, and gleam'd in winter's ray.

He clamber'd up my couch, and eyed me long.
 'Show me thy skates,' said I; 'for once, alas!
  I too could skate. What pixie mayst thou be?'
'I am the king', he answered, 'of the throng
 Called Winter Elves. We live in roots, and pass
  The summer months asleep. Frost sets us free.'

II

'We find by moonlight little pools of ice,
  Just one yard wide,' the imp of winter said;
  'And skate all night, while mortals are in bed,
In tiny circles of our elf device;
And when it snows we harness forest mice
  To wee bark sleighs, with lightest fibrous thread
  And scour the woods; or play all night instead
With snowballs large as peas, well patted thrice.

But is it true, as I have heard them say,
  That thou canst share in winter games no more,
    But liest motionless, year in, year out?
That must be hard. Today I cannot stay,
  But I'll return each year, when all is hoar,
    And tell thee when the skaters are about.'

EUGENE LEE-HAMILTON (1845–1907)

From *The Pickwick Club*

'Now,' said Wardle, after a substantial lunch, with the agreeable items of strong beer and cherry-brandy, had been done ample justice to; 'what say you to an hour on the ice? We shall have plenty of time.'

'Capital!' said Mr Benjamin Allen.

'Prime!' ejaculated Mr Bob Sawyer.

'You skate, of course, Winkle?' said Wardle.

'Ye-yes; oh, yes,' replied Mr Winkle. 'I—I—am *rather* out of practice.'

'Oh, *do* skate, Mr Winkle,' said Arabella. 'I like to see it so much.'

'Oh, it is *so* graceful,' said another young lady.

A third young lady said it was elegant, and a fourth expressed her opinion that it was 'swan-like'.

'I should be very happy, I'm sure,' said Mr Winkle, reddening; 'but I have no skates.'

This objection was at once overruled. Trundle had a couple of pair, and the fat boy announced that there were half-a-dozen more down stairs: whereat Mr Winkle expressed exquisite delight, and looked exquisitely uncomfortable.

Old Wardle led the way to a pretty large sheet of ice; and the fat boy and Mr Weller, having shovelled and swept away the snow which had fallen on it during the night, Mr Bob Sawyer adjusted his skates with a dexterity which to Mr Winkle was perfectly marvellous, and described circles with his left leg, and cut figures of eight, and inscribed upon the ice, without once stopping for breath, a great many other pleasant and astonishing devices, to the excessive satisfaction of Mr Pickwick, Mr Tupman, and the ladies: which reached a pitch of positive enthusiasm, when old Wardle and Benjamin Allen, assisted by the aforesaid Bob Sawyer, performed some mystic evolutions, which they called a reel.

All this time, Mr Winkle, with his face and hands blue with the cold, had been forcing a gimlet into the soles of his feet, and putting his skates on, with the points behind, and getting the straps into a very complicated and entangled state, with the assistance of Mr Snodgrass, who knew rather less about skates than a Hindoo. At length, however, with the assistance of Mr Weller, the unfortunate skates were firmly screwed and buckled on, and Mr Winkle was raised to his feet.

'Now, then, sir,' said Sam, in an encouraging tone; 'off vith you, and show 'em how to do it.'

'Stop, Sam, stop!' said Mr Winkle, trembling violently, and clutching hold of Sam's arms with the grasp of a drowning man. 'How slippery it is, Sam!'

'Not an uncommon thing upon ice, sir,' replied Mr Weller. 'Hold up, sir!'

This last observation of Mr Weller's bore reference to a demonstration Mr Winkle made at the instant, of a frantic desire to throw his feet in the air, and dash the back of his head on the ice.

'These—these—are very awkward skates; ain't they, Sam?' inquired Mr Winkle staggering.

'I'm afeerd there's a orkard gen'l'm'n in 'em, sir,' replied Sam.

'Now, Winkle,' cried Mr Pickwick, quite unconscious that there was anything the matter. 'Come; the ladies are all anxiety.'

'Yes, yes,' replied Mr Winkle, with a ghastly smile. 'I'm coming.'

'Just a goin' to begin,' said Sam, endeavouring to disengage himself. 'Now, sir, start off!'

'Stop an instant, Sam,' gasped Mr Winkle, clinging most affectionately to Mr Weller. 'I find I've got a couple of coats at home that I don't want, Sam. You may have them, Sam.'

'Thank'ee sir,' replied Mr Weller.

'Never mind touching your hat, Sam,' said Mr Winkle, hastily. 'You needn't take your hand away to do that. I meant to have given you five shillings this morning for a Christmas-box, Sam. I'll give it you this afternoon, Sam.'

'You're wery good, sir,' replied Mr Weller.

'Just hold me at first, Sam; will you?' said Mr Winkle. 'There—that's right. I shall soon get in the way of it, Sam. Not too fast, Sam; not too fast.'

Mr Winkle stooping forward, with his body half doubled up, was being assisted over the ice by Mr Weller, in a very singular and un-swan-like manner, when Mr Pickwick most innocently shouted from the opposite bank:

'Sam!'

'Sir?'

'Here. I want you.'

'Let go, sir,' said Sam. 'Don't you hear the governor a callin'? Let go, sir.'

With a violent effort, Mr Weller disengaged himself from the grasp of the agonised Pickwickian, and, in so doing, administered a considerable impetus to the unhappy Mr Winkle. With an accuracy which no degree of dexterity or practice could have insured, that unfortunate gentleman bore swiftly down into the centre of the reel, at the very moment when Mr Bob Sawyer was performing a flourish of unparalleled beauty. Mr Winkle struck wildly against him, and with a loud crash they both fell heavily down. Mr Pickwick ran to the spot. Bob Sawyer had risen to his feet, but Mr Winkle was far too wise to do anything of the kind, in skates. He was seated on the ice, making spasmodic efforts to smile; but anguish was depicted on every lineament of his countenance.

'Are you hurt?' inquired Mr Benjamin Allen, with great anxiety.

'Not much,' said Mr Winkle, rubbing his back very hard.

'I wish you'd let me bleed you,' said Mr Benjamin, with great eagerness.

'No, thank you,' replied Mr Winkle hurriedly.

'I really think you had better,' said Allen.

'Thank you,' replied Mr Winkle; 'I'd rather not.'

'What do *you* think, Mr Pickwick?' inquired Bob Sawyer.

Mr Pickwick was excited and indignant. He beckoned to Mr Weller, and said in a stern voice, 'Take his skates off.'

'No; but really I had scarcely begun,' remonstrated Mr Winkle.

'Take his skates off,' repeated Mr Pickwick firmly.

The command was not to be resisted. Mr Winkle allowed Sam to obey it in silence.

'Lift him up,' said Mr Pickwick. Sam assisted him to rise.

Mr Pickwick retired a few paces apart from the by-standers; and, beckoning his friend to approach, fixed a searching look upon him, and uttered in a low, but distinct and emphatic tone, these remarkable words:

'You're a humbug, sir.'

'A what?' said Mr Winkle, starting.

'A humbug, sir. I will speak plainer, if you wish it. An impostor, sir.'

With those words, Mr Pickwick turned slowly on his heel, and rejoined his friends.

While Mr Pickwick was delivering himself of the sentiment just recorded, Mr Weller and the fat boy, having by their joint endeavours cut out a slide, were exercising themselves thereupon, in a very masterly and brilliant manner. Sam Weller, in particular, was displaying that beautiful feat of fancy-sliding which is currently denominated 'knocking at the cobbler's door', and which is achieved by skimming over the ice on one foot, and occasionally giving a postman's knock upon it with the other. It was a good long slide, and there was something in the motion which Mr Pickwick, who was very cold with standing still, could not help envying.

'It looks a nice warm exercise that, doesn't it?' he inquired of Wardle, when that gentleman was thoroughly out of breath, by reason of the indefatigable manner in which he had converted his legs into a pair of compasses, and drawn complicated problems on the ice.

'Ah, it does indeed,' replied Wardle. 'Do you slide?'

'I used to do so, on the gutters, when I was a boy,' replied Mr Pickwick.

'Try it now,' said Wardle.

'Oh do please, Mr Pickwick!' cried all the ladies.

'I should be very happy to afford you any amusement,' replied Mr Pickwick, 'but I haven't done such a thing these thirty years.'

'Pooh! pooh! Nonsense!' said Wardle, dragging off his skates with the impetuosity which characterized all his proceedings. 'Here; I'll keep you company; come along!' And away went the good tempered old fellow down the slide, with a rapidity which came very close upon Mr Weller, and beat the fat boy all to nothing.

Mr Pickwick paused, considered, pulled off his gloves and put them in his hat: took two or three short runs, baulked himself as often, and at last took another run, and went slowly and gravely down the slide, with his feet about a yard and a quarter apart, amidst the gratified shouts of all the spectators.

'Keep the pot a bilin', sir!' said Sam; and down went Wardle again, and then Mr Pickwick, and then Sam, and then Mr Winkle, and then Mr Bob Sawyer, and then the fat boy, and then Mr Snodgrass, following closely upon each other's heels, and running after each other with as much eagerness as if all their future prospects in life depended on their expedition.

It was the most intensely interesting thing, to observe the manner in which Mr Pickwick performed his share in the ceremony; to watch the torture of anxiety with which he viewed the person behind, gaining upon him at the imminent hazard of tripping him up; to see him gradually expend the painful force he had put on at first, and turn slowly round on the slide, with his face towards the point from which he had started; to contemplate the playful smile which mantled on his face when he had accomplished the distance, and the eagerness with which he turned round when he had done so, and ran after his predecessor: his black gaiters tripping pleasantly through the snow, and his eyes beaming cheerfulness and gladness through his spectacles. And when he was knocked down (which happened upon the average every third round), it was the most invigorating sight that can possibly be imagined, to behold him gather up his hat, gloves, and handkerchief, with a glowing countenance, and resume his station in the rank, with an ardour and enthusiasm that nothing could abate.

The sport was at its height, the sliding was at the quickest, the laughter was at the loudest, when a sharp smart crack was heard. There was a quick rush towards the bank, a wild scream from the ladies, and a shout from Mr Tupman. A large mass of ice disappeared; the water bubbled up over it; Mr Pickwick's hat, gloves, and handkerchief were floating on the surface; and this was all of Mr Pickwick that anybody could see.

Dismay and anguish were depicted on every countenance, the males turned pale, and the females fainted, Mr Snodgrass and Mr Winkle grasped each other by the hand, and gazed at the spot where their leader had gone down, with frenzied eagerness: while Mr Tupman, by way of rendering the promptest assistance, and at the same time conveying to any persons who might be within hearing, the clearest possible notion of the catastrophe, ran off across the country at his utmost speed, screaming 'Fire!' with all his might.

It was at this moment, when old Wardle and Sam Weller were approaching the hole with cautious steps, and Mr Benjamin Allen was holding a hurried consultation with Mr Bob Sawyer, on the advisability of bleeding the company generally, as an improving little bit of professional practice—it was at this very moment, that a face, head, and shoulders, emerged from beneath the water, and disclosed the features and spectacles of Mr Pickwick.

'Keep yourself up for an instant—for only one instant!' bawled Mr Snodgrass.

'Yes, do; let me implore you—for my sake!' roared Mr Winkle, deeply affected. The adjuration was rather unnecessary; the probability being, that if Mr Pickwick had declined to keep himself up for anybody else's sake, it would have occurred to him that he might as well do so, for his own.

'Do you feel the bottom there, old fellow?' said Wardle.

'Yes, certainly,' replied Mr Pickwick, wringing the water from his head and face, and gasping for breath. 'I fell upon my back. I couldn't get on my feet at first.'

The clay upon so much of Mr Pickwick's coat as was yet visible, bore testimony to the accuracy of this statement; and as the fears of the spectators were still further relieved by the fat boy's suddenly recollecting that the water was nowhere more than five feet deep, prodigies of valour were performed to get him out. After a vast quantity of splashing, and cracking, and struggling, Mr Pickwick was at length fairly extricated from his unpleasant position, and once more stood on dry land.

CHARLES DICKENS, *Pickwick Papers*

Tuesday, 27 December 1870

After dinner drove into Chippenham with Perch and bought a pair of skates at Benk's for 17/6. Across the fields to the Draycot water and the young Awdry ladies chaffed me about my new skates. I had not been on skates since I was here last, 5 years ago, and was very awkward for the first ten minutes, but the knack soon came again. There was a distinguished company on the ice, Lady Dangan, Lord and Lady Royston and Lord George Paget all skating. Also Lord and Lady Sydney and a Mr Calcroft, whom they all of course call the Hangman. I had the honour of being knocked down by Lord Royston, who was coming round suddenly on the outside edge. A large fire of logs burning within an enclosure of wattled hurdles. Harriet Awdry skated beautifully and jumped over a half sunken punt. Arthur Law skating jumped over a chair on its legs.

Wednesday, 28 December

An inch of snow fell last night and as we walked to Draycot to skate the snow storm began again. As we passed Langley Burrell Church we heard the strains of the quadrille band on the ice at Draycot. The afternoon grew murky and when we began to skate the air was thick with falling snow. But it soon stopped and gangs of labourers were at work immediately sweeping away the new fallen snow and skate cuttings of ice. The Lancers was beautifully skated. When it grew dark the ice was lighted with Chinese lanterns, and the intense glare of blue, green, and crimson lights and magnesium riband made the whole place as light as day. Then people skated with torches.

Thursday, 19 December

Skating at Draycot again with Perch. Fewer people on the ice today. No quadrille band, torches or fireworks, but it was very pleasant, cosy and sociable. Yesterday when the Lancers was being skated Lord Royston was directing the figures. Harriet Awdry corrected him in one figure and he was quite wrong. But he immediately left the quadrille and sat down sulking on the bank, saying to one of his friends, 'Those abominable Miss Awdrys have contradicted me about the Lancers.' This was overheard and repeated to Harriet by a mutual friend, and the next time she saw him she said meaningly, 'Lord Royston, sometimes remarks are overheard and repeated,' or something to that effect. However soon after he wanted to make it up and asked her to skate up the ice hand in hand with him. 'Certainly *not*, Lord Royston,' she said. Lady Royston skates very nicely and seems very nice. A sledge chair was put on the ice and Lady Royston and Lady Dangan, Margaret, Fanny, Maria and Harriet Awdry were drawn about in it by turns, Charles Awdry pushing behind and Edmund and Arthur and Walter pulling with ropes. It was a capital team and went at a tremendous pace up and down the ice. A German ladies' maid from Draycot House was skating and making ridiculous antics.

FRANCIS KILVERT, *Diary*

The Midnight Skaters

The hop-poles stand in cones,
  The icy pond lurks under,
The pole-tops steeple to the thrones
  Of stars, sound gulfs of wonder;
But not the tallest there, 'tis said,
Could fathom to this pond's black bed.

Then is not death at watch
  Within those secret waters?
What wants he but to catch
  Earth's heedless sons and daughters?
With but a crystal parapet
Between, he has his engines set.

Then on, blood shouts, on, on,
  Twirl, wheel and whip above him,
Dance on this ball-floor thin and wan,
  Use him as though you love him;
Court him, elude him, reel and pass,
And let him hate you through the glass.

EDMUND BLUNDEN (1896–1974)

Under the Ice

Like Coleridge, I waltz
on ice. And watch my shadow
on the water below. Knowing that
if the ice were not there
I'd drown. Half willing it.

In my cord jacket
and neat cravat, I keep
returning to the one spot.
How long, to cut
a perfect circle out?

Something in me
rejects the notion.
The arc is never complete.
My figures-of-eight
almost, not quite, meet.

Was Raeburn's skating parson
a man of God, poised
impeccably on the brink;
or his bland stare
no more than a decorous front?

If I could keep my cool
like that. Gazing straight ahead,
not at my feet. Giving
no sign of knowing
how deep the water, how thin the ice.

Behind that, the other
question: whether the real you
pirouettes in space,
or beckons from under the ice
for me to come through.

STEWART CONN (b. 1936)

Sailing

Another popular amusement upon the water is sailing, and many persons have pleasure boats for this purpose; I do not mean the open boats which are usually let out for hire by the boat-builders for the purpose of sailing, but vessels of much greater magnitude, that are covered with a deck, and able with skilful management to weather a rough storm; many large bets are frequently dependant upon the swiftness of these boats, and the contest is sometimes determined at sea.

A society, generally known by the appellation of the Cumberland Society, consisting of gentlemen partial to this pastime, give yearly a silver cup to be sailed for in the vicinity of London. The boats usually start from the bridge at Blackfriars, go up the Thames to Putney, and return to Vauxhall, where a vessel is moored at a distance from the stairs, and the sailing boat that first passes this mark upon her return obtains the victory.

JOSEPH STRUTT

'An Elfin Pinnace'

The moon was up, the Lake was shining clear
Among the hoary mountains; from the Shore
I push'd, and struck the oars and struck again
In cadence, and my little Boat mov'd on
Even like a Man who walks with stately step
Though bent on speed. It was an act of stealth
And troubled pleasure; not without the voice
Of mountain-echoes did my Boat move on,
Leaving behind her still on either side
Small circles glittering idly in the moon,
Until they melted all into one track
Of sparkling light. A rocky Steep uprose
Above the Cavern of the Willow tree
And now, as suited one who proudly row'd
With his best skill, I fix'd a steady view
Upon the top of that same craggy ridge,
The bound of the horizon, for behind
Was nothing but the stars and the grey sky.
She was an elfin Pinnace; lustily
I dipp'd my oars into the silent Lake,
And, as I rose upon the stroke, my Boat
Went heaving through the water, like a Swan;
When from behind that craggy Steep, till then
The bound of the horizon, a huge Cliff,
As if with voluntary power instinct,
Uprear'd its head, I struck, and struck again.
And growing still in stature, the huge Cliff
Rose up between me and the stars, and still,
With measur'd motion, like a living thing,
Strode after me.

WILLIAM WORDSWORTH, *The Prelude*

The Yacht

The vessel that rests here at last
Had once stout ribs and topping mast,
And, whate'er wind there might prevail,
Was ready for a row or sail.
It now lies idle on its side,
Forgetful o'er the stream to glide.

And yet there have been days of yore,
When pretty maids their posies bore
To crown its prow, its deck to trim,
And freighted a whole world of whim.
A thousand stories it could tell,—
But it loves secrecy too well.—
Come closer, my sweet girl, pray do!
There may be still one left for you.

WALTER SAVAGE LANDOR (1775–1864)

'Racing in Cutters'

Days of endeavour have been good; the days
Racing in cutters for the comrade's praise,
The day they led my cutter at the turn
Yet could not keep the lead and dropped astern
The moment in the spurt when both boats' oars
Dipped in each other's wash and throats grew hoarse
And teeth ground into teeth and both strokes quickened
Lashing the sea, and gasps came, and hearts sickened
And coxswains damned us, dancing, banking stroke,
To put our weights on, though our hearts were broke
And both boats seemed to stick and sea seemed glue,
The tide a mill-race we were struggling through
And every quick recover gave us squints
Of them still there and oar-tossed water-glints,
And cheering came, our friends, our foemen cheering,
A long, wild, rallying murmur on the hearing
'Port Fore!' and 'Starboard Fore!' 'Port Fore!' 'Port Fore!'
'Up with her, Starboard,' and at that each oar
Lightened, though arms were bursting, and eyes shut
And the oak stretchers grunted in the strut
And the curse quickened from the cox, our bows
Crashed, and drove talking water, we made vows,
Chastity vows and temperance; in our pain
We numbered things we'd never eat again
If we could only win; then came the yell
'Starboard,' 'Port Fore,' and then a beaten bell
Rung as for fire to cheer us. 'Now.' Oars bent
Soul took the looms now body's bolt was spent,
'Give way, come on now!' 'On now!' 'On now!' 'Starboard.'
'Port Fore!' 'Up with her, Port!' each cutter harboured

Ten eye-shut painsick strugglers, 'Heave, oh, heave!'
Catcalls waked echoes like a shrieking sheave.
'Heave!' and I saw a back, then two. 'Port Fore.'
'Starboard!' 'Come on!' I saw the midship oar
And knew we had done them. 'Port Fore!' 'Starboard!' 'Now!'
I saw bright water spurting at their bow,
Their cox' full face an instant. They were done.
The watchers' cheering almost drowned the gun.
We had hardly strength to toss our oars; our cry
Cheering the losing cutter was a sigh.

JOHN MASEFIELD, from *Biography*

At Putney

When eight strong fellows are out to row,
With a slip of a lad to guide them,
I warrant they'll make the light ship go,
Though the coach on the launch may chide them,
With his 'Six, get on to it! Five, you're late!
Don't hurry the slides, and use your weight!
You're bucketing, Bow, and, as to Four,
The sight of his shoulders makes me sore!'

But Stroke has steadied his fiery men,
And the lift on the boat gets stronger;
And the Coxswain suddenly shouts for 'Ten!
Reach out to it, longer, longer!'
While the wind and the tide raced hand in hand
The swing of the crew and the pace were grand;
But now that the two meet face to face
It's buffet and slam and a tortoise-pace;

For Hammersmith Bridge has rattled past,
And, oh, but the storm is humming.
The turbulent white steeds gallop fast;
They're tossing their crests and coming.
It's a downright rackety, gusty day,
And the backs of the crew are drenched in spray;
But it's 'Swing boys, swing till you're deaf and blind,
And you'll beat and baffle the raging wind.'

They have slipped through Barnes; they are round the bend;
  And the chests of the eight are tightening.
'Now spend your strength, if you've strength to spend,
  And away with your hands like lightning!
Well rowed!' —and the coach is forced to cheer—
'Now stick to it, all, for the post is near!'
And lo, they stop at the coxswain's call,
With its message of comfort, 'Easy all!'

So here's to the sturdy undismayed
  Eight men who are bound together
By the faith of the slide and the flashing blade
  And the swing and the level feather;
To the deeds they do and the toil they bear;
To the dauntless mind and the will to dare;
And the joyous spirit that makes them one
Till the last fierce stroke of the race is done.

R. C. LEHMANN (1856–1929), from *Punch*, 16 March 1910

The Old Yacht

Proud is Phaselus here, my friends, to tell
That once she was the swiftest craft afloat;
No vessel, were she winged with blade or sail,
Could ever pass my boat.
Phaselus shunned to shun grim Adria's shore,
Or Cyclades, or Rhodes the wide renowned,
Or Bosphorus, where Thracian waters roar,
Or Pontus' eddying sound.
It was in Pontus once, unwrought, she stood,
And conversed, sighing, with her sister trees,
Amastris born, or where Cytorus' wood
Answers the mountain breeze.
Pontic Amastris, boxwood-clad Cytorus!—
You, says Phaselus, are her closest kin:
Yours were the forests where she stood inglorious:
The waters yours wherein
She dipped her virgin blades; and from your strand
She bore her master through the cringing straits,
Nought caring were the wind on either hand,
Or whether kindly fates

Filled both the straining sheets. Never a prayer
For her was offered to the gods of haven,
Till last she left the sea, hither to fare,
And to be lightly laven
By the cool ripple of the clear lagoon.
This too is past; at length she is allowed
Long slumber through her life's long afternoon,
To Castor and the twin of Castor vowed.

JAMES ELROY FLECKER (1884–1915)

XI

We Run because We Must

Foot-Racing

There is no kind of exercise that has more uniformly met the approbation of authors in general than running. In the middle ages, foot-racing was considered as an essential part of a young man's education, especially if he was the son of a man of rank, and brought up to a military profession.

It is needless, I doubt not, to assert the antiquity of this pastime, because it will readily occur to every one, that variety of occasions continually present themselves, which call forth the exertions of running even in childhood; and when more than one person are stimulated by the same object, a competition naturally takes place among them to obtain it. Originally, perhaps, foot-races had no other incitement than emulation, or at best the prospect of some small reward: but in process of time the rewards were magnified, and contests of this kind were instituted as public amusements; the ground marked out for that purpose, and judges appointed to decide upon the fairness of the race, to ascertain the winner, and to bestow the reward.

In former times, according to Comenius, it was customary for the places appropriated to pedal races to be railed in on either side, and the prize-giver stood at the goal, to deliver the reward to the person who should first touch it. I suppose he means at the Olympic games, among which foot-racing was one. In the present day foot-races are not much encouraged by persons of fortune, and seldom happen but for the purpose of betting, and the racers are generally paid for their performance. In many instances the distance does not exceed one hundred yards. At fairs, wakes, and upon many other occasions where many people are assembled together, this species of amusement is sometimes promoted, but most frequently the contest is confined to the younger part of the concourse.

Two centuries back running, according to Peacham, was thought to be an exercise by no means derogatory to the rank of nobility; and a poetical writer in the Cotton manuscript, 'Of Knyghthode and Batayle', before cited, written early in the fifteenth century, recommends it strongly to the practice of the soldiery: his words are these,

> In rennynge the exercise is good also,
> To smyte first in fight, and also whenne,
> To take a place our foemen will forrenne

And take it erst, also, to serche or sture,
Lightly to come and go, rennynge is sure.
Rennyng is also right good at the chase,
And for to lepe a dike is also good;
For mightily what man may reune and lepe,
May well devict, and safe is party kepe.

JOSEPH STRUTT

From *Atalanta's Race*

There with the others to a seat he gat,
Whence he beheld a broidered canopy,
'Neath which in fair array King Schœneus sat
Upon this throne with councillors thereby;
And underneath his well-wrought seat and high,
He saw a golden image of the sun,
A silver image of the Fleet-foot One.

A brazen altar stood beneath their feet
Whereon a thin flame flickered in the wind;
Nigh this a herald clad in raiment meet
Made ready even now his horn to wind,
By whom a huge man held a sword, entwined
With yellow flowers; these stood a little space
From off the altar, nigh the starting place.

And there two runners did the sign abide
Foot set to foot,—a young man slim and fair,
Crisp-haired, well knit, with firm limbs often tried
In places where no man his strength may spare;
Dainty his thin coat was, and on his hair
A golden circlet of renown he wore,
And in his hand an olive garland bore.

But on this day with whom shall he contend?
A maid stood by him like Diana clad
When in the woods she lists her bow to bend,
Too fair for one to look on and be glad,
Who scarcely yet has thirty summers had,
If he must still behold her from afar;
Too fair to let the world live free from war.

She seemed all earthly matters to forget;
Of all tormenting lines her face was clear,
Her wide grey eyes upon the goal were set
Calm and unmoved as though no soul were near,
But her foe trembled as a man in fear,
Nor from her loveliness one moment turned
His anxious face with fierce desire that burned.

Now through the hush there broke the trumpet's clang
Just as the setting sun made eventide.
Then from light feet a spurt of dust there sprang,
And swiftly they were running side by side;
But silent did the thronging folk abide
Until the turning-post was reached at last,
And round about it still abreast they passed.

But when the people saw how close they ran,
When half-way to the starting-point they were,
A cry of joy broke forth, whereat the man
Headed the white-foot runner, and drew near
Unto the very end of all his fear;
And scarce his straining feet the ground could feel,
And bliss unhoped for o'er his heart 'gan steal.

But midst the loud victorious shouts he heard
Her footsteps drawing nearer, and the sound
Of fluttering raiment, and thereat afeard
His flushed and eager face he turned around,
And even then he felt her pass him bound
Fleet as the wind, but scarcely saw her there
Till on the goal she laid her fingers fair.

There stood she breathing like a little child
Amid some warlike clamour laid asleep,
For no victorious joy her red lips smiled,
Her cheek its wonted freshness did but keep;
No glance lit up her clear grey eyes and deep,
Though some divine thought softened all her face
As once more rang the trumpet through the place.

But her late foe stopped short amidst his course,
One moment gazed upon her piteously,
Then with a groan his lingering feet did force
To leave the spot whence he her eyes could see;
And, changed like one who knows his time must be
But short and bitter, without any word
He knelt before the bearer of the sword;

Then high rose up the gleaming deadly blade,
Bared of its flowers, and through the crowded place
Was silence now, and midst of it the maid
Went by the poor wretch at a gentle pace
And he to hers upturned his sad white face;
Nor did his eyes behold another sight
Ere on his soul there fell eternal night.

WILLIAM MORRIS (1834–96)

The Song of the Ungirt Runners

We swing ungirded hips,
And lightened are our eyes,
The rain is on our lips,
We do not run for prize.
We know not whom we trust
Nor whitherward we fare,
But we run because we must
Through the great wide air.

The waters of the seas
Are troubled as by storm.
The tempest strips the trees
And does not leave them warm.
Does the tearing tempest pause?
Do the tree-tops ask it why?
So we run without a cause
'Neath the big bare sky.

The rain is on our lips,
We do not run for prize.
But the storm the water whips
And the wave howls to the skies.
The winds arise and strike it
And scatter it like sand,
And we run because we like it
Through the broad bright land.

CHARLES HAMILTON SORLEY (1895–1915)

Coach and Slowcoach

We had our local Marathon;
  Dick entered for the race;
Five others ran; and strange to say
  He took the seventh place.

Yes, truly, seventh out of six;
  He had a friend who ran
Beside him in a sweater, crying
  'Keep it up, old man!'

Had he had four pacemakers more,
  Instead of being seventh,
Beyond a doubt the plodding youth
  Would have come in eleventh.

NICARCHUS (*fl.* AD 70), trans. Walter Leaf

To an Athlete Dying Young

The time you won your town the race
We chaired you through the market-place;
Man and boy stood cheering by,
And home we brought you shoulder-high.

Today, the road all runners come,
Shoulder-high we bring you home,
And set you at your threshold down,
Townsman of a stiller town.

Smart lad, to slip betimes away
From fields where glory does not stay
And early though the laurel grows
It withers quicker than the rose.

Eyes the shady night has shut
Cannot see the record cut,
And silence sounds no worse than cheers
After earth has stopped the ears:

Now you will not swell the rout
Of lads that wore their honours out,
Runners whom renown outran
And the name died before the man.

So set, before its echoes fade,
The fleet foot on the sill of shade,
And hold to the low lintel up
The still-defended challenge-cup.

And round that early-laurelled head
Will flock to gaze the strengthless dead,
And find unwithered on its curls
The garland briefer than a girl's.

A. E. HOUSMAN

The Hurdlers' Headlong Rush

Hurdling is a pretty sport. But beauty lurked in the eye of the beholder in the days immediately after hurdling ceased to be a combined test of running and jumping ability. That it undoubtedly was in the first quarter of the nineteenth century, when hurdling races at Eton College were held for the boys of the Tutors' and Dames' Houses.

The idea, in those days, was to make speed between fences and to ensure safety by jumping well clear of each obstacle. That meant landing fairly and squarely on both feet after taking each hurdle, and, consequently, a dead stop before a boy could again get into his running. But the application of mechanics to the hurdler's art soon followed. So men sailed over their fences, trunk almost upright, leading leg tucked up well in front and parallel to the top rail of the hurdle, with the rear leg trailing. They looked 'pretty' but, to quote Kipling, 'The devil whispered softly, it's pretty, but is it art?'

The 'devil' did not think so, and the particular 'devil' in question was A. C. M. Croome, the great Oxonian, who achieved Blues for athletics and cricket and was also a distinguished golfer. He held the theory that hurdlers who looked pretty hurdled the wrong way, and his theory it was that put the punch into the modern hurdlers' devastating headlong rush, with every hurdle doing duty as a winning-post.

Croome liked hurdling. His perfectly logical conclusions, after studying style and the event exhaustingly, were that the bent-leg form was bad—firstly because the upright torso offered too great a surface to wind-resistance, and therefore, reduced the speed of the athlete; and secondly because, in his opinion, mighty few men were supple enough—and 'supple' is the executive word—in the hip and knee joints to raise the foot of the leading leg up to the level of the crutch. For every inch the ankle was below that level, so many inches higher was it necessary for the hurdler to rise from the ground in affecting the clearance of each of the ten hurdles. This, of course, constituted an unnecessary waste of time. Croome also held that if a bent-legger did tap timber he would be bowled right over and put clean out of the race.

In support of his new straight-leg style he argued that in his way of hurdling the seat of the athlete's shorts cleared the top rail of the hurdle by an appreciably small margin, that the forcing of the body forward above the thigh of the rising leg drove the leading foot more quickly to ground after hurdle clearance, and that, should the hurdler hit the top rail in rising to it, the heel of his shoe would push the barrier over. The straight-legged hurdler would, therefore, not be put out of the race.

When demonstrating this principle upon one occasion the knee of Croome's leading leg made such violent contact with his own out-thrust chin that he knocked himself out and came to all mixed up with the fragments of the next fence.

He was of the opinion also that hurdling success requires more brains, patience and courage than any other athletic event; and certainly the attainments of the four hurdlers who started in the Oxford and Cambridge race of 1886, which Croome won in 16.4 sec., seemed to prove his contention.

F. A. M. WEBSTER, from *Great Moments in Athletics* (1947)

The Sports

All the school and several local visitors were assembled in the field. Grimes stood by himself, looking depressed. Mr Prendergast, flushed and unusually vivacious, was talking to the Vicar. As the headmaster's party came into sight the Llanabba Silver Band struck up *Men of Harlech*.

'Shockin' noise,' commented Lady Circumference graciously.

The head prefect came forward and presented her with a programme, beribboned and embossed in gold. Another prefect set a chair for her. She sat down with the Doctor next to her and Lord Circumference on the other side of him.

'Pennyfeather,' cried the Doctor above the band, 'start them racing.'

Philbrick gave Paul a megaphone. 'I found this in the pavilion,' he said. 'I thought it might be useful.'

'Who's that extraordinary man?' asked Lady Circumference.

'He is the boxing coach and swimming professional,' said the Doctor. 'A finely developed figure, don't you think?'

'First race,' said Paul through the megaphone, 'under sixteen, Quarter-mile!' He read out Grimes's list of starters.

'What's Tangent doin' in this race?' said Lady Circumference. 'The boy can't run an inch.'

The silver band stopped playing.

'The course,' said Paul, 'starts from the pavilion, goes round that clump of elms . . .'

'Beeches,' corrected Lady Circumference loudly.

'. . . and ends in front of the band-stand. Starter, Mr Prendergast; timekeeper, Captain Grimes.'

'I shall say, "Are you ready? one, two, three!" and then fire,' said Mr Prendergast. 'Are you ready? One'—there was a terriffic report. 'Oh dear! I'm sorry'—but the race had begun. Clearly Tangent was not going to win; he was sitting on the grass crying because he had been wounded in the foot by Mr Prendergast's bullet. Philbrick carried him, wailing dismally into the refreshment tent, where Dingy helped him off with his shoe. His heel was slightly grazed. Dingy gave him a large slice of cake, and he hobbled out surrounded by a sympathetic crowd.

'That won't hurt him,' said Lady Circumference, 'but I think some one ought to remove the pistol from that old man before he does anything serious.'

'I knew that was going to happen,' said Lord Circumference.

'A most unfortunate beginning,' said the Doctor.

'Am I going to die?' said Tangent, his mouth full of cake.

'For God's sake, look after Prendy,' said Grimes in Paul's ear. 'The man's as tight as a lord, and on one whisky, too.'

'First blood to me!' said Mr Prendergast gleefully.

'The last race will be run again,' said Paul down the megaphone. 'Starter, Mr Philbrick; timekeeper, Mr Prendergast.'

'On your marks! Get set.' Bang went the pistol, this time without disaster. The six little boys scampered off through the mud, disappeared behind the beeches and returned rather more slowly. Captain Grimes and Mr Prendergast held up a piece of tape.

'Well run, sir!' shouted Colonel Sidebotham. 'Jolly good race.'

'Capital,' said Mr Prendergast, and dropping his end of the tape, he sauntered over to the Colonel. 'I can see you are a fine judge of a race, sir. So was I once. So's Grimes. A capital fellow, Grimes; a bounder, you know, but a capital fellow. Bounders can be capital fellows; don't you agree, Colonel Slidebottom? In fact, I'd go further and say that capital fellows *are* bounders. What d'you say to that? I wish you'd stop pulling at my arm, Pennyfeather. Colonel Shybotham and I are just having a most interesting conversation about bounders.'

The silver band struck up again, and Mr Prendergast began a little jig, saying: 'Capital fellow! Capital fellow!' and snapping his fingers. Paul led him to the refreshment tent.

'Dingy wants you to help her in there,' he said firmly, 'and, for God's sake, don't come out until you feel better.'

'I never felt better in my life,' said Mr Prendergast indignantly. 'Capital fellow! capital fellow!'

'It is not my affair, of course,' said Colonel Sidebotham, 'but if you ask me I should say that man had been drinking.'

'He was talking very excitedly to me,' said the Vicar, 'about some apparatus for warming a church in Worthing and about the Apostolic Claims of the Church of Abyssinia. I confess I could not follow him clearly. He seems deeply interested in Church matters. Are you quite sure he is right in the head? I have noticed again and again since I have been in the Church that lay interest in ecclesiastical matters is often a prelude to insanity.'

'Drink, pure and simple,' said the Colonel. 'I wonder where he got it? I could do with a spot of whisky.'

'Quarter-mile Open!' said Paul through his megaphone.

Presently the Clutterbucks arrived. Both the parents were stout. They brought with them two small children, a governess, and an elder son. They debouched from the car one by one, stretching their limbs in evident relief.

'This is Sam,' said Mr Clutterbuck, 'just down from Cambridge. He's joined me in the business, and we've brought the nippers along for a treat. Don't mind, do you, Doc? And last, but not least, my wife.'

Dr Fagan greeted them with genial condescension and found them seats.

'I am afraid you have missed all the jumping-events,' he said. 'But I have a list of the results here. You will see that Percy has done extremely well.'

'Didn't know the little beggar had it in him. See that, Martha? Percy's won the high-jump and the long-jump and the hurdles. How's your young hopeful been doing, Lady Circumference?'

'My boy has been injured in the foot,' said Lady Circumference coldly.

'Dear me! Not badly, I hope? Did he twist his ankle in the jumping?'

'No,' said Lady Circumference, 'he was shot at by one of the assistant masters. But it is kind of you to inquire.'

'Three miles open!' announced Paul. 'The course of six laps will be run as before.'

'On your marks! Get set.' Bang went Philbrick's revolver. Off trotted the boys on another race.

'Father,' said Flossie, 'don't you think it's time for the tea interval?'

Nothing can be done before Mrs Beste-Chetwynde arrives,' said the Doctor.

Round and round the muddy track trotted the athletes while the silver band played sacred music unceasingly.

'Last lap!' announced Paul.

The school and the visitors crowded about the tape to cheer the winner. Amid loud applause Clutterbuck breasted the tape well ahead of the others.

'Well run! Oh, good, jolly good, sir!' cried Colonel Sidebotham.

'Good old Percy! That's the stuff,' said Mr Clutterbuck.

'Well run, Percy!' chorused the two little Clutterbucks, prompted by their governess.

'That boy cheated,' said Lady Circumference. 'He only went round five times. I counted.'

'I think unpleasantness so mars the afternoon,' said the Vicar.

'How dare you suggest such a thing?' asked Mrs Clutterbuck. 'I appeal to the referee. Percy ran the full course, didn't he?'

'Clutterbuck wins,' said Captain Grimes.

'Fiddlesticks!' said Lady Circumference. 'He deliberately lagged behind and joined the others as they went behind the beeches. The little toad!'

'Really, Greta,' said Lord Circumference, 'I think we ought to abide by the referee's decision.'

'Well, they can't expect me to give away the prizes, then. Nothing would induce me to give that boy a prize.'

'Do you understand, madam, that you are bringing a serious accusation against my son's honour?'

'Serious accusation, fiddlesticks! What he wants is a jolly good hidin'.'

'No doubt you judge other people's sons by your own. Let me tell you, Lady Circumference. . .'

'Don't attempt to browbeat me, sir. I know a cheat when I see one.'

At this stage of the discussion the Doctor left Mrs Hope-Browne's side, where he had been remarking upon her son's progress in geometry, and joined the group round the winning post.

'If there is a disputed decision,' he said genially, 'they shall race again.'

'Percy has won already,' said Mr Clutterbuck. 'He has been adjudged the winner.'

'Splendid! splendid! A promising little athlete. I congratulate you, Clutterbuck.'

'But he only ran five laps,' said Lady Circumference.

'Then clearly he has won the five furlongs race, a very exacting length.'

'But the other boys,' said Lady Circumference, almost beside herself with rage, 'have run six lengths.'

'Then they,' said the Doctor imperturbably, 'are first, second, third, fourth and fifth respectively in the Three Miles. Clearly there has been some confusion. Diana, I think we might now serve tea.'

Things were not easy, but there was fortunately a distraction, for as he spoke an enormous limousine of dove-grey and silver stole soundlessly on to the field.

'But what could be more opportune? Here is Mrs Beste-Chetwynde.'

Three light skips brought him to the side of the car, but the footman was there before him. The door opened, and from the cushions within emerged a tall young man in a clinging dove-grey overcoat. After him, like the first breath of spring in the Champs Elysées, came Mrs Beste-Chetwynde—two lizard-skin feet, silk legs, chinchilla body, a tight little black hat, pinned with platinum and diamonds, and the high invariable voice that may be heard in any Ritz Hotel from New York to Buda-Pesth.

'I hope you don't mind my bringing Chokey, Dr Fagan?' she said. 'He's just crazy about sport.'

'I sure am that,' said Chokey.

'Dear Mrs Beste-Chetwynde!' said Dr Fagan; 'dear dear Mrs Beste-Chetwynde!' He pressed her glove, and for the moment was at a loss for words of welcome, for 'Chokey', though graceful of bearing and irreproachably dressed, was negro.

EVELYN WAUGH (1903–66), *Decline and Fall*

From *The Loneliness of the Long-Distance Runner*

I trotted on along the edge of a field bordered by the sunken lane, smelling green grass and honeysuckle, and I felt as though I came from a long line of whippets trained to run on two legs, only I couldn't see a toy rabbit in front and there wasn't a collier's cosh behind to make me keep up the pace. I passed the Gunthorpe runner whose shimmy was already black with sweat and I could just see the corner of the fenced-up copse in front where the only man I had to pass to win the race was going all out to gain the half-way mark. Then he turned into a tongue of trees and bushes where I couldn't see him anymore, and I couldn't see anybody, and I knew what the loneliness of the long-distance runner running across country felt like, realizing that as far as I was concerned this feeling was the only honesty and realness there was in the world and I knowing it would be no different ever, no matter what I felt at odd times, and no matter what anybody else tried to tell me. The runner behind me must have been a long way off because it was so quiet, and there was even less noise and movement than there had been at five o'clock of a frosty winter morning. It was hard to understand, and all I knew was that you had to run, run, run, without knowing why you were running, but on you went through fields you didn't understand and into woods that made you afraid, over hills without knowing you'd been up and down, and shooting across streams that would have cut the heart out of you had you fallen into them. And the winning post was no end to it, even though crowds might be cheering you in, because on you had to go before you got your breath back, and the only time you stopped really was when you tripped over a tree trunk and broke your neck or fell into a disused well and stayed dead in the darkness forever. So I thought: they aren't going to get me on this racing lark, this running and trying to win, this jog-trotting for a bit of blue ribbon, because it's not the way to go on at all, though they swear blind that it is. You should think about nobody and go your own way, not on a course marked out for you by people holding mugs of water and bottles of iodine in case you fall and cut yourself so that they can pick you up—even if you want to stay where you are—and get you moving again.

On I went, out of the wood, passing the man leading without knowing I was going to do so. Flip-flap, flip-flap, jog-trot, jog-trot, crunchslap-crunchslap, across the middle of a broad field again, rhythmically running in my greyhound effortless fashion, knowing I had won the race though it wasn't half over, won it if I wanted it, could go on for ten or fifteen or twenty miles if I had to and drop dead at the finish of it, which would be the same, in the end, as living an honest life like the governor wanted me to. It amounted to: win the race and be honest, and on trot-trotting I went, having the time of my life, loving my progress because it did me good and set me thinking which by now I liked to do, but not caring at all when I remembered that I had to win this race as well as run it. One of the two, I had to win the race or run it, and I knew I could do both because my legs had carried me well in front—now coming to the short cut down the bramble bank and over the sunken road—and would carry me further because they seemed made of electric cable and easily alive to keep on slapping at those ruts and roots, but I'm not going to win because the only way I'd see I came in first would be if winning meant that I was going to escape the coppers after doing the biggest bank job of my life, but winning means the exact opposite, no matter how they try to kill or kid me, means running right into their white-gloved wall-barred hands and grinning mugs and staying there for the rest of my natural long life of stone-breaking anyway, but stone-breaking in the way I want to do it and not in the way they tell me.

ALAN SILLITOE (b. 1928)

XII
Men and Mountains

'Great Things are Done'

Great things are done when men and mountains meet;
This is not done by jostling in the street.

WILLIAM BLAKE, *Gnomic Verses*

'Oh! When I have Hung'

Oh! when I have hung
Above the raven's nest, by knots of grass
And half-inch fissures in the slippery rock
But ill sustained, and almost (so it seemed)
Suspended by the blast that blew amain,
Shouldering the naked crag, oh, at that time
While on the perilous ridge I hung alone,
With what strange utterance did the loud dry wind
Blow through my ear! the sky seemed not a sky
Of earth—and with what motion moved the clouds!

WILLIAM WORDSWORTH, *The Prelude*

From *Reflections*
On having left a Place of Retirement

But the time, when first
From that low Dell, steep up the stony Mount
I climb'd with perilous toil and reach'd the top,
Oh! what a goodly scene! *Here* the bleak mount,
The bare bleak mountain speckled thin with sheep;
Grey clouds, that shadowing spot the sunny fields;
And river, now with bushy rocks o'er-brow'd,

Now winding bright and full, with naked banks;
And seats, and lawns, the Abbey and the wood,
And cots, and hamlets, and faint city-spire;
The Channel *there*, the Islands and white sails,
Dim coasts, and cloud-like hills, and shoreless Ocean—
It seem'd like Omnipresence! God, methought,
Had built him there a Temple: the whole World
Seem'd *imag'd* in its vast circumference:
No *wish* profan'd my overwhelméd heart.
Blest hour! It was a luxury,—to be!

SAMUEL TAYLOR COLERIDGE (1772–1832)

Climber, An Amateur

Eskdale, Friday, Augt 6th (1802) at an Estate House called Toes.

There is one sort of Gambling, to which I am much addicted; and that not of the least criminal kind for a man who has children & a Concern.—It is this. When I find it convenient to descend from a mountain, I am too confident & too indolent to round about & wind about 'till I find a track or other symptom of safety; but I wander on, & where it is first possible to descend, there I go—relying upon fortune for how far down this possibility will continue. So it was yesterday afternoon. I passed down from Broad-crag, skirted the Precipices, and found myself cut off from a most sublime Crag-summit, that seemed to rival Sca'Fell Man in height, & to outdo it in fierceness. A Ridge of Hill lay low down, & divided this Crag (called Doe-crag) & Broad-crag—even as the Hyphen divides the words broad & crag. I determined to go thither; the first place I came to, that was not Direct Rock, I slipped down, & went on for a while with tolerable ease—but now I came (it was midway down) to a smooth perpendicular Rock about 7 feet high—this was nothing—I put my hands on the Ledge, & dropped down / in a few yards came just such another / I dropped that too / and yet another, seemed not higher—I would not stand for a trifle / so I dropped that too / but the stretching of the muscle(s) of my hand & arms, & the jolt of the Fall on my Feet, put my whole Limbs in a Tremble, and I paused, & looking down, saw that I had little else to encounter but a succession of these little Precipices—it was in truth a Path that in a very hard Rain is, no doubt, the channel of a most splendid Waterfall. / So I began to suspect that I ought not to go on / but then unfortunately tho' I could with ease drop down a smooth Rock 7 feet high, I could not climb it / so go on I must / and on I went / the next 3 drops were not half a Foot, at least not a foot more than my own height / but every Drop increased the Palsy of my Limbs—I shook all over, Heaven knows without the least influence of Fear / and now I had only two more to drop down / to return was impossible—but of these two the first was tremendous / it was twice my own height, & the Ledge at the bottom was (so) exceedingly narrow, that if I dropt down upon it I must of necessity have fallen backwards & of course killed myself. My Limbs were all in a tremble—I lay upon my Back to rest myself, & I was beginning according to my Custom to laugh at myself for a Madman, when the sight of the Crags above me on each side, & the impetuous Clouds just over them, posting so luridly & so rapidly northward, overawed me / I lay in a state of almost prophetic Trance & Delight—& blessed God aloud, for the powers of Reason & the Will, which remaining no Danger can overpower us! O God, I exclaimed aloud—how calm, how blessed am I now / I know not how to proceed, how to return / but I am calm & fearless & confident / if this reality were a Dream, if I were asleep, what agonies had I suffered! what screams!—When the Reason & the Will are away, what remains to us but Darkness & Dimness & a bewildering Shame, and Pain that is utterly Lord over us, or fantastic Pleasure, that draws the Soul along swimming through the air in man shapes, even as Flight of Starlings in a Wind.—I arose, and looking down saw at the bottom a heap of stones—which had fallen abroad—and rendered the narrow Ledge on which they had been piled, double dangerous / at the bottom of the third Rock that I dropt from, I met a dead Sheep quite rotten— This heap of Stones, I guessed, & have since found that I guessed aright, had been piled up by the Shepherd to enable him to climb & free the poor creature whom he had observed to be crag-fast—but seeing nothing but rock over rock, he had desisted & gone for help—& in the mean time the poor creature had fallen down & killed itself. —As I was looking at these I glanced my eye to my left & observed that the Rock was rent from top to bottom—I measured the breadth of the Rent, and found that there was no danger of my being wedged in / so I put my Knap-sack round to my side, & slipped down as between two walls, without any danger or difficulty—the next Drop brought me down on the Ridge called the How / I hunted out my Besom Stick, which I had flung before me when I first came to the Rocks—and wisely gave over all thoughts of ascending Doe-Crag—for the Clouds were again coming in most tumultuously—so I began to descend / when I felt an odd sensation across my whole Breast—not pain nor itching— & putting my hand on it I found it all bumpy—and on looking saw the whole of my Breast from my Neck (to my Navel)— & exactly all that my Kamell-hair Breast-shield covers, filled with great red heatbumps, so thick that no hair could lie between them. They still remain / but are evidently less— & I have no doubt will wholly disappear in a few Days. It was however a startling proof to me of the violent exertions which I had made. —I descended this low Hill which was all hollow beneath me—and was like the rough green Quilt of a Bed of waters—at length two streams burst out & took their way down, one on (one) side a high Ground upon this Ridge, the other on the other—I took that to my right (having on my left this high Ground, & the other Stream, & beyond that Doe-crag, on the other side of which is Esk Halse, where the head-spring of the Esk rises, & running down the Hill & in upon the Vale looks and actually deceived me, as a great Turnpike Road—in which, as in many other respects the Head of Eskdale much resembles Langdale & soon the channel sank all at once, at least 40 yards, & formed a magnificent Waterfall—and close under this a succession of Waterfalls 7 in number, the third of which is nearly as high as the first. When I had almost reached the bottom of the Hill, I stood so as to command the whole 8 Waterfalls, with the great triangle-Crag looking in above them, & on the one side of them the enormous more than perpendicular Precipices & Bull's-Brows, of Sc'Fell! And now the Thunder-storm was coming on, again & again! —Just at the bottom of the Hill I saw on before me in the Vale, lying just above the River on the side of a Hill, one, two, three, four Objects, I could not distinguish whether Peat-hovels, or hovel-shaped Stones—I thought in my mind, that 3 of them would turn out to be stones—but that the fourth was certainly a Hovel. I went on toward them, crossing & recrossing the Becks & the River & found that they were all huge Stones—the one nearest the Beck which I had determined to be really a Hovel, retained It's likeness when I was close beside / in size it is nearly equal to the famous Bowder stone, but in every other respect greatly superior to it—it has a complete Roof, & that perfectly thatched with wees, & Heath, & Mountain-Ash Bushes—I now was obliged to ascend again, as the River ran greatly to the Left, & the Vale was nothing more than the Channel of the River, all the rest of the interspace between the mountains was a tossing up and down of Hills of all sizes—and the place at which I am now writing is called—Te-as, & spelt, Toes—as the Toes of Sc'Fell—. It is not possible that any name can be more descriptive of the Head of Eskdale—I ascended close under Sca'Fell, & came to a little Village of Sheep-folds / there were 5 together / & the redding Stuff, & the Shears, & an old Pot, was in the Passage of the first of them. Here I found an imperfect Shelter from a Thunder-shower—accompanied with such Echoes! O God! what thoughts were mine! O how I wished for Health & Strength that I might wander about for a Month together in the stormiest month of the year, among these Places, so lonely & savage & full of sounds!

After the Thunder-storm I shouted out all your names in the Sheep-fold—when Echo came upon Echo / and then Hartley & Derwent & then I laughed and shouted Joanna / it leaves all the Echoes I ever heard far far behind, in number, distinctness & humanness of Voice— & then not to forget an old Friend I made them all say Dr. Dodd & c.—

SAMUEL TAYLOR COLERIDGE

Climber, A Professional

The Summit

There was no one to tell about it. There was, perhaps, nothing to tell. All the world we could see lay motionless in the muted splendor of the sunrise. Nothing stirred, only we lived; even the wind had forgotten us. Had we been able to hear a bird calling from some pine-tree, or sheep bleating in some valley, the summit stillness would have been familiar; now it was different, perfect. It was as if the world had held its breath for us. Yet we were so tired . . . the summit meant first of all a place to rest. We sat down just beneath the top, ate a little of our lunch, and had a few sips of water. Ed had brought a couple of firecrackers all the way up; now he wanted to set one off, but we were afraid it would knock the cornices loose. There was so little to do, nothing we really had the energy for, no gesture appropriate to what we felt we had accomplished: only a numb happiness, almost a languor. We photographed each other and the views, trying even as we took the pictures to impress the sight on our memories more indelibly than the cameras could on the film. . . . I thought then, much as I had when Matt and I sat on the glacier just after flying in, that I wanted to know how the others felt and couldn't. Trying to talk about it now would have seemed profane; if there was anything we shared, it was the sudden sense of quiet and rest. For each of us, the high place we had finally reached culminated ambitions and secret desires we could scarcely have articulated had we wanted to. And the chances are our various dreams were different. If we had been able to know each other's, perhaps we could not have worked so well together. Perhaps we would have recognised, even in our partnership, the vague threats of ambition, like boats through a fog: the unrealisable desires that drove us beyond anything we could achieve, that drove us in the face of danger; our unanswerable complaints against the universe—that we die, that we have so little power, that we are locked apart, that we do not know. So perhaps the best things that happened on the summit were what we could see happening, not anything beneath. Perhaps it was important for Don to watch me walk across the top of the east ridge; for Matt to see Ed stand with a cigarette in his mouth, staring at the sun; for me to notice how Matt sat, eating only half of his candy bar; for Ed to hear Don insist on changing to black-and-white film. No one else could see these things; no one could even ask whether or not they were important. Perhaps they were all that happened.

David Roberts (b. 1943)

Tuesday, 13 June 1871

Up at 5.30. Not a soul stirring in the house, the front door locked and the key gone. I got out by the garden door and through the wicket into the Marian Mawr. There was the caravan. The people were all asleep, but the lions were rustling and growling about their dens hungry for breakfast. The caravans were full of strange noises of the different beasts. I knocked at the lions' door and at the door of the ostriches, gnus and antelopes, eliciting divers roars, groans, howls, hoots and grunts. In the town I met the guide, old Pugh, coming to meet me. He took me to his house and furnished me with an alpenstock while his good wife gave me some tea and bread and butter for I could get nothing at the inn.

As we went towards the mountain my old guide told me how Mr Smith (Tom Colborne's clerk at Newport), was lost on Cader Idris some 6 years ago. He was on a tour in N. Wales, walking with his knapsack and had come to Machynlleth. He wanted the guide on the Machynlleth side to go over the mountain with him and offered him 2/6. The guide refused, saying his fee to go to the top of the mountain was 5/- and if we went on down the other side it was 10/-. Moreover the guide strongly advised Mr Smith not to attempt the ascent alone that evening, for night would soon fall and the weather was bad. However Mr Smith persisted in going on and the guide went a little way with him to put him in the right road. Two days after this guide was in Dolgelly and meeting my guide, old Pugh, he asked if he had seen anything of the gentleman who had crossed the Cader from Machynlleth to Dolgelly two days before. Pugh said he had neither seen nor heard anything of him although he had been up Cader Idris twice that day, one time being late in the evening. So they supposed Mr Smith had changed his mind and had gone down from the top of the mountain to Towyn. But 6 weeks passed. Nothing was heard of him and his wife grew very uneasy. His brother came to Machynlleth, Towyn, and Dolgelly to make inquiries but could hear nothing, and the mountain was searched without result. Mr Smith disappeared in September, and in the following May a man was up on Cader Idris looking for a quarry. He heard his dog bark suddenly and looking over a precipice he saw a dead body. He hurried back to Dolgelly and fetched a doctor and a policeman and the coroner, and Pugh came along with them. When the body was turned over Pugh was horrified. He said he never saw such a sight and he hoped he should never see such another. It was what had been Mr Smith. It was a skeleton in clothes. The foxes and ravens had eaten him. His eyes were gone. His teeth were dashed out by the fall and lay scattered about the mountain. His head was bent double under him and crushed into his chest so that his neck was broken. The only piece of flesh remaining on the bone was where the coat buttoned over the chest. One leg was gone and one boot. Pugh looked up and saw something white lying on a ledge above where the body lay. It was his knapsack. When it was brought down there were his things, his papers, his money. Then his stick was found.

And some months afterwards Pugh found his hat. Pugh said he had probably tried to come down a short way to Dolgelly and must have fallen down a precipice in the mist and growing darkness. He showed me the place where the body was found. He found the marks the body had made in falling and knew exactly the point it had fallen from. He had carefully measured the distance and declared the body must have fallen 440 yards.

My old guide comes of a family of Welsh harpers. His brother is now harper to [ ] Sir Watkin's sister. Another brother who is dead won a silver harp at an Eisteddfod and was one of the best harpers in Wales. Pugh said there was a harper at Corwen and another at Llangollen and he knew an old bard at Corwen. He told me he had once been up Cader Idris 4 times in one day for a £10 wager against a reading party of 4 or 5 Cambridge men who declared he could not do it. On the last day of September a pouring wet day he did it and won the wager easily. He could have gone up the 5th time. A man on each side was posted on the top of the mountain and a man on each side at the bottom to see fair play and that Pugh did not ride up. It was stipulated that he should go up by the pony road and come down any way he liked. Coming down the first time he nearly came to trouble and was delayed 20 minutes in this way. He had noticed often when on the mountain that at a particular place his dog usually put up a fox and that the fox always disappeared down a cleft in the rocks. When walking for the wager he thought of this fox path and thought it would take him down quicker. Supposing that he could go where a fox went he slid down the narrow chasm and found that it led to the brink of a precipice. He could not go back and he was obliged to go on so taking off his boots and slinging them round his neck he clambered down. He did not try that way again.

By this time we had come to a place where was a lake by the roadside and in a boat on the lake were two men fishing. Leaving the road here we turned up a rough lane and crossing a little brook by a farm house were on the open mountain. As we sloped up the mountain side we had beautiful views of the Harlech mountains opposite, blue Cardigan Bay and dim Snowdon. The zig-zag path was steep in parts and a great wind blew over the mountain so that I had to sit down in a sheltered place and tie the band of my hat to my button-hole with the old guide's neckerchief, for, said the old man, 'Many hats have been lost on this ridge.' We aimed for a great stone on the top of the first ridge. After this the climbing was not so severe. The old man came up very slowly. Soon after we passed the great stone we passed through a gateway the posts of which were large basaltic pillars. Here we saw a mountain standing apparently close by waiting upon Cader Idris. It was Plynlimmon. Here we passed round over the back of the mountain and began ascending the summit from the S. We came to a little round pool or rather hole full of water. The old man pulled a little tumbler out of his pocket rinsed it and gave me a glass of the clear bright water. It was delicious. Then he drank himself. He said the pool was the head water or spring of the Dysyni River. He had never known it dry in the driest summers. We saw from the spring the winding gleam of the Dysyni wandering down a desolate valley to join the Dyfi, its sister stream.

About this time the wind changed and flew suddenly round into the S. The head of Idris, which had been cowled in cloud, had cleared for a while, but now an impenetrable dark cloud settled down upon it and the mist came creeping down the mountain. The sky looked black and threatened rain. Now there lay before us vast tracts and belts of large stones lying so close together that no turf could be seen and no grass could grow between them. It was broken basalt, and huge lengths of basalt, angled, and some hexagonal, lay about or jutted from the mountain side like enormous balks of timber and with an unknown length buried in the mountain. We passed quarries where some of the great columns had been dug out to be drawn down the mountain on sledges. Cader Idris is the stoniest, dreariest, most desolate mountain I was ever on. We came now to the edge of a vast gulf or chasm or bason almost entirely surrounded by black precipices rising from the waters of a small black tarn which lay in the bottom of the bason. Here the guide showed me the place at the foot of an opposite precipice where Mr Smith's body had been found. Then we stumbled and struggled on again over rough tracts and wildernesses of slate and basalt. The sun was shining on the hills below, but the mist crawled down and wrapped us as if in a shroud blotting out everything. The mists and clouds began to sweep by us in white thin ghostly sheets as if some great dread Presences and Powers were going past and we could only see the skirts of their white garments. The air grew damp and chill, the cloud broke on the mountain top and it began to rain. Now and then we could discern the black sharp peak which forms the summit looming large and dark through the cloud and rain and white wild driving mist, and it was hidden again. It is an awful place in a storm. I thought of Moses on Sinai.

The rain grew heavier. The old guide could not get on very fast and told me to go on alone to the top and shelter in the hut as I could not miss the path. So I went on up the last sharp peak looming black through the dark mist and cloud, by a winding path among the great rocks and wildernesses of loose stone. For a few minutes I was alone on the top of the mountain. The thought struck me, suppose the old man should be seized with cramp in the stomach here, how in the world should I get him down or get down myself in the blinding mist? The cloud and mist and rain swept by and drove eddying round the peak. I could hear the old man chinking his iron-shod staff among the rocks and stones, as he came up the path, nearer and nearer, but till he got close to me I could not discern his white figure through the dense mist. 'This is the highest point of *Cader Idris*', he said, laying his hand upon a peak of wet living rock, 'not *that*', looking with contempt at the great conical pile of stones built upon the peak by the sappers and miners during the Ordnance Survey. He said, 'The Captain of the surveying company had his tent pitched on the top of Cader Idris for 3 summer months and never left the place. He had 18 men to wait upon him. And how many clear views do you think he got in that time?' 'Twelve', I hazarded. 'Nine', he said.

He took me down to a rude 2-roomed hut built of huge stones by his father just under the shelter of the peak, and produced for my benefit a hard-boiled egg and some slices of bread and butter. Also he gave me a woollen comforter to wrap round my neck. Then he vanished. The mist drove in white sheets and shapes past the doorless doorway and past the windows from which the window frames had been removed and the wind whistled through the chinks in the rude walls of huge stones. A large flat block of stone in the middle of the room on which I sat formed the table. It is said that if any one spends a night alone on the top of Cader Idris he will be found in the morning either dead or a madman or a poet gifted with the highest degree of inspiration. Hence Mrs Hemans' fine song 'A night upon Cader Idris'. The same thing is said of the top of Snowdon and of a great stone at the foot of Snowdon. Old Pugh says the fairies used to dance near the top of the mountain and he knows people who have seen them.

Presently I heard the old man clinking his stick among the rocks and coming round the hut. He came in and lighted his pipe and we prepared to go down by the 'Foxes' Path'. And indeed it was a path fit only for foxes. After leading me a few steps he began to go over what seemed to me to be the edge of a precipice, depth unknown and hidden in the mist. The side of the mountain was frightfully steep here and required great care in going down. Suddenly the old man stopped at a beautiful little spring in the almost perpendicular bank, pulled out his tumbler and gave me a draught of the clear sparkling water, much colder than the water from the spring of Dysyni. About the spring the grass grew brilliant green and there was a long winding riband of bright green where the waters overflowing from the spring trickled down through the grass stems to feed the lake at which the foxes drink just below. Next we came to a broad belt of loose rocks lying close together which the guide cautioned me to beware of and not without reason saying they were as slippery as glass and that a sprained ancle was an awkward thing on the mountain. Down, down and and out of the cloud into sunshine, all the hills below and the valleys were bathed in glorious sunshine — a wonderful and dazzling sight. Above and hanging overhead the vast black precipices towered and loomed through the clouds, and fast as we went down the mist followed faster and presently all the lovely sunny landscape was shrouded in a white winding sheet of rain. The path was all loose shale and stone and so steep that planting our alpenstocks from behind and leaning back upon them Alpine fashion we glissaded with a general landslip, rush and rattle of shale and shingle down to the shore of the Foxes' Lake. The parsley fern grew in sheets of brilliant green among the grey shale and in the descent we passed the largest basaltic columns of all protruding from the mountain side. In the clefts and angles of the huge grey tower columns grew beautiful tufts and bunches of parsley fern. We passed another lake and after some rough scrambling walking over broken ground at the mountain foot we came back into the turnpike road at the lake that we had passed in the morning. As we entered Dolgelly the old man said, 'You're a splendid walker, Sir', a compliment which procured him a glass of brandy and water.

FRANCIS KILVERT, *Diary*

Ad Comitem

Old friend, how many a strenuous day
  Have you and I, with axe and guide
And spirits innocent and gay,
    Spent on the mountain side!

Away from city fume and fret
  And cares about the market price,
You know how glad I was to get
    My foot upon the ice,

Where life is strong and runs apace
  And simple joys can please, to know
The wild-flower's hue and scent, or trace
    The marmot on the snow.

The shadows fell, and then we turned
  To seek a shelter for the night,
And found it where the wood-fire burned
    With embers warm and bright;

Where herdmen went their cheerful round,
  And hay was plentiful and dry;
Or else we slept upon the ground
    Beneath the open sky

But when the loaf and cheese were gone,
  And morning peak no more to win,
When sunset came, we sauntered down
    Towards the friendly inn.

On sunlit hours upon the heights,
  Where pulse beat firm and eye was clear,
Where sleep came bountiful o'nights,
    And all the world was dear!

Life passes on, but, ere it goes,
One other summer may we taste
That bright, free life upon the snows
We knew in summers past.

A. C. DOWNER (published privately, 1905)

'A Hairbreadth Escape'

It has fallen to my lot to be indirectly concerned in a few hairbreadth escapes. Probably the most astounding and remarkable of these was that which happened on the Pillar Rock during the Easter holidays of 1903. A party of four arrived at the north side of the rock on Good Friday morning. Two of them were novices; the others had some knowledge of climbing, though they knew nothing of the intricacies of this course. It was decided that the three strongest climbers should start the ascent, and their erstwhile companion should carry two of the rücksacks and other luggage around the mountain to the south side of the rock to meet the others later in the day. The climbers had a 100-foot length of rope, and O. G. Jones's book on rock-climbing; and the last view their comrade obtained of them was at some point high up on the rock, where they were consulting the well-known work. Then he walked around to the appointed meeting-place, waited vainly till darkness fell, and finally reached Wastdale much concerned for the safety of his friends.

We did our utmost to soothe his misgivings, yet not very successfully. Such questions as these were constantly recurring: 'Do you think there is any danger?' 'Can an accident have happened?' 'Could they have hurt themselves on that climb?' Before answering, I jokingly told him of a previous journey from Keswick to rescue a party who had spent a New Year's night and day high up on the same climb; on my arrival at Wastdale, they were safe and sound asleep in bed. Nevertheless, I had to admit that a slip might have awkward results on the North Climb. 'Yes,' came the answer, 'but surely they couldn't slip. They had Jones's book and a rope!' This reply was a good excuse for merriment; if a man could cling to Jones's book and a rope, all would be well. Some of the listeners seemed to think that the best of the books would be a poor substitute for an air-ship should impromptu flight down that hopeless precipice be necessary. However, though everybody grew gradually anxious, we kept all going merrily till midnight, when we retired to bed for a short rest, after promising that a search-party should start about 4 a.m.

Meanwhile, fearful events were happening on the Pillar Rock. Before telling the story, a few topographical details might well be noted. The north face of the Pillar Rock is, roughly speaking, split vertically by a deep rift which extends from base to summit of the Low Man. This is known as

Savage Gully; it forms the key to the ascent by the North Climb. The route begins in the foot of the gully, but about 150 feet higher, a fearsome, vertical rise of nearly 200 feet necessitates a way being made out of the gully on the right. The rocks here on its right side are much broken up, and the ascent is made thereon until gradually a wall of overhanging rock rises overhead, and a way has to be made back to the left into the upper easy part of Savage Gully above the 200-foot drop. But an almost impracticable buttress of rock bars the return. This is the Nose, and to force a way up and beyond it requires circuitous and complicated methods. As the leader cannot usually climb or lead over the Nose, he has to be lowered on the rope—without this support the descent is unjustifiable—down a 25-foot crack into the depths of Savage Gully. The steep finish of the well-named rift rises over his head, but he must not climb this; rather should he cross Savage Gully by a broad grassy ledge, after pulling down the whole of the rope. Then he can scramble up the easy left wall until it is possible to walk without trouble back to the top of the Nose. After lowering the rope, he can now safeguard and assist his companions' ascent.

Now let us return to the adventurers. They reached the Nose in safety; the way ahead seemed blocked, so they consulted Jones's book, and as a result the leader and second man were lowered carefully into Savage Gully. Now, instead of going round to the left, the leader started straight up Savage Gully. Above the difficult part he found his length of rope exhausted. After calling down instructions to the second man to stand still, he unroped and was going forward to prospect, with the rope held loosely in his hand to allow more length. But the second man—by the way, the novice of the party— did not hear or understand. He started to climb up the gully, slipped off at the crucial point, and fell crashing down the terrific chasm for about 40 feet. The rope was jerked instantly out of the leader's fingers; its end flew loose. But the other end was held by the last man, who was standing up on the right wall of Savage Gully and below the Nose. He could not see round the corner, but heard the uproar, and suddenly the rope began to rush through his fingers till the blood ran, and he felt a dreadful wrench as it tightened around his waist.

He was dragged off his feet and almost over the edge, but just managed to seize the outstanding spike of rock below the Nose with his right hand, and with the other a convenient niche in the rock.

Then followed a desperate struggle for life; the fall was arrested, but the victim hung stunned over the sheer depths of Savage Gully. The strain was horrible. Just as the human anchor felt that he must give way, and be dragged down into the cruel, gaping gulf, the dangling climber recovered his full senses, and eased the strain by stepping upon a ledge, which luckily happened to be within reach. The position was still terrifying. Eventually the last man was able to secure his rope around the small belaying-pin below the Nose and collect his shattered nerves. Meanwhile, the leader, by a remarkable *tour de force*, had descended the gully to the bottom of the crack below the Nose, where he could reach the rope that led to the fallen man, who was still invisible over the edge. After noting a suitable rock spillikin, he cut the rope which held the cause of the trouble and tied it securely around the belay. The upper part of the cut rope was still fixed up above, and by this means the last man, though torn, cut, and damaged by his struggle up above, was able to join the leader in Savage Gully. The work ahead of the two men seemed impossible. There they were, crawling about like two spiders, but without the spider's natural advantages, on a sloping edge of the precipice with a 13-stone damaged companion below them. He was out of sight, and standing on a narrow ledge with a vertical drop of some hundreds of feet below him. It seemed at first impossible to try to move him without a horrible tragedy, so they shouted as loudly as possible, hoping some party might be near. All in vain: there was no response save the echo of their plaintive voices among the desolate crags.

For some time they were at their wits' end. Suddenly they remembered the loose end of the rope hanging down below the lowest man. They managed to communicate with the victim, and ultimately a remarkable plan of rescue was evolved. The leader unravelled a woollen garter he had worn, and, with a small stone tied to the end of this frail but veritable lifeline, it was lowered until the suspended man could reach it. Then, after some exciting moments, he was able to pull up the end of the rope, tie it to the wool, and the others gradually and gingerly hauled it up to their level. Now, with the second rope to haul on, and the other end fixed on the belay, they slowly hoisted up their companion.

G. D. Abraham, *Mountain Adventures* (1912)

The Cragsman

In this short span
between my finger tips on the smooth edge
and these tense feet cramped to the crystal ledge
I hold the life of man.
Consciously I embrace
arched from the mountain rock on which I stand
to the firm limit of my lifted hand
the front of time and space:—
    For what is there in all the world for me
      but what I know and see?
    And what remains of all I see and know,
      if I let go?

With this full breath
bracing my sinews as I upward move
boldly reliant to the rift above
I measure life from death.
With each strong thrust
I feel all motion and all vital force
borne on my strength and hazarding their course
in my self-trust:—
    There is no movement of what kind it be
        but has its source in me;
    and should these muscles falter to release
        motion itself must cease.

In these two eyes
that search the splendour of the earth, and seek
the sombre mysteries on plain and peak,
all vision wakes and dies.
With these my ears
that listen for the sound of lakes asleep
and love the larger rumour from the deep,
the eternal hears:—
    For all of beauty that this life can give
        lives only while I live;
    and with the light my hurried vision lends
        all beauty ends.

GEOFFREY WINTHROP YOUNG (1876–1958)

What It Feels Like to Fall

The first book which I spelled out for myself as a child was Edward Whymper's *Scrambles Amongst the Alps*. The first picture which left a permanent impression on my mind was the engraving of Whymper falling head first down the icy slopes below the Col du Lion. He fell 200 ft. in seven or eight bounds, and was finally brought to rest, the blood spurting out of more than 20 cuts. He clamped a big lump of snow on his head as a plaster, scrambled up to a place of safety, and fainted away. 'I was perfectly conscious,' he writes:

'and felt each blow; but, like a patient under chloroform, experienced no pain. Each blow was, naturally, more severe than that which preceded it and I distinctly remember thinking, "Well, if the next is harder still, that will be the end!" Like persons who have been rescued from drowning, I remember that the recollection of a multitude of things rushed through my head, many of them trivialities or absurdities, which had been forgotten long before; and, more remarkable, this bounding through space did not feel disagreeable. But I think that in no very great distance more, consciousness, as well as sensation, would have been lost, and upon that I base my belief, improbable as it seems that death by a fall from a great height is as painless an end as can be experienced.'

Whymper fell about 200 ft. Squadron-Leader F. L. Robinson survived a sliding fall on ice which carried him down a vertical distance of 2,000 ft. His was, perhaps, the most remarkable escape in mountaineering history. His guide was cutting steps down a steep ice slope on the Gabelhorn, a famous peak near Zermatt, when a small snow avalanche dragged the party from their holds and swept them down the ice slope, across crevasses and over a small ice cliff. Their injuries were serious, but no bones were broken, and, as the accident was fortunately observed through a telescope by the Keeper of the Mountet hut, they were rescued in due course from their perilous position. Squadron-Leader Robinson was knocked silly by the fall, and was therefore not in a position to corroborate or refute this theory that death by falling is perhaps the pleasantest method of passing from this world to the next. But having studied the records left by climbers who survived long falls, and having myself survived seven mountaineering falls, two of which should have been, and all of which might have been, fatal, I am convinced that Whymper's experience was by no means abnormal.

Frank Smythe, for instance, describes in one of his books a long fall in the Alps. He felt as if he were watching with complete detachment his own body somersaulting down from crag to crag. It was as if the real Smythe was no longer connected with his body, as if this thing making feeble, convulsive movements was something which had once belonged to him, something which he had discarded like an old suit of clothes or his first set of teeth. This body did not matter, it could be scrapped without damage to the personality which had used it as a temporary habitation. This experience, he told me, convinced him beyond all need of proof that he, himself, would survive the death of his body.

Many years ago I fell 100 ft. while descending alone a rocky ridge. A monolith of rock detached itself from the rock face to which I was clinging. Fear vanished when the fall began. I struck the face of the cliff three or four times, and each time I somersaulted off into space I felt the same angry disappointment that my fall had not been finally checked. An impression of the mountains apparently hanging upside down in the sky etched itself in my mind. I remember keen disappointment every time I struck the rock and failed to stop, but perhaps the basic reaction was one of mild indignation, almost of injured vanity. 'You can't do this to me . . . You CAN'T DO THIS TO *ME*.'

If the last enemy be death, the last friend and ally is vanity. The vanity motive, so much more important in history than the profit motive, persists in the most discouraging circumstances. A case in point was another fall of mine, this time on ice.

A friend and I were descending an icy slope covered by a shallow layer of soft snow. We cut no steps, but drove the ice claws, which we were wearing, into the underlying ice. My right leg, which as a result of the fall described above, is short and misshapen, was hurting abominably, and I warned my friend to keep the rope taut. Suddenly I slipped on my bad leg, fell and dragged my friend from his hold. He shot past me head first down an icy slope leading to the glacier 500 ft. below.

Even the apparent certainty of death did not prevent vanity getting to work, on the usual process of self-justification. 'I did warn him. . . . Why the devil didn't he keep the rope taut!' I wish I could feel certain that I also felt genuine contrition for involving my friend in what looked like proving a fatal accident. We shot past two other friends on another rope at an accelerating speed. There was nothing they could do to save us; but somehow I resented their maddening impassivity. Some kind of gesture would have been welcome—the removal of their hats, if not to a corpse, at least to prospective corpses.

200 ft. lower down, the rope caught round a little knob of rock projecting about 3 inches above the surface of the ice; the soft snow which was swept off the ice by the rope, packed against the rock, with the result that one thread of the rope remained uncut. As my friend collected himself together he remarked with quiet pride, 'I never dropped my axe.' 'Damn you!' I answered irritably. 'You dropped ME.'

It is difficult to understand why one should feel no fear when one is falling to what seems to be certain death. I can best explain my own tentative solution by means of an analogy. The unborn child may fear birth as we fear death, knowing nothing of the life to come, may cling tenaciously to the only existence which it knows. Fear may be Nature's device for preventing premature birth and premature death. Where the issue between life and death is in doubt, fear often invokes a dynamic and superhuman effort; but in the experience I have described, no effort could have had the slightest influence on the result. Whymper, Smythe and I were as helpless as falling stones—because fear was useless, fear ceased to be.

On the other hand, my son, Peter, who was a parachutist, tells me that a doctor who saw four men killed because their parachutes failed to open, said that in every case, the unfortunate man was heard to scream with fear before he hit the ground.

Jowett has defined tragedy as: 'A beautiful hypothesis killed by a fact.' My hypothesis is at least weakened by the fact my son mentioned.

Perhaps somebody else can produce a better explanation.

ARNOLD LUNN (1888–1974)

Levanna

Jagged above the cloud, the ridge, the scramble in the sun,
The rocks sound, a climber's paradise,
Turrets, slabs, a delicate cornice, three rappels,
And the blue, clear, spectroscopic—

Northward the ridges radiate like fingers;
Dazzles, high over Monte Viso, the Italian sun;
Vivid, intangible as music, Cervin, Monte Rosa,
The etherial skyline, Monte Bianco.

Printed on burning air or shimmering frost, the world is order,
Time is a simple map, the streams are frozen:
Orco, the chestnut valley, Valsavaranche, the groves of walnut,
And Val Grisanche, a rocky desert.

The eyes are bright with vision,
Clutching the fiery rock the fingers burn,
Intense the burning limbs, knowing the world of ice,
The mountain, and the dark cloud under.

And these descending: Paradiso,
Gran Nomenon, Grivola, fading, sinking—
The hills are twisted cloud, the eyes are puzzled,
Our muffled voices echo in the couloir.

The summit world is lost, the map is crumpled,
Folds become clouded hills and brittle shale;
Here in the minute saxifrage and ghostly gentian,
The rock disintegrates.

Thin windflower, soldanelle, wizened aconite,
These are our limbs, our hands, our eyes;
Here in our finite sorrow, vision withers;
Winter forbids return, with bulging ice.

Here on the long moraine, these have their wisdom,
Their root, their form and limit,
And over these the century towers,
Prouder, darker.

MICHAEL ROBERTS (1902–48)

Mountain View

Can those small hills lying below
Be mountains that some hours ago
I gazed at from beneath?
Can such intense blue be the sea's
Or that long cloud the Hebrides?
Perhaps I prayed enough
By crawling up on hands and knees
The sharp loose screes,
Sweat dripping on the lichen's scurf,
And now in answer to my prayer
A vision is laid bare;
Or on that ledge, holding my breath,
I may have even slipped past Death.

ANDREW YOUNG (1885–1971)

ACKNOWLEDGEMENTS

The editor and publisher are grateful for permission to include the following copyright material:

G. D. Abraham: 'A Hairbreadth Escape' from *Mountain Adventures* (Methuen, 1912).

Dannie Abse: 'A Note Left on the Mantelpiece' and 'The Game' from *Collected Poems* (Hutchinson, 1977). Reprinted by permission of Anthony Sheil Associates.

Anon: 'The Old Race Horse', trans. Humbert Wolfe, from *Others Abide* (Ernest Benn, 1927). Reprinted by permission of Miss Ann Wolfe.

John Arlott: 'Cricket at Worcester, 1938' from *Of Period and Place* (Cape). Reprinted by permission of the author.

W. H. Auden: 'Hunting Season' from *Collected Poems*. Reprinted by permission of Faber & Faber Ltd.

Sir John Betjeman: 'Seaside Golf', 'Pot Pourri from a Surrey Garden', and 'East Anglian Bathe' from *Collected Poems*. Reprinted by permission of John Murray (Publishers) Ltd.

Elizabeth Bishop: 'The Fish' from *The Complete Poems 1927–1979*. Copyright 1940 and copyright renewed © 1968 by Elizabeth Bishop. Reprinted by permission of Farrar, Straus & Giroux, Inc.

Edmund Blunden: 'The Midnight Skaters' from *Poems of Many Years* (Collins). Reprinted by permission of A. D. Peters & Co. Ltd.

Neville Cardus: 'Hutton, Hobbs and the Classical Style'. Reprinted by permission of Margaret Hughes, literary executor.

Stewart Conn: 'Under the Ice' from *Under the Ice*. Reprinted by permission of Century Hutchinson Ltd.

Bernard Darwin: extract from 'Unforgettable Days' from *The Saturday Book* (5th Year) (Hutchinson, 1945). Reprinted by permission of Century Hutchinson Ltd.

Walter de la Mare: 'The Old Angler'. Reprinted by permission of the Literary Trustees of Walter de la Mare and the Society of Authors as their representative.

Patric Dickinson: 'University Match of '35' from *The Good Minute*. Reprinted by permission of Victor Gollancz Ltd.

Michael Henry: 'Stagnant Pond'. © 1987 Michael Henry. Reprinted by permission of the author.

David Jacobs: 'Park Tennis' from *Terminus* (Peterloo Poets, 1984). Reprinted by permission of Harry Chambers/Peterloo Poets.

Francis Kilvert: from *Kilvert's Diary*, ed. William Plomer. Reprinted by permission of Jonathan Cape Ltd., on behalf of the editor and Mrs Sheila Hooper.

Philip Larkin: 'At Grass' from *The Less Deceived* (The Marvell Press, 1950).

Arnold Lunn: 'What It Feels Like to Fall' from *Bedside Lilliput* (Hulton Press). Reprinted by permission of David Higham Associates Ltd.

A. G. Macdonell: 'The Cricket Match' from *England, their England*. Reprinted by permission of Macmillan, London and Basingstoke.

John Masefield: 'Partridges', and extracts from *The Everlasting Mercy* ('Eighteen Rounds'), *Biography* ('Racing in Cutters'), and *Reynard the Fox*. Reprinted by permission of the Society of Authors as the literary representative of the Estate of John Masefield.

Will H. Ogilvie: 'The Stable Path' and 'A Single Hound' from *Collected Sporting Verse* (Constable Publishers).

Craig Raine: 'A Hungry Fighter' from *Rich* (1984). Reprinted by permission of Faber & Faber Ltd.

David Roberts: 'The Summit' from *The Mountain of My Fear*. Reprinted by permission of Laurence Pollinger Ltd.

Michael Roberts: 'Levanna' from *The Year's Poetry 1934–36* (The Bodley Head Ltd.).

Alan Ross: 'Stanley Matthews' from *Collected Poems* (Eyre & Spottiswoode, 1967). Reprinted by permission of the author.

Siegfried Sassoon: extract from *The Weald of Youth* and 'The Blues at Lord's' from *Collected Poems* (Faber, 1961). Reprinted by permission of George Sassoon.

William Scammell: 'Golden Dawn' from *Jouissance* (Peterloo Poets, 1985). © 1985 William Scammell. Reprinted by permission of the author.

Vernon Scannell: 'Peerless Jim Driscoll' and 'Comeback' from *New and Collected Poems*, 'Mastering the Craft' from *Winterlude*, and 'Wicket Maiden' from *The Loving Game*. All reprinted by permission of Robson Books Ltd.

Alan Sillitoe: extract from *The Loneliness of the Long-Distance Runner* (W. H. Allen, 1959). Reprinted by permission of Tessa Sayle, Literary & Dramatic Agency.

David Storey: extract from *This Sporting Life* (Longman, 1960). Copyright © David Storey, 1960. Reprinted by permission of Penguin Books Ltd.

Evelyn Waugh: 'The Sports' from *Decline and Fall* (Chapman & Hall Ltd.). Reprinted by permission of A. D. Peters & Co. Ltd.

F. A. M. Webster: 'The Hurdlers' Headlong Rush' from *Great Moments in Athletics* by Lt.-Col. F. A. M. Webster, published by Country Life Ltd. Reproduced by permission of Newnes Books, a Division of The Hamlyn Publishing Group Ltd.

P. G. Wodehouse: 'Scientific Golf' and 'Tea and Tennis' from *Love Among the Chickens*, and 'The Great Day'. Reprinted by permission of A. P. Watt Ltd., on behalf of the Trustees of Wodehouse Trust No. 3 and Century Hutchinson Ltd.

Kit Wright: 'The Captain' and 'Packer's Circuit' from *The Bear Looked over the Mountain* (1977). Reprinted by permission of the author.

W. B. Yeats: 'At Galway Races', 'The Ballad of the Foxhunter', and 'The Fisherman' from *Collected Poems*. Reprinted by permission of A. P. Watt Ltd., on behalf of Michael B. Yeats and Macmillan London Ltd.

Andrew Young: 'Mountain View' from *The Poetical Works of Andrew Young*. Reprinted by permission of Secker & Warburg Ltd.

Geoffrey Winthrop Young: 'The Cragsman' from *Poems of Today* (Sidgwick & Jackson, 1930). Reprinted by permission of Sidgwick & Jackson Ltd.

In a few instances it has not been possible to make contact with the copyright holder. If notified, the publisher will rectify any errors or omissions in future editions.

INDEX OF AUTHORS

Authors' dates are given on their first appearance in the book